IMISCOE Research Series

This series is the official book series of IMISCOE, the largest network of excellence on migration and diversity in the world. It comprises publications which present empirical and theoretical research on different aspects of international migration. The authors are all specialists, and the publications a rich source of information for researchers and others involved in international migration studies.

The series is published under the editorial supervision of the IMISCOE Editorial Committee which includes leading scholars from all over Europe. The series, which contains more than eighty titles already, is internationally peer reviewed which ensures that the book published in this series continue to present excellent academic standards and scholarly quality. Most of the books are available open access.

For information on how to submit a book proposal, please visit: http://www.imiscoe.org/publications/how-to-submit-a-book-proposal.

More information about this series at http://www.springer.com/series/13502

Peter Scholten • Mark van Ostaijen
Editors

Between Mobility and Migration

The Multi-Level Governance of Intra-European Movement

Springer Open

Editors
Peter Scholten
Department of Public Administration and Sociology
Erasmus University Rotterdam
Rotterdam, The Netherlands

Mark van Ostaijen
Tilburg Institute of Governance
Tilburg University
Tilburg, The Netherlands

ISSN 2364-4087 ISSN 2364-4095 (electronic)
IMISCOE Research Series
ISBN 978-3-030-08593-3 ISBN 978-3-319-77991-1 (eBook)
https://doi.org/10.1007/978-3-319-77991-1

Printed on acid-free paper

This Springer imprint is published by the registered company Springer International Publishing AG part of Springer Nature.
The registered company address is: Gewerbestrasse 11, 6330 Cham, Switzerland

Contents

Chapter 1
Between Mobility and Migration: The Consequences and Governance of Intra-European Movement

Mark van Ostaijen and Peter Scholten

One of the cornerstones of the development of the European Union is the principle of free movement within the EU. The EU has created an unprecedented area in which not just capital, goods and services but also people can move around relatively freely. This freedom of movement is guaranteed by EU law and enshrined in the principles of the Lisbon strategy with the objective of creating 'more and better jobs, by reducing obstacles to mobility' (European Commission 2004, 2007). Especially after the EU enlargements in 2004 and 2011 with various Central and Eastern European (CEE) countries, the scale of EU movement has grown significantly. Migration from the EU Member States in Central and Eastern-Europe (CEE) has evolved into one of the main migration flows within Europe (Black et al. 2010). For instance, it resulted in more than 2.2 million people from Poland engaged in international migration or mobility between 2004–2007 (Grabowska-Lusinska et al. 2009). This contributed to a 'new face' of East-West migration in Europe (Favell 2008; Favell and Recchi 2010). It is therefore important to know more about migration from Central and Eastern to Western parts of Europe. Because this 'new face' has not remained without consequences (Van Ostaijen et al. 2017).

This 'new face' triggered for instance national Ministers to call for attention that "*this type of immigration burdens the host societies with considerable additional costs*" (Mikl-Leitner et al. 2013) and ask to combat 'the improper and abusive use' of the Posted Workers Directive (Hundstorfer et al. 2015). In a response, the then Home Affairs Commissioner, Cecilia Malmström, criticized this outcry and stated that: "*they are mixing apples and oranges*" by "*mixing up internal EU mobility and immigration*" (Hansen 2015). By an external research report, the European Commission concluded that: "*the overall evidence suggests that this situation is not*

M. van Ostaijen (✉)
Tilburg Institute of Governance, Tilburg University, Tilburg, The Netherlands
e-mail: m.vanostaijen@uvt.nl

P. Scholten
Erasmus University Rotterdam, Rotterdam, The Netherlands

P. Scholten, M. van Ostaijen (eds.), *Between Mobility and Migration*, IMISCOE Research Series, https://doi.org/10.1007/978-3-319-77991-1_1

placing major issues and burdens" (EY 2014, p. 2). This makes visible that this 'new face' caused contestation, in many member-states. For example, in France, the 'Polish plumber' played a significant role in the public debate that led to the rejection of the EU constitution in 2005, in Sweden there were fierce debates around 'new' beggars and homeless people (Favell and Nebe 2009) and the Dutch Deputy Prime Minister called upon a 'Code Orange' for a better awareness on the 'shadow sides' of free movement (Asscher and Goodhart 2013). This reveals a paradigm conflict between the European Commission versus its member-states and local municipalities regarding free movement as a clearly contested issue and a site of policy conflict.

But next to its political and policy relevance, there are a number of theoretical questions regarding this 'new face' of 'East-West migration' (Friberg 2012; Black et al. 2010; Favell 2008; Düvell and Vogel 2006; Okolski 2001; Wallace and Stola 2001). First of all, how should we understand this new European free movement? Do we need to understand this as more permanent settlement or as more flexible, circular and temporary migration? Secondly, since certain local authorities point at issues in their territories, what are the specific social consequences for (urban) municipalities? And thirdly, how do local authorities react to this and what kind of policy networks and governance approaches have evolved as effective responses?

Therefore, the key objective of this book is to develop a better theoretical and empirical understanding of the consequences of European free movement, with a particular focus on the significance of East-West migration. In other words, a focus on migration from Central and Eastern to Western parts of Europe. To meet this aim, this book has a threefold structure: first a section on 'types of intra-European movement and their consequences', followed by a section on 'multi-level governance' which is complemented with a section on 'perspectives from sending and receiving regions'.

Guided by this structure, the book first conceptualizes European free movement and this 'new face' of East-West migration as 'CEE migration' by distinguishing different *types* of CEE migrants to understand the range of consequences. Furthermore, it relates to how policies responded to these consequences, so it investigates the governance responses to CEE migration. In order to connect 'both sides' of the story, it also incorporates the Eastern or sending countries perspective of emerging and new migration corridors in and outside Europe, including Poland, the Czech Republic and Turkey. As such, this book addresses central questions as whether free movement or 'East-West migration' can be empirically understood as either mobility or migration, what this means in terms of the social and economic implications for the host area as well as the area of origin, and what type of governance approaches are associated with these implications.

1.1 Conceptualizing Free Movement and Its Consequences

In migration and integration studies it has remained unclear how we could understand 'European free movement'. Should it be perceived as a 'new' type of migration, as permanent settlement or as more flexible, circular and temporary migration?

As Adrian Favell argues: "*Within this, European citizens –old and new- can move freely against a wider, transnational horizon that encourages temporary and circular migration trends, and demands no long term settlement or naturalisation in the country of work*" (Favell 2008: 705–706). However, this contrasted with studies acknowledging a more diversified picture including the more permanent settlement migration as well (Engbersen et al. 2013; Friberg 2012, 2013). These studies show that beyond the seasonal and circular forms of migration, other types of migration have emerged which involves a more permanent presence of CEE migrants in the receiving regions. Some migrants maintain transnational connections that connect them to their region of origin as well as their host regions. Some settle permanently in their receiving societies and bring over or found new families, while in other cases, migrants move on to other parts in Europe (Glorius et al. 2013; Lafleur and Stanek 2016). Thus, we see a diversifying picture in European free movement, with a large variety between individual citizens.

Therefore, this book starts with explicating *two important assumptions*. First of all, based on previous research (Engbersen et al. 2013; Friberg 2012, 2013), we assume that European free movement towards Western Europe is characterized by significant diversity and heterogeneity in socio-economic status and time-span. This means that although there are many CEE migrants working in low-qualified and low-paid jobs, there are also medium-skilled and highly skilled migrants working at, for instance, universities or in the (medical) business industry. This *socio-economic diversification* includes a varied perspective on socio-economic status which leads to a socio-economic differentiation of CEE migrants in types of migrants, such as: 'knowledge workers', 'entrepreneurs', 'manual workers', 'persons working in private households', 'sex workers', 'trafficked persons', 'students', 'non-working spouses/partners and children' and 'beggars and homeless people'.

Next to the socio-economic differentiation, European free movement is characterized by variation in time, in the temporality of stay. This includes a wide range between temporary flexible categories and permanent settlement. This variation could lead to large differences concerning to what extent host societies develop extra procedures, policies and legislation. Both diversifications are visualized in the figure below, which visualizes the socio-economic and temporal differentiation in two axes and shows a variety of different types of CEE migrants that one could associate with the varieties considered. While we are sensitive for the mobility versus migration language debate, for aims of academic clarity, we stayed close to the body of literature on migration studies here, to be able to give our fieldwork the most effective and feasible starting point possible. Because the Fig. 1.1 below has been used as a heuristic device in this project to sensitize the research focus for the varieties involved, not to (normatively) depict specific categories for this research. The empirical chapters will give substance to the specific 'corners' of this figure.

Besides the socio-economic diversification, this research presumes that European free movement is spatially 'unevenly distributed' (Gijsberts and Lubbers 2015; 25). This implies that CEE populations tend to be *spatially concentrated* in specific rural and urban areas. As such, a second expectation is that, given the '*uneven distribution*'

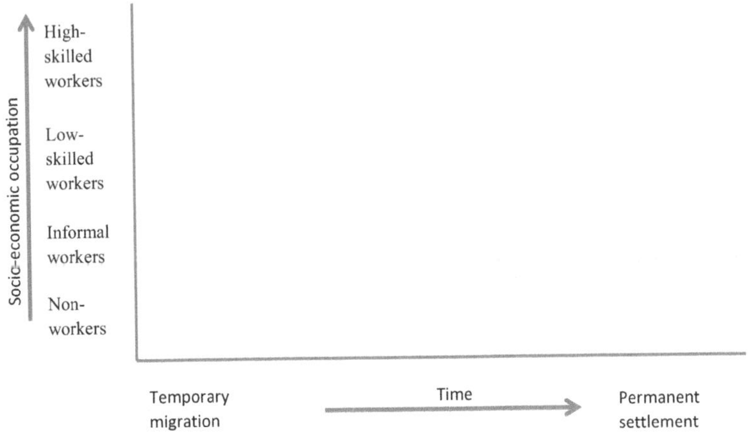

Fig. 1.1 Socio-economic and temporal differentiation of CEE migrants

of migrants in specific localities, the diversification of intra-European movement also leads to a *diversification of local consequences*: not only in terms of labour market issues, but a wide range of issues that evolve from short-term (housing) to long-term implications (language and education) in the receiving and sending countries. We assume that different types of CEE migrants have different social implications on the receiving urban and rural regions. This holds importance for the social consequences related to European free movement, since implications of circular and footloose migration can be expected to be primarily socio-economic, concentrating particularly on labour market incorporation and housing issues. While implications of settlement migration can be expected to be more of a socio-cultural character, raising issues like language skills, education and participation. Therefore, this points to issues of integration, segregation and social cohesion in urban regions. An important issue is the effect of CEE migrants in disadvantaged neighbourhoods in their contribution to strengthen or weaken the social cohesion within these neighbourhoods (Musterd et al. 2016). Therefore, to study this spatial specificity and concentration of CEE migrants in specific urban and rural spaces, we distinguished several 'domains' regarding socio-economic, socio-cultural and legal-political issues, in which we expected that European free movement could cause implications. For that aim we comparatively studied implications regarding labour market, registration (socio-economic); education, language, communication, societal participation, housing and neighbourhood issues (socio-cultural); and social security, health care and political participation issues (legal-political). We expected that European free movement could cause implications in all these domains, differentiated by the spatial context in which CEE migrants reside or work. With this division we aimed to guide and structure our analysis primarily on the social consequences in the urban regions.

1.2 Governance of Free Movement in a Multi-Level Setting

The second part of the book focuses on how local, national and European (governmental) authorities responded on features related to 'European free movement' in its multi-level setting. Since European free movement is clearly related to European Union regulations of free movement, adopted by member-state permissions in the 'opening' of their labour markets and faced by local municipalities in terms of housing and neighbourhood consequences (Black et al. 2010; Van Puymbroeck et al. 2011; Engbersen and Snel 2012), this can clearly be seen as a topic in a multi-level setting. And since multiple governmental bodies are involved in this issue, it holds importance to stress the differences between the governance structures of Sweden, Turkey, the Netherlands and Austria. The four selected countries represent four distinctly different political-administrative institutional models, spanning multi-level to unitary organization of decision-making. They range from Austria's formally federal system with strong elements of multi-level corporatism and extensive social partnership participation in decision-making to Turkey's unitary state system with policy-making set in a highly hierarchical top-down institutional framework (Sert et al. 2015: 8). Between these two cases, Sweden and the Netherlands display elements of lingering – but different - traditions of corporatism and social partnership decision-making located within unitary state systems that feature strong aspects of a local decision-making capacity. At an overarching level, three of the countries, Austria, Netherlands and Sweden, are well-established democracies (Lijphart 2012) and EU members while Turkey is from a strict institutional European perspective and with regard to intra-European movement an 'outlier case' since Turkey has an 'EU Candidate' status. But for a variety of reasons, that will be explained at length later on, Turkey has relevance. Because of historical (ethinc ties with Bulgaria), geographical (proximity of large urban regions) and legislative (non-EU member-state but importance on European migration flows) reasons, Turkey has relevance and importance. Thus, from a strict institutional European perspective, what could be defined as an 'outlier' case, contains multiple reasons why Turkey is an important and relevant case for this research. The table below outlines the variances in the case-studies selected, particularly regarding the outlook of governance structures Table 1.1.

Table 1.1 Governance contexts

Governance context parameters				
Degree of freedom	Partly free	Free		
Politico-administrative institutional model	Unitary	Federal	Unitary decentralised	Unitary
State – Social partners relation	Top-Down	Corporatist	Semi corporatist	Post corporatist
Type of welfare state	Welfare state	Conservative	Mixed	Social democratic
Country	**Turkey**	**Austria**	**Netherlands**	**Sweden**

Table 1.2 selected urban regions in the country cases

Country	Urban region I	Urban region II
Austria	Vienna	Linz
Netherlands	Rotterdam	The Hague
Sweden	Stockholm	Gothenburg
Turkey	Istanbul	Edirne

Table 1.2 shows the differences between the cases, based on centralized state traditions. Most relevant is to what extent his variances are of influence in how the local, national and European authorities interact with each other on the issue of CEE migration. The literature, which outlines this multi-level setting, observes a growing role of local governments in general and cities in particular in global and multi-level systems (Brenner 2004; Holston and Appadurai 1999; Isin 2000; Le Gales 2002; Sassen 1999). It has become manifest that in the context of 'glocalization', cities are becoming hubs for innovation in governance networks. Therefore, cities should not only be studied as subnational governments that are affected by Europeanization (Emelianoff 2013), but as key players in multi-level networks and as motors of policy dynamics 'from below', also within the topic of 'European free movement'. From this perspective, local governments develop various strategies to influence national and EU policymaking (Heinelt and Neiderhafner 2008; Scholten et al. 2017). One strategy involves lobbying or negotiating policy preferences at other levels of government, also described as 'vertical venue shopping' (Pralle 2003; Guiraudon 2000). *Vertical venue shopping* means that if local governments cannot achieve certain policy preferences at their own level, they can act as policy entrepreneurs in relation to other levels of government. This venue shopping can take place via formal channels where governments of different levels meet, but also via informal policy lobbying or political networks. Such efforts can influence governance processes at other levels which involves networking and coalition building with other cities or local governments (Gustavsson et al. 2009) and transnational municipal networks (Kern and Bulkeley 2009). These actions can be considered as horizontal governance processes of local authorities interacting and developing relationships with each other. Next to these horizontal interactions, local governments can also interact vertically with more central or national located authorities to adopt or modify policies, laws and legislation.

To understand the role of local authorities in their responses towards European free movement, we will focus on the policy networks and governance approaches in relation with other public, private and NGO stakeholders. For that aim we developed a conceptual frame to understand the policy networks and governance approaches in its multi-level setting (Scholten 2013). With a typology of four theoretical ideal types of governance approaches we aim to understand to what extent public authorities constructed horizontal and vertical relations to develop policies, laws and legislation on CEE related topics:

1. Multi-level governance
   Characterized by a more or less equal relationship in terms of engagements and participation among the various levels that are relevant to a specific governance

situation. In multi-level governance situations, policies at various levels are synchronized without a clear hierarchy. In the case of intra-European movement, the concept multi-level governance would apply in particular to situations where the local, national and European level are involved. When one of these levels is missing, we can also speak of 'multiple level governance.'

2. Top-down governance
   Characterized by a hierarchical relationship in which the highest level steers the overall governance response for actors from all other involved layers. 'Lower' policy levels are primarily involved in terms of policy implementation, not policy formulation.
3. Bottom-up governance
   Characterized by a leading role of local governments in agenda setting and formulating policy solutions that require policy actions also at other 'higher' levels of governance. In the literature, this model has also been described as the 'localist' model.
4. Disjointed governance
   Characterized by 'horizontal' governance processes at various levels, without actual vertical relations between the different levels. In this model, the policy-making logics at different levels are largely decoupled.

To address European free movement in its multi-level setting, the case studies are analysed by the above-distinguished ideal types of governance.

1.3 Outline of the Book

The aim of this book is to comprehensively address a theoretical and empirical understanding of the consequences of intra-European movement in general and CEE migration in particular, in terms of variety of types of migration and social implications and its linkage with governance approaches. Whereas the current state of the art in the literature provides a good overview of migration flows and the varying types of migration from CEE countries, the social implications of CEE migration for urban regions and how urban regions deal with this from a governance perspective have been relatively unexplored (Friberg 2012; Black et al. 2010; Düvell and Vogel 2006; Okólski 2001; Wallace and Stola 2001; Geddes and Boswell 2011). In the sections that follow we will elaborate on these elements and further develop the expectations that guide us throughout this book. This leads us to the following sections:

1) **'Types of intra-European movement and their consequences'.** This part addresses the size and types of CEE migration, addressing the more sociological and migration studies questions to understand European free movement more as a circular, permanent or more flexible phenomenon; addressing the social consequences perceived by stakeholders in the urban regions, addressing geographic, sociological and migration issues to understand the spatial implications of European free movement;

2) **'Multi-level governance'**. This part addresses the policy networks and governance responses, including political science, public administration and governance studies issues to understand European free movement as a multi-level phenomenon;
3) **'Perspectives from sending and receiving regions'**, addressing the consequences for sending regions such as Poland, Czech Republic and Turkey

It is important to mention that especially the first two parts are guided by theoretically or conceptually informed notions on 'consequences' and 'governance'. As such, the first section in the book is guided by a typology of different types of free moving EU citizens. The introduction elaborates on this typology, based on previous studies of free movement in the EU (such as Black et. al. 2010). Chapter 2 by Deniz Sert distinguishes eight types of 'EU free moving citizens' based on two dimensions, including the time-specificity of movement. In her contribution she observes that creating a typology of CEE migration and including a diversified picture of types of migrants in this research as a heuristic device for comparison creates a tool with an exploratory value for answering research questions in a valuable way. The added value of this heuristic device can be seen in Chap. 3 in which Ursula Reeger shows, guided by the diversification of CEE migration, what kind of social- and economic implications free movement has regarding stakeholders. This has been studied with a focus on its urban specificity, acknowledging that free movement is 'unevenly spread' amongst specific rural and urban municipalities. It shows that a detailed look at the implications in various domains for different types of migrants reveals that these are often interrelated with each type displaying its own "chain of implications". For some types of migrants, these linkages result in vicious cycles difficult to escape or a domino effect of implications, multiplying their effects due to their social or economic position. These empirical chapters are complemented by Chaps. 4 and 5 by Godfried Engbersen en Rinus Penninx. In Chap. 4, Godfried Engbersen translates the empirical data to the broader debates within sociological theory on liquid modernity (Engbersen 2012). By his concept of liquid migration he concludes that the findings show that this liquidity or temporality of mobility does not cover the full story. More long term or settlement types show that there is more to say than only the 'new face' of East-West fluidity could suggest. In Chap. 5, Rinus Penninx questions the 'newness' of this migration and compares this with other migration regimes in the past. He concludes that comparisons are hard because of the changed and different regulatory context, legal instruments and the position of private organisations in the management of this migration. As such, he provides some context embeds the findings in a historical framework.

The second section on 'governance' focuses on how local, national and European (governmental) authorities responded to the types of free movers and their social- and economic implications. This is also guided by a conceptual frame, a typology of five theoretical ideal types of governance approaches to map the horizontal and vertical relations in which policies, laws and legislation on CEE related topics are developed. In her Chap. 6, Karin Zelano shows the story from 'inside Brussels' and how free movement and its governance has been perceive by stakeholders on EU level. She reveals a more top-down approach and a governance gap between the EU, member-states and local municipalities on this issue. In Chap. 7 by Gregg Bucken-Knapp, Jonas Hinnfors, Andrea Spehar and Karin Zelano, they show the empirical governance variety between the selected cases of The Netherlands, Sweden, Austria and Turkey. And despite the institutional and political difference between the cases, multi-level governance seems to be absent in most instances. In his Chap. 8, Dion Curry develops indicators to understand multi-level governance in much more detail and embedded in the multi-level governance literature. He reveals how the findings develop this strand of literature for instance by showing the need to separate out multi-level contexts from multi-level governance. Finally, in Chap. 9 Alex Balch observes the central role of national governments on European decision-making. He sees a lot of political conflict and contestation which causes social denizenship for some citizens in Europa. Highlighting the politicized character of this topic, he shows how the findings could be understood in relation to political science literatures and beyond.

In the third section 'perspectives from sending and receiving regions' it connects the findings on intra- European movement to the literature on Central and Eastern European countries such as Poland and the Czech Republic, which are important 'sending' countries of intra- European movement, as well as Turkey as a new emergent destination country of migration from Central and Eastern Europe. In Chap. 10, Marta Kindler shows in detail the positive and negative effects of free movement for Poland as a sending and receiving country. By a detailed analysis of what is going on in Poland she shows the 'double governance challenge' evolving in Poland. By focussing on Czech careworkers in Austrian regions, Dusan Drbohlav and Lenka Pavelkova show in Chap. 11 a new emerging type of MICO, of migration and commuting, in-between old notions of settlement, transborder movement and mobility. And finally, in Chap. 12, Deniz Karci Korfali and Tugba Acar show how a diversification of migration affects the regions of Edirne and Istanbul and how this contributes to the 'key importance' of governance challenges. They also explain the specificities of the Turkish case as a state centred hierarchal order and top-down approach on policy, to better understand the position of Turkey as case within European free movement. Finally, in the Chaps 13 and 14, Mark van Ostaijen, Peter Scholten and Adrian Favell formulate concluding thoughts on the project of IMAGINATION, the empirical and theoretical contributions and how this can be interpreted into larger bodies of knowledge. More specifically, Adrian Favell concludes on the whole volume with an epilogue reflecting on the contributions of the book to the literature on European free movement.

As can be understood from previous notions on the subsequent chapters, this book is set-up to relate the empirical data gathering with broader theoretical debates. As such, the first two parts: 'consequences' and 'governance', are finalized with theoretical chapters. As such, in the first 'consequences' part, the debate is focussing on the body of literature in migration studies and beyond, questioning if this is an 'exceptional' phenomenon, can we see it as 'liquid migration' or is this 'new face' of East-West or CEE migration more 'old wine in new bottles'? In the 'governance' section, the debate focuses on Europeanization literature and governance studies, contesting the multi-level character of this governance setting and discussing the European politics and policymaking processes of free movement. These chapters are written by scholars who are experts in their field, invited to reflect on the empirical contributions and to embed this into a number of thematically related theoretical discussions. The authors of these chapters were not involved in the IMAGINATION project, but do reflect on the IMAGINATION findings in their contributions. All these chapters were discussed during a workshop in Gothenburg in December 2015 by the authors.

1.4 IMAGINATION Project

The empirical material stems from a research project funded by the Joint Programing Initiative (JPI) Urban Europe: IMAGINATION, 'Urban Implications and Governance of CEE migration'. This 3-year project of empirical research was carried out between June 2013 and June 2016, implemented by interdisciplinary teams in Turkey, Sweden, Austria, the Czech Republic, Poland and The Netherlands including sociologists, political scientists, geographers and public administration scholars. This interdisciplinary approach of the IMAGINATION research project also stimulated the confrontation of the empirical findings on European free movement with broader literatures from migration studies, geography, sociology, political sciences and public administration theory.

The project followed an innovative approach in terms of methodology. The empirical analyses in the book are based on comparative large-scale in-depth interviews with various stakeholders, as well as a systematic data collection effort, document analyses and literature review. In terms of interviews, stakeholders were involved from very different positions, in order to allow for a multiple perspective analysis of CEE migration. This includes policymakers from different levels, but also representatives from migrant organizations, NGO's, housing corporations, labour recruitment agencies and business associations. We believe that this not only allows for a more balanced 'multi-actor' view on CEE migration, it also provides a more comprehensive, valid and reliable method for the study of a topic on which official data is often lacking or incomplete. This applies in particular to the case of CEE migration, as many migrants are not registered.

Thus, as primary unit of analysis not countries or cities, but *urban regions* were selected as most significant objects of research. Since European free movement is not only an urban but also a rural phenomenon, local consequences are often not limited by the city boundaries where many migrants live, but also located into nearby suburban and rural areas where CEE migrants work. The notion of urban regions thus focuses on cities together with their suburban areas and nearby rural areas to capture the complementary social implications within *daily urban systems* of labour, housing and leisure. Urban regions were selected from three countries

(The Netherlands, Sweden and Austria), which received relatively large numbers of CEE migrants but 'opened' their labour market borders to CEE countries in different periods and in different ways. Next to this we selected one non-European 'outlier case' (Turkey) to study the consequences of EU laws and regulations on the urban cases in a non-EU member state. The selected urban regions were Fig. 1.2.

It is worth to mention some important considerations in the case study selection process. First of all, as important selection criterion, Austria, the Netherlands and Sweden are representations of different *transition regimes* in Europe. They all opened their borders at different points in time (Sweden in 2004; the Netherlands in 2007; Austria in 2011 for A8 countries), which allowed the project to study the effects of this variety. But in this book, also other cases are included, such as:

a) A most-likely case (Poland);
b) A least-likely case (Czech Republic)
c) An outlier case (Turkey)

We will explain this rationale first. Because first of all, Poland and the Czech Republic are two important sending (and receiving) regions of CEE migrants. Especially Poland has been the most significant sending country during the free movement regulations. As mentioned before, with more than 2.2 million people between 2004–2007, Poland can be considered as a very significant and 'most-likely case' to study this phenomenon (Grabowska-Lusinska et al. 2009). The Czech Republic instead, has always been a rather reluctant case of international migration. Czechs seem to be well rooted and reluctant in moving out. The overall Czech emigration is relatively low compared with some of the other countries in this book (see the chapter of Drbolav and Pavelkova in this book). However, statistics are rather unreliable since most movement is not formally registered. This can be seen by other, estimated, stock data of 13,000 Czechs working in Austria in 2014 (see Chap. 11 of Drbolav and Pavelkova). According to this data, Austria is an important and significant rising country for transborder movement and Czechs working abroad. This raises various questions regarding the drivers and opportunities of these movers and how they do not comply with the general reluctance of Czechs. This legitimates the significance of this least-likely case of Czech Republic in this volume. And finally, the fourth section is completed by the case study on Turkey. First of all, from a strict institutional European perspective, Turkey could be seen as an 'outlier' case. However, for a number of reasons, Turkey has relevance and importance to gain knowledge about this emerging phenomenon. First of all, because of historical interrelations and legacies, a significant number of Bulgarians have a Turkish passport. This has historically evolved into a stable amount of transborder movements between Bulgaria and Turkey. It is interesting to see to what extent this historical migration corridor changes by new regulatory legacies from the EU. Next to this, from a geographical point of view, and with a focus on urban consequences, one of the most proximate and largest urban regions outside the European territory is, next to for instance Saint Petersburg, the Istanbul urban region. Next to this, Edirne is selected as a more rural and border region, to gain a better understanding of

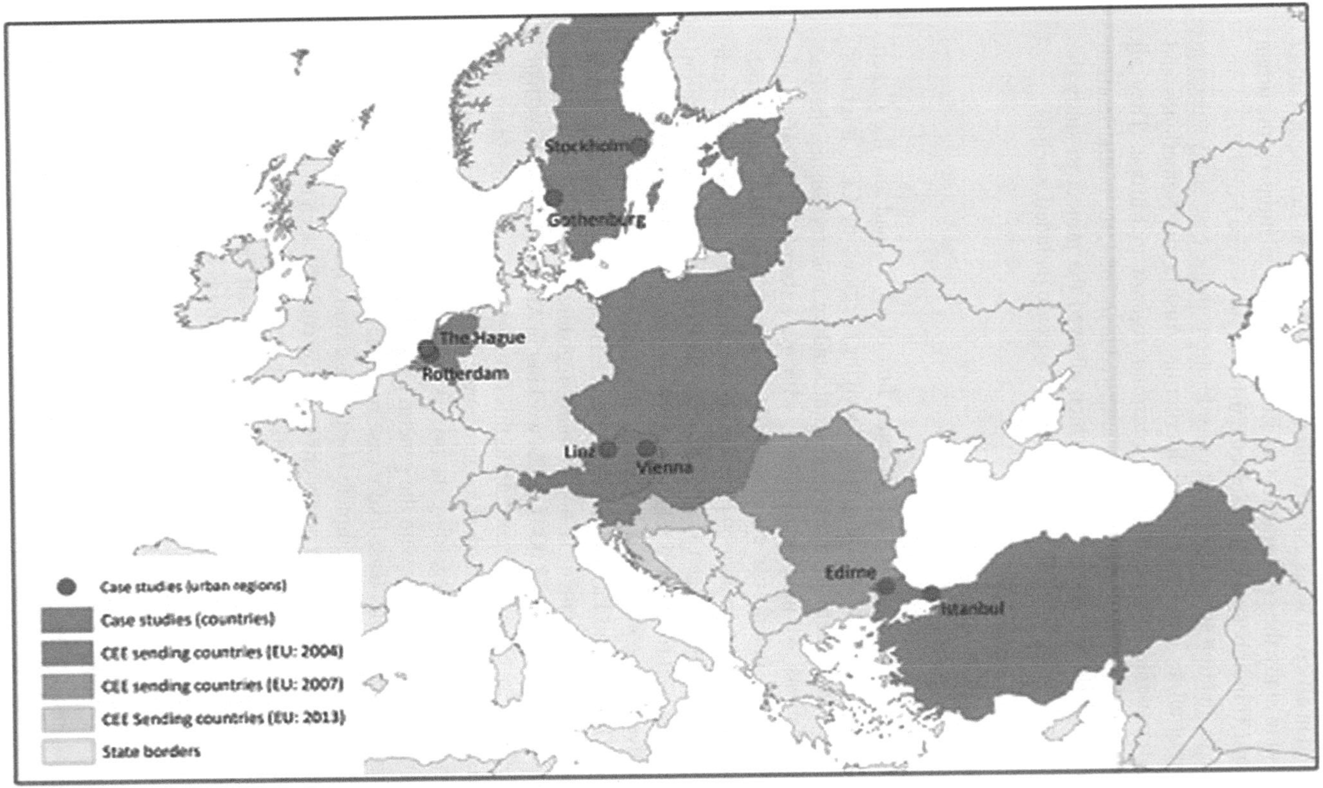

Fig. 1.2 Overview cases included (Important to mention is that there is a *double inclusion* on CEE countries in this study. In the first place, the study interprets 'CEE' by the countries Bulgaria, Croatia, Czech Republic, Estonia, Hungary, Latvia, Lithuania, Poland, Romania, Slovakia and Slovenia, Albania, Belarus, Bosnia Herzegovina, Kosovo, Macedonia, Moldova, Montenegro and Serbia. Secondly, given this overview, there is a focus applied to the most significant and important countries (in terms of population size) for sending and receiving regions in Europe. The selected countries for this book are shown in the map above). (Source: Korfali et al. 2014)

transborder movements. Edirne maintains a large Bulgarian-Turkish community and the region of Edirne is one of the most important entry points of Turkey. As illustration, in 2010, 1.5 million people from CEE countries entered Turkey via the region of Edirne on a total of 2.5 million and 600.000 CEEs entered Istanbul on a total of seven million people (Korfali et al. 2014). To conclude, it holds relevance to study the impact of EU rules and regulation on Turkey and the eventual effects on migration from CEE to EU and vice versa. Are these figures in- or decreasing, why and what are the consequences for both sending and receiving regions? Thus, from a strict institutional European perspective, what could be defined as an 'outlier' case, there are multiple reasons to include Turkey as an important and relevant case for this research.

1.5 Methodological Considerations

While this book is built upon the comparative framework outlined above and the data collected in the context of the IMAGINATION project, it is worth considering some methodological issues here. To overcome a repetition of argumentation, specific issues of methodology are considered in the forthcoming chapters. However, the chapters share an overall methodological framework that will be discussed in the following.

First of all, to make a systematic comparison, and to select case studies, all research went through a bibliographic and statistical analysis of secondary data sources which enabled a preliminary comparative setting. For that aim, the research teams have collected available data on CEE migration pertaining to their respective countries, and tried to synchronize these figures. *First*, they utilized secondary sources, reviewing the literature of previous research as well as available official statistics. This provided with a valuable source on stocks and flows of migrants including basic demographic features such as age and gender, but lacks important information on education, professional background or legal status. Additionally, especially where no official data were available, teams conducted semi-structured interviews with different stakeholders to get estimates of the scale of CEE migration and to discover different types of migration. These included representatives of the CEE migrants mostly from different migrant organizations, officials from local governments, relevant private agencies such as labour recruitment agencies, and NGOs involved in the related areas of migration like housing corporations and educational institutions. The analysis in Chap. 2 contains the key features of this first data-gathering step. As mentioned in that chapter it shows the outcome of exploring, classifying and summarising quantitative data that could be gathered around the selected cases in this project.

Secondly, the study included a multi-level stakeholder analysis to capture the perceptions of stakeholders in various positions concerning the consequences as well as the governance of intra- European movement. In all case studies, the survey was distributed amongst experts, local and national policymakers as well as NGO's.

Table 1.3 Overview respondents

	Urban region	Online survey	Expert interviews	Urban living lab
Austria	Linz	n = 23	n = 8 (9)	n = 8
	Vienna	n = 23	n = 5 (7)	
	National level	—	n = 1	
The Netherlands	The Hague	n = 15	n = 5	n = 16
	Rotterdam	n = 15	n = 5	
	National level	n = 16	n = 2	
Sweden	Gothenburg	n = 22	n = 8 (12)	n = 30
	Stockholm	n = 15	n = 5 (7)	
	National level	—	n = 4	
Turkey	Edirne	n = 24	n = 7	n = 11
	Istanbul	n = 21	n = 7	
	National level	—	—	

The strength of a multiple stakeholder analysis is that it enables the project to capture a variety of perspectives, from different positions as well as focussing on different elements of governance. The multiple-stakeholder analysis involved three interrelated stages of data gathering (Table 1.3) (see: Enengel and Reeger 2015) of:

(1) *Online survey* (primary inventory of implications, N = 174)
(2) *Expert interviews* (qualitative in-depth information on stage 1, N = 57)
(3) *Focus groups* (reflection of the findings from stages 1 and 2, N = 65)

As a first step, the online survey was implemented as a 'mapping exercise', to establish a primary inventory of relevant issues and types of migration. The design was comparatively developed and implemented during spring 2014 in all eight urban regions and resulted in 174 returned questionnaires. The people selected for this questionnaire was based on our previous experience working in the research domain of CEE migration, having done the desk research of phase one and the informal interviews. The professionals that came up from that work have been consulted in this explorative phase. Content-wise, the questionnaires were built up, just like the interviews and focus groups, on the three main pillars of this research. Respondents were asked about a) types of CEE migration b) urban consequences of CEE migration and c) governance issues relating to CEE migration.

Secondly, after mapping the outcomes of the survey, additional expert interviews were set up to delve deeper into what has been mentioned in the online survey. Similar to the online survey, experts were selected according to predefined criteria based on variety of 1) their relationship to the respective urban regions 2) their professional affiliation (NGO, public, private). The interviews were held during autumn and fall of 2014 and involved 57 expert interviews with 66 interviewed participants. With the explicit aim to follow-up on the online survey, especially those were selected who indicated interest in future participation, complemented with those unable or not initially approached for the survey. The interviews were transcribed and a systematic grid of codes and sub-codes enabled a comparative analysis.

Finally, the multi-stakeholder analysis was complemented by *Urban Living Labs*, focus groups of deliberative exchange of ideas and reflections on preliminary research findings. This method enabled to validate some initial findings and bring further and deepen ideas about data found. Participants were selected based on the interviews and the people mentioned. Since much depended on the professional involvement of stakeholders in this issue and the knowledge they have, all three phases were layers of chronological snowball sampling strategies. This contains clear biases for which the research was sensitive, but was chosen in order to get the most relevant expertise on board as possible. All Living Labs were held in December 2014 on four sites and were recorded, transcribed and analysed in a comparative fashion. As such, all data collection carried out in all six urban regions was guided by a strict common framework. In total, more than 250 contacts with key stakeholders from the public sector, semi-public, private institutions and with NGOs have taken place.

References

Asscher, L. and Goodhart, D. (2013). Code oranje voor vrij werkverkeer binnen de EU. *De Volkskrant* 17-08-2013.

Black, R., Engbersen, G., Okolski, M., & Pantiru, C. (Eds.). (2010). *A continent moving west? EU enlargement and labour migration from central and eastern Europe*. Amsterdam: Amsterdam University Press.

Brenner, N. (2004). *New state spaces: urban governance and the rescaling of statehood*. Oxford: Oxford University Press.

Düvell, F., & Vogel, D. (2006). Polish migrants: Tensions between sociological typologies and state categories. In A. Triandafyllidou (Ed.), *Contemporary polish migration in Europe. Complex Patterns of Movement and Settlement* (p. 26789). Lewiston: Edwin Mellen Press.

Emelianoff, C. (2013). Local energy transition and multilevel climate governance: the contrasted experiences of two pioneer cities. *Urban Studies, 51*, 1–16.

European Commission. (2004). *Report on the implementation of the Commission's action plan for skills and mobility, COM 72*. Brussels: EC.

European Commission. (2007). *Mobility: An instrument for more and better jobs: European job mobility action plan 2007–2010, COM 773*. Brussels: EC.

Enengel, M. L. and U. Reeger, 2015. *Urban implications of CEE migration in Austrian urban regions*. Country report Austria. IMAGINATION Working Paper.

Engbersen, G. (2012). Migration transitions in an era of liquid migration. In M. Okolski (Ed.), *European immigrations: Trends, Structures and Policy Implications, IMISCOE Research* (pp. 91–105). Amsterdam: Amsterdam University Press.

Engbersen, G. and Snel, E. (2012). Lokaal bestuur en de uitbreiding van Europa. De bestuurlijke aanpak van de arbeidsmigratie uit Midden- en Oost-Europa, Bestuurskunde (1), pp. 25–32.

Engbersen, G., Leerkes, A., Grabowska-Lusinska, I., Snel, E., & Burgers, J. (2013). On the differential attachments of migrants from Central and Eastern Europe. *Journal of Ethnic and Migration Studies, 39*(6), 959–981.

EY. (2014). *Evaluation of the impact of free movement of EU citizens at local level – Final report*. Brussels: Ernst and Young.

Favell, A. (2008). The new face of east–west migration in Europe. *Journal of Ethnic and Migration Studies, 34*(5), 701–716.

Favell, A., & Recchi, E. (Eds.). (2010). *Pioneers of European identity: Citizenship and mobility in the EU*. Northampton: Edward Elgar.
Favell, A., & Nebe, T. (2009). Internal and external movers: East-West migration and the impact of EU enlargement. In E. Recchi & A. Favell (Eds.), *Pioneers of European integration* (pp. 205–223).
Friberg, J. H. (2012). The guest-worker syndrome revisited? *Nordic Journal of Migration Research, 2*(4), 316–324.
Friberg, J. H. (2013). The stages of migration. From going abroad to settling down: Post-Accession Polish workers in Norway. *Journal of Ethnic and Migration Studies, 38*(10), 1589–1605.
Geddes, A., & Boswell, C. (2011). *Migration and Mobility in the European Union*. Houndmills: Palgrave Macmillan.
Grabowska-Lusinska, I., Lesinska, M., & Okólski, M. (2009). *Transformacja nieoczywista. Polska jako kraj imigracji* (pp. 69–124). Warszawa: Wydawnictwa Uniwersytetu Warszawskiego.
Glorius, B., Grabowska-Lusinska, I., & Rindoks, A. (Eds.). (2013). *Mobility in transition: Migration patterns after EU-enlargement*. Amsterdam: Amsterdam University Press.
Gijsberts, M., & Lubbers, M. (2015). *Langer in Nederland*. SCP: Den Haag.
Guiraudon, V. (2000). European integration and migration policy: Vertical policy-making as venue shopping. *Journal of Common Market Studies, 38*(2), 251–271.
Gustavsson, E., Elander, I., & Lundmark, M. (2009). Multilevel governance, networking cities, and the geography of climate-change mitigation: Two Swedish examples. *Environment and Planning C: Government and Policy, 27*, 59–74.
Hansen, P. (2015). Undermining free movement: Migration in an age of austerity, *Eurozine*. http://www.eurozine.com/articles/2015-02-06-hansenp-en.html
Holston, J., & Appadurai, A. (1999). Introduction: Cities and citizenship. In J. Holston (Ed.), *Cities and citizenship* (pp. 1–18). Durham: Duke University Press.
Heinelt, H., & Neiderhafner, S. (2008). Cities and organised interest intermediation in the EU multi-level system. *European Urban and Regional Studies, 15*(2), 173–187.
Hundstorfer, R., Peeters, K., Rebsamen, F., Nahles, A., Schmit, N., Asscher, L., Johansson, Y. (2015). Letter to Ms. Thyssen. Posting of workers Directive. 18-06-2015.
Isin, E. F. (2000). Introduction: Democracy, citizenship and the city. In E. F. Isin (Ed.), *Democracy, citizenship and the global city* (pp. 1–21). London: Routledge.
Kern, K., & Bulkeley, H. (2009). Cities, Europeanization and multi-level governance: Governing climate change through transnational municipal networks. *Journal of Common Market Studies, 47*, 309–332.
Korfali, D. Sert, D., and T. Acar, (2014) Mapping and analysis of types of migration from CEE countries: Country report Turkey, IMAGINATION Working Paper.
Lafleur, J. M., & Stanek, M. (Eds.). (2016). *South-north migration of EU citizens in times of crisis*. Cham: Springer.
Le Gales, P. (2002). *European cities: social conflicts and governance*. New York: Oxford University Press.
Lijphart, A. (2012). *Patterns of democracy. Government forms and performance in thirty-six countries*. New Haven: Yale University Press.
Musterd, S., Murie, A., & Kesteloot, C. (2016). *Neighbourhoods of poverty*. Palgrave Macmillan.
Mikl-Leitner, J., H.P. Friedrich, F. Teeven, and H.T. May. 2013. Letter to Alan Shatter, Presidency of European Council.
Okolski, M. (2001). Incomplete migration. A new form of mobility in central and Eastern Europe. The case of Polish and Ukrainian migrants. In C. Wallace & D. Stola (Eds.), *Patterns of migration in Central Europe*. Houndmills/Basinstoke: Palgrave Macmillan.
Ostaijen, M. M. A. C., van Reeger, U., & Zelano, K. (2017). The commodification of mobile workers in Europe. A comparative perspective on capital and labour in Austria, the Netherlands and Sweden. *Comparative Migration Studies, 5*(6).
Pralle, S. B. (2003). Venue shopping, political strategy, and policy change: The internationalization of Canadian forest advocacy. *Journal of Public Policy, 23*(3), 233–260.

van Puymbroeck, N., van de Pol, S., & Oosterlynck, S. (2011). Oost-West mobiliteit en de bestuurlijke europeanisering van steden. Een vergelijkende studie van de cases Gent en Rotterdam. *Tijdschrift voor Sociologie, 32*(3–4), 291–326.

Sassen, S. (1999). Whose city is it? Globalization and the formation of new claims. In J. Holston (Ed.), *Cities and citizenship* (pp. 177–194). Durham: Duke University Press.

Scholten, P. W. A. (2013). Agenda dynamics and the multi-level governance of migrant integration. The case of Dutch migrant integration policies. *Policy Sciences, 46*, 217–236.

Scholten, P., Engbersen, G., van Ostaijen, M., & Snel, E. (2017). Multilevel governance from below: How Dutch cities respond to intra-European mobility. *Journal of Ethnic and Migration Studies*, 1–23.

Sert, D., Korfali, D., & Acar, T. (2015). *Urban implications of CEE migration in Turkish urban regions. Country report Turkey*. IMAGINATION Working Paper.

Wallace, C., & Stola, D. (Eds.). (2001). *Patterns of Migration in Central Europe*. Houndmills/Basinstoke: Palgrave Macmillan.

Part I
Types of Intra-European Movement and Their Consequences

Chapter 2
The Diversification of Intra-European Movement

Deniz Sert

2.1 Introduction

The literature on free movement among the 28 member states of the European Union (EU) divides along two main themes. The first set of studies analyses the nature and type of intra-European movement. Here, the central focus tends to be one of the main migration flows within Europe – namely, the movement of Central and Eastern Europeans (CEE) who are mostly citizens of the EU (Black et al. 2010). In migration studies, this freedom of movement within the EU is increasingly articulated in terms of 'East' to 'West' migration. Many studies show how this migration pattern within Western Europe is expanding beyond the seasonal and circular forms of labour migration that initially characterized CEE migration, to one characterized by more permanence (e.g., Recchi 2008; Favell 2008; Eade et al. 2006; Düvell and Vogel 2006; Engbersen et al. 2011, 2013; Castro-Martin and Cortina 2015). To illustrate, Engbersen et al. (2011; Engbersen et al. 2013) contend that along the two axes of attachment to country of origin and destination, there are now four categories of intra-European movement: (1) bi-national; (2) circular; (3) settlement and; (4) "footloose". This typology captures the fact that some migrants preserve transnational ties that attach them to their region of origin as well as their host countries while others remain permanently in receiving societies, later reuniting with family members or establishing new families in the receiving country (ibid.). Others still may continue their expedition to other parts of Europe or may rather end up "footloose", experiencing problems accessing the labour market in the receiving country as their ties with the home country fade (ibid.). Studies also show that different types of migration are related to different stages of migration, moving from an initial stage of temporary work abroad, through transnational commuting to permanent

D. Sert (✉)
Oyzegin University Istanbul, Istanbul, Turkey

P. Scholten, M. van Ostaijen (eds.), *Between Mobility and Migration*, IMISCOE Research Series, https://doi.org/10.1007/978-3-319-77991-1_2

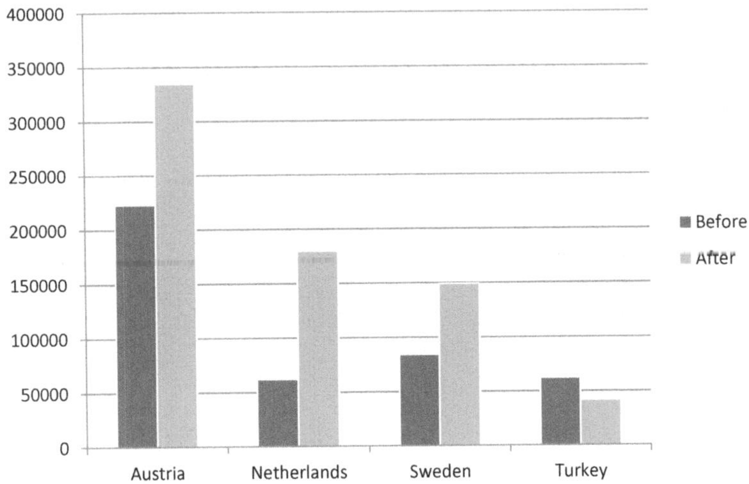

Fig. 2.1 CEE migration before and after the 2004 and 2007 enlargements
Country (Before/After): Austria (2002/2013), Netherlands (2003/2013), Sweden (2000/2012), Turkey (2003/2012)
Source: Sert (2014), updated by the author

settlement, where these phases largely depend on the labour market opportunities in the destination regions (Friberg 2012).

A second set of studies considers this free movement as a form of socio-economic participation on the European labour market, where migrants are seen as a key driver of economic integration. This stream in the literature focuses more on the subsequent *effects* of free movement, largely taking it for granted that this movement is essentially about 'labour migration' (Pascouau 2013; Martín and Venturini 2015; Barslund et al. 2015). While some studies underline the phenomenon of "social dumping" produced by migrants' readiness to work for low wages in bad working conditions (Amelina and Vasilache 2014), others question if this is a form of welfare – rather than labour – migration. Still others argue that liberalization of movement in the EU is producing a workforce that is more aware of the European dimension of the labour market (Andrijasevic and Sacchetto 2015).

Based on a research conducted in Austria, Sweden, the Netherlands and Turkey in 2013–2016, this chapter largely contributes to the first line of literature on intra-European movement with one key argument: diversification of CEE migration. While drawing the main migration corridors from CEE countries to the less-focused cases of Austria, Sweden, the Netherlands, and Turkey, we argue that migration patterns within these corridors are diversified on two levels: time (i.e., temporary versus permanent migration), and; socio-economic status (i.e., high-skilled workers versus non-workers). This typology is also presented in Chap. 1, as Fig. 2.1. Consequently, in that typology we choose eight categories or types of migrants (TOMs) that cover most of the surface of the typology. These are: 1) knowledge workers; (2) entrepreneurs; (3) manual workers; (4) persons working in private households; (5) sex workers and trafficked persons; (6) students; (7) non-working spouses and children, and; (8) beggars and homeless people. This categorization on time and socio-economic status is an important contribution to the literature as it avoids the typical singular reliance on migrants' ethnicity/national citizenship (which holds limited analytical relevance) to focus on their labour-market position instead.

Migration corridors are utilized here as frames of observation. The concept of corridors enables us to observe different forms of asymmetry in movement (Carling 2015). The destination countries chosen for this research represent different stages in relation to CEE migration. To illustrate, while Austria and the Netherlands issued transitional arrangements concerning intra-European 'labour migration' during the 2004 and 2007 enlargements, Sweden opted out of such a policy choice. Turkey is included in the analysis as a case study with a very different immigration regime, since the EU regulations on CEE migration are not applicable. Moreover, the corridors are not evaluated solely at the country level. Different urban regions were also included in the analysis adding leverage to the analysis of the diversity of CEE migration. Two urban regions were included for each country: Vienna and Linz in Austria, The Hague and Rotterdam (the Netherlands), Stockholm and Gothenburg (Sweden), and Edirne and Istanbul (Turkey). The concentration on urban regions uncovered further diversification of CEE migration, since we observed more transnational patterns in bordering urban regions, such as Linz and Edirne. Still, considering a multilevel perspective, the country level is more determinant than the specific urban level to identify responses, policies and even consequences of CEE migration, where cities located in the same country often seem to display similar responses and register the same consequences.

The chapter proceeds as follows. The first section presents the methodology, underlining the issues of inaccessibility and incomparability of available data. The second part provides a brief outline of the historical background of East-West migration before the 2004 and 2007 enlargements. Subsequently, the effects of the eastern enlargement of the EU are analysed with a specific focus on the transitional arrangements where the four countries chosen for the research represent comparable cases. The fourth section defines and details the main migration corridors. The fifth part depicts the types of migrants involved in each country and urban region, with a focus on the feminization of migration. The final section presents some concluding remarks.

2.2 Methodology and Issues

As outlined in the methodological considerations of Chap 1, research teams in Austria, Sweden, the Netherlands and Turkey collected available data on CEE migration pertaining to their respective countries, and tried to synchronize these figures to produce systematic comparisons. Each research team outlined and analysed existing data on the number of CEE migrants across four data clusters: (1)

country of origin, gender, educational levels, stocks and flows; (2) migration motives (i.e., labour, family, and/or study); (3) duration of migration (i.e., temporary versus permanent), and; (4) labour market participation (i.e., whether employment was formal or informal). All the teams followed a dual approach on methodology.

First, as mentioned in Chap. 1, they utilized secondary sources, reviewing the literature of previous research as well as available official statistics. This provided with a valuable source on stocks and flows of migrants including basic demographic features such as age and gender, but lacks important information on education, professional background or legal status. As such, although CEE migration in Europe is a highly debated issue, finding comparable data proved difficult. To demonstrate, the Central Population Register (CPR) in Austria works with a system of continuous reporting on the changes of main residences at the municipal level covering all persons who have registered a main residence in Austria for more than 90 consecutive days. This provides a valuable source for an overview on stocks and flows of migrants including basic demographic features such as age and gender, but lacks important information on education, professional background or legal status. In the Netherlands, population statistics provide reliable information about the registered 'migrants' in the country. However, only those migrants who intend to stay in the Netherlands more than 4 months need to register, making statistics incomplete and socially selective. There are analyses of CEE migration derived from representative samples from these population registers, but the problem remains that many CEE migrants are not registered. There are also survey studies based on non-representative sampling of CEE migration, which provide better insight into the more volatile category of temporary (and often less integrated) CEE migrants in the Netherlands, but the unemployed and other non-working migrants tend to be absent in these. In Sweden, data on CEE migration were derived from official statistics (i.e., from Statistics Sweden, the Swedish Work Environment Authority, the National Board of Health and Welfare, and the Swedish Higher Education Authority). Like the Netherlands, there is a time dimension in the population registers where only those migrants who declare their intention to stay for at least one year in Sweden are included in the population statistics. Moreover, like in Austria the official data hardly provide any information on the educational levels of CEE migrants. In Turkey, the problem of availability of data is more critical than other cases. International migration in Turkey became a policy concern only in the late '90s, and collection and distribution of data have been considered as statistically important only after the establishment of the Directorate General of Migration Management in 2014, as envisioned by Law 6458 on Foreigners and International Protection (YUKK) adopted in 2013.

Secondly and additionally – especially where no official data were available – teams conducted qualitative interviews to estimate the scale of CEE migration and to uncover the different types of migration. Within this second approach, semi-structured interviews with different stakeholders were conducted. These included representatives of CEE migrants in the different migrant organizations, officials from local government, relevant private outfits (e.g., labour recruitment agencies), and NGOs involved in migration-related areas (e.g., housing and education). In that regard the upcoming paragraphs are the outcome of the exploring, classifying and summarising quantitative data gathering steps in this project. But overall, although CEE migration in Europe is a highly debated issue, finding data – especially *comparable* data – proved difficult.

2.3 CEE Migration Before the Enlargements

Migration from CEE countries to Austria, Sweden, the Netherlands, and Turkey occurred long before the EU enlargements. In Austria, two groups of CEE migrants have been of particular importance. The first are refugees from the communist countries (who continued to arrive until the late 1980s) and the second are labour migrants and their families. Due to its neutrality during Cold War, Austria received three major waves of refugees: from Hungary in 1956, Czechoslovakia (1968) and Poland (1981). For many, Austria was only a transit country on their way to other destinations (Enengel et al. 2014). At the beginning of the 1960s, Austria was confronted with a growing need of additional labour and started to recruit workers from countries such as Turkey and Yugoslavia (ibid.). Despite the original model – a rotation of temporary 'guest workers' – many of these migrants stayed and brought their families to Austria. To this day, Turkish- and Balkan-origin workers comprise the most important and growing foreign-born groups in the country (ibid.).

Like Austria, the Netherlands also received refugees from Hungary, Czechoslovakia, and Poland during the same periods (1956, 1968 and 1981, respectively) (Bonjour 1980: 48; also cited in Ostaijen et al. 2014). Unlike other countries, the Netherlands also faced a unique type of movement of those Polish soldiers who had fought with the Allied forces to liberate the Netherlands from German occupation during World War II. These soldiers often stayed and married Dutch women. There was also marriage migration of women from CEE countries, particularly from Poland, who married Dutch men, the so-called 'Polish brides' (Dagevos 2011; also cited in Ostaijen et al. 2014). Again, like Austria the Netherlands has also been an important destination for labour migration. Even before and shortly after World War II several thousand CEE nationals, mainly from Poland and Slovenia, arrived to work in the Dutch mines (Brassé and Van Schelven 1980; also cited in Ostaijen et al. 2014). 50,000 Poles were estimated to work as seasonal workers in Dutch horticulture in the late 1980s (Dagevos 2011: 31; also cited in Ostaijen et al. 2014).

Like Austria and the Netherlands, Sweden was (and still is) a destination for humanitarian immigration, and in increasing numbers (Boguslaw 2012; also cited in Zelano et al. 2014). Unlike the two other cases, Sweden followed a more cautious immigration policy in terms of labour migration. In the wake of the economic downturn at the beginning of the 1970s, Sweden allowed labour migration only if demand could not be met by the existing domestic workforce. These obstacles for free movement were removed with Sweden's accession into the EU in 1995 (Zelano et al. 2014).

Immigration from CEE followed a different trajectory in Turkey. In the Early Republican Period, usually categorized under Balkan migrations, there were large influxes from Bulgaria, Romania, and Yugoslavia. After the war of independence, as part of its nation and state building efforts, the country needed human capital to build a homogenous nation state and welcomed migrants of Sunni-Islam origin from countries such as Bulgaria, Romania and Yugoslavia. In the period of 1940 and 1945, more than 20,000 people migrated to Turkey with Bulgarians, Romanians and Yugoslavians representing 73%, 19% and 8% of this migrant community, respectively (Korfalı et al. 2014). During the Cold War, a similar trend was observed. Approximately 800,000 migrants entered Turkey, those from Bulgaria forming the largest group followed by those coming from Yugoslavia (ibid.). Large-scale migration from Bulgaria during this time was due to Bulgaria's negative policies against its minorities, including those of Turkish ethnicity. Overall, the history of CEE migration to Turkey has been dominated by migration of people of Muslim origin from Bulgaria, Yugoslavia and Romania, usually looking for a safe haven. This pattern thus somehow resembles the humanitarian migrations in other countries under research. Lately, with the neo-liberal economic policies of governments in Turkey after 1990, different types of migration have been observed.

2.4 Enlargements, CEE Migration, and Transitional Arrangements

The EU enlargements bringing in the mostly Eastern European countries of the A10 in 2004 and Bulgaria and Romania in 2007 (the EU-2), had significant effects on both the mobility of people within the EU and near abroad (i.e., Turkey). Figure 2.1 depicts the volume of CEE migration in the four countries under research before and after the 2004 and 2007 enlargements, showing a substantial increase in the number of CEE migrants in Austria, Sweden, and the Netherlands, but a decrease in Turkey.

Accordingly, as of 2013 there were a total of 330,000 officially registered persons in Austria who were born in the CEE enlargement countries. This figure was one third higher compared to 2002. The number of CEE migrants has also risen in the Netherlands. Just before the EU enlargement of 2004, in 2003, there were about 62,000 CEE residents in the country. This number was only 50,000 in the 1990s. As of 2013, the number of CEE migrants in the Netherlands increased to almost 180,000, three times more than the same figure in 2003. Sweden also faced an increasing number of CEE migration. From 2000 to 2012, the number of individuals born in one of the CEE EU member states increased by almost 80%, from 80,000 to 150,000.

In Turkey, there was a reverse pattern: the proportion of CEE migrants of the total number of regular migrants who received residence permits in Turkey declined from 40% in 2003 and to 22% in 2011. This can be explained by two factors. *First*,

Table 2.1 Transitional arrangements (Source: Sert (2014), updated by the author)

Country	Policy	Years of application
Austria	Workers from the new member states require a work permit sponsored by their employer. After one year of legal employment, workers free to move within the labour market. After 18 months, those family members residing with the worker also receive this right.	EU-8: 2004–11
		EU-2: 2007–13
Netherlands	Workers from the new member states require a work permit for the first two years of employment.	EU-8: 2004–07
		EU-2: 2007–13
Sweden	No transitional restrictions were applied.	Not applicable.
Turkey	Not applicable.	Not applicable.

Turkey has begun to receive higher numbers of migrants from non-CEE countries in general, likely causing the ratio of migrants from the CEE countries to fall. *Second*, the number of CEE migrants has declined as they have shifted their migration destination towards the EU following the home country's EU accession. The finding reiterates the position of Turkey as a reference case in the IMAGINATION research.

Following the two enlargements, the number of CEE migrants in Austria, Sweden and the Netherlands did not increase overnight. Some member states opted for transitional restrictions, which allowed member states to temporarily restrict the right of workers from the new member states to move freely to another member state to *work*. Such transitional arrangements had been applied in most of the previous enlargements of the EU. Among the four countries under research here, it was Austria and the Netherlands that have issued such transitional arrangements in relation to intra-European movement (See Table 2.1).

Austria put in place transitional rules during both the 2004 and 2007 enlargement processes. Concerning the labour market access of CEE migrants, Austria declared that workers from the new member states needed a work permit sponsored by the employer. After one year of legal employment, workers were free to move within the labour market. After 18 months, those family members residing with the workers also received this right. The restrictions were lifted for the EU-10 in May 2011 and for Romania and Bulgaria by the end of 2013. In fact, transitional rules had not restricted freedom of settlement in Austria where the citizens of the new EU-member states could arrive as students, retirees or to join family members. They also had the right to found businesses, where they could be self-employed.

A year after lifting the transitional rules (2012), net migration from the CEE to Austria reached a zenith of 20,000. Because there is not municipal-level, register-based census that provides figures on employment of individuals during this time, the effects of the end of the transitional rules in May 2011 can only be made based on employment data and extensive in-depth analysis provided by the Federal Ministry of Labour, Social Affairs and Consumer Protection (Enengel et al. 2014).

Hence, the impact of liberalization one year after the end of the transitional provisions amounted to an increase of almost 27,000 persons or in relative terms about a one-third increase compared to April 2011 (ibid.). Based on the expert interviews conducted in Austria, some of these workers were not new immigrants, but had already been in Austria and had only legalized their existing employment. Interestingly, almost half of these new workers were commuters who did not move to Austria (ibid.).

Similarly, the Netherlands also issued transitional restrictions, which required that workers from the new member states obtain a work permit for the first two years of their employment. After 2007, when the restrictions for Poles and residents from the other new member states of 2004 were revoked, the figure of migrants from these countries rose. Studies conducted in the Netherlands during this time illustrate the implications of the transitional restrictions on CEE immigration and give a sense of comparison between the cases of 2004 and 2007, as transitional restrictions were still in effect in the latter case (e.g., Weltevrede et al. 2009, Engbersen et al. 2011, Engbersen et al. 2013, Snel et al. 2014, also cited in Ostaijen et al. 2014). Focusing both on registered and non-registered CEE labour migrants, these studies show that because of the transitional regulations that were still effective towards the citizens of EU-2 enlargement countries of 2007, many Romanian and Bulgarian respondents were often self-employed rather than holding formal jobs (ibid.).

Contrasting the Austrian and Dutch cases, Sweden did not employ any transitional restrictions during either enlargement. In 2004, Sweden was the only EU member state that refrained from implementing transitional rules, where the UK and Ireland implemented minor ones to moderate the impact of the prospective immigration flows. Similarly, in 2007 Sweden again elected not to apply restrictions. Additionally, in 2008 Sweden liberalized its labour migration policy. With the change, instead of having state institutions evaluate the demand for immigrant labour via labour market tests, authorization to conduct the assessment was delegated to employers (Zelano et al. 2014). Having a work permit in Sweden now only depends on having a job offer with a wage that is in accordance with a collective agreement or at the same level as collective agreements in the industry concerned (Wadensjö and Gerdes 2013). Despite cautionary calls that insisted on transitional restrictions, studies by Doyle et al. (2006), Ruist (2013) and Wadensjö and Gerdes (2013) have proved that the fears of welfare abuse were exaggerated; immigrants from the expanded EU show no dramatic deviation in earnings, work conditions, educational levels or social welfare provisions (Zelano et al. 2014).

Overall, in Sweden – where no transitional restrictions were applied – the reservations on CEE immigration proved entirely unfounded. In Austria and the Netherlands, where transitional restrictions were employed, the restraints only affected formal employment. Immigrants from the CEE member states still arrived in both countries, working on a self-employed basis.

Table 2.2 Main migration corridors (Ranking) (Source: Sert (2014), updated by the author)

	Poland	Romania	Bulgaria	Hungary	Others	
Austria	2	1		3	4[a]	
Netherlands	1	4	2	3		
Sweden	1	2		3	4[b]	5[c]
Turkey		4	1		2[d]	3[e]

[a]Czech Republic
[b]Estonia
[c]Lithuania
[d]Ukraine
[e]Moldova

2.5 Main Migration Corridors

Migration corridors are tracks that form under specific conditions and enable movement of people within a geographical setting, in our case between the CEE countries and Austria, Sweden, the Netherlands, and Turkey. Inspecting the four country cases under research, the emergence of different migration corridors facilitating the movement of migrants can be explained by the classic push–pull factors theory, where migration is determined by the presence of attracting pull factors at destination, and repelling push factors at origin (Lee 1966). Demographic growth, low living standards, lack of economic opportunities, and political repression are typically cited push factors in the place of origin. Demand for labour, availability of land, good economic opportunities, and political freedoms that attract migrants to certain receiving countries are common examples of pull factors (Castles and Miller 1998; Sert 2010). Regarding CEE migration towards our four country cases, geographical proximity, historical ties, and political conditions such as endorsement of transitional periods are also among the facilitating conditions of movement. Table 2.2 identifies the main migration corridors between the CEE countries and Austria, Sweden, the Netherlands and Turkey based on the volume of immigrants from these countries.

In view of that, Austria's main migration corridors are with Romania, Poland, Hungary, and the Czech Republic. An analysis of the Statistics Austria Population Register shows that immigrants from the new EU member states – the EU-10 of 2004 and EU-2 of 2007 – comprised almost 300,000 persons in 2013, with growth in 2002–13 being 26% for the EU-10, and 95% for the EU-2 (Enengel et al. 2014). The increase of migrants from Romania and Bulgaria was much more noticeable compared to immigrants coming from bordering countries: the Czech Republic, Hungary, Slovakia as well as Poland, who had already been arriving in Austria in larger numbers during the 1990s (ibid.). While geographical proximity and historical and transnational ties seem to play a more important role in creation of migration corridors with Hungary, Poland, and the Czech Republic, political conditions (i.e., accession to the EU) appear to be also relevant for movement originating in Romania.

Like in Austria, Poland, Hungary, and Romania constitute important migration corridors to the Netherlands. Bulgaria is an additional important corridor. In the Netherlands, the number of immigrants from Poland almost tripled in 2004–13, from approximately 60,000 to 110,000, while the number of Hungarians grew one-third to almost 20,000 persons (Ostaijen et al. 2014). In 2013, almost 21,000 Bulgarians arrived in the Netherlands, a five-fold increase since the 2007 enlargement (ibid.). Romanian migrants, comprising almost 18,000 people the same year, nearly doubled after the enlargement (ibid). These figures are derived from the Dutch Population Registers. As many labour migrants do not register in the Netherlands, it is assumed that the actual number of CEE migrants is probably much higher (ibid.). Recent studies, operating advanced statistical estimation techniques, projected that in 2010 about 340,000 CEE nationals (both registered and not) were present in the Netherlands, either temporarily or permanently (Van der Heijden et al. 2013, also cited in Ostaijen et al. 2014).

Like in Austria and the Netherlands, Poland, Romania and Hungary form the major migration corridors to Sweden, followed by Estonia and Lithuania. Based on figures provided by Statistics Sweden, there are almost 75,000 Polish, 22,000 Romanians, 16,000 Hungarians, 10,000 Estonians and 9000 Lithuanians in Sweden (Zelano et al. 2014). Like in Austria, geographical and political factors are important in the formation of these corridors.

Like in other countries, Romania is a main migration corridor also towards Turkey, along with Bulgaria, Ukraine and Moldova (Korfalı et al. 2014). Partially because of its location and partially because of its status, Turkey has rather different migration corridors than other countries under research here (i.e., countries like Ukraine and Moldova). While the link with Moldova can be explained by the historical and linguistic closeness of the Gagauz people living there (they speak Turkish), the corridor with Ukraine is mostly the result of economic factors.

2.6 Types of Migration (TOMs) and the Feminization of Migration

Based on earlier studies, comparative insight and inductive reasoning, we can categorize migration patterns within these corridors on two levels: duration (i.e., temporary versus permanent migration), and; socio-economic status (i.e., high- versus low-skilled migration). Consequently, a typology of CEE migration is fashioned depicting eight different categories or types of migrants (TOMs). These are: (1) knowledge workers; (2) entrepreneurs; (3) manual workers; (4) persons working in private households; (5) sex workers and trafficked persons; (6) students; (7) non-working spouses and children and; (8) beggars and homeless people. The typology is structured following an account of abductive reasoning (Yanow 2012), which is formed along formal–informal non-employment levels, taking into consideration different characteristics such as migrants' skills, the sectors in which they are employed, their vulnerability as well as the duration of their migration (i.e. temporary versus permanent). The typology shows that CEE migrants should not be considered a homogenous category, but rather a highly differentiated one. As previous studies such as Engbersen et al. (2013) have proposed, the typology here also includes high- and low-skilled migrants as well as temporary versus permanent ones. Unlike previous studies, though, the effort of creating a typology of CEE migration here is realized not within a single country but in four different countries (and eight different urban regions). Regarding the typology, there are some major findings relevant for all four countries and urban regions (See Table 2.3). Table 2.3 provides a comparative synthesis of the typology with certain drawbacks on internal coherence. There is an asymmetry of information, for instance, for the same category of migrants, the main activity sectors for some countries and urban regions, and about chronological evolution.

To begin, there is a small presence of *knowledge workers* in all countries, but there are more differences than similarities. In Austria, high-skill positions in the labour market are usually reserved for Austrian citizens, with a certain level of improvement in this situation (Enengel et al. 2014). With regard to the urban regions of Linz and Vienna, we have less region-specific information. In the Netherlands, despite the conventional belief that CEE migrants hold low-skill jobs, there is an observed heterogeneity in the labour market positions of the migrants from the CEE, where migrants also have high-skill employment (Ostaijen et al. 2014). While there is less region-specific information with regard to Rotterdam, we observe Romanians and Hungarians taking on some positions in international organizations in The Hague. Contrary to Austria and the Netherlands, the highest shares within the skill-level distributions in occupations of migrants in Sweden are detected in high- and medium-skill jobs (Zelano et al. 2014). While high-skill jobs are accessible for migrants in Sweden, we observe a decreasing pattern in Stockholm compared to Gothenburg. Although migrants taking high-skill positions are exceptional in Turkey, Istanbul is considered to attract highly skilled migrants. The conventional wisdom especially in Edirne holds that migrants from the CEE have higher skills than the local population.

Because of the legal conditions that determine the entry to the formal labour market, the category of *entrepreneurs* is observed as an important path for formal employment in all four countries. In Linz and Vienna, there are many one-person companies especially in the construction and care sectors. Similarly, in Rotterdam and The Hague, self-employment in the construction sector is common. Self-employment as a means of formal employment is also observed in Sweden, where Estonians have a higher share. Interestingly, in Sweden the number of self-employed female migrants is increasing both in Stockholm and Gothenburg, pointing to a feminization of CEE migration in this category. Self-employment as

Table 2.3 TOMs within countries and urban regions (Source: Sert (2014))

	Austria		Netherlands		Sweden		Turkey	
	Vienna	Linz	Rotterdam	The Hague	Stockholm	Gothenburg	Istanbul	Edirne
Knowledge workers	High-skill positions exceptional		High-skill positions exceptional		High-skill positions accessible		High-skill positions exceptional	
	Less region-specific information	Less region-specific information	Less region-specific information	Some positions in international organizations (Romanians and Hungarians)	Decreasing	Stable	Attracting highly skilled migrants	Conventional belief that migrants have higher skills than locals
Entrepreneurs	Mostly small enterprises as a means of entering labour market during transitional period		Self-employment as a means of entering labour market during transitional period		Self-employment as a means of formal employment (Estonians with a higher share)		Mostly small enterprises	
	One-person companies (e.g., construction, care)	One-person companies (e.g., construction, care)	Construction sector	Construction sector	Number of self-employed female migrants increasing	Number of self-employed female migrants increasing	Mostly small enterprise	Mostly small enterprise
Manual workers	Tourism, construction and agricultural sectors		Seasonal workers in horticulture and agriculture, mainly Polish		Low skilled workers in both formal and informal labour market in construction, cleaning and welding		Internal migration supplying the demand for manual workers in urban areas	
	Gastronomy sector and viticulture, mostly by Slovakians and Hungarians	Agricultural workers in rural areas	Less region-specific information	Less region-specific information	Number of young male migrants increasing since 2004	Number of young male migrants increasing since 2004	A few cases of young Moldovan males in construction sector	Not relevant

Persons working in private households	Circular migration of females especially in the care sector for the elderly; informal employment as cleaners		Usually informal arrangements in domestic care and cleaning sectors		A small immigrant overrepresentation in the health sector, but information about unregistered migrants rather patchy		Irregular domestic labour both in temporary and permanent arrangements	
	Relevant, Poland and Slovakia, increasingly Romania	Relevant, Poland and Slovakia, increasingly Romania	Mostly Bulgarians –may change with end of transitional arrangements	Mostly Bulgarians–may change with end of transitional arrangements	7% of registered migrants in nursing & cleaning	9% of registered migrants in nursing and cleaning	Bulgarian and Moldovan females	Not relevant
Sex workers and trafficked persons	Both registered and unregistered, sometimes forced prostitution		Prostitution legalized under certain conditions, but no official statistics; CEE migrants also as victims of trafficking		Young women staying short periods of time		Human trafficking especially from Moldova	
	Majority of registered sex workers Hungarian and Romanian	Limited data	Limited data	Limited data: 25% of registered sex workers from CEE	Few women from Romania, Hungary, Bulgaria, Moldova, the Baltic countries and Poland	Roma minority	Relevant, but less known	Relevant, but less known
Students	Numbers are increasing where Bulgarians constitute a large category		Several CEE students		Numbers are increasing with gender differences		Numbers are high	
	75% of CEE students in Austria concentrated in Vienna	Minor role as education location	Erasmus University Rotterdam	Delft University	Number of females decreasing	Number of females decreasing	Many private and public universities	University of Thrace

(continued)

Table 2.3 (continued)

	Austria		Netherlands		Sweden		Turkey	
	Vienna	Linz	Rotterdam	The Hague	Stockholm	Gothenburg	Istanbul	Edirne
Non-working spouses and children	Children a small portion of CEE migration		Family related migration increasing and mostly led by females, which is different than migration of single males historically		Second largest reason for registering for residence permit is intention of family members to accompany their spouses and parents		Highest proportion of residence permits granted upon education is in primary education	
	7931 children registered, cross-border school attendance an emerging issue	Minor relevance, mostly Romanians	Large scale of CEE migration related to families	Number of children going to school doubled since 2010	Relevant, but less region-specific information	Relevant, but less region-specific information	Relevant, but less region-specific information	Relevant, but less region-specific information
Beggars and homeless people	Begging is a sensitive public issue, but no reliable figures		Numbers are low and decreasing		379 homeless EU citizens, the majority being males with an average age of 38 years old from Romania as well as Poland, Bulgaria, Slovakia and Spain		Beggars and homeless from CEE are rare	
	Often commuting from the neighbouring countries, especially from Slovakia & Hungary	Growing number of Roma descent	Non-registered Bulgarians selling journals, or street musicians	Public debate about homeless CEE nationals, mainly Poles	NGO Crossroads receives on average 120 visits every day	Numbers are increasing, majority females	With the conflict in Syria, a visible increase of Syrians in the streets	Not relevant

a means of formal status in the labour market is also detected in Edirne and Istanbul, mostly in the form of small enterprises. Thus, there is a clear relationship between the presence of legal restrictions on employment in the formal labour market in the host country and the use of self-employment as strategy of migrants to achieve formal status. To illustrate, as the transitional rules were lifted in Austria and the Netherlands, there was – as expected – a decrease in the trend of self-employment. Similarly, as more regulations were applied in the berry-picking market in Sweden, the number of self-employed migrants in this sector rose (Zelano et al. 2014).

Manual workers are commonly observed in the cases under research except for Turkey. In Austria, the tourism, construction and agricultural sectors employ large segments of CEE migrants, both in the formal and informal employment schemes. In Vienna, there are mostly Slovakians and Hungarians taking on jobs in the gastronomy sector and viticulture. In Linz, there are more agricultural workers in the rural areas. In the Netherlands, there are seasonal workers in horticulture and agriculture, mainly composed of Polish migrants. Regarding Rotterdam and The Hague, we have less region-specific information due to the lack of data. In Sweden, there are low-skilled workers in both the formal and informal labour market in construction, cleaning and welding. Both in Gothenburg and Stockholm, we observe that the number of young, male migrants has been increasing since 2004. While there are a few cases of young Moldovan males in the construction sector in Istanbul, generally in Turkey internal migration of the local Kurdish population – and lately the increasing number of asylum seekers from Syria – supply the demand for manual workers.

Persons working in private households as a category are identified in all four countries. In Austria, there is a trend of circular migration of females especially in the care sector for the elderly as well as informal employment of migrants as cleaners. The category is observed both in Vienna and Linz, where migrants from Poland, Slovakia (and increasingly Romania) work in private households. Similarly, in the Netherlands there are also migrants who usually work in informal arrangements in the domestic care and cleaning sectors. Both in Rotterdam and The Hague, the category is mostly composed of Bulgarians, which is expected to change with the end of transitional arrangements. With regard to the care sector in Sweden, while official numbers show a small immigrant overrepresentation in the health sector, information about unregistered migrants is rather patchy at best. In Stockholm 7% and in Gothenburg 9% of registered migrants work in the nursing and cleaning sectors. In Istanbul, irregular domestic labour – both in temporary and permanent arrangements – is common and is largely dominated by female Bulgarian and Moldovan migrants. In all four cases, a dominant issue in relation to migrants working in private households as care workers, nannies, cleaning persons, and gardeners is the problem of registration, where the distinction between regular versus irregular migrants becomes difficult to distinguish.

Another category where the distinction between formal and informal arrangements is hard to differentiate is *sex workers and trafficked persons*. In Austria, there are both registered and unregistered sex workers, and forced prostitution can be observed in both cases. While most registered sex workers in Vienna are Hungarian and Romanian, there is insufficient information about the urban region of Linz. In the Netherlands, prostitution is legalized under certain conditions and CEE migrants are known to be victims of trafficking, but there are no official statistics. In The Hague, 25% of registered sex workers are known to be from CEE countries. In Sweden, there are young women staying for short periods of time. In Stockholm, there are few women from Romania, Hungary, Bulgaria, Moldova, the Baltic countries and Poland working in the sector. In Gothenburg, the Roma from Bulgaria and Romania are more visible. In Turkey, human trafficking, especially from Moldova, is a known phenomenon and for both urban regions the category is relevant, but less is known. Overall, on the one hand some sex workers are not registered and working informally. On the other hand, there are many registered sex workers that may represent a voluntary choice of profession in a formal setting. Within this latter group there are also many that are forced into prostitution. Thus, sex workers and trafficked persons are usually mixed in this category.

Students as a category of CEE migration are rising in volume in all four countries. In Austria, the number of CEE students is increasing where Bulgarians constitute a large category. In the Netherlands and Turkey, there are also many CEE students. In Sweden, the number of CEE students is also increasing with gender differences. Student mobility is an expanding phenomenon not only among the member states of the EU, but also in Turkey (Findlay et al. 2012; Van Mol and Timmerman 2013). Students may utilize education as a means of access to permanent residency within a country (Gribble 2008), but further research is needed to understand the motivations and future plans of CEE students in the four countries.

Less is discerned about the qualitative features of the migration of *non-working spouses and children*, but quantitatively this category is visible in numbers in all four countries, while receiving less attention both in policy and academic circles. In Austria, children constitute a small portion of CEE migration. In Vienna, there are 7931 children registered, where cross-border school attendance is an emerging issue. In Linz, the category has minor relevance, mostly dominated by Romanians. In the Netherlands, family-related migration is increasing and mostly led by females, i.e., women migrating first and husbands joining later, which is very different than the historical migration of single males. In Rotterdam, a large share of CEE migration is related to families. In The Hague, the number of CEE children going to school has doubled since 2010. In Sweden, the second largest reason for registering for a residence permit is intention of family members to accompany their spouses and parents. Similarly, in Turkey the highest proportion of residence permits granted upon education is at the primary level (i.e., mostly children). For the latter two cases, region-specific information is not available regarding this category.

In contrast to the category of *non-working spouses and children* – which receives little policy and academic attention – the category of *beggars and homeless people* emerges as a sensitive issue that attracts public debate, although the numbers of this type of migration are rather low compared to the other categories. In Austria, begging is a sensitive public issue, but there are no reliable figures. In Vienna, beggars are often commuting from the neighbouring countries, especially from Slovakia and Hungary. In Linz, a growing number of beggars of Roma descent are observed. In the Netherlands, the number of beggars and homeless people are low and decreasing. In Rotterdam, there are non-registered Bulgarians selling journals, or street musicians. In The Hague, there is a public debate about homeless CEE nationals, mainly Polish. In Sweden, there are 379 homeless EU citizens; the majority are males with an average age of 38 years old from Romania as well as Poland, Bulgaria, Slovakia and Spain (Zelano et al. 2014). In Stockholm, NGO Crossroads receives on average 120 visits every day. In Gothenburg, the numbers are increasing with the majority being female migrants. In Turkey, beggars and homeless from CEE is a rare phenomenon.

Overall, within many categories there is an observed feminization of migration, which is described here as an increasing number of female migrants in CEE migration. In Austria, the gender composition of CEE migration has changed a lot since the end of the Cold War. Female migrants from CEE (being 15 years and older) have an increasing presence and importance, clearly outnumbering males. In 1991, the proportion of male migrants among all CEE-migrants ranged at around 70% with only little variation between the sending countries and with around one third not having reached the age of 30 years Today, young and middle-aged female migrants have gained importance and visibly exceed the number of males. Women from CEE are more visible in the service sector, in child care as well as caring for old-aged people in private households. These occupations have strong demand in Austria, thus providing a considerable number of jobs, but generally pay modest incomes and are often organized on an informal basis. The urban regions of Vienna and Linz do not show a variance from this trend on the national level. While the figures of residents that were born in the EU-8 do not show big differences in gender patterns in the whole of Vienna urban region, the study by Lechner et al. (2010) referring primarily to the (daily) commuters in the Austro-Hungarian border region (south-eastern parts of the region of Vienna) show clear gender- and age- specific patterns. Accordingly, about 75% of the Hungarian workers are male. Many of these migrants choose to commute to Austria daily, as they can stay and live in western Hungary (with lower living and residential costs) and work in the border regions of Austria for higher wages than they would earn at home. Thus, geographical proximity is a determining factor of this type of migration, where males show a stronger presence than females.

In the Netherlands, there is also a tendency towards feminization of migration, where the majority (albeit a small portion in some cases) of the officially registered

CEE migrants are females (51% of Polish and Bulgarian, 54% of Hungarian, and 60% of Romanians). While the proportion of females among the *labour* migrants is low (Nicolaas 2011, Jennissen 2011), females are overrepresented in migration for family motives (Gijsberts and Lubbers 2013). Looking at the ratios at the level of urban regions, in Rotterdam the total percentage of females is more than the males in all three municipalities. The difference is profound among Romanian migrants, where females are overrepresented in all municipalities (63% in Rotterdam; 62% in Schiedam and 72% in Lansingerland). Similarly, the male-female ratio in The Hague region is also in favour of the female migrants, where the total percentage of females is more than the males in all three municipalities. In the municipalities of The Hague and Westland, women are overrepresented among both Romanians (59–60% female) and Hungarians (63–4% female). In the municipality of Delft, a similar overrepresentation is true for the Polish (62% female).

In Sweden, gender distribution shows a variance between registered and unregistered migrants. While the flows of regular and registered CEE migrants are characterized by a rather even gender distribution, the group of CEE immigrants overlooked by the official records is dominantly male. In 2012, of the 148,998 individuals living in Sweden born in one of the EU-10 countries the gender distribution was 45% male and 55% female. For the CEE as a whole, the gender distribution has been more or less the same throughout the period 2000–12, with a somewhat larger share of women than men (an average of 42% men, 58% women). The same is true for the five largest immigrant populations, with the exception for the Polish and Lithuanian ones, where the share of males have increased slightly during the 10 years period between 2000–2012 (Statistics Sweden 2013b). Of the 2732 citizens from the CEE region who obtained Swedish citizenship in 2012, 1627 were women and 1105 were men (Statistics Sweden 2013a). Polish women consist the largest category representing 36% (975) of all CEE naturalizations in Sweden in 2012. In the urban region of Stockholm, women had a larger share than men in both the municipality of Haninge and Stockholm (51 and 56% respectively). In Södertälje, the ratio was 48% women, 52% men. In the region of Gothenburg, women were the larger category in all three municipalities ranging from 53 to 60%.

In Turkey, the number of female CEE migrants with residence permits in 2011 was approximately 59% of total regular CEE migrants. In previous years, the share of residence permits given to women was 55% in 2008, 54% in 2009, and 55% in 2010. These high percentages of female migrants among the CEE migrants were also higher than the averages of female migrants among total migrants in Turkey. For rge same years, female migrants constituted 50% (2008), 51% (2009), 52% (2010) and 54% (2011) of total migrants in Turkey, which are below the proportion of women among CEE migrants. In a more detailed analysis, it is demonstrated that there was a gender balance of CEE migration between 2003 and 2005, male predominance in 2006 and 2007, and female predominance after 2008. A similar trend of increasing female domination is also observed, when we look at the work permits. An analysis of gender distribution of CEE migrants with work permits in the year 2008 shows that female migrants constitute only 37% of the CEE community holding employment permits. However, the difference between women and men with employment permits started closing in 2009 when women constituted almost half of the CEE migrants with work permits. Moreover, in an increasing trend the proportion of women among CEE migrants with employment permits in 2010, 2011 and 2012 rose to 52%, 65% and 67%, respectively.

However, like in Sweden the gender distribution may show a variance between registered and unregistered migrants. While the flows of regular and registered CEE migrants are characterized by recent female predominance, looking at the apprehension data (a basic variable for estimation of unofficial migration) especially in Edirne, we see that it is predominantly male. However, there is also a variance among unregistered migration between irregular labour migrants and irregular transit migrants. While female CEE migrants may largely dominate the former (like in Austria, there is a strong demand for domestic female workers), the latter is largely a male-dominated phenomenon. In Istanbul, the variance is also visible between different types of migration.

2.7 Conclusions

Regardless of the variances in accessibility, type and disposition of data in the four countries, the exercise of mapping of migration corridors and analysis of types of migration from CEE countries to Austria, the Netherlands, Sweden, and Turkey see interesting conclusions develop. International comparisons are challenging, where disparities in data-collection practices between countries, the changing nature of political unions (in our case for example, being a member of the EU or applying transitional rules), and informal paths of migration all contribute to the problem. The lack of data is observed on the international level, as well as supranational, regional and local levels. On the supranational level, even though CEE migration is mostly about intra-European movement, unavailability of comparable data among the EU member states on the movement of EU citizens deserves policy attention. On a regional level, inaccessibility of comparable data between urban regions in a given country also demands further elaboration. There is a need to build mechanisms that enhance data collection at these different levels.

Within this context, creating a typology of CEE migration as a heuristic device for comparison produces a tool with great exploratory value for answering further research questions. To illustrate, the almost trivial presence of knowledge workers in high-skill jobs in all four countries is instructive both for understanding dequalification of migrants from the CEE countries in the labour market and recognizing the glass ceiling created by established structures. There is room for further research about this group, such as collecting information about their patterns of integration or modes of professional advancement. In all four countries, self-employment seems to be a useful instrument for migrants from different CEE countries to overcome the limitations created by the recognized structures, such as transitional rules in the case of Austria and the Netherlands and strict labour market regulations in the case of Sweden and Turkey.

Whether there are signs of emerging ethnic economies in these countries also remains to be explored. In Austria, the Netherlands, and Sweden, manual workers are taking seasonal jobs mostly in the agricultural sector, implying that we can predict new routines of circular migration, where the difference between registered/unregistered migrants is blurred. In all four cases, persons working in private households are parts of unregistered or irregular migration patterns, leaving room for further research to understand both the scale and nature of this type of migration. A similar reflection can be made about sex workers and trafficked persons, non-working spouses and children, and beggars and homeless people. All three groups include at-risk persons, and more research needs to be done to recognize the level and character of their vulnerabilities. The number of foreign students is increasing in all four countries, also opening a rather new venue for research.

The typology created here shows that the labour market remains an important governing factor in this specific types of CEE migration, but that new and changing patterns of free movement within the migration corridors are also in evidence, leaving room for more analytical insights and interpretation about the drivers, impacts, and modes of integration of migrants. The typology confirms that 'CEE migrants' should not be considered as a homogenous, but rather as a highly differentiated category with high and low skilled, as well as temporary and permanent migrants. There is also a need to address the feminization of migration, which is described here as increasing number of female migrants in CEE migration, an observed phenomenon in all four countries, maybe more in some than others. Very basically, we still do not know much about the gender relations among CEE migrants or the changing profile of female CEE migrants.

The country cases selected for this research also help us to draw conclusions about migration corridors. The cases illustrate the importance of historical context. Certain migration corridors have always been active. For example, the migration corridors between Poland and the Netherlands, or Bulgaria and Turkey have seen flows that have not eroded but rather transformed over time. In many ways, institutional regimes, rather than geographical proximity, have played a larger role in these transformations. The country cases with their different applications of transitional restrictions create specifically interesting comparisons. In Sweden, where no transitional restrictions were applied, concerns about the costs of admitting CEE migrants proved groundless. In Austria and the Netherlands, where transitional restrictions were in place, the limits only had consequences for formal employment. Deploying different tactics, such as self-employment, migrants from the CEE member states still arrived and worked in both countries. Taking everything into account, today we see a diversification of intra-European movement, where historical context, institutional structures and individual schemes have all contributed to the alteration of existing migration corridors.

References

Amelina, A., & Vasilache, A. (2014). The shadows of enlargement: Theorizing mobility and inequality in a changing Europe. *Migration Letters, 11*(2), 109–124.

Andrijasevic, R., Sacchetto, D. (2015). *From labour migration to labour mobility? the spectre of the multinational worker in Europe*, paper presented at the Inequality in the 21st Century Conference, The London School of Economics & Political Science, London, UK, July 2–4.

Barslund, M., Busse, M., & Schwarzwälder, J. (2015). *Labour mobility in Europe: An untapped resource?* (Vol. 327). Brussels: Centre for European Policy Studies Policy Brief.

Black, R., Engbersen, G., Okolski, M., & Pantiru, C. (2010). *A continent moving west? EU enlargement and labour migration from central and eastern Europe*. Amsterdam: AUP.

Boguslaw, J. (2012). *Svensk invandringspolitik under 500 år: 1512–2012*. Lund: Studentlitteratur.

Brassé, P., Van Schelven, W. (1980). Assimilatie van vooroorlogse immigranten: Drie generaties Polen, Slovenen, Italianen in Heerlen. Den Haag: Ministerie van Cultuur, Recreatie en Maatschappelijk Werk.

Carling, J. (2015). Exploring 12 migration corridors: Rationale, methodology and overview. In O. Bakewell, G. Engbersen, L. Fonseca, & C. Horst (Eds.), *Beyond networks: Feedback in international migration* (pp. 18–46). Basingstoke: Palgrave.

Castles, S., & Miller, M. J. (1998). *The age of migration*. New York: Guilford Press.

Castro-Martin, T., & Cortina, C. (2015). Demographic issues of Intra-European migration: Destinations, family and settlement. *European Journal of Population/Revue européenne de Démographie, 31*, 109–125.

Dagevos, J. (2011). *Poolse migranten*. The Hague: Sociaal en Cultureel Planbureau.

Doyle, N., Hughes, G., Wadensjö, E. (2006) Freedom of Movement for Workers from Central and Eastern Europ: Experiences in Ireland and Sweden *SIEPS*, the University of Stockholm: Swedish Institute for European Policy Studies.

Düvell, F., & Vogel, D. (2006). Polish migrants: Tensions between sociological typologies and state categories. In A. Triandafyllidou (Ed.), *Contemporary Polish migration in Europe complex patterns of movement and settlement* (p. 26789). Lewiston: Edwin Mellen Press.

Eade, J., Drinkwater, S., Garapich, M. (2006) *Class and Ethnicity: Polish Migrant Workers in London*, Swindon: Economic and Social Research Council, End of Award Report No. RES-000-22-1294.

Enengel, M. L., Fassmann, H., Kohlbacher, J., Reeger, U. (2014) *Mapping and analysis of types of migration from CEE countries: Country report Austria*, IMAGINATION Working Paper No. 1.

Engbersen, G., Ilies, M., Leerkes, A., Snel, E., & Van der Meij, R. (2011). *Arbeidsmigratie in vieren. Bulgaren en Roemenen vergeleken met Polen*. Rotterdam: EUR.

Engbersen, G., Leerkes, A., Grabowska-Lusinska, I., Snel, E., & Burgers, J. (2013). On the differential attachments of migrants from Central and Eastern Europe: A typology of labour migration. *Journal of Ethnic and Migration Studies, 39*(6), 959–981.

Favell, A. (2008). The new face of East-West migration in Europe. *Journal of Ethnic and Migration Studies, 34*(5), 701–716.

Findlay, A. M., King, R., Smith, F. M., Geddes, A., & Skeldon, R. (2012). World class? An investigation of globalisation, difference and international student mobility. *Transactions of the Institute of British Geographers, 37*(1), 118–131.
Friberg, J. H. (2012). The stages of migration: From going abroad to settling down: Post-accession Polish migrant workers in Norway. *Journal of Ethnic and Migration Studies, 38*(10), 1589–1605.
Gijsberts, M., & Lubbers, G. (2013). *Nieuw in Nederland.* The Hague: Sociaal en Cultureel Planbureau.
Gribble, C. (2008). Policy options for managing international student migration: The sending country's perspective. *Journal of Higher Education Policy and Management, 30*(1), 25–39.
Jennissen, R. (2011). Ethnic migration in Central and Eastern Europe: Its historical background and contemporary flows. *Studies in Ethnicity and Nationalism, 11*, 252–270.
Korfalı, D. K., Sert, D. S., Acar, T. (2014) Mapping and analysis of types of migration from CEE countries: Country report Turkey, IMAGINATION Working Paper No. 4.
Lechner, F., Major, A., Matt, I. & Willsberger, B. (2010). *Ungarische GrenzgängerInnen in Wien. Studie im Auftrag von EURES-T Pannonia.* [online], available: http://media.arbeiterkammer.at/noe/pdfs/broschueren/ungar_grenzgaenger.pdf
Lee, S. E. (1966). A theory of migration. *Demography, 3*(1), 47–57.
Martín, I., Venturini, A. (2015). 'A Comprehensive Labour Market Approach to EU Labour Migration Policy' Migration Policy Centre, EUI Policy Brief 2015/07 doi: https://doi.org/10.2870/753878.
Nicolaas, H. (2011). Poolse migratie. Voorbode voor gezingshereniging? *Demos, 27*(10), 5–7.
Ostaijen, M., Snel, E., Hart, M., Faber, M., Engbersen, G., Scholten, P. (2014) *Mapping and analysis of types of migration from CEE countries: Country report the Netherlands.* IMAGINATION Working Paper No. 2.
Pascouau, Y. (2013) *Intra-European mobility: The 'second building block' of EU labour migration policy.* European Policy Center Issue Paper No. 74.
Recchi, E. (2008). Cross-State mobility in the EU. *European Societies, 10*(2), 197–224.
Ruist, J. (2013) *Immigration, work and welfare.* Unpublished PhD Thesis, University of Gothenburg, Gothenburg.
Sert, D. (2010). Explaining why people move: Intra and interdisciplinary debates about the causes of international migration. In R. A. Denemark (Ed.), *The International Studies Encyclopaedia.* Wiley.
Sert, D. (2014) *Mapping and analysis of types of migration from CEE countries: Comparative report.* IMAGINATION Comparative Project Report No. 1 and Policy Brief No. 1, August 2014.
Snel, E., Faber, M., & Engbersen, G. (2014). Civic stratification and social positioning: CEE labour migrants without a work permit. *Population, Space and Place.* https://doi.org/10.1002/psp.1846.
Statistics Sweden. (2013a). *Antal personer som fått svenskt medborgarskap efter medborgarskapsland, kön och år (2000, 2002, 2004, 2006, 2008, 2010, 2012).* Retrieved 20140110, from Statistiska Centralbbyrn (SCB).
Statistics Sweden. (2013b). *Utrikes födda efter födelseland, ålder, kön och tid.* Retrieved 20131025, from Statistiska Centralbbyrn (SCB)
Van der Heijden, P. G. M., Cruijff, M., & Van Gils, G. (2013). *Aantallen geregistreerde en niet-geregistreerde burgers uit MOE-landen die in Nederland verblijven, Rapportage schattingen 2009 en 2010.* Utrecht: Universiteit Utrecht.
Van Mol, C., & Timmerman, C. (2013). Should I stay or should I go? An analysis of the determinants of intra-European student mobility. *Population, Space, and Place.* https://doi.org/10.1002/psp.1833.
Wadensjö, E., Gerdes, C. (2013) *Immigration to Sweden from the New EU Member States, SIEPS,* the University of Stockholm: Swedish Institute for European Policy Studies.

Weltevrede, A., De Boom, J., Rezai, S., Zuiderwijk, L., & Engbersen, G. (2009). *Arbeidsmigranten uit Midden-en Oost-Europa: Een profielschets van recente arbeidsmigranten uit de MOE-landen*. Rotterdam: Risbo.

Yanow, D. (2012). Organizational ethnography between toolbox and world-making. *Journal of Organizational Ethnography, 1*(1), 31–42.

Zelano, K., Bucken-Knapp, G., Hinnfors, J., Spehar, A. (2014) *Mapping and analysis of types of migration from CEE countries: Country report Sweden*. IMAGINATION Working Paper No. 3.

Chapter 3
Consequences of Intra-European Movement for CEE Migrants in European Urban Regions

Ursula Reeger

3.1 Introduction – Setting the Scene

In Europe today, EU citizens are free to move within the entire EU and may take up jobs, enter universities, enjoy retirement or try their luck wherever they want to. As many scholars have pointed out (Favell 2008, 2009; Ciupijus 2011; Castro-Martin and Cortina 2015) this complete freedom of movement marks a turning point in European history, and the predominant direction of movement is currently from East to West. Post-accession migration from Central and Eastern Europe (CEE) thus brings back old European migration patterns, in which CEE migrants are making use of this still quite new freedom of movement. So, being mobile as such is simple and easy without any legal constraints whatsoever, as nowadays even more sceptic EU 15 countries like Austria and Germany have abolished most of the transitional provisions regulating access to their labour markets. One might exaggerate and say that the official term "mobility" implies that internal EU migrants never really arrive anywhere, but are rather floating freely through the EU, which of course is a completely inaccurate picture. With the national level becoming less important in the present setting, having been "taken out of the equation", CEE migrants are arriving at and settling within varying periods of time in cities and urban regions, which are still the most important destinations, though rural areas, e.g. in Southern Europe, are also becoming more attractive destinations (see Caglar 2014). Still, CEE migration to Western Europe is to a large extent an urban issue.

From the EU's point of view, free intra-European movement between Central-Eastern and Western Europe is praised as a win-win-win situation with gains for Western economies, higher wages for migrants and returning capital and talent for Eastern economies (Favell 2008: 705). But it is clearly necessary to look at this phenomenon from a more nuanced perspective (1) in terms of potential barriers in

U. Reeger (✉)
Institute for Urban and Regional Research, Austrian Academy of Sciences, Vienna, Austria
e-mail: ursula.reeger@oeaw.ac.at

P. Scholten, M. van Ostaijen (eds.), *Between Mobility and Migration*, IMISCOE Research Series, https://doi.org/10.1007/978-3-319-77991-1_3

different fields CEE migrants may face in their new destinations and (2) in terms of different groups of CEE migrants and their access to local resources. This will make it possible to overcome the rather one-dimensional view on an in fact rather heterogeneous group of people.

This chapter is going to explore the accessibility of CEE migrants to the labour market, housing, the welfare system, the school system and society as such. The previous chapters outline a definition as well as the actual presence of different groups of CEE migrants in urban regions in Austria, the Netherlands and Sweden. We will be looking at groups of migrants who are present on the labour market, both formally and informally employed (knowledge workers, entrepreneurs, manual workers, persons working in private households, sex workers), and at groups whose primary purpose of staying abroad is not work-related (students, partners or spouses, children as well as beggars and homeless persons).

This chapter presents both the obverse and the reverse side of free movement by looking at the pathways of these different types of CEE migrants into various domains and their access to local resources in six target urban regions based on qualitative empirical data. Details on methodology and the stakeholder-based approach can be found in Chap. 1. The question is, whether the access to and provision of local resources – which in the present context is understood as functional integration – runs as easily and seemingly smoothly as the freedom of movement promoted by the EU indicates. How are CEE migrants impacted by free movement in terms of inclusion and exclusion in central domains, and do migrant groups differ in this respect? If yes, in what way? This chapter provides a multidimensional synthesis pertaining to patterns of consequences for different types of CEE migrants based on assessments from key stakeholders across six urban regions in Austria, the Netherlands and Sweden. Implications of CEE migration in the Turkish urban regions of Istanbul and Edirne are analysed in Chap. 11. Nevertheless, references will be made as to a comparison between urban regions within and outside the EU.

3.2 State of the Art: Studies on CEE Migration

During the past 25 years, the vast body of literature on the renewed European East-West migration has oftentimes focussed on analysing stocks and flows, on migration patterns, contributions to and advancements in migration theory, on labour migration and on facets of integration (in different fields like the labour market or housing). In geographical terms this has mostly been done for (a) single sending countries, with Poland being the most important as well as the most investigated country, and (b) single receiving countries, regions or cities (e.g. in the UK and in Germany). With the aforementioned paradigm shift in the legal-political framework and the emergence of free movement, scientific interest has moved on to post-accession migration and its particularities (Black et al. 2010; Glorius et al. 2013). It is still concentrating on distinct types and patterns of EU-internal East-West movement but is also addressing issues of functional integration in the receiving regions such as labour market segmentation, inclusion, exclusion, and de-qualification. There is a growing awareness among migration scholars that even though European 'mobile citizens' nowadays basically have the same rights as citizens of the receiving EU countries, they still may face pronounced barriers and experience "integration needs" (Collett 2013) similar to those of migrants from outside of the EU, usually on the local level of regions and cities. Furthermore, the national frameworks in the receiving member states may still determine registration requirements, for example, which are connected to accessing the welfare system or the labour market in those countries that implemented transitional provisions.

While in-depth analyses of implications related to lacking language skills and subsequent difficulties in finding proper information by accessing local resources are rarely available, issues concerning the labour market situation of CEE migrants have remained in the centre of scientific attention (e.g. Drinkwater et al. 2010; Ciupijus 2011). In this context, de-qualification is one of the key aspects that has already been analysed from various perspectives since the re-emergence of European East-West migration in the wake of the fall of the Iron Curtain more than 25 years ago (Fassmann et al. 2014). Compared to other immigrant groups like guest workers in the 1960s and 1970s, CEE migrants display an above-average level of education which they oftentimes cannot translate into corresponding positions in the receiving labour market. To give an example from Austria: According to the Labour Force Survey (Statistics Austria 2015), the share of university graduates in the Austrian born population aged 15–64 was 15 per cent in 2014 compared to 23 per cent for CEE migrants.

Apart from the analysis of factors that explain the ongoing de-qualification of CEE workers, it has been shown that precarious work associated with downward occupational mobility is the price CEE migrants are willing to pay to gain higher wages in the "West" (Voitchovsky 2014). For Romanians and Bulgarians, who were shut out from some Western national labour markets for a longer period of time, bogus self-employment was an important pathway into these labour markets and often resulted in an even more pronounced precariousness combined with wage competition (Ciupijus 2011: 546). Being known, described and used as "hard workers" hinders CEE migrants from social participation and language learning, as described in the British context (MacKenzie and Forde 2009): "certain workplaces, particularly those embodying classical features of secondary labour market jobs, do not facilitate overcoming social and cultural exclusion", which might be passed on to the children of CEE migrants, as many temporary migration projects become more permanent (Ciupijus 2011: 546).

Though scholars are increasingly aware of the fact that CEE migrants are a very heterogeneous group, many recent studies still focus on migrant workers in danger of facing rather unfavourable conditions. Still, some scholars have looked into distinct groups of mobile CEE citizens. Favell (2009), to give an example, has elaborated on elite professional movers whom he calls "Eurostars" in "Eurocities", a predominantly urban hub phenomenon, where "an invisible migration of West Europeans has laid path now for young, talented and educated Poles, Hungarians, Romanians and others heading in the same direction" (ibid: 178 f.). Comparing their situation in London, Amsterdam and Brussels, Favell sees mobile EU elite professionals in general as blocked to some extent. Even though the official barriers inhibiting their movement have been abolished completely, they still face serious long-term consequences of social isolation and local as well as national barriers (e.g. in housing) related to language and the "the internal secrets of a national 'culture' reserved to native speakers" (ibid: 180). Turning from these successful CEE migrants to those finding themselves in a destitute position, Garapich (2014) looks at street homeless in London among migrants from Poland and distinguishes between two types: The first one comprises persons who fled from a troubled history in some way (unemployment, homelessness and substance abuse in the country of origin), while the second one "is composed of people, who have descended into poverty and subsequent substance abuse after migrating to Britain". The latter type is linked to structural features like their weak position in the labour market and their subsequent loss of housing in the tight and expensive London housing market. Garapich found that "structurally rejected people ... form strong ties despite (or because of) a hostile exclusionary and hegemonic social environment of the neoliberal order" (ibid.).

Other bodies of literature look at different domains of functional integration rather than at distinct groups of CEE migrants. Concerning the situation on the housing market, Ciupijus (2011: 542) points out that although they nominally have the right to access social housing in Britain, the general scarcity in this housing segment "left many mobile CEEs (most of them employed in poorly paid, secondary labour market jobs) with the unattractive option of expensive private accommodation". The question of whether this concentration in a certain segment of the housing market leads to residential segregation has been addressed by Sabater (2015), who has shown that in the UK EU 'mobile' citizens from Poland – in comparison to those from Spain, Italy and Portugal – are overrepresented in disadvantaged neighbourhoods.

3.3 Empirical Results: Implications of CEE Migration in Selected Urban Regions

3.3.1 Preliminary Remarks: Urban Regions and the Notion of Space

The main focus of this chapter is the analysis of the consequences of intra-European movement for various types of CEE migrants in European urban regions. These consequences are by and large related to the labour market, housing, the welfare system, the school system, and societal participation. Generally speaking, there are two different angles from which the implications can be looked at: that of the individual migrants and that of the cities and urban regions. To give an example: Children from CEE in schools may have difficulties following the lessons due to lacking language skills, which is a problem on the individual level. From the urban regions' point of view, the presence of migrant children in schools may lead to changing needs and focuses and thus represent a cause for action, which in turn has urban consequences. Both kinds of implications are to some extent interlinked but they can be clearly distinguished. This contribution focuses on the individual perspective, which the experts have frequently elaborated on, with eventual side glances at the urban perspective.

From the perspective of European receiving cities, CEE migration adds to the ever-growing migration-related diversity that urban regions across Europe have been facing during the past decades. This fact changes and challenges cities and their subsystems. Cities cannot steer immigration as such, as this is dealt with on the national level and in the case of intra-European movement on the European level, but they are the places where migrants actually arrive and where integration needs and challenges become visible. The urban regions that are going to be explored include two capital cities (Stockholm and Vienna) that are at the same time the largest cities in the respective countries, the second and third largest cities of the Netherlands, Rotterdam and The Hague, and two smaller urban regions in Sweden and Austria (Gothenburg and Linz). Generally speaking, the urban regions concerned vary significantly in size but display a common main feature, namely a considerable inflow of CEE migrants over the past decade, and even earlier, to both the core cities and the surrounding areas. The latter areas also attract CEE migrants because housing might be cheaper, the city is still easily accessible, and because rural areas offer employment opportunities (e.g. in agriculture). We expect distinctive implications in the core cities with a larger experience of immigration and a more differentiated labour market compared to the surrounding municipalities, where (CEE) migration may not be that "common" and where migrant labour is often concentrated in one specific sector.

A central discriminating factor between the urban regions that shapes both the extent and the variation of types of migration and subsequently – such is the assumption – of the implications is that of spatial proximity. While Sweden and the Netherlands do not share any common borders with one of the CEE sending countries, Austria directly neighbours on four CEE countries, which literally surround its entire eastern part and with which it shares a long common history, not only regarding migration. A similar situation can be found the Edirne urban region (see Chap. 12). Short-term mobility is thus much more likely in this central European area because the related risks and costs for the migrants are comparably low. For CEE migrants from neighbouring countries, Austria is a kind of lab "for trying out" migration or simply for working "abroad" and living at home (e.g. daily commuting). This makes a huge difference to the other destinations in Sweden and the Netherlands, where larger distances have to be overcome and where the related risks and costs are higher. So there are two facets of the notion of "space" that have to be taken into account, namely (1) the factual distance between origin and destination and (2) spatial variations in labour market structures and job opportunities within the receiving urban regions.

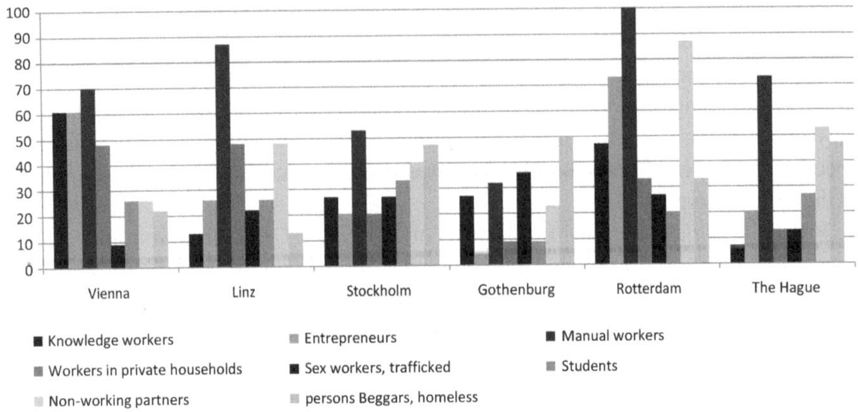

Fig. 3.1 Relevance of eight types of CEE migration for the stakeholders' work in six urban regions (Source: IMAGINATION online survey 2014. N = 113. Note: In each city individually, stakeholders were asked about the relevance of the different groups in their work)

3.3.2 Relevance of Different Types of CEE Migration in European Urban Regions

Before actually starting to answer the core research question, one needs to know, whether and to what extent the different types of CEE migrants defined in the present context are relevant for the stakeholders' work in the six urban regions. Results from the online survey that aimed at gathering first insights into relevant themes show the following: All groups have been mentioned as relevant by the local stakeholders across all urban regions (see Fig. 3.1), which is not surprising because the groups were pre-defined based on the assessment and analysis during the mapping exercise (see Chaps. 1 and 2).

A closer look reveals both similarities and differences between (1) groups of CEE migrants and (2) urban regions. The relevance of a specific group in the stakeholders' work furthermore provides a preliminary indication as to the urban consequences felt in specific contexts. As a majority, manual workers occupy much of the stakeholders' engagement; they are the most important group in all urban regions except for Gothenburg. In Linz, Rotterdam and The Hague this goes hand in hand with a pronounced relevance of accompanying family members, which is discussed in terms of housing and consequences for the school system. Knowledge workers and entrepreneurs have been particularly relevant in Vienna and Rotterdam, though with varying urban consequences: While knowledge workers are mostly associated with positive outcomes for the urban regions, entrepreneurs may find themselves in difficult situations and may display detrimental outcomes for the urban labour market, as will be described later. Interestingly enough, only Austrian stakeholders are also dealing with consequences of CEE workers in private households, which is probably due to spatial proximity and the presence of commuting care workers. Beggars and homeless persons, who receive a lot of media attention and are often in the focus of discussions of intra-European movement as such throughout Western Europe, were mostly mentioned by Swedish and Dutch respondents. More importantly, and this was revealed later during the expert interviews and the focus groups, there are enormous differences in the stakeholders' perceptions and narratives as to who is "really important" in the respective urban setting, which leads to varying urban consequences that were raised. In the Netherlands, stakeholders were mostly concerned with temporary manual workers having a low socio-economic status and tended to neglect the fact that some CEE migrants stay for longer periods of time or even for good, while Swedish stakeholders were more concerned with beggars and homeless persons.

In Austria, given the specificity of spatial proximity, both temporary and permanent forms of CEE migration were discussed. Another divergence in the stakeholders' assessments pertains to the definition of the "urban region". While Austrian and Swedish experts did not elaborate on the big picture and oftentimes discussed only the spatial entity they were concretely working in, Dutch stakeholders often discussed rural surroundings, where – and this is the link – most temporary workers find jobs in horticulture. This needs to be mentioned as a limitation to the data as it has probably resulted in a bias.

3.4 Consequences for Different Types of CEE Migrants

In the following, a basic distinction will be made between labour migrants and those not economically active in the receiving urban regions. Further refinements as to the various types of CEE migration will then be displayed throughout the discussion of the results. Implications will be presented for the position on the labour market, the fields of housing and the local level of the neighbourhood, registration and social security, social participation, and the school system. Furthermore, we will take a closer look at potential interconnections between implications in these domains.

3.4.1 The Situation of Economically Active CEE Migrants: A Question of Legal Status

Though the freedom of movement has led to a pronounced diversification of types of CEE migration, taking up a job in order to escape unemployment, hoping for higher wages or broadening one's experience still are the predominant reasons to go abroad. Within the group of labour migrants, there are short-term and long-term forms including eventual fluent transitions that mainly depend on the success and prospects on the receiving labour market. Another distinctive feature shaping the trajectories in the receiving urban region is the legal status on the labour market ranging from informal to formal to mixed forms, as some CEE migrants hold both a formal and an informal job.

Next, the individuals' level of qualification has to be taken into account: It has oftentimes been proven that a large share of CEE migrants is highly qualified, with knowledge workers per definition being the only group able to translate their qualifications into adequate positions on the receiving labour market. Their presence has mainly been assessed as positive for urban regions – in terms of economic gains and filling gaps on the labour market, a fact that also holds true for Edirne in Turkey (see Chap. 12) – and for individual migrants in terms of broadening their experience and gaining higher wages. Compared to the other groups, knowledge workers have rarely been mentioned by the stakeholders across urban regions and thus appear to be "invisible" because they are capable of navigating the different parts of the system easily. Being formally employed translates into an unproblematic registration, and the related access to welfare benefits works somewhat automatically. Due to comparatively high salaries, their access to decent housing merely depends on the general availability of flats, which appears to be difficult in the urban regions in Sweden and Austria (most of all in the capital cities), where the overall situation on the housing market is rather tight. Nevertheless, many find housing in better-off neighbourhoods where they – again – remain invisible. For them, even the contested field of language competence is not seen as particularly relevant from the point of view of the stakeholders because their English is oftentimes sufficient, at least in the workplace. Concerning this group, the stakeholders were mainly concerned about their need for better information regarding rules and regulations in the different fields and also regarding the transfer of welfare benefits once they decide to move to another country or return to their country of origin.

Continuing with the individuals' level of qualification, a central issue potentially applying to all other CEE migrant groups on the labour market irrespective of their length of stay and to some extent interlinked with their legal status is de-qualification, which is defined as a mismatch between the qualification "brought along" and the skill level acquired in the job at the destination. Since CEE migrants are oftentimes very qualified, the risk of doing de-qualifying work is high. A lack of information about the recognition of qualifications, weak networks and insufficient language skills are decisive reasons for this risk. Stakeholders have discussed this issue from extremely different perspectives, with the national specificities playing a more important role than differences between urban regions in the same country. It is a top-priority for Austrian stakeholders, who consider it a negative consequence for many CEE migrants that is closely connected to complex regulations concerning the nostrification of qualifications and lacking language skills. Not mentioned at all by Swedish stakeholders, the issue was discussed in the Netherlands from an entirely different perspective: CEE migrants may actually do de-qualified work but at the same time they qualify themselves in terms of tacit skills, international perspective and portfolio-building, a line of argumentation that once more proves the dominance of the "temporary view" in the Dutch context.

In order to understand the situation of CEE entrepreneurs in the urban regions one has to keep in mind that the majority of them chose self-employment (1) as a strategy to enter the labour market as long as the transitional provisions in Austria and the Netherlands were applied, with Sweden refraining from this post-accession strategy to protect the labour market, and (2) as a strategy to be employed in a sector where gainful employment is not feasible. From the point of view of the stakeholders in the Dutch and Austrian urban regions, this resulted in high numbers of self-employed CEE citizens, many of whom are still marginalised one-person companies facing unfavourable situations in many respects, even though the transitional restrictions have been lifted. Thus, self-employed work is often linked to wage dumping, exploitation and de-qualification. Beyond that, some CEE migrants are essentially pushed into self-employment (concentrated in some branches like construction, care work, and taxi driving), an issue linked to an even higher risk of (self-)exploitation and less secure working conditions. Local employers in this way reduce personnel costs and avoid administrative burdens aggravating both short- and long-term gainful employment. Blurred lines between self-employment and informal work may reduce the claims regarding welfare benefits. Furthermore, the low socio-economic status of these entrepreneurs decreases their chances on the housing market, and long working hours are detrimental to language learning and societal participation as such.

Many of these CEE entrepreneurs are in fact manual workers, a group that obviously displays various strategies as to length of stay and legal status on the regional labour markets, which in turn results in different trajectories of inclusion and exclusion in the central domains. In the Netherlands, stakeholders have addressed this group mainly in terms of short-term gainfully employed manual workers subject to clustered contractual relationships. In this context, temporary employment agencies act as gatekeepers. They are very much interested in managing and controlling these migrants in terms of wages and regarding security issues but also regarding travel costs and housing. These short-term workers are hired on the basis of all-inclusive package deals and are mostly employed in the rural surroundings of the cities, which display a more monocultural economic profile. Migrants may profit from the conditional services that the agencies and employers offer as they do not have to take care of housing and transport. However, the issue becomes negative, when their autonomy and private behaviour are dictated by labour conditions (compare van Ostaijen et al. 2015). All-inclusive package deals are likely to result in multiple dependencies, which can imply that employees are in a vulnerable position towards their employers. Discrimination or intimidation could cause employees to feel unable to speak up about their rights and labour situation or feel afraid to empower themselves. Further consequences include wage discrimination, labour discrimination and intimidation by fines for breaching rules set out for housing behaviour as well as by threatening to terminate labour contracts if employees speak up about improper labour conditions. For Sweden and Austria, this sort of all-encompassing relationship between employers and employees in short-term agricultural work has only been marginally touched upon.

Though identified as an important part of CEE migration, the type "persons working in private households" has not been elaborated on much by Dutch and Swedish stakeholders, while Austrian and Turkish stakeholders have put a lot of emphasis on it (for details on Turkey see Chap. 12 and Sert et al. 2015). Usually involving women, the ever-growing demand for care work and domestic work in mostly middle-class households has attracted a growing number of persons, thus contributing to the ongoing feminisation of CEE migration. In this field, two major types have been discussed by the experts: (1) care workers who go back and forth on a bi-weekly basis, by and large only feasible in the Austrian urban regions as they are spatially close enough to CEE for this kind of strategy (compare Enengel and Reeger 2015), and (2) women in informal cleaning jobs as well as males engaging in gardening and renovation work in private households, also mostly in an informal way and scrutinized in all urban regions. Care workers constantly commute between their life at home and a household in Austria, where they take care of sick and elderly persons 24/7. Although there are many positive stories to be told including benefits for both the women (in terms of higher wages) and the persons being cared for (as they can stay at home in their familiar surroundings), some care workers may find themselves in situations where various detrimental factors coincide: Living with their employers may result in a pronounced dependence with eventual cases of exploitation when they are asked to carry out domestic work not in their remit and furthermore keep them away from a broader societal participation. According to the stakeholders, this group is hard to reach and kind of hidden in the private households. Nevertheless, most of this work is carried out in a formal way (mostly self-employed, rarely employed by an agency or the household itself), with full access to welfare benefits, though the transfer of claims is still often unclear. The second group comprises all other forms of domestic help, carried out mainly by CEE citizens already residing in the urban regions who sometimes engage both in an official, formal job and in informal domestic work to earn some extra money. These kinds of services are in high demand with "these ambitious 'new Europeans' being in danger of becoming a new Victorian servant class" (Favell 2008: 711). In the following, a closer look will be taken at the general implications of informal work regarding the domestic sector as well as other parts of the economy.

Generally speaking, informal workers (in construction, the service sector, private households) are in a very vulnerable position as these kinds of work arrangements are often associated with exploitation and a pronounced dependence on the employer. This assessment also holds true e.g. for informal work in Istanbul (see Chap. 12). Yet, these types of jobs still seem to offer an alternative way to earn money for those who are not able to find or are kept away from a formal job. But on the labour market they are affected by de-qualification, competition and eventual displacement, e.g. due to an even cheaper labour force from more Eastern parts of CEE, wage-related discrimination, a complete lack of labour rights, poor working conditions and long working hours. Beyond these effects regarding the labour market, informal work results in a spiral of negative interrelated effects in terms of inclusion, or rather exclusion, regarding other resources: a weak position on the housing market with few choices, no access to welfare benefits (including accident insurance), social marginalisation due to long working hours, and limited chances to learn the language.

The situation of CEE sex workers is again characterized by a spiral of effects mostly depending on their status in terms of formal and informal work and also as to whether sex work is prohibited in the respective urban setting or not. Sex work in areas where it is officially forbidden is driven underground or online, sometimes related to human trafficking, and reinforces the exploitative structure of this activity. Due to the stigmatised position, access to housing may be difficult, as can be access to social benefits, which in turn leads to general marginalisation and hardly any societal participation.

3.4.2 The Situation of Family Members: Depending on the Single Earner

Though the majority of CEE migrants enter Western European urban regions in order to find an employment, there are also groups not primarily pursuing economic goals. Accompanying partners and spouses who are themselves not (officially) participating in the labour market have as such not been discussed much in terms of consequences by the experts. Their situation largely depends on the socio-economic position of their partner, which may leave them either in a weak position if their partner is part of the informal labour market or in a satisfactory situation if their partner has a well-paying, formal job. Access to social benefits also depends on this, since family members are able to apply for financial aid and benefits only if their partner is formally employed. For the Austrian case, stakeholders elaborated that access to the labour market is particularly difficult for this group because they face childcare duties that are often difficult to combine with a job. Consequently, this non-participation in the labour market has wide-ranging consequences for them, their children and also for the economically active partner, who may have to work longer and harder in order to provide for the family. Non-working spouses and partners have more difficulties learning the language as they lack social contacts because their childcare duties hinder them from spending time attending language training.

Across all urban regions family reunification is an ongoing process which clearly affects the schools in the receiving areas and puts attention on the role of CEE children in families and the education system. Schools face challenges resulting from the notion of "mobile EU-citizens". In the Netherlands, the assessment once again concentrates on the temporality of stays and on children entering and leaving schools frequently. Furthermore, a lack of knowledge about regulations regarding the school age has been addressed as has the situation that parents simply leave their children at home instead of sending them to school because they are more inclined to take care of them in the family.

Spatial proximity once more shapes the assessments in the Austrian urban regions: Recently, some CEE children and teenagers have been heading to Austria to attend compulsory or vocational schools in the border region while still residing in their country of origin or attending boarding schools. CEE pupils therefore lead to changing needs and focuses at school, which has been particularly underlined in the case of the fast-growing urban region of Vienna. CEE citizens acknowledge the positive effects of sending their children to Austrian schools in terms of a later entry into the Austrian labour market. On the other hand, the more peripheral schools benefit from additional pupils and do not run the risk of being closed down.

In terms of education-related implications the Austrian example shows the need for a differentiation between two groups of CEE pupils: Children who migrate in early childhood usually integrate very quickly and more easily into the education system as they learn the language at kindergarten and school in a "hands on" fashion. Older newcomers (such as teenagers) accompanying their parents face more difficulties in following the lessons due to insufficient German language proficiencies and diverging curricula. This problem is aggravated by the fact that most measures are implemented within compulsory education but would also be necessary in vocational schools where school attendance is no longer compulsory. Moreover, academic high schools do not offer substantial supporting measures and it is therefore often recommended that these newcomers attend ordinary schools. Many of them have little or no knowledge of German and are therefore particularly challenging to include into the education system. These problems discourage many teenaged newcomers from attending vocational schools, which leads to a subsequent loss of individual future opportunities and human capital.

The Swedish results do not offer any indication that CEE migration has major implications for the education sector. Education for the younger CEE citizens, i.e. under the age of 18, seems to work well. This can result from the fact that, e.g., Gothenburg has an established practice of offering schooling to the children of rejected asylum seekers, and the public administration representatives were almost puzzled by the respective question. CEE pupils are not considered a problematic group, maybe partly due to the rather permanent presence of CEE citizens in the region. Children accompanying homeless CEE citizens are welcome to attend primary and secondary schools and this process seems to work well.

3.4.3 The Situation of Students: Rarely Discussed by the Experts

Just like in the case of knowledge workers, stakeholders did not elaborate much on students from CEE, who have been assessed as a rather positive facet of intra-European movement. With many of them being embedded in European schemes like ERASMUS and being present on a temporary basis, they are seen as an enrichment of urban society and the university scene. Nevertheless, they also may face problems, e.g., on the housing market, where many find themselves in a disadvantaged position lacking relevant social connections and information on how the system works and how to navigate bureaucratic formalities. The latter also applies to finding adequate jobs alongside their studies, and CEE students run the risk of taking on informal work and being faced with the related disadvantages like discrimination and exploitation with a similar situation for CEE students in Turkey (see Chap. 12). Language proficiency and the necessity to learn the new language were discussed rather divergently: While Dutch stakeholders argued that students were exempt from having to learn Dutch if their English was sufficient, Swedish and Austrian stakeholders viewed local language proficiency as a necessary requirement to enter the labour market after graduation and also during their studies. In this respect, Austrian stakeholders diagnosed a lack of specialised language courses.

3.4.4 The Situation of Destitute CEE Migrants: A "Special Challenge"

Though in quantitative terms they make up very small groups, beggars and homeless CEE migrants are in the focus of a lot of public and political discussions in all of the urban regions explored. Basically, there are two different, albeit overlapping, groups which have in common that they are (1) excluded from access to all central dimensions and that they (2) have been assessed as a group facing as well as causing problems and thus represent a challenge for the receiving systems. Beggars, mostly of Roma descent, often lead their own structured lives and do not access night shelters etc. Both groups are concentrated in the core cities, where homeless find shelters and where begging is feasible in shopping streets with many passers-by, for example.

Welfare provision and return counselling remains a constant task in the receiving cities, and the health care system is overburdened with homeless EU citizens lacking health insurance. Stakeholders have elaborated on the lack of supportive facilities for homeless persons including easier and cheaper access to housing. Neighbourhood consequences of CEE migration were also largely associated with beggars and homeless CEE citizens. The visibility of these groups may increase generalised negative attitudes on migration from CEE as such.

The "catch 22" of being a homeless EU-citizen in Western Europe has been described for Sweden (compare Zelano et al. 2015) but this description can be expanded to all urban regions: Without a social security number, they have difficulties opening a bank account and getting formal employment. As they need to earn a living, they are more likely to work in the informal labour market, where there is a lack of transparency and an increased risk of exploitation. Moreover, homelessness and social marginalisation also creates a spiral of effects stretching beyond the obvious ones. In order to be entitled to assistance, the jobseeker must regularly visit the employment agency and account for the efforts made to get a job. Therefore, staying in the job-seeking process requires an address, or at least a reliable contact point, where they can be reached by the agency. Without a way to get in touch with the jobseeker, the employment agency cannot fulfil the controls required, and the jobseeker is excluded from the process. The uncertainty of not having a place to live also hampers the educational attainment of accompanying children. In the worst case, this marginalisation will be inherited by the next generation.

3.5 The Crucial Interface: Access to Information and Individual Language Skills

There are two comprehensive factors shaping the effects described so far as explanatory variables that need to be discussed in more detail: access to information and individual language skills. Across urban regions and the various types of migration, stakeholders have emphasised a lack of information about specificities of the labour market, the situation regarding housing but also in the fields of registration, social security and education. CEE migrants definitely need more and better information, and the stakeholders suggest a clear need for improving routines and facilitating information flows. First of all, it would benefit the migrants themselves: Easy access to information on registration, on how the social security system works, on the labour and housing market as well as on the school system is necessary to manoeuvre within the receiving society in general. There are several factors that explain why CEE migrants lack proper information, the most important one being a lack of language skills, since oftentimes in-depth information is only available in the local language. Second, information on the specificities of the labour market or regarding social security, for example, has been reported to be contradicting when addressing different institutions and often causes confusion as to which rules actually apply. Third, there is some indication that CEE migrants rely on the information they get from family and friends rather than from official channels, which has been discussed in relation with a generalized avoidance of official authorities. Last but not least, Dutch experts elaborated on a certain interest of some employers to keep temporary workers uninformed, which is a clear sign of discrimination and intimidation (compare van Ostaijen et al. 2015).

However, an increase in information would also benefit the authorities and society at large, since it improves supervision, which in turn minimises the scope for criminal activities such as labour exploitation (compare Zelano et al. 2015). There also seems to be a need for better information before migrants actually decide to move. In the case of the Netherlands and Austria some stakeholders argued that different types of CEE migrants are often not well prepared and may have unrealistic expectations (for example, regarding chances on the labour market or the availability of housing) before actually starting their migration process.

Individual language skills were seen as the second prerequisite to success in every-day-life as well as in the working sphere. Lacking language skills hinder CEE migrants from getting adequate information, with the exception of knowledge workers, for whom English may suffice. However, language acquisition is a matter of length of stay: It may not be worthwhile for short-term migrants like seasonal workers but is seen as absolutely necessary for all migrants staying for a longer period of time or permanently. Not all types of migrants have easy access to language courses or are encouraged to learn the new language in the receiving urban regions. Access to language courses may be a problem in more rural areas in particular, and funding appears to be insufficient in all urban regions. There is also a clear need for more job-related language courses as well as evening courses that meet the needs of working CEE migrants.

3.6 Conclusion

Taking a comparative look at different types of migrants from CEE revealed enormous differences between them in terms of access to and provision of local resources, the respective trajectories and positions as well as the barriers they are facing. Knowledge workers and students as the least problematized categories are comparatively better off or, in other words, they have rarely been mentioned by the stakeholders and thus seem to be capable of navigating the different parts of the system with comparative ease. In contrast, many manual workers, entrepreneurs and domestic helpers face de-qualification, competition, wage dumping and exploitation with the disadvantages progressively intensifying in informal employment. This furthermore goes hand in hand with a complete lack of social security and, generally speaking, more barriers in accessing all other central domains. Finally, we saw that the most vulnerable groups – beggars and homeless persons – find themselves completely excluded and have been defined by the stakeholders as a "special challenge" for the urban regions. The present approach, offering a more nuanced perspective on intra-European movement, proves that the triple-win scenario promoted by the EU (Favell 2008: 705) does not entirely hold true. Migrants may be among the "winners" in terms of higher wages but the circumstances under which they are working and living in Western European urban regions are oftentimes rather unfavourable.

Furthermore, a detailed look at the implications in various domains for different types of migrants (see also Reeger and Enengel 2015) quickly reveals that these are often interrelated and that each type of migration has its own "chain of implications". For some types of migrants, these linkages may result in a vicious cycle that is difficult to escape, and many of these have a domino effect of implications that multiply their effects due to their chained patterns.

Some of the stories that have been told by the stakeholders regarding the implications in various domains and their chained patterns obviously also apply to migrants from outside of the EU and not just to mobile EU-citizens enjoying their freedom of movement. This leads to the conclusion that having the same rights as nationals and being treated like them legally does not necessarily result in positive outcomes, as has been shown in previous studies on CEE migration (e.g. Favell 2009; Ciupijus 2011; MacKenzie and Forde 2009; Sabater 2015). Yes, EU citizens are free to live and work wherever they want to but they may still face obstacles and be in need of help and guidance at least at the beginning of their stay, especially in terms of the "crucial interface": sufficient, pinpoint information, and opportunities to learn the language in case they intend to stay longer. This is where they do not differ from third country nationals. But contrary to them, they are, at least up to now, often not subject to integration policies due to the principle of non-discrimination of EU citizens, which may have some unfortunate effects. As indicated by the experts, they are often not covered by specific integration efforts and programmes and lack financial support on the EU, the national, and the local level.

The stakeholders' tasks regarding and their engagement with CEE migrants and their narratives concerning consequences for them in the urban regions show a lot of similarities and differences that can be defined and framed along several lines. Some of these variations are related to spatial differences, namely to distance and proximity between origin and destination and the resulting structure and extent of CEE migration. In the Austrian urban regions, which are the closest to the CEE countries, display the highest shares of CEE migrants, offer the most pronounced variety in types of migrants' projects and share a long common (migration) history, stakeholders drew a nuanced picture of both positive and negative outcomes of intra-European movement for both the individual migrants and the cities and their economies. In Sweden, being further away and experiencing comparatively less CEE immigration, though transitional provisions were not applied, stakeholders also had a differentiated view on various types of CEE migration with the general conclusion being that the vast majority integrates well and contributes to both economy and society, which was also argued by Austrian stakeholders. In the Dutch case, stakeholders elaborated mostly on temporary migrants with a low socio-economic status, thus to some extent neglecting issues regarding long-term migrants, though they are present in both of the Dutch urban regions as well. On this level of comparison it thus became obvious, that urban consequences are to some extent determined by the national level with urban regions in the same country displaying a lot of similarities. There are two further explanations: 1) The national level plays a crucial role in the basic design of governance in the domains explored. The functioning of the labour market, the welfare system and the school system and the rules applied are to a large extent top down with only slight regional and local variations. Matters of the housing market and societal participation on the other hand are more in the area of responsibility of the local level. 2) As shown above, the stakeholder-based approach revealed a kind of "national narrative" when it comes to distinct aspects of CEE migration and its consequences as experts engaged in this field are connected through local and national networks active in various domains and share their views and experiences.

Another notion – again from a spatial perspective – is that differences in consequences occur rather within than between urban regions in the same national context, as was illustrated by Dutch and Austrian stakeholders pointing to the importance of future research on the spatial specificities of CEE migration in urban and rural areas. Cities seem to be better suited to welcoming newcomers and providing them with an adequate infrastructure and diverse offers. On the one hand, they are attractive to all types of CEE migration also regarding existing migrant networks, on the other hand, they appear to be limited to influencing domains like housing and community cohesion. They cannot steer immigration as such, matters of the labour market or registration, which are designed on the national level, nor social security in the broad sense. More rural municipalities on the outskirts of urban regions are often less well prepared and equipped for catering to the needs of mobile EU citizens due to their smaller population size and due to having less experience with immigration.

The present analysis of the obverse and reverse side of free movement proves that there are problem areas to be considered and challenges to be solved when it comes to intra-European movement. These problems and challenges are mostly felt on the local level of urban regions as cities are and will continue to be migration magnets for all migrants irrespective of their origin, among them EU citizens. The ever-growing migration-related diversity puts new socio-political challenges that need to be resolved urgently. For many CEE migrants, transitions into the local fabric work smoothly, as the interviewees argued, but still there is a lot to be done in terms of policy responses. The sheer multitude of negative implications in single domains as well as their interconnectedness leads to the expectation that there are not many structured governance approaches – at least not on the local level of urban regions – to the implications of CEE migration, but rather ad-hoc arrangements and reactions instead of proactive procedures. Chap. 7 will discuss, whether this assumption is correct or whether it can be rejected.

References

Black, R., Engbersen, G., Okolski, M., & Pantiru, C. (Eds.). (2010). *A continent moving west? EU enlargement and labour migration from central and Eastern Europe*. Amsterdam: Amsterdam University Press.

Caglar, A. (2014). *Urban migration trends, challenges and opportunities in Europe*. Background Paper, World Migration Report 2015. IOM, Geneva.

Castro-Martin, T., & Cortina, C. (2015). Demographic issues of intra-European migration: Destinations, family and settlement. *European Journal of Population, 31*(2), 109–125.

Ciupijus, Z. (2011). Mobile central eastern Europeans in Britain: Successful European Union citizens and disadvantaged labour migrants? *Work, Employment and Society, 25*(3), 540–550.

Collett, E. (2013). *The integration needs of mobile EU citizens. Impediments and opportunities*. Brussels: Migration Policy Institute Europe.

Drinkwater, S., Eade, J., & Garapich, M. (2010). What's behind the figures? An investigation into recent Polish migration to the UK. In R. Black, G. Engbersen, M. Okolski, & C. Pantiru (Eds.), *A continent moving west? EU enlargement and labour migration from central and Eastern Europe* (pp. 73–88). Amsterdam: Amsterdam University Press.

Enengel, M. L., & Reeger, U. (2015). *Urban implications of CEE migration in Austrian urban regions. Country report Austria*. IMAGINATION Working Paper. Online: http://www.project-imagination.eu.

Fassmann, H., Kohlbacher, J., & Reeger, U. (2014). The re-emergence of European East-West migration – the Austrian example. *Central and Eastern European Migration Review, 3*(2), 1–21.

Favell, A. (2008). The new face of East-West migration in Europe. *Journal of Ethnic and Migration Studies, 34*(5), 701–716.

Favell, A. (2009). Immigration, migration, and free movement in the making of Europe. In J. T. Checkel & P. J. Katzenstein (Eds.), *European identity* (pp. 167–189). Cambridge: Cambridge University Press.

Garapich, M. P. (2014). Homo Sovieticus revisited – Anti-institutionalism, alcohol and resistance among Polish homeless men in London. *International Migration, 52*(1), 100–117.

Glorius, B., Grabowska-Lusinska, I., & Kuvik, A. (Eds.). (2013). *Mobility in transition. Migration patterns after EU enlargement. IMISCOE research*. Amsterdam: Amsterdam University Press.

MacKenzie, R., & Forde, C. (2009). The rhetoric of the "good worker" versus the realities of employers' use and the experiences of migrant workers. *Work, Employment and Society, 23*(1), 142–159.

Reeger, U., & Enengel, M. L. (2015). *Implications of CEE migration in European urban regions. The socio-economic, socio-cultural and legal-political implications in comparison.* IMAGINATION Comparative Report 2. Vienna. Online: http://www.project-imagination.eu.

Sabater, A. (2015). Between flows and places: Using geodemographics to explore EU migration across neighbourhoods in Britain. *European Journal of Population, 31*(2), 207–230.

Sert, D., Korfali, D., & Acar, T. (2015). *Urban implications of CEE migration. Country report Turkey*. IMAGINATION Working Paper. Online: http://www.project-imagination.eu.

van Ostaijen, M. M. A. C., Faber, M., Scholten, P., & Engbersen, G. (2015). *Social consequences of CEE migration. Country report the Netherlands*. IMAGINATION Working Paper. Online: http://www.project-imagination.eu.

Voitchovsky, S. (2014). Occupational downgrading and wages of new member states immigrants to Ireland. *International Migration Review, 48*(2), 500–537.

Zelano, K., Bucken-Knapp, G., Hinnfors, J., & Spehar, A. (2015). *Urban implications of CEE migration in Gothenburg and Stockholm. Country report Sweden*. IMAGINATION Working Paper. Online: http://www.project-imagination.eu.

Chapter 4
Liquid Migration and Its Consequences for Local Integration Policies

Godfried Engbersen

4.1 Introduction

This chapter addresses the notion of 'liquid migration' in relation to intra-European movement. Does intra-European movement challenge our conventional understanding of temporary versus permanent intra-European migration? And what does this mean in terms of the central dilemma of 'mobility' versus 'integration'?

The EU enlargements of 2004 and 2007 led to an unexpected scale of labour mobility within the enlarged EU (mainly from Poland, the Baltic States, Romania, Bulgaria and Slovakia) (Black et al. 2010). Within the 10 years following the 2004 EU enlargement, the total number of nationals from the new member states residing in the 'old' member states increased more than fivefold, from 1.1 million in 2004 to 6.1 million in 2014. This is a total net inflow of 5 million migrants from Central Europe (Fihel et al. 2015), most of whom went to the UK, Ireland, Germany, Austria, Italy, Spain, the Scandinavian countries and the Netherlands.

The EU expansion is an interesting case, not just because it resulted – in absolute numbers – in a substantial increase in migration from specific East European to specific West European countries, but also for the nature of the new labour migration (Krings et al. 2013). Favell (2008: 701) has claimed that the East-West migration associated with the EU enlargement process has resulted in "the emergence of a new migration system in Europe" that forces us to rethink standard theories and conceptions on immigration, integration and citizenship, as these are mainly tied up with post-colonial, guest worker and asylum migration. In my own work I have previously proposed that this new migration system can be described as 'liquid migration' (Engbersen 2013; Engbersen and Snel 2013). The main feature of liquid migration is its temporary, flexible and unpredictable character, with workers

G. Engbersen (✉)
Erasmus University Rotterdam, Rotterdam, The Netherlands
e-mail: engbersen@fsw.eur.nl

P. Scholten, M. van Ostaijen (eds.), *Between Mobility and Migration*, IMISCOE Research Series, https://doi.org/10.1007/978-3-319-77991-1_4

'trying their luck' in different European labour markets before settling or moving on or moving home. One consequence of liquid migration is that many intra-European labour migrants only partially and temporarily integrate in the destination countries.

My analysis also led to the position that many destination locations were insufficiently equipped to deal with these patterns of liquid migration (Engbersen 2013). Despite experiences with temporary labour migration in West European countries (particularly with seasonal labour) and with intra- European movement (especially between the original EU member states), many cities and regions did not seem capable of responding adequately to the structural temporariness associated with liquid migration (Grzymała-Kazłowska 2005).

The introduction of the concept of liquid migration has met various objections, for instance that the extent of temporary and unpredictable intra-European movement was being overestimated. After all, there are also patterns of settlement migration in West European countries. A second objection concerned the local consequences of intra-European movement. Do any serious consequences actually occur at the local level, or are unwelcome consequences restricted to very specific groups and very specific problems?

In this Chap. I shall explore the nature of intra- European movement and the relevance of the concept of liquid migration, confronted with the IMAGINATION findings. I will also consider the consequences of intra- European movement for local integration policy. The chapter is structured as follows. First I will describe the features of liquid migration and the impact thereof at the local level. Next, I confront these features with the typology of intra- European movement as developed in Chap. 1 and with the findings on local consequences (Reeger, Chap. 3). I conclude with a discussion of liquid migration.

4.2 Liquid Migration and its Local Consequences

4.2.1 Liquid Migration as an Ideal Type

The concept of liquid migration is an ideal type. Ideal types draw attention to the typical features of a specific phenomenon, in order to build a picture of its key characteristics (Ringer 1997). An ideal type is a conceptual construct in order to unveil and explain social phenomena. Ideal types are, in the famous words of Max Weber (2002: 55) "constructed concepts endowed with a degree of consistency, seldom found in actual history.".[1]

The concept of liquid migration was formulated to capture the nature of intra EU-mobility, especially after the EU enlargements of 2004 and 2007. A key principle

[1]This quotation is from Max Weber's (2002: 55) *The Protestant Ethic and the Spirit of Capitalism*. He continues as follows: "Precisely because of the impossibility of drawing sharp boundaries in historical reality, our only hope of identifying the particular effects of these religious ideas must come through an investigation of their most consistent (or "ideal") forms."

underlying the concept of liquid migration is that migration forms an intrinsic part of wider social transformations within origin and destination countries in Europe. These transformations are related to several institutional changes:

- The transition by former communist countries to liberal democracies, giving citizens more freedom to migrate;
- The expansion of the European Union in 2004 and 2007 and the abolishment of internal borders;
- The increase in flexible, temporary and uncertain labour in many OECD and West European countries. Non-standard work, such as temporary work, part-time work and self-employment account for about a third of total employment in OECD countries. Since the mid-1990s, more than half of all job creation was in the form of non-standard work (OECD 2015);
- The individualisation of family relations, offering more freedom to individual members (especially the children) to go their own way (Beck and Beck-Gernsheim 2002);
- Technological changes, especially the growth of social media, which have facilitated new and unconventional means of finding potential migration destinations (Dekker and Engbersen 2014).

Furthermore, the EU is characterised by substantial inequalities between the member states, particularly between the old and new member states, making migration an attractive option for many. Obviously, the concept of liquid migration was inspired by Zygmunt Bauman's work (1999; 2003; 2005; 2007) on liquid modernity. Central to the notion of liquidity is the transformation of "solid" institutions (class, family, labour, community, neighbourhood, welfare state and nation state) into to more flexible and loose institutions. These institutions lose their power to interconnect individual choices and collective projects. They become less solid and less predictable, and in the melting pot of modern society, they lose their compelling and self-evident character.[2] As Bauman (2005: 1) notes:

> Liquid modern is a society in which the conditions under which its members act change faster than it takes the ways of acting to consolidate into habits and routines. Liquidity of life and that of society feed and reinvigorate each other. Liquid life, just like liquid modern society, cannot keep its shape or stay on course for long.

These insights are relevant to understanding contemporary patterns of labour mobility in Europe. Migration has always been strongly embedded in rather strong and stable institutions (the family, local community and local labour markets, and the nation state (Portes 1995; Boyd and Nowak 2013; Goldin et al. 2011). The transformation of these institutions, together with advanced communications technologies and the disappearance of internal borders due to the EU enlargements,

[2] Bauman (2007: 6) writes in *Liquid Modernity*: 'The solids whose turn has come to be thrown into the melting pot and which are in the process of being melted at the present time, the time of fluid modernity, are the bonds which interlock individual choices in collective projects and actions – the patterns of communication and co-ordination between individually conducted life policies on the one hand and political actions of human collectivities on the other.'

Overview 4.1 The characteristics of liquid migration

1	**Settlement**	Temporality of migration and stay Invisibility of stay (non-registration)	Temporal migration
			Economic integration in destination country
2	**Type of migration**	Labour and student migration	Labour migrants
			Student migrants
3	**Status**	Legal residential status	Regular labour migration
			Temporary work permit holders
4	**Destination**	No predestined receiving country	Multiple receiving countries
			New receiving countries
5	**Family**	Individualised life strategy (limited family obligations)	Individualised forms of migration
			First generation pattern
6	**Migratory habitus**	Intentional unpredictability	No fixed migration aspirations
			Open options

has changed migration patterns in post-industrial societies and has made migration more flexible, and less visible and predictable.

In earlier publications on the nature of CEE labour mobility I highlighted six dimensions (Engbersen 2013; Engbersen and Snel 2013) (see Overview 4.1). The first dimension is the temporality of a stay abroad. Migrants do not settle permanently, but move back and forth from their origin country to receiving countries (circular migration), operate in in-between situations that are neither wholly temporary nor wholly permanent, or move to multiple destination countries. Their stays abroad may differ from migrant to migrant and from group to group. Some stay briefly (for example seasonal workers), others will opt for a medium long stay or a longer-term stay (for example highly skilled workers). The temporal nature of residence often goes hand in hand with non-registration, which contributes to the invisibility of liquid migration.

A second dimension is that liquid migration is predominantly labour migration. Student migration may be seen as a minor supplement to this labour migration (short term labour migration is sometimes the true motive behind forms of student migration) (Ivancheva 2007).

A third dimension is that liquid migration is a regular form of migration. Mobile EU citizens formally have the same rights and duties as the native citizens in the destination Member State, and they should not be treated differently in comparison to the native citizens. However, before 2014 many EU migrants needed a work permit in order to access the labour market. Without such a work permit they could become irregular workers. This transition period, in which restrictions were imposed on workers from the A-8 and A-2 countries, ended on 1 January 2014.

A fourth dimension of liquid migration is that intra-European movement has become more unpredictable. Some categories of labour migrants work and reside in well-established destination countries (such as Germany), while others travel to new destinations countries such as the UK but also to Belgium, Denmark, Ireland,

Norway and the Netherlands (Fihel et al. 2015). A crucial aspect of intra-European movement is that it partly ignores the political and economic factors that shaped migration flows in the past.

A fifth dimension concerns the role of family. International migration has always been stimulated and facilitated by networks of family (Tilly 1990; Massey et al. 2005; Palloni et al. 2001; Massey et al. 2005; Epstein 2008). Households develop strategies to maximise the household income. These classical forms of migration rely on the solidarity between generations and on extended family patterns. However, next to this classical pattern, new patterns are emerging that are much more individualised. Family ties have become looser and more fragile, not only in West European societies but also in Central and Eastern European societies.

A sixth dimension is that the social position of migrants and the migration field in which they strategically operate, generates a specific migratory habitus of 'intentional unpredictability'. This is especially true for young single migrants (Eade et al. 2007). This migratory habitus expresses the more individualistic ethos of migrants who are less bound by family obligations and also less constrained by borders and local labour markets than previous generations of migrants. Among the more highly educated migrants, the desire to experience a metropolitan lifestyle may also play a role (Drinkwater and Garapich 2015).

The concept of liquid migration has met with some criticism. First, there is the question whether it actually represents a new phenomenon, or whether, instead, it's a matter of old wine in new bottles? (Penninx, Chap. 5). Temporary, short-term, seasonal and circular forms of migration are nothing new. They have occurred throughout (European) history (Moch 1992) and are particularly visible in migration flows in Africa and China, but also between Mexico and the US (Chapman and Prothero 1983/84; Massey et al. 2005). Worth mentioning here is the work by Okolski (2012) on incomplete migration, which was an important phenomenon in post-war Poland, before the EU expansion. Incomplete migration concerns the trans-national circularity of people, on the one hand seeking employment and on the other pursuing a household risk minimisation strategy.

Second, the concept seems to pay little attention to the dynamics of migration, culminating in settlement migration. Thus, Friberg (2012) shows that the labour migration from Poland to Norway displays various phases, from circulation to trans-national commuting and finally to settlement. On the other hand, Recci (2015) draws attention, not so much to the dynamics of intra- European movement but to the co-existence of old and new patterns of migration. This position is more in line with my own work on the heterogeneity of EU labour migration (Engbersen et al. 2013).

Third, the notions of the free-moving lifestyle and the migratory habitus of intentional unpredictability are questioned. Most mobile workers are in search of a possibility to settle down and live grounded, secure and stable lives (Bygnes and Erdal 2017). This observation – based on an analysis of the future narratives of Polish and Spanish migrants in Norway – is partly supported by the work by King et al. (2015) into the position of highly educated young adults from the Baltic states in the city of London. The researchers confirm the relevance of the concept of liquid migration for its acknowledgement of aspects such as self-development, life style, metropolitan culture and the open-ended character of migration (King 2017). Yet they also point to "a young adult transition or a process of adult 'becoming' (hence, not yet complete) - from an individualised life style, with few family obligations, to a life-stage which combines thoughts on family formation with a possible return to the home country." To what extent a return ever materialises is an open question, but a longing for a more secure and stable social life is also found among Baltic graduates. Yet as King et al. note (2015: 2): "Where a stable home will be, however, is often not very clear in migrants' mind." Incidentally, it applies for all groups that a stable job with a decent income and 'normal' working life conditions are seen as important ingredients of a grounded life or stable home, in either the origin or the destination country.

The critical comments concerning the concept of liquid migration relate to the theme of structure and agency. However, liquid migration does not entail that migrants are free to choose the life they want and that they have a natural inclination towards the adventurous life. Liquid migration instead implies that keeping your options open is a rational attitude developed by intra-European mobile citizens in response to the institutional uncertainties and opportunities that they encounter. This pertains especially to uncertainties and opportunities in the labour market. Many mobile workers have temporary jobs and work below their actual educational qualifications in European countries, but they also have limited opportunities in the labour markets of their origin countries (Nowicka 2012; Verwiebe et al. 2014; Voitchovsky 2014; McCollum and Findlay (2015). This contributes to a liquid life: "lived under conditions of constant uncertainty" (Bauman 2005:2). Nevertheless, there are differences concerning the extent to which individuals have different options to choose from. Some individuals can afford to take more risks and to develop an adventurous lifestyle, for example graduates who are supported by wealthy parents or highly skilled workers who wish to gain experience working abroad. Low educated labour migrants who must depend on (temporary) work, offered by temporary work agencies (and who may have to sustain a family), are not as free to pursue an adventurous life style and to aspire to a rich cultural life. Their main concern is to find a reliable job with decent wages.

The question now is what insights the IMAGINATION project has produced with respect to the theme of liquid migration. We will address this question below, after we look into a related conceptual question, that is the implications of liquid migration for (local) integration policies.

4.2.2 *Inplications of Liquid Migration for Local Integration Policies*

In the introduction we cited Favell's claim (2008) that we need to rethink standard theories on immigration and integration as they are strongly related to post-colonial, guest worker and asylum migration. In Europe, integration policy has mainly focused on third-country nationals (TCNs) who settle in West European countries, such as (former) guest workers and the following family migrants, post-colonial migrants and asylum migrants. Intra-European movement was never part of the domain of integration, also because of the small size of intra-European mobility.

With the EU enlargements, intra-European mobility has become a dominant phenomenon; in part due to the increasing size it. Specific countries and cities are receiving significant numbers of mobile EU citizens, without being adequately equipped to do so (Black et al. 2010). Besides, intra-European mobility challenges established integration policies due to its unpredictable and dynamic nature. Accordingly, we see that the arrival of large numbers of labour migrants is producing specific social problems for urban regions, for instance with regard to housing but also in the areas of registration, education and health care (see Chap. 3).

However, the gravity of these problems is assessed differently in the countries affected. In some European cities – such as Rotterdam and The Hague in the Netherlands – policy makers use strong metaphors (e.g. "a tsunami of Polish migrants") to focus attention on issues of housing and disorder in neighbourhood. But in other European cities that also faced a substantial influx of mobile EU citizens, the political idiom is more moderate. Nonetheless, cities like Antwerp, Berlin, Brussels, Dublin, Ghent, London, Oslo, and Manchester also report problems of housing and homelessness (Broadway 2011; Garapich 2011; Crellen 2010; Mostowska 2011).

Furthermore, in many European cities a debate is ongoing whether an integration policy ought to be pursued for specific categories of mobile EU citizens (Van Puymbroeck et al. 2011; Engbersen et al. 2017). Various considerations play a role here. On the one hand, policy makers wish to prevent that the arrival of mobile European citizens causes problems for settled citizens. On the other hand, they incorporate a timeline in respect of integration policy for mobile EU citizens. Thus, cities are developing language facilities for mobile workers who have taken up residence for the longer term. In sum: the co-existence of old and new forms of mobility – expressed in new forms of temporality – raises new questions for cities and local authorities. For this theme, too, it is important to examine the IMAGINATION findings.

4.3 Liquid Migration in the Light of the IMAGINATON Findings

How does the concept of liquid migration relate to the empirical findings of the IMAGINATION project, especially to the typology (see Chap. 1), and to integration issues encountered at the local level (see Chap. 3)?

4.3.1 On the Concept of Liquid Migration

When we apply the concept of concept liquid to the IMAGINATION data we see:

- the centrality of temporality: many CEE persons are working and residing temporarily in West-European urban regions or are in an in-between position;

- the dominance of labour migration as the main motive of intra EU movement;
- the importance of being an EU citizen that enables to cross borders in a regular way. However, some categories are not able to get access to regular labour and housing markets and rely on informal institutions (informal economy, informal housing markets and migrant networks);
- the changing nature of intra EU-movement. In the post second world period, there has been (temporal and circular) labour and asylum migration from specific Central and Eastern European countries to Austria, but this was less the case in the Netherlands and Sweden. The EU Enlargements created new migration corridors, and resulted in substantial migration flows from new origin regions of CEE countries to urban regions in Austria, Sweden and the Netherlands. The scale of these migration flows was not foreseen.
- the effects of the individualization process in family relations. Many temporary migrants are working in West-European urban regions to support a family back home, but we also see young couples and singles (students) who do not have these traditional obligations. They are taking care of themselves without having specific family responsibilities.
- the unpredictability of migrant's behaviour, especially in the big cities. One simple indicator of this unpredictability is that many CEE migrants do not register, making policies of registration one of the top priorities of local policies.

However, the key dimension of the concept of liquid migration is the temporal nature of movement. As we have seen, The IMAGINATION typology (TOMs) is based on two dimensions: socio-economic status and a temporal dimension (see Fig. 1.1 in Chap. 1). The concept of liquid migration mainly pertains to the left-hand side of Fig. 1.1 and on in-between situations, between temporariness and settlement.

To understand the dynamics of intra EU-movement, we should also incorporate a temporal dimension on the vertical axis. Unfortunately, the IMAGINATION data does not offer this longitudinal option. There are clear indications that settlement migration, circular or a return to the home country relate also to the (in-)ability to achieve a stable socio-economic position. To achieve this position often requires social mobility and this takes time (e.g. going from informal worker to a regular worker or from student to highly skilled), but finding a stable job with decent wages is more important. For this is what enables them to settle in the expensive European cities. Yet this goal is out of reach for many entrepreneurs, manual workers, persons working in private households, sex workers, trafficked persons, students and beggars. Moreover, many in these categories lack access to social security, so that they lack the financial resources to support a sustainable residence. For these categories, circular migration or temporary labour mobility offers better opportunities to achieve their aims and targets. The IMAGINATION project shows clearly that new routines of circular migration have evolved in Europe, with manual workers in Austria, the Netherlands and Sweden taking seasonal jobs mainly in the agricultural sector. In Austria, circular migration of mainly women appears to be a dominant pattern in the care sector for the elderly.

Still, we also see categories of migrants with marginal labour market positions managing to settle (Ciupijus 2010; Fox et al. 2014). This category has been typified as a 'new informal urban lower class' or as the 'precariat' (cf. Standing 2011; Savage 2015), which is settling in urban areas and is managing to survive through access to informal institutions of work and housing (and to migrant networks). These informal institutions are typical of big cities like Vienna, Rotterdam, The Hague, Stockholm and Istanbul (Saunders 2010).

The concept of liquid migration was formulated in relation to the EU's eastern enlargements, and one of the defining characteristics is its legal character. EU citiziens are free to move to other members-states, and have full rights to residence, work and study. This is often not the case with the CEE-Turkey migration corridors. The Edirne and Istanbul areas have seen a gradual increase of migration from Central and Eastern Europe. This migration includes labour migrants as well as students. However, espcially, the CEE-Istanbul corridor is characterised by substantial irregular migration (see Chap. 12). But due to an implicit policy of toleration irregular migrants are rather free to engage in back and forth migration and develop liquid patterns of migration that have a resemblance with intra-European movement patterns. To conclude: the IMAGINATION findings particularly reveal a heterogeneity in forms of movement. Intra EU-movement includes all forms of migration: from very temporary to settlement. There are no clear, unambiguous processes. Temporary mobility does not necessarily culminate in permanent settlement. Circular mobility does not carry on perpetually. And temporary mobility is not necessarily coupled to circular mobility; there are also forms of once-only or twice-only mobility. Different patterns also occur simultaneously.

The concept of liquid migration does not cover the whole field of labour mobility within the EU. It relates to patterns of temporary and in-between patterns of mobility. The IMAGINATION project offers a further understanding of new temporalities of migration – circular, temporary, seasonal and short-term – and of the underlying institutional factors driving these temporalities. It also shows how the migratory habitus of keeping options open is a rational response to structural constraints and opportunities.

4.3.2 *On Liquid Migration and Local Integration Policies*

The consequences of these diverse temporalities of mobility for local integration policy are described in Chap. 3. Although there are differences between urban regions, the following policies issues are encountered:

- The issue of registration, particularly keeping track of workers that stay temporarily;
- Providing adequate housing, both for those who settle permanently and those who stay (very) briefly. Most workers do not have access to public housing and rely on the private housing sectors, where (abusive) landlords may charge exces-

sive rental prices. A new phenomenon for many cities is the need to realise short-stay facilities for temporary and circular labour migrants;

- Preventing homelessness and forms of public nuisance as a result of overcrowded housing. Homelessness is partly an inevitable consequence of temporary labour and temporary accommodation, as to lose one's job means to lose one's housing. Various European cities are now developing voluntary return programmes;
- Education and language acquisition, for both adults and young children. Cities may experience a sudden influx of new school pupils (especially in primary school). Making sure that labour migrants' children do enrol in schools and don't drop out of schools is an important issue.
- Access to health care and claims on social assistance and other public provisions. Some mobile EU citizens lack health care insurance, and rely on NGO's often supported by central and local state policies (Fermin 2016). Besides, there are concerns about growing claims on local social assistance schemes.

The extent to which such issues occur varies from city to city. The IMAGINATION project reveals that in cities like Vienna and Stockholm, the intra-European mobility is not treated or portrayed as a problem as much as in cities like The Hague and Rotterdam (Reeger and Enengel 2015). The project also reveals that it is crucial for cities like Vienna, Stockholm, The Hague and Rotterdam to monitor the new temporalities of intra-European mobility in order to develop effective measures regarding registration, housing, education, health care and public order. It requires a flexible structure to cope with temporary, short-term and circular migration (especially in the sphere of housing), but also with middle long-term mobility that is related to the in-between category of mobile EU citizens (between temporality and settlement).

4.4 Conclusions

This chapter has confronted the concept of liquid migration with the findings of the IMAGINATION project. This confrontation reveals that liquid migration pertains to a part of intra EU-mobility. It focuses on the complex temporalities of intra-European movement – circular, temporary, seasonal, short-term – associated with various social groups. These temporalities have been described previously in migration literature, for instance in the European migration literature on the mobile nineteenth century and in post-war literature on guest workers. One new aspect is that migration movements have become more individualised and less predictable, and that new migration destinations are more easily found. The increased opportunities for free movement, the availability of strategically important knowledge (thanks to social media), the reduced costs of travel and the greater role of international recruitment agencies facilitate finding new and multiple destinations more quickly.

A second aspect of the concept of liquid migration is that it acknowledges the institutional changes that create opportunities and impose restrictions on (potential) mobile EU citizens. The EU expansion with its principle of freedom of movement has brought more freedom to migrate, but other institutional changes have created more uncertainties: the growth of non-standard labour, structural unemployment, individualisation of family relations and welfare state retrenchment. Liquid migration can be seen as a product of these institutional changes.

The consequences of intra-European movement are apparent in specific regions, as the results of IMAGINATION show. These findings indicate that part of the mobile EU citizens easily find their way in the new destination locations (e.g. in family households or in highly skilled jobs), but that some problems do occur. The complex temporalities raise questions about the relevance of contemporary integration policies and compel cities to develop new approaches for the integration of intra-European mobile citizens.

The local policies and governance strategies described in this study seem to develop along three lines: (1) Prevention: prevent that natives and established citizens (including migrants) are confronted with the influx of intra-European mobile workers in a negative manner. This implies providing for an adequate (flexible) infrastructure of housing, education and health care. This can help prevent unwelcome effects of intra-European movement such as overcrowded neighbourhoods, houses and schools, homelessness and health risks. (2) Non-discrimination and equal treatment: prevent that intra-European mobile workers are exploited and treated unequally. In this regard, local authorities do have some authority to counter and control abusive landlords, but hardly any authority to counter unfair treatment and exploitation in the domain of work, as this is a national policy domain. The same applies for policy that should prevent EU mobile workers of unfairly competing with established citizens by being much cheaper; (3) Incorporation: developing programmes targeting EU mobile workers who remain for extended periods or who repeatedly return. Since these are EU citizens, mandatory programmes cannot offer a solution here. Many cities have begun offering voluntary integration programmes, and language courses in particular have proved to be popular.

To maintain public support for intra-European movement, it is essential that these three policy lines are developed further. Local authorities cannot do so wholly on their own, but must be able to rely on the support of the state government and of the EU.

References

Bauman, Z. (1999). *Liquid modernity*. Oxford: Polity Press.
Bauman, Z. (2003). *Liquid love: On the frailty of human bonds*. Cambridge: Polity Press.
Bauman, Z. (2005). *Liquid life*. Oxford: Polity Press.
Bauman, Z. (2007). *Liquid times. Living in an age of uncertainty*. Cambridge: Polity Press.

Beck, U., & Beck-Gernsheim, E. (2002). *Individualization*. London: Sage.
Black, R., Engbersen, G., Okolski, M., & Pantiru, C. (2010). *A continent moving west? EU enlargement and labour migration from central and Eastern Europe*. Amsterdam: Amsterdam University Press.
Boyd, M., & Nowak, J. (2013). Social networks and international migration. In M. Martinello & J. Rath (Eds.), *An introduction to international migration studies. European perspectives* (pp. 79–105). Amsterdam: Amsterdam University Press.
Broadway (2011). *Street to home annual report*, 1st April 2011 to 31st March 2012. Broadway: London.
Bygnes, S., & Erdal, M. B. (2017). Liquid migration, grounded lives: Coniderations about future mobility and settlement among Polish and Spanish migrants in Norway. *Journal of Ethnic and Migration Studies, 43*(1), 102–118.
Chapman, M. and Prothero, R.M. (1983/84) Themes on circulation in the third world. International Migration Review, 17(4): 597–632.
Ciupijus, Z. (2011). Mobile central eastern Europeans in Britain: Successful European Union citizens and disadvantages labour migrants*? Work Employment and Society, 25*(3), 540–550.
Crellen, J. (2010). Sharing solutions; How can we support central and eastern Europeans who become homeless in the UK? In *Homeless in Europe* (pp. 16–18). The Magazine of FEANTSA (Summer): Homelessness and migration in Europe.
Dekker, R., & Engbersen, G. B. M. (2014). How social media transform migrant networks and facilitate migration. *Global networks: A journal of transnational affairs, 14*(4), 401–418.
Drinkwater, S., & Garapich, M. (2015). Migration strategies of Polish migrants: Do they have any at all? *Journal of Ethnic and Migration Studies, 41*(12), 1909–1931.
Eade, J., Drinkwater, S. and Garapich, M. (2007) *Class and ethnicity: Polish migrant Workers in London*. End of award research report, ESR. Economic and Social Research Council: Swindon.
Engbersen, G. (2013). Labour migration from central and Eastern Europe and the implications for integration policy. In J. W. Holtslag, M. Kremers, & E. Schrijvers (Eds.), *Making migration work. The future of labour migration in the European Union* (pp. 104–121). Amsterdam, Amsterdam University Press.
Engbersen, G., & Snel, E. (2013). Liquid migration: Dynamic and fluid patterns of post-accession migration flows. In B. Glorius, I. Grabowska-Lusińska, & A. Rindoks (Eds.), *Mobility in transition: Migration patterns after EU enlargement* (pp. 21–40). Amsterdam University: Amsterdam.
Engbersen, G., Leerkes, A., Grabowska-Lusinska, I., Snel, E., & Burgers, J. (2013). On the differential attachments of migrants from central and Eastern Europe: A typology of labour migration. *Journal of Ethnic and Migration Studies, 39*(6), 959–981.
Engbersen, G., Leerkes, A., Scholten, P., & Snel, E. (2017). The intra-EU mobility regime: Differentiation, stratification and contradictions. *Migration Studies, 5*(3), 337–355.
Epstein, G. S. (2008). Herd and network effects in migration decision-making. *Journal of Ethnic and Migration Studies, 34*(4), 567–583.
Favell, A. (2008). The new face of East–West migration in Europe. *Journal of Ethnic and Migration Studies, 34*(5), 701–716.
Fermin, A. (2016). *Handbook of urban governance of free movement in the EU: Facts, implications and policies*. The Hague: European Urban Knowledge Network.
Fihel, A., Janicka, A., Kaczmarczyk, P., & Nestorowicz, J. (2015). *Free movement of workers and transitional arrangements: Lessons from the 2004 and 2007 enlargements*. Brussels: DG Employment.
Fox, J. E., Morşoanu, L., & Szilassy, E. (2014). Denying discrimination: Status, 'race', and the whitening of Britain's new Europeans. *Journal of Ethnic and Migration Studies, 41/5*, 729–748.
Friberg, J. H. (2012). The stages of migration. From going abroad to settling down: Post-accession Polish migrant Workers in Norway. *Journal of Ethnic and Migration Studies, 38/10*, 1589–1605.

Garapich, M. (2011). Of alcohol and men. Survival, masculinities and anti-institutionalism of Polish homeless men in a global city, Migration between Poland and United Kingdom. *Special issue of Studia Migracyjne-Przeglad Polonijny, 1*, 309–330.

Goldin, I., Cameron, G., & Balarajan, M. (2011). *Exceptional people: How migration shaped our world and will define our future*. Princeton: Princeton University Press.

Grzymała-Kazłowska, A. (2005). From ethnic cooperation to in-group competition: Undocumented polish Workers in Brussels. *Journal of Ethnic and Migration Studies, 31*(4), 675–697.

Ivancheva, M. (2007). Strawberry fields forever? Bulgarian and Romanian student workers in the UK, *Focaal. European Journal of Anthropology, 49*, 110–117.

King, R. (2017). Theorising new European youth mobilities. *Population, Space and Place*. https://doi.org/10.1002/psp.2117.

King, R. A. Lulle, V. Parutis and M. Saar (2015). *Young Baltic graduates living adn working in London: from Peripheral Region to Escaltor RFegion in Europe*. Working paper 2015, Sussex Centre for Migration Research.

Krings, T., Moriarty, E., Wickham, J., Bobek, A., & Salamonska, J. (2013). *New mobilities in Europe. Polish migration to Ireland post-2004*. Manchester: Manchester University Press.

Massey, D. S., Arango, J., Hugo, G., Kouaouci, A., Pellegrino, A., & Taylor, J. E. (2005). *Worlds in motion: Understanding international migration at the end of the millennium*. Oxford: Clarendon Press.

McCollum, D., & Findlay, A. (2015). 'Flexible' workers for 'flexible' jobs? The labour market function of A8 migrant labour in the UK. *Work, Employment and Society, 29*(3), 427–443.

Moch, L. P. M. (1992). *Moving Europeans. Migration in Western Europe since* (p. 1650). Bloomington and Indianopolis: Indiana University Press.

Mostowska, M. (2011). Services for homeless immigrants: The social welfare capital of polish rough sleepers in Brussels and Oslo. *European Journal of Homelessness, 5*(1), 27–47.

Nowicka, M. (2012) *Deskilling in migration in transnational perspective: The case of recent Polish migration to the UK: Working Paper 112/2012*. Center on Migration, Citizenship and Development: Bielefeld.

OECD. (2015). *In it together. Why less inequality benefits all*. Paris: OECD.

Okólski, M. (2012). Spatial mobility from the perspective of the incomplete migration concept. *Central and Eastern European Migration Review, 1*(1), 11–35.

Palloni, A., Massey, D. S., Ceballos, M., Espinosa, K., & Spittel, M. (2001). Social capital and international migration: A test using information on family networks. *The American Journal of Sociology, 106*(5), 1262–1298.

Portes, A. (1995). Economic sociology and the sociology of immigration: A conceptual overview. In A. Portes (Ed.), *The economic sociology of immigration* (pp. 1–41). New York: Russell Sage Foundation.

Recci, E. (2015). *Mobile Europe. The theory and practice of free movement in the EU*. London: Palgrave Macmillan.

Reeger, U. and Enengel, M.L (2015) *Implications of CEE migration in European urban regions*. IMAGINATION comparative project report 2. Vienna: Institute for Urban and Regional Research/Austrian Academy of Sciences.

Ringer, F. (1997). *Max Weber's methodology. The unification of the cultural and social sciences*. Cambridge: Harvard University Press.

Saunders, D. (2010) Arrival city. Alfred A. Knopf.

Savage, M. (2015). *Social class in the 21st century*. London: Penquin Books.

Standing, G. (2011). *The precariat; the new dangerous class*. London: Bloomsbury Academic.

Tilly, C. (1990) Transplanted networks. In V. Yans-McLaughlin (red.), *Immigration reconsidered: History, sociology, and politics*, 79–95. New York: Oxford University Press.

Van Puymbroeck, N., Van de Pol, S., & Oosterlynck, S. (2011). Oost-West mobiliteit en de bestuurlijke europeanisering van steden. *Een vergelijkende studie van de cases Gent en Rotterdam, Tijdschrift voor Sociologie, 32*(3–4), 291–326.
Verwiebe, R., Wiesböck, L., & Teitzer, R. (2014). New forms of intra-European migration, labour market dynamics and social inequality in Europe. *Migration Letters, 11*(2), 125–136.
Voitchovsky, S. (2014). Occupational downgrading and wages of new member states immigrants to Ireland. *International Migration Review, 48*(2), 500–537.
Weber, M. (2002). *The Protestant ethic and the Spirit of capitalism. New translation and introduction by Stephen Kalberg*. Los Angeles: Blackwell Publishers.

Chapter 5
Old Wine in New Bottles? Comparing the Post-War Guest Worker Migration and the Post 1989 Migration from CEE-Countries to EU-Member Countries

Rinus Penninx

5.1 Introduction

In the absence of a substantial theory for international migration that would enable to predict how a migration movement would develop, researchers and policymakers have often used migration movements in the past in comparison with those in the present time as a predictive instrument. In this light, the movement of workers from ten Central and Eastern European (CEE) countries to European Union member states in Western and Southern Europe (henceforth the CEES system) after 1990 is often compared to the post-war Guest Worker System (henceforth GWS). In policy circles such an approach is often called: lessons learned from the past.

This approach of using comparison-based predictions is based on the assumption that the units compared are indeed of the same nature. In this case, the first question is whether the two movements that we compare are in point of fact two cross-border labour migration systems that follow the same mechanisms and happened under similar conditions. We will turn to this question in the next section, where I will outline the contours of the two labour migration systems to establish comparability in a broader sense.

For a detailed comparison of the two cases, which will follow in Sect. 5.3 of this chapter, we need a more refined analytical instrument. To establish such an instrument, I draw on the literature on migration theory and, more specifically, on migration systems theory (Fawcett 1989). This literature refers to three sets of factors that are essential for the emergence and continuation of migration systems. The first set implies that there need to be push and pull factors for labour migration to emerge. Push and pull factors encourage individuals to move from one place to another. Economists measure these factors in general terms like wage differentials and work opportunities, where low wages locally act as a push factor and higher wages

R. Penninx (✉)
University of Amsterdam, Amsterdam, The Netherlands
e-mail: M.J.A.Penninx@uva.nl

P. Scholten, M. van Ostaijen (eds.), *Between Mobility and Migration*, IMISCOE Research Series, https://doi.org/10.1007/978-3-319-77991-1_5

elsewhere as a pull factor; high unemployment rates and decreasing job opportunities act as a push factor and the availability of work elsewhere as a pull factor. These factors are necessary conditions for a labour migration system to emerge. But they are not sufficient in and of itself: their mere existence does not lead to migration and not in all cases.

The second set of factors specifies how individuals – existing in the above-mentioned economic circumstances – are actually brought into a labour migration system: candidates for migration have to be aware of their own economic situation and of alternatives elsewhere; there have to be networks – often of emigrants that went before them – that help new migrants, as well as intermediaries and facilitators that take away barriers and thus trigger and sustain movements. In well-established labour migration systems such informational and facilitating functions become institutionalised in recruitment systems that involve sending and receiving states, employers and trade unions, employment agencies, et cetera.

The third set of factors refers to regulatory systems of international migration in the countries of origin as well as in the countries of destination. The countries of origin have to allow the exit of citizens on principle (non-exit was rule in communist countries behind the Iron Curtain up until 1989) and in actual practice (e.g. by giving out passports). They may even facilitate labour migration by assisting in recruitment. Countries of destination, for their part, have policies that 'control and regulate' labour inflows: targets or quota may be established for selective groups of workers, as well as for their duration of stay and the conditions of their work set.

These three sets of factors will be described and compared for both labour migration systems. This will enable us to establish if the two systems differ, and on what points and with what consequences.

5.2 The Contours of Two Labour Migration Systems

5.2.1 The Guest Worker Labour Migration System: 1955–1974

In the immediate aftermath of World War II, Europe had to 'resettle' some 20 million people on the newly established political map (Bonifazi et al. 2008: 113). Apart from these significant internal movements, Europe was predominantly an emigration continent at that time: pre-war emigration to classical destinations like the USA, Canada, Australia, New Zealand and Latin America was resumed in North Western European countries.

This situation started to change in the mid-1950s. Emigration decreased and immigration gained importance, in the form of temporary labour migration. The economic reconstruction after the war was so successful in several Western and North Western European countries that their labour markets needed more workers than available. Particularly unskilled and low-skilled workers were sought for labour-intensive Fordist production processes, such as mining and manufacturing. Some Western European countries, such as Switzerland, Luxembourg, Belgium and

France, resumed pre-war labour immigration to fill the vacancies at the lower end of their labour markets. For the Federal Republic of Germany, Austria, the Netherlands and Sweden this experience of being attractive for migrant workers was a relatively new concept.

From the mid-1950s on, a labour migration system was built up gradually, attracting workers from the nearest countries in the south – Italy, Spain, Greece and Portugal – and the east – until 1961 from East Germany and following the closing of the Iron Curtain from Yugoslavia (Van Mol and de Valk 2015: 32/33). In the 1960s the system expanded to include Morocco, Algeria, Tunisia and Turkey. While growing, it also became more organised: rules, conditions and procedures were agreed upon in bilateral agreements between the recruiting and sending countries and institutional arrangements and policies were elaborated, both in the sending and in the receiving countries.

The framing of this labour migration as a temporary solution for labour market shortages and the designation of the workers as 'temporary guests' are important characteristics of GWS. All destination countries defined themselves as 'non-immigration countries' and stressed the temporary nature of the work contracts. The label 'guest worker' openly expressed such expectations. The migrants also saw their work and stay in Europe as temporary. When the number of temporary workers that returned home during the economic recession of 1966–67 turned out to be rather limited, the response of European countries was to develop stricter rules for entrance and access to the labour market (issuing fewer permits) and to start a discussion on the rotation principle to increase the return. Nevertheless, those of the 'temporary workers' who stayed and brought their families grew larger and the resident immigrant population accumulated over the course of time.

The exact number of migrant workers who were involved in this GWS system is difficult to establish. Estimates of the numbers of individuals that left Italy, Spain, Greece, and Portugal alone between 1950 and 1970 vary from 7 to 10 million (Okolski 2012: 33). The number of migrants from Yugoslavia, Turkey and North Africa who travelled to Western Europe for work is probably equally large, or maybe slightly less so because their migration movement started somewhat later. When looking at the whole period, most of the workers returned, yet a significant foreign labour force was built up: Cohen estimates that at the end of the period, in 1974, the FRG counted 2.2 million foreign workers; France 1.9 million; Switzerland 1.0 million; Belgium 0.22 million, and the Netherlands 0.12 million (Cohen 1987: 111–112).

In the early 1970s the limits of the growth of the Fordist industrial economies became manifest and the need to restructure North Western European economies was evident. The first oil crisis of 1973 sped up this restructuring: the closing of certain sectors like mining, the relocation of other labour intensive sectors to low-wage countries and the automation of still other sectors led to a fall in demand for low-skilled work and thus for migrant workers. Switzerland (1970) and Sweden (1972) were the first countries to install an immigration stop for workers, followed by the FRG (1973), the Benelux countries and France in 1974 (Van Mol and de Valk 2015: 35).

By the mid-1970s GWS as a system of rotating workers had ceased to exist. The halted recruitment and the various policies to promote the return of migrant workers had specific effects for the different immigrant groups. Migrant workers from Southern European countries did return to their countries of origin more often, while those from the Maghreb countries and Turkey did significantly less so. Quite the contrary happened: they started to bring their families to Europe whenever possible. In the FRG, the Netherlands, Belgium, Austria and France populations from North Africa and Turkey grew significantly under the policy category of 'family reunification' and 'family formation' in the second half of the 1970s and in the 1980s.

5.2.2 *Migration from CEE Countries to EU Member Countries: 1989 – Present*

The collapse of the Iron Curtain in 1989 and the subsequent opening up of the borders for exit induced significant new migration flows from Central and East European (CEE) countries that took various forms and different directions (Black et al. 2010; Okolski 2012; Glorius et al. 2013). First there was a migration corridor to the 'old immigration countries' in North Western Europe, in which two forms of movements took place: that of well-organised legal, albeit limited, bilateral programmes for temporary employment in Germany and other North-Western European countries (Glorius et al. 2013: 7/8) on the one hand, and short-term irregular circular migration – within the bounds of tourist visa – on the other hand. A second migration corridor was one of mostly irregular flows to the new immigration countries in the South: Greece, Italy, Spain and Portugal. These were popular destinations for migrant workers from Romania, Ukraine, Albania and Bulgaria, because they had easy entry and tolerated irregular residence and clandestine work (Engbersen et al. 2010a, b: 8 ff). Estimates suggest that a net migration outflow of around 3.2 million took place from the ten CEE states via the two migration corridors between 1989 and 2004 (Engbersen et al. 2010a: 9).

The accession of ten new members to the European Union in 2004 marked the beginning of another new era. Eight of these were CEE countries that had been part of the communist bloc: Poland, the three Baltic States, Slovakia, Slovenia, the Czech Republic and Hungary (the A8). Three years later, in 2007, Bulgaria and Romania (the A2) also joined the EU. The effect of these accessions was twofold: on the one hand the migration that had taken place from the ten CEE countries to Western and Southern Europe since 1989 was redefined as EU-internal mobility and legalised under the new regime. On the other hand, the new regime reinforced migration flows from some new member states, particularly Poland, Romania and Bulgaria, to member states in the Western part of the EU whose labour markets attracted workers.

The EU15 countries responded differently to the accessions: the UK, Ireland, Sweden and Norway (the latter country is not an EU member, but is part of the European Economic Area) opened up their borders immediately in May 2004. Other countries – often backed up by national trade unions – opted for a transition period of five years in which access of workers of the ten accessory countries to the labour market was subject to permits. Some countries even opted for an additional two years extension. These national policies of immediate or delayed free access have shaped intra-European movement significantly.

In terms of flow, Van Mol and De Valk (2015: 43–49) show, first of all, that the scale of intra-European movement increased significantly in the period 2004–08. In 2008 alone, nearly two million EU-citizens moved within the EU (Eurostat 2011), Polish and Romanian migrants making up the bulk of it. Net flows of intra-European migration (immigration minus emigration) amounted to nearly 1.2 million in 2008 (Dhéret et al. 2013: 10). For the whole period and calculated in absolute numbers, Polish migration (primarily to and from Germany and the UK) makes up for the largest share, followed by Romanian migration (primarily to and from Italy and Spain).

As a result migrant populations of the A8 and A2 countries, particularly from Poland and Romania, grew significantly in all of the EU15 member states: while the immigrant population with A8 and A2 origin in the EU15 states amounted to approximately 1.9 million in 2004, this population had grown to 5.2 million in 2010 (SVR 2013: 51). The case of Poland, having the largest emigration of all CEE countries in absolute terms, reflects this growth: the number of Polish citizens residing in other EU countries rose from 451,000 in May 2002 to 1,860,000 by the end of 2007; of which 690,000 lived in the UK, 490,000 in Germany and 200,000 in Ireland (Fihel and Okolski 2009: 189).

During the economic crisis of 2009–10 net inflows were reduced from 1.2 million to some 300,000. For CEE migration this meant that the migration corridors to the West and to the South were both affected: net emigration was low or negative and immigrant populations in destination countries were somewhat stabilised. After 2010, when the crisis in Southern Europe continued but Northern countries were much less affected, the southern corridor continued to have negative or low net flows (Spain became an emigration country again: Arango 2016), but flows in the western corridor recovered (Dhéret et al. 2013: 10). However, the CEES system as a whole had ceased to grow.

5.3 Comparing Two Labour Migration Systems

The brief outlines of the GWS and the CEES do indeed suggest that these systems have some common characteristics that make them comparable at face value. The two systems connect sending countries that have less developed economies, redundant labour and low wages, with receiving countries that have developed economies, labour shortages and attractive wages. The flow sizes of the two systems are also significantly alike (both involving millions of workers), although the CEES system was somewhat smaller than the GWS system. And in terms of length of time there is similarity as well: the GWS system covered 2.5 to 3 decades before it stopped as a labour migration system; the CEES system, starting in 1990, until the present day also covers a period of 2.5 decades.

Accepting this comparability at first glance, I will analyse and compare the three sets of factors that are essential for the emergence and continuation of migration systems in more detail: economic development, differences in wages, and (un-) employment in origin and destination countries; systems of information, networks, intermediaries and organisations that mobilise and steer the migration movements, and the national regulatory systems of sending and receiving countries and their differential effects.

5.3.1 The Development of Economic Push and Pull Factors

The starting point in both labour migration systems has been a significant difference in economic development and concomitant wage and employment differentials. First we will compare the economic development of the most important countries involved in the two labour migration systems,[1] using Gross Domestic Product per Capita (ERS International Macro-economic data set that starts in 1969[2]) as a rough indicator of development: see Table 5.1.

In 1969, Morocco had the lowest GDP within the GWS system, only 5.3 per cent of the GDP of its major country of destination: France. In 1969 the Turkish GDP was 20.2 per cent of that of Germany, the most important country of destination for Turkish workers. The Southern European countries did have better statistics than Morocco and Turkey in that same year, although the numbers varied considerably: Portugal had the lowest GDP, while Italy had reached the highest level of GDP of the Southern European countries (see also Akgündüz 2008: 18 and Rist 1978: 102).

When it comes to other indicators such as unemployment or the activity rate of the population, the data are not truly comparable because they measure different factors in the various countries, but the literature suggests that unemployment (including hidden unemployment) was high in countries like Turkey (Akgündüz 2008; Abadan-Unat et al. 1976) and Morocco, while this was much less the case in the more developed economies of the Southern European countries such as Italy. This smaller potential of migrant workers in the Southern European countries made the official recruitment of guest workers shift to Morocco and Turkey in the late 1960s.

[1] Ideally, the average GDP of all countries of destination would be the best quantity to measure: the EU15 average for the CEES system. For the GWS, such data were not available. The next best comparison was the GDP of the largest destination country: the FRG for Turkish migration, and France for migration from Morocco.

[2] At www.ers.usda.gov

Table 5.1 Gross domestic product per Capita in GWS and CEES origin and destination countries: absolute in US $ and relative (1969–2014). Source: ERS International macro-economic data set at www.ers.usda.gov

Country (/Destin.)	1969	%	1974	%	1990	%	2004	%	2014	%
Morocco (/France)	1001	**5,3**	1110	**4,7**	1766		2351		3175	7,7
Turkey (/FRG)	3912	**20,2**	4417	**20,0**	6194		8258		11,104	24,9
Portugal (/France)	7182	**37,8**	10,840	**45,6**	16,790		21,795		20,613	
Greece (/FRG)	12,061	**62,3**	15,741	**71,3**	19,456		28,288		22,929	
Spain (/France)	12,847	**67,7**	16,771	**70,6**	22,190		30,451		29,224	
Italy (/FRG)	16,354	**84,4**	20,537	**93,0**	30,857		36,439		33,008	
FRG	19,374		22,081		32,345		38,641		44,554	
France	18,987		23,759		32,742		39,998		41,196	
EU15	17,362		21,273		30,070		38,076		39,351	
EU28	14,497		17,660		24,863		31,937		33,888	
Slovenia (/EU15)	8420	48,5	9540		15,558	**51,7**	21,051	**55,3**	24,016	**61,0**
Czech Rep. (/EU15)	8109	46,7	9283		13,980	**46,5**	16,831	**44,2**	19,953	**50,7**
Estonia (/EU15)	6768	39,0	7441		9187	**30,6**	13,473	**35,4**	17,997	**45,7**
Hungary (/EU15)	5267	30,3	6921		9952	**33,1**	12,428	**32,6**	13,787	**35,0**
Romania (/EU15)	3887	22,4	4307		5599	**18,6**	6174	**16,2**	8200	**20,8**
Poland (/EU15)	3795	21,9	4241		5925	**19,7**	9487	**24,9**	13,854	**35,2**
Bulgaria (/EU15)	2695	15,5	2897		4045	**13,5**	5206	**13,7**	7093	**18,0**

At the receiving end of the GWS, the North Western European countries had recovered from the economic recession of 1966–67 and unemployment was lower than ever and labour shortages were unprecedented. The period 1968–73 became the summit of the GWS system: official recruitment following strict rules had become the dominant way of migrating and Turkey and the Maghreb countries were by now the most important countries of origin.

By 1974, at the end of the GWS system, the relative differences in GDP of Morocco and Turkey had not changed as compared to 1969. By contrast, the Southern European countries had improved their figures significantly, Italy having a GDP that was as almost as high as that of Germany: 93 per cent. The gap between Morocco and Turkey and the destination countries was clearly of a different order than the gaps between the countries in Southern Europe and their destination countries.

Thus, the movement of workers stopped around 1974 by the sudden disappearance of the demand for labour in destination countries, which was followed by a recruitment stop and policy measures to stimulate return. At that moment the push factors (expressed as relative GDP figures) in Morocco and Turkey were equally strong as five years before. In the Southern European countries, however, they had become less compelling. This explains the different reactions of migrant populations after the recruitment stop: fewer migrants from Morocco and Turkey returned than migrants from Southern European countries.

If we compare such relative figures of the GWS system with those in the CEES system (using the average EU15 GDP for destination countries), we see that the relative differences between Bulgaria, Romania and Poland in 1990 compare to Turkey in the GWS system in 1969 to a certain extent; the figures for Slovenia and the Czech Republic in 1990 are somewhere between those of Portugal and Greece in 1969, but below the figures for Spain and Italy in that same year.

Between 1990 and 2004, these relative gaps did not change for Bulgaria and Romania: these countries still had the lowest GDP of the CEE countries in 2004. But the relative difference of Poland (25.5 per cent) had changed in a positive way. At the other end of the spectrum, Slovenia and the Czech Republic had the highest GDP.

Ten years later, in 2014, Bulgaria, Romania and Poland still had the lowest GDP of the CEE countries, but the relative differences had diminished, particularly for Poland (35.2 per cent). Slovenia and the Czech Republic had the highest GDP: 61.0 and 50.7 per cent respectively of the average GDP of EU15 countries. (For comparable data in the literature, but with slightly different indicators, see: Galgóczi et al. (2009: 8 ff) and Dhéret et al. (2013: 17 ff) on all CEE countries; on Hungary see Hars 2009; on Romania see Potot 2010; on Bulgaria see Markova 2010).

These figures make clear that within the GWS and CEES systems there were significant differences between the countries of origin: the relative figures of Bulgaria, Romania and Poland were low (meaning wide gaps) and compare well with those of Turkey between 1969–1974 (though Poland did improve significantly over the course of time). The differences between Slovenia's and the Czech Republic's GDP with the average GDP of EU15 countries at the other end are relatively small and quite comparable with the Southern European countries in the GWS system between 1969 and 1974.

The significant GDP differences above are "translated into significant income differentials, which were clearly an important pull factor for EU-10 nationals" (Galgóczi et al. 2009: 10). By contrast, unemployment seems to be a relatively less important driver for movement in these countries, as unemployment rates were more or less in line with the EU average of 9.2 per cent, Poland being the exception with an unemployment rate of 17.9 per cent in 2005. However, Poland reduced its unemployment from 19.1 in 2004 to 7.1 per cent in 2008.

In the receiving countries, complementary observations on pull factors indicate that these operated quite differently within the two migration corridors of the CEES system. In the North Western European countries unemployment was relatively high in the 1990s and labour shortages appeared in specific sectors, for which bilateral labour migration programmes were organised. At the same time, these specific labour shortages, specifically in agriculture and horticulture, were filled by irregular short-term work on tourist visa. The migration corridor to the Southern countries, however, was of a different nature: migrants moved irregularly, attracted by work opportunities in the informal sector of the economies of the Southern European countries. The pull factor here was not so much the low unemployment and high wages, but the comparatively easy way to enter a country, find (informal) work and earn a (relatively low) wage. The accession of the A8 and A2 countries in 2004 and 2007 in point of fact regularised the irregular work and residence situation of CEE migrants if that had not happened by amnesties before.

After the accession of the CEE countries, some countries in the north-west migration corridor allowed full access in 2004 and argued that very low unemployment and a great demand for mainly unskilled and low-skilled labour were the reason. This was particularly the case for the UK, Ireland and Norway that became the new target countries of the CEES system. (Sweden also opened its borders immediately, but had a relatively high unemployment and attracted much less CEE migrants). Other countries like Austria, Germany and the Netherlands, having relatively high unemployment rates, chose for transitional arrangements in order to protect their labour markets. Even more countries chose for transitional arrangements in 2007 when Bulgaria and Romania became EU-members.

The 2009 economic crisis changed the balance of push and pull factors completely. In the destination countries, the first crisis of 2009–10 hit both the west and south migration corridors of the CEES system; unemployment increased and the demand for workers fell. Inflow of foreign workers decreased and return grew. After 2010 the situation changed again: some north western countries, Germany particularly, emerged from the crisis and attracted CEE migrants again, albeit on a more modest scale than before. This was in sharp contrast with the countries in the south where economic crisis deepened, leading to huge unemployment numbers and an increasing emigration of both native and immigrant workers (Arango 2016).

This was the mirror image of the perspective of the emigration countries where "outflows from Poland decreased substantially (...) after 2008, when better domestic employment rates were recorded at the same time as the deterioration of the economic situation in receiving countries such as Ireland" (Dhéret et al. (2013: 17). Other indicators of labour market drivers had also converged significantly between 2004 and 2007: In Poland for example, wage differentials increased from 21.5 to 25.4 per cent in EUR at exchange rate (with average EU15); employment rose from 51.2 to 57.0 per cent and unemployment decreased from 17.9 to 9.6 per cent. These observations make Galgóczi et al. (2009: 11) conclude that "differences in overall labour market performance, initially substantial, have shown remarkable convergence between A8 and EU15 countries". This is surely the case, but on balance it seems fair to conclude that the strong changes in the CEES system since 2008 have been caused more by pull factors falling away than by decreasing push factors.

5.3.2 The Organisation and Selectivity of Labour Migration

How were individuals – in situations where the economic conditions of push and pull are fulfilled – drawn into a labour migration system. How were supply of and demand for work brought together? What did the organisation of labour migration mean for those who moved when, under what conditions and with what strategy?

In the case of the GWS system, the literature suggests that there were two main ways of getting into the system. The first was based on informal networks between individuals in sending and receiving countries through which information was passed on possibilities to work elsewhere; people in such networks received and supported new arrivals and mediated in finding work. There is an abundance of descriptions in the literature of the 'pioneers' who came 'spontaneously' (i.e. without a prior invitation for work), found work (and received a work and a residence permit) and started to bring over kin and fellow countrymen on request of their employer, leading to strong concentrations of workers from the same villages and regions in certain cities in receiving countries on the aggregate level (see Abadan-Unat et al. 1976 and Den Exter 1993 for Turks in the Netherlands and Engelbrektsson 1978 for Turks in Gothenburg, Sweden). From a broader perspective, it also tells us that earlier migrations from certain regions in sending countries, such as pre-war labour migration from Southern Europe to Switzerland, France and Belgium could easily be revived on the basis of networks stemming from these earlier migrations.

The second way of entering the system was through the institutionalised system of labour recruitment. This system involved strong governmental participation of both sending and receiving countries through bilateral agreements on how and under what conditions workers would be recruited. It might even imply – as in the case of Turkey – that sending countries registered candidates and selected them to be sent to recruitment offices of destination countries. For those who were selected, special cheap worker passports were issued. It also implied approval of demands for recruitment by governments of receiving countries. For the selected workers contracts, work and residence permits were pre-arranged.

The Turkish case (Abadan-Unat et al. 1976; Akgündüz 2008) shows how the originally spontaneous character of migration through informal networks was gradually incorporated in the official system through the so-called 'nominative contracts' (through which an employer could officially recruit a certain person whom he knew through workers he already employed). Nevertheless, the official system did not replace the spontaneous migration completely, because the waiting list for official recruitment in Turkey grew so long that the chances to be recruited became slim. Going as a 'tourist' and using the informal system thus remained in place so long as there were lenient policies to get a work and residence permit in destination countries. However, in the late 1960s such policies became stricter, thereby creating the phenomenon of illegal work (no work permit) and illegal workers (no residence permit) for the first time.

The organisation of migration as described above had consequences for the selection of migrants involved. Migration originally started in cities, but spread to rural areas later; in Morocco and Turkey this was also a consequence of the sending governments' policy. In general, the work for which guest workers were sought was production work in well-regulated industrial sectors for which no or limited skills were needed. In general, male workers were sought and recruited; female workers only in special cases for specific work. Official recruiters in Turkey and Morocco preferred married men, who were looked upon as more responsible than unmarried youngsters. Spontaneous migration could lead to over-qualification, particularly when migrants were pushed out of their country for reasons other than work but used the guest worker status to leave, such as those who fled the authoritarian regimes of Salazar, Franco or the Greek colonels in the 1960s and early 1970s.

The official recruitment system, however, did not lead to large-scale placement of workers below their qualification level.

The development of the organisation of labour migration is different in the case of the movements from CEE countries to Western and Southern Europe and thus the selection of movers differs. When the exit opportunity opened in CEE countries after 1989, certain specific groups could and did use historical links to move. This was the case with certain regions in the CEE countries with German-speaking people who had either migrated from Germany in the past or had other ties with Germany. (Germany's *Aussiedler* return policy made it possible for some people of such regions, particularly in Poland, to come to Germany before 1989). Most migrants, however, had to find new routes or destinations without historical ties to guide and support them.

The movements of such new migrants from CEE countries in the period of 1989 to 2004 have followed distinctive patterns within the two migration corridors, when it comes to the question of how the migration was organised. In the first corridor of movements to Western European countries, destination countries put in place strict regulated labour recruitment programmes, mostly for temporary or seasonal work. Germany developed such migrant workers' programmes, particularly for workers from Poland, but other countries too, like France, Belgium and Switzerland; later Spain,[3] Greece, Norway and the Netherlands also introduced specific bilateral programmes to facilitate temporary labour migration, often for the purposes of seasonal work (Engbersen et al. 2010a: 8 Glorius et al. 2013: 7/8). This pattern of regulated programmes resembled the official recruitment and deployment of guest workers two decades earlier.

Within this first corridor a less formal, partially legal and mostly unregistered way of work migration was practised as well, as described by Fihel and Grabowska-Lusinska (2014: 23):

> "Institutional barriers introduced (...) by key receiving countries located in Western Europe and North America imposed a specific pattern of mobility on Polish nationals: migration comprised repetitive, short stays abroad that coincided with seasonal and temporary employment of migrants in agriculture, construction or domestic services (...). In order to not exceed the three-month (non-visa) stay in Western European countries, Polish nationals temporarily returned home only to re-embark, soon afterwards or following a short lag, depending on economic circumstances, on another trip abroad". This has been named 'incomplete migration' by Okolski (2001).

In the second corridor of movements, to the Southern European countries, migration took an entirely different form: irregular flows. Italy, Spain, Portugal and Greece had become attractive not only to returning emigrants in the 1980s, but also to migrants from Eastern Europe in the 1990s. The large informal sector (agriculture, building, tourism and domestic work) and the labour-intensive manufacturing

[3] For Spain and Greece these state-led labour migration programmes have been only a small part of the total CEE labour immigration; by far most labour migrants followed the irregular pattern; see below.

sector of their economies attracted many migrants from Romania, Ukraine, Albania and Bulgaria (King et al. 1997; Peixoto et al. 2012). These flows resembled the spontaneous migration of the GWS system in its first phase: informal networks providing information and support and building up chains between regions of origin and destinations. Lenient admission regimes made it easy to enter the southern destination countries. Frequent and massive regularisations legalised most of these migrants over the course of time. In addition to informal networks, intermediaries and agencies in the private sector developed to connect the demand and supply. State regulation and control were nearly absent, apart from the small quota for recruitment (see above).

The accession to the EU of eight CEE countries in 2004 and of Bulgaria and Romania in 2007 changed the patterns outlined above significantly. First of all, it legalised the migrant populations that had reached the EU15 countries in irregular ways before, particularly in the southern countries. Secondly, it created new flows to those EU15 members that opened their borders without transitional arrangements within a short time. The pull factor of low unemployment and ample opportunities for work (until the economic crisis in 2009) in the UK, Ireland and Norway particularly attracted many workers from CEE countries. In this new context of great demand for workers, the absence of restrictions on entrance and access to the labour market and a neo-liberal political climate of deregulation, private agencies quickly found a new market of connecting demand and supply; they mushroomed "and made a lot of money" (Jones 2014).

Flows to EU15 countries that had opted for transitional arrangements for the introduction of free movement of workers also increased after 2004, notwithstanding the delayed free movement. The population of Polish workers in the FRG and the Netherlands, for example, increased significantly between 2004 and 2008. Newcomers often used alternative strategies to circumvent the limitations to free movement, such as coming as self-employed entrepreneurs or being sent as posted workers (in both cases using the freedom of service provision in the EU: see Galgóczi and Leschke 2015: 8). In such cases, the social networks of the resident immigrant population and the infrastructure of intermediaries and work agencies were used to employ posted and self-employed workers.

Literature on the consequences of the way migration was organised in the CEES system is ever growing and it poses the following questions: who moved, with what motivation and strategy, and with what intentions for the future. Our central question remains: what makes the movements in the CEES system different from those in the GWS system?

The first element of difference is the less prominent – and sometimes even completely absent – roles of state control and regulation on the one and the significance of private- or market-driven intermediaries and work agencies (including smugglers and traffickers in some circumstances) on the other hand. The latter organise the connection between supply and demand, often resulting in less protected ways of labour migration or work mobility. In comparison with the GWS system only a small portion of CEE labour migration went through official, state-led or controlled programmes that not only connected supply and demand, but also clearly regulated legal statuses, work conditions and remuneration – on a par with local conditions for natives. The CEES has a multitude of legal statuses (including a large portion who lack a legal status at least temporarily), many of these imply a great vulnerability on the routes toward and on the new labour markets. In CEES private intermediaries (who are sometimes illegal) and agencies operating in both sending and receiving countries discovered a profitable market. These agencies played an important role, not only in connecting supply and demand, but also in actively recruiting workers. Furthermore the work that they offered more often than not was located in new and (for workers) less protected segments of the labour market.

Such a system is attractive and profitable for candidate migrants in a different way than GWS. The GWS system was more demand-driven in its organisation and future employers recruited selected workers under conditions that implied more protective elements: for workers there was less choice, but relatively more certainty and protection. In the CEES system, there seemed to be more options and alternatives for workers, but the options were less certain and unprotected. The selectivity among the candidates in the CEES system is therefore based on the question of who sees advantages in work abroad that is temporary and uncertain, and how does a choice for such work fit into the migrant's plan for the future.

That leads to another characteristic of CEE migration, namely the multitude of (labour market) strategies that migrant workers follow. For example, Glorius et al. (2013: 315 ff) mention 'target earners' and 'circular migrants' that seem to fit within the concept of temporary labour migration, but they also find 'career seekers', students and young (often urbanized) educated migrants ('adventure seekers' or 'drifters') whose migration trajectory is different and unpredictable.

According to Fihel and Grabowska-Lusinska (2014: 23), characteristics of incomplete migration and the unpredictability of migrant decisions to remain in a host country, return home or move to another country are also valid after 2004, as is the uncertainty of the meaning of return. This uncertainty is reflected in the various strategies that migrants have, such as a) reconciling employment opportunities in Poland and abroad; b) giving up jobs in Poland to work abroad temporarily; c) replacing inactivity in Poland with work abroad; d) starting a business at home after migration (Fihel and Grabowska-Lusinska 2014: 28–30).

The typologies above are based on the labour market perspective of the country of origin. Engbersen et al. (2013) made a typology of migrants in which strong or weak ties with the countries of origin and destination are combined and they have come up with four types: circular migrants; bi-national migrants; footloose migrants and settlement migrants. All four types can be found, although sometimes in unexpected combination with, for example education.

This hints at yet another characteristic of CEE migrants: their level of education. In literature we have found that also students and professionals participated in the temporary and seasonal work programmes before 2004. After 2004, the average educational level of movers seems to have increased: "An important new trend of post-2004 labour mobility is the fact that migrants from low-wage countries [within the EU] generally have comparably high educational profiles, also in relation to nationals in the receiving countries" (Galgóczi and Leschke 2015: 8–23).

The high educational levels combined with labour markets that offer low-skilled jobs lead to the claim that "skills/occupation mismatch is an important characteristic of post-2004/2007 intra-EU migration; this claim has been substantiated by the current sectoral distribution of migrant labour, which focuses overwhelmingly on sectors that do not require a higher education" (Galgóczi and Leschke 2015: 8–23).

Researchers looking at the aggregate flows and at the motivations and strategies of the migrants involved have stressed that east-west labour migration in Europe "is becoming increasingly diverse, fluid and sub-regionalised in nature (Napierala and Trevena 2010)." Engbersen et al. (2010a: 11 ff) have coined the concept 'liquid migration' for such diverse and unpredictable migrations (see also Engbersen in Chap. 4 of this volume).

5.3.3 National and EU Systems of Regulating Cross-Border Migration and Mobility

In the preceding two sections, states and their regulatory systems have been alluded to several times. In this paragraph we will look explicitly at state regulatory systems of international migration and see whether they have played a different role in the GWS and CEES migration systems.

When the demand for migrant workers emerged in the 1950s and 1960s, they were defined as foreigners, or foreign workers, from the point of view of the migration regulatory system. Apart from Switzerland, that had a stricter policy of old, most North Western European countries had simple and lenient admission procedures in the beginning. Migrant workers came 'spontaneously', as tourists; if they found work they would be given a work permit. Having a work permit would enable them to get a residence permit. After the economic recession of 1966/67 however, most destination countries started to apply more control to the system of admission. In the Netherlands, for example, permission for legal entrance and a residence permit had to be arranged with a Dutch Embassy or Consulate in the country of origin before arrival in the Netherlands since 1969. Introducing this new system of control also made it possible to implement the actual labour migration stops between 1972 and 1974. In the second half of the 1970s these stricter policies for residence and work permits, combined with the stop on labour migration, led to the emergence of undocumented migrants and the call for regularisations.

Within the legal regulatory system described above, the state (i.e. the ministry responsible for employment) gradually built an institutional system for recruitment and deployment of workers from abroad: bilateral agreements between recruiting and sending countries were concluded in which rules, conditions and procedures were established. Institutional arrangements and policies were elaborated at the sending and the receiving side. Turkey gave emigration a place in its national economic planning, for example, and developed a registration system for candidate migrant workers and proposed selected candidates to foreign recruitment offices (Akgündüz 2008). At the receiving end, recruitment procedures were developed by state agencies and implemented by recruitment or immigration offices. In countries where trade unions had acquired strong positions in tripartite socio-economic decision-making, such as Austria, the FRG, the Netherlands and Sweden, labour unions were actively involved in controlling and setting the conditions for recruitment and employment of these migrant workers (Penninx and Roosblad 2000; Rist 1978).

The regulatory system of the CEES system saw a completely different development than that of the GWS system. In the early 1990s the legal infrastructure still resembled the one that was in place towards the end of the GWS system. On the one hand, CEE countries of origin had opened the exit option for its citizens after the fall of the Iron Curtain (which before had been open only for migrant workers from Yugoslavia in the GWS system). On the other hand, European Community countries (totalling 12 in 1990) theoretically installed the same restrictive immigration policies for third-country nationals (TCNs) that had been developed in the destination countries of the former GWS system: new EC members, like Greece, Spain and Portugal, had created similar legal regulatory systems as part of the requirements to become an EU member: the *acquis*.

However, under this formally unitary legal system, two quite different implementation regimes developed within the European Community and later the EU (Doomernik and Bruquetas-Callejo 2015: 61ff). The first is the North Western European regime that had developed from an initially open 'guest worker system' in the 1960s towards an increasingly controlled, restrictive and selective admission policy for foreign workers after 1974. CEE labour migration to these countries under this regime in the period 1990–2004 took the form of specific but limited labour immigration programmes on the one hand, and short-term circular labour on tourist visa and irregular work migration on the other.

The second implementation regime in that same period was established in the Southern European countries (see chapters on Italy and Spain in Zincone et al. 2011). In the words of Doomernik and Bruquetas-Callejo (2015: 61), this regime is characterized "by a predominance of labour and family migration, scarcity of asylum seekers, illegality as an endemic feature, and the combination of restrictive admission and citizenship policies with frequent amnesties." Under this regime labour migrants were mainly attracted and absorbed by the informal economy. The state is not an actor in the regulation of migration, while private intermediaries and agencies play an important role in the organisation.

In previous analyses of labour migration policies in Europe, states were the basic units for analysis, workers were defined as international migrants who cross state borders and states had the sovereign right to decide whether foreign workers are allowed to reside and work there. Over the course of time, however, a completely different legal regime for mobility has been developed for and within a supranational unit in Europe: the European Union (Penninx 2014). Its predecessors, the European Coal and Steel Community (ECSC, since 1951), the European Economic Community (EEC, since 1968), and the European Community (EC, since 1985) had gradually created an area in which former international migration between member states was actually transformed into internal migration and mobility. This process was finalised in the European Union (EU, since 1993) that gave all citizens (and long-term legally residing TCNs) complete freedom of movement and the freedom to work in all member states.

This new intra-European movement regime was in place when the EU expanded from 15 members (since 1995) to 25 members in 2004, to 27 in 2007 and to 28 in 2013, when Croatia joined the EU. Although many EU15 member states delayed free access of citizens to the labour market of these new members for some years, by 2014 the freedom to work had been realised in all 28 EU-countries, except Croatia. This changed the basics of the regulatory system and the role of states in migration and mobility in general, and of labour migration systems in particular. In the economy-driven ideology of the EU, the national labour markets of all EU countries have merged into a single market where market mechanisms and agencies are supposed to do their work without the hindrance of borders and of national authorities and legislations. International migration has become internal mobility: an economically profitable and desirable situation. Ideally, it means that individual citizens have an unlimited choice – on principle – to go and work elsewhere in the EU for whatever reason, with whatever intention to stay or return; and employers, agencies and intermediaries, in turn, are working in an open competitive market, unhindered by protective state or national labour market regulations.

In actual practice, however, the picture is somewhat different: the unrestricted choice for the worker should be put in the perspective of the greater precariousness of the work on offer (as compared between the CEES and the GWS). At the same time, the absence of national restrictions to open, intra-European competition is resisted vehemently by trade unions and sometimes even national governments. Using national protective systems they want to defend equality of workers against 'social dumping', such as the posting of workers under foreign rules, outsourcing work to agencies or the use of 'bogus self-employed entrepreneurs'.

All in all, it is clear that the principles, regulations and practical mechanisms of free movement of workers in deregulated and segmented labour markets are quite different from the ones that governed the Guest Worker System. The outcomes in terms of the nature and direction of flows, of who participates in the movement with which motivation and which strategy, and where participants in the movement ultimately end up are bound to be different.

This fundamental difference between the GWS and CEES systems, in terms of state regulation also had consequences for the cities and towns in which migrants came to work. The strong involvement of the state and social partners in the regulation and control of guest workers deployment implied an employers' and state responsibility for the housing of recruited workers. Big companies often built residential accommodation (sometimes on the premises of the work place) or hired these elsewhere, and the national state could take the initiative to build special residences within national building plans, as was the case in the Netherlands in the 1970s. Furthermore, the state subsidised social and welfare work for guest workers, in the Dutch case for example through a network of regional Foundations for Assistance to Foreign Workers and its umbrella organisation LSBBW (later NCB). In the case of migrant workers from CEE countries, particularly after 2004, employers or the state did not take on such responsibilities. Cities and towns had to deal with the housing and social demands of these migrant workers, using their own services and budgets. Claims of local governments on state budgets for costs of such services to CEE migrants have been to no avail generally speaking.

5.4 Conclusion

At face value, the guest worker migration system of 1955–1974 and the migration system from CEE countries to EU15 countries in the period 1990–2015 do have some basic resemblances: both entail a number of sending countries with economies and labour markets that push workers to go elsewhere. These countries are connected to a number receiving countries that have healthy economies and (selective) labour market shortages that pull workers. In both the GWS system and the CEES system millions of workers have been involved, often including periods of work that were followed by a definitive return. The time frame of 2.5 decades in both systems also led to resident immigrant populations of not only workers in receiving countries, partially settling immigrants.

Comparing economic and labour market factors that form a necessary condition for the emergence and continuation of labour migration systems in more detail, we see a strong resemblance again. The differential development gaps (measured in GDP per capita) between sending and receiving countries in both systems during and at the end of both systems are strikingly similar. Even the differentiation of countries at the sending side is comparable: in the GWS system Turkey compares with Poland, Romania and Bulgaria in the CEES, as they are all countries with a GDP per capita of around 20% of the destination countries. The Southern European countries within the GWS also had comparable gap figures as the better-performing countries in the CEES like Slovenia and the Czech Republic. Other indicators, such as unemployment and activity rate, suggest a comparability of the two systems as well. The ending of the GWS system in 1974 and the end of the growth of the CEES system in 2009 are not so much caused by changes at the push side (with decreasing GDP- and wage differentials) in sending countries, as by a sudden disappearance of pull factors in destination countries during the economic crises starting in 1974 and 2008 respectively.

Nevertheless, when comparing the organisation of the migration movements in combination with the legal regulatory framework and state policies regarding labour migration, we see very different regimes of regulating labour migration, going together with very different forms of the practical organisation of flows. The GWS had started as a movement of workers moving along informal networks that connected workers and future employers in a context in which the spontaneous arrival could be legalised easily and under regular conditions of the labour market. In the course of time, this labour migration became institutionalised, implying a state-led – often tripartite – decision-making on recruitment and on conditions for regular work and residence. That system was also able to canalize to a great extent the informal system through nominative recruitment. It could imply involvement of the sending state in recruitment, regulation and protection, as was the case in Turkey. Private intermediaries and work agencies were virtually absent in this institutionalised system.

In the CEES system both the legal context and the organisation were different. In the first period of 1990 to 2004 there were at least three quite different ways of participating in labour migration: in the North Western European corridor there were (limited) formalised labour migration programmes that resembled the official recruitment of the GWS system, but the bulk of labour migration consisted of the quasi-legal short-term and repeated work visits that was coined incomplete migration. Private market intermediaries and work agencies (both legal and illegal) played an important role in these movements. In the southern migration corridor, movements took the form of irregular labour migration through informal channels, and became increasingly organised and assisted by (illegal) intermediaries and agencies, without involvement, consent or cooperation of authorities in destination countries. This labour migration mainly served the informal and low-wage sectors of the economies in the south.

After the accession of CEE states in 2004 and 2007, the legal context changed drastically in the sense that legal barriers for movement gradually disappeared. In the new free mobility market, connecting the supply of workers in CEE countries with a growing demand for flexible work in the booming neo-liberal economies of the west and south, was a profitable activity for intermediaries and work agencies. Regulation and control of movement by national authorities was supposed to be absent after transitional periods (but even before that time), even when migrant workers' protection became endangered by new practices of deploying foreign workers by posting or so-called self-employment. This heyday of the CEES ended abruptly in 2009 by the economic crisis.

The literature documents the differential effects of the new legal framework and the different organisation that came with it: who was selected, who made himself available as a migrant in the system, and how did migrants use that system for their short and long-term future? The GWS generally brought in low-skilled, predominantly male migrants for certain periods for regular jobs at the lower end of the formal labour market for relatively well-protected contract work. In the CEES the regular organised labour migration programmes were a minor part of the movement and only in the first phase. In the first phase, until 2004, most of the movement was irregular – in the sense that a pre-organised legal frame was absent – and not officially organised – in the sense that demand and supply was connected through informal networks or (often irregular) private intermediaries and agencies. The actual work obtained was often irregular, less protected and certain, and low paid.

Such different opportunities have obviously attracted different candidates who could fit these opportunities to their varied migration strategies. Women participated much more than in GWS. The age variation is larger. Migrants in CEES turn out to be relatively well educated, but work below their skills. These trends seem to be reinforced after 2004, when the legal barriers obstructing labour mobility had disappeared. The result is an increasingly heterogeneous movement of people who use temporary, uncertain work in the west or south as a means of exploring how their future might look and where it could happen. It is certainly not a labour migration system as the one defined in the literature: not only the new bottles of the CEES are different from the older ones of the GWS, the wine tastes different as well.

The outcome, where these mobile people of the CEES will end up establishing themselves is rather unpredictable. The ones who are successful in their new places of residence will probably be inclined to stay. But who knows the percentage of successful migrants (basically those that find a steady job corresponding with the skill level and ambition of the migrant and better than staying in their home country)? In the North Western European countries and economies, chances of success do not appear to be any better now than they were for guest workers in the past. In the crisis-ridden Southern European countries, chances seem even slimmer. One basic difference with the GWS system is that none of the CEE migrants will stay in destination countries because a return home would make it impossible to depart anew. Free mobility within the EU will prevent that unexpected outcome of strict regulation (for Turks and Moroccans) after the end of the GWS system in 1974.

References

Abadan-Unat, N., Keleş, R., Penninx, R., van Renselaar, H., van Velzen, L., & Yenisey, L. (1976). *Migration and development: A study of the effects of international labor migration on Boğazlıyan district*. NUFFIC: Den Haag/Ankara.

Akgündüz, A. (2008). *Labour migration from Turkey to western Europa, 1960–1974; a multidisciplinary analysis*. Aldershot: Ashgate.

Arango, J. (2016),*Spain: New Emigration Policies Needed for an Emerging Diaspora*. At: http://www.migrationpolicy.org/research/spain-new-emigration-policies-needed-emerging-diaspora

Black, R., Engbersen, G., Okolski, M., & Pantiru, C. (Eds.). (2010). *A continent moving west? EU enlargement and labour migration from central and Eastern Europe*. Amsterdam: Amsterdam University Press.

Bonifazi, C., Okolski, M., Schoorl, J., & Simon, P. (Eds.). (2008). *International migration in Europe: New trends and new methods of analysis*. Amsterdam: Amsterdam University Press.

Cohen, R. (1987). *The new helots; Migrants in the international division of labour*. Vermont: Gower.

Den Exter, J. (1993), Regionale herkomst van Turken in Nederland, in: *Migrantenstudies* 9, nr 3, 18–34.

Dhéret, C., A. Lazarowicz, F. Nicoli, Y. Pascouau & F. Zuleeg (2013), *Making progress towards the completion of the Single European Labour Market*. Brussels: European policy Centre, EPR Issue Paper no. 75.

Doomernik, J., & Bruquetas-Callejo, M. (2015). National immigration and integration policies in Europe since 1973. In B. Garcés-Mascareñas & R. Penninx (Eds.), *Integration processes and policies in Europe. Contexts, levels, actors* (pp. 57–76). Dordrecht: Springer Open.

Engbersen, G., Okolski, M., Black, R., Godfried, E., & Pantiru, C. (2010a). Introduction: Working out a way from east to west: EU enlargement and labour migration from central and Eastern Europe. In R. Black, G. Engbersen, M. Okolski, & C. Pantiru (Eds.), *A continent moving west? EU enlargement and labour migration from central and Eastern Europe* (pp. 7–22). Amsterdam: Amsterdam University Press.

Engbersen, G, E. Snel & J. de Boom (2010b), A van full of poles': Liquid migration from central and Eastern Europe'. In: R. Black, G. Engbersen, M. Okolski & Chr. Pantiru (Eds), A continent moving west? EU enlargement and labour migration from central and Eastern Europe. Amsterdam: Amsterdam University Press, pp. 115–140.

Engbersen, G., Leerkes, A., Grabowska-Lusinska, I., Snel, E., & Burgers, J. (2013). On the differential attachments of migrants from central and Eastern Europe: A typology of labour migration. *Journal of Ethnic and Migration Studies, 39*(6), 1–23.
Engelbrektsson, U.-B. (1978). *The force of tradition; Turkish migrants at home and abroad.* Gothenburg: Acta Universitatis Gothoburgensis.
Eurostat. (2011). *Migrants in Europe. A statistical portrait of the first and second generation.* Luxembourg: Publications Office of the EU.
Fawcett, J. T. (1989). Networks, linkages, and migration systems. *The International Migration Review, 23*(3), 671–680.
Fihel, A., & Grabowska-Lusinska, I. (2014). Labour market Behaviours of back-and-forth migrants from Poland. *International Migration, 52*(1), 2014.
Fihel, A., & Okolski, M. (2009). Dimensions and effects of labour Migrtaion to EU countries: The case of Poland. In B. Galgóczi, J. Leschke, & A. Watt (Eds.), *EU labour migration since enlargement: Trends, impacts and policies* (pp. 185–210). Aldershot: Ashgate.
Galgóczi, B, & J. Leschke (2015). *Free movement of labour in Europe: a solution for better labour allocation?* Brussels: ETUI, Working Paper 2015.06.
Galgóczi, B., Leschke, J., & Watt, A. (2009). Intra-European labour migration – Flows and policy responses. In B. Galgóczi, J. Leschke, & A. Watt (Eds.), *EU labour migration since enlargement: Trends, impacts and policies* (pp. 1–28). Aldershot: Ashgate.
Glorius, B., Grabowska-Lusinska, I., & Kuvik, A. (Eds.). (2013). *Mobility in transition; migration pattern after EU enlargement.* Amsterdam: Amsterdam University Press.
Hars, A. (2009). Dimensions and effects of labour migration to EU countries: The case of Hungary. In B. Galgóczi, J. Leschke, & A. Watt (Eds.), *EU labour migration since enlargement: Trends, impacts and policies* (pp. 229–252). Aldershot: Ashgate.
Jones, K. (2014, December). 'It was a Whirlwind. A lot of people made a lot of money': The role of agencies in facilitating migration from Poland into the UK between 2004 and 2008. *Central and Eastern European Migration Review, 3*(2), 105–125.
King, R., Fielding, A., & Black, R. (1997). The international migration turnout in Southern Europe. In R. King & R. Black (Eds.), *Southern Europe and the new immigrations* (pp. 1–25). Brighton: Sussex Academic Press.
Markova, E. (2010), Optimising migration effects: A perspective from Bulgaria, In: R. Black, G. Engbersen, M. Okolski & Chr. Pantiru (Eds), *A continent moving West? EU enlargement and labour migration from central and Eastern Europe.* Amsterdam: Amsterdam University Press, pp. 207–230.
Napierala, J., & Trevena, P. (2010). Patterns and determinants of sub-regional migration: A case study of Polish contruction workers in Norway. In R. Black, G. Engbersen, M. Okolski, & C. Pantiru (Eds.), *A continent moving west? EU enlargement and labour migration from central and Eastern Europe* (pp. 51–72). Amsterdam: Amsterdam University Press.
Okolski, M. (2001). Incomplete migration. A new form of mobility in central and Eastern Europe. The case of Polish and Ukrainian migrants. In C. Wallace & D. Stola (Eds.), *Patterns of migration in Central Europe*. Houndmills/Basinstoke: Palgrave Macmillan.
Okolski, M. (Ed.). (2012). *European immigrations: Trends, structures and policy implications.* Amsterdam: Amsterdam University Press.
Peixoto, J., J. Arango, C. Bonifazi, C. Finotelli, C. Sabino, S. Strozza & A. Triandafyllidou (2012),'Immigrants, markets and policies in Southern Europe; the making of an immigration model?. In: B. Glorius, I. Grabowska-Lusinska & Aimee Kuvik (Eds) (2013),*Mobility in transition; Migration pattern after EU enlargement.* Amsterdam: Amsterdam University Press, pp. 107–148.
Penninx, R. (2014). Regional economic integration and migration: Lessons from the case of Europe. In G. Battistella (Ed.), *Global and Asian perspectives on international migration* (pp. 183–196). Cham: Springer International Publishing.

Penninx, R., & Roosblad, J. (Eds.). (2000). *Trade unions, immigration, and immigrants in Europe, 1960–1993: A comparative study of the attitudes and actions of trade unions in seven Western European countries*. New York/Oxford: Berghahn Books.

Potot, S. (2010). Transitioning strategies of economic survival: Romanian migration during the transition process. In R. Black, G. Engbersen, M. Okolski, & C. Pantiru (Eds.), *A continent moving West? EU enlargement and labour migration from Central and Eastern Europe* (pp. 249–270). Amsterdam: Amsterdam University Press.

Rist, R. C. (1978). *Guestworkers in Germany; The prospects for pluralism*. New York: Praeger Publishers.

SVR (Sachverständigenrat deutscher Stiftungen für Integration und Migration). (2013). Erfolgsfall Europa? Folgen und Herausforderungen der EU-Freizügigkeit für Deutschland. In *Jahresgutachten 2013 mit Migrationsbarometer*. Berlin: SVR.

Van Mol, C., & de Valk, H. (2015). Migration and immigrants in Europe: A historical and demographic perspective. In B. Garcés-Mascareñas & R. Penninx (Eds.), *Integration processes and policies in Europe. Contexts, Levels, Actors* (pp. 31–55). Dordrecht: Springer Open.

Zincone, G., Borkert, M., & Penninx, R. (Eds.). (2011). *Migration policymaking in Europe; The dynamics of actors and contexts in past and present*. Amsterdam: Amsterdam University Press.

Part II
Multi-Level Governance

Chapter 6
Governance of the Free Movement of Workers and Persons at the European Level

Karin Zelano

6.1 Introduction

A Brussels correspondent allegedly described the general impression of the EU as 'an animal that lives in Brussels'. Given that most EU regulations are implemented at national and subnational levels of government, it may be tempting to discard the metaphor as a misconception. But it is not entirely false. Governance, in the sense of negotiations and decisions guiding implementation, does take place in the corridors and conference rooms in Brussels. This chapter describes and analyses governance processes at the EU level in matters that relate to the free movement of workers and persons (hereafter free movement).

During the past 10 years, the European Union[1] has introduced open and flexible modes of governance that diverge from the more traditional top-down steering. More than any other idea, the term multilevel governance has come to represent that change. Overall, there seems to be an emerging consensus about the desirability of multilevel governance and increased partnership in EU policy making (e.g. van den Brande 2014).

Prima facie, to increase cooperation may seem like a straightforward strategy to facilitate member state collaboration where legislation is neither possible nor desired. Yet the institutional structure of the EU suggests the opposite. Inclusive multilevel governance is set out to take place in those policy areas where the EU does not enjoy full competence. At the same time, the shared competence is in itself the result of explicit member state and/ or EC preferences. Among the reasons for wanting to keep a policy area under national competence may be specific national interests or a general preference for customised solutions.

[1] The terms 'the European Union' and 'the EU' will be used interchangeably throughout the chapter.

K. Zelano (✉)
University of Gothenburg, Gothenburg, Sweden
e-mail: karin.zelano@gu.se

P. Scholten, M. van Ostaijen (eds.), *Between Mobility and Migration*, IMISCOE Research Series, https://doi.org/10.1007/978-3-319-77991-1_6

To summarise, competence is more likely to be shared in policy areas where member states, for one reason or another, perceive the stakes to be high. Issues relating to the free movement of labour and persons across the EU are prime examples of such matters. This is particularly so after the accession of countries in Central and Eastern Europe (CEE).

Before the first Eastern accession in 2004, statements about the need to protect national welfare systems came thick and fast in the western and northern parts of the EU (Council of the European Union 2015; Doyle et al. 2006; EC 2016; European Commission 2014b). At the same time, the Eastern and Central European member states were eager to join the inner market. The enlargements generated new labour mobility patterns within the EU, predominantly running from East to West (European Committee of the Regions 2015a). As a result, regions and cities in host member states faced a series of social and economic consequences (Reeger and Enengel 2015). In parallel to diverging perspectives at the European and national levels about, for example, labour market standards and wage levels, insufficient political and socio-economic institutions obstruct a satisfactory compliance of the free movement regulatory regime (European Commission 2010; Svetlozar 2009). Nevertheless, the free movement of persons is a European reality. In 2013, more than 7 million European citizens lived and worked in another member state and over one million European citizens crossed the border to work in a neighbouring country every day (Your Europe 2015).

The free movement of workers and people relates to policy areas of exclusive EU competence and policy areas that are dominated by an outspoken ideal of multi-level, non-hierarchical governance. The combination creates a multifaceted arena for governance solutions at the European level. In addition, several policy areas are of a politically delicate nature. Potential gains and losses for the involved parties are likely to influence governance outcomes.

This chapter provides a picture of how governance of this free movement is constructed, managed and negotiated at the European level. The aim is to supplement the previous chapters focusing on governance in European urban regions. A first section presents the data collection and methodology applied. Then follows a presentation of the primary tool of analysis (a modified version of the typology used in Chap. 5) and the foundational theoretical assumptions. The empirical results are analysed in two sections. The first categorises governance structures from what emerged in the data as major thematic areas. A subordinate, second empirical part zooms in on the formal and informal interactions taking place *within* governance structures. This part investigates the working methods of the European Commission,[2] the Permanent Representations of host member states (PR) and to some extent, the Committee of the Regions (CoR). A final paragraph summarises the main results and discusses the present and future role of the EU level in free movement governance.

[2] The terms the European Commission, the Commission and the EC will be used interchangeably throughout the chapter.

Table 6.1 In-depth interview respondents[a]

Permanent Representations to the EU (PR)	European Commission
Permanent Representation of Austria to the EU (1)	DG Internal Market and Services (1)
Permanent Representation of the Netherlands to the EU (1)	DG Internal Market and Services (2)
Permanent Representation of Sweden to the EU (1)	DG Employment, Social Affairs and Inclusion (1)
Permanent Representation of Sweden to the EU (1)	DG Employment, Social Affairs and Inclusion (2)
	DG Justice and Consumers (2)

[a]The number within () refers to the number of respondents present during the interview

6.1.1 Methodology and Data

The chapter uses the term *free movement governance at the EU level*. The concept refers to the general exercise of authority within the multilevel institutional structure of the European Union, namely taking place in the relations and regulations within which institutions, public, private or both, operate (based on Lynn 2012).

The data analysed consist of ten in-depth interviews and written materials. Interview respondents were officials at the EU level working either in the European Commission or at national permanent representations. The selection of member state representations includes countries that have experienced a significant inflow of mobile EU citizens since 2004. In that capacity these member states are considered central to governance relating to the urban implications of free movement. The interviews took place during 2015 and were subsequently recorded and transcribed. Table 6.1 provides an overview of expert respondents:

The actors included in the analysis were chosen on the basis of their position in the formal structures of free movement governance. Member states have a formalised position in the legislative structure of the EU, namely via Comité des représentants permanents (COREPER). In addition, the permanent representations are thought to function as the extension of national governments into the corridors of Brussels. The European Commission in turn is expected to use the permanent representations as channels to national administrations. In addition to the interviewees, two other actors were also included. European Regional and local governments are primarily represented through the Committee of the Regions (CoR), while the European Parliament is the voice of the EU's' citizens. Indisputably, each one of those actors has a strong interest in the processes relating to free movement. However, depending on whether one takes a neo-functionalist or more intergovernmentalist approach to European integration, the relative power of the involved parties varies.

Further data sources consist of official documents from the EU institutions themselves: e.g. legislative acts, press releases, reports and opinions. The data also include the program declarations and mission letters of the two most recent Presidents of the European Commission, as well as open letters to the Commission from member states with regards to the free movement under discussion.

6.2 Governance Modes at the EU Level

This first empirical section (categorisation) is structured using a typology of governance modes. The typology departs from the one introduced in Chap. 5, being moderated to suit the European focus of this chapter.

The point of departure is an institutional setting comprising of four possible governance levels: the EU, national, regional and local. The actors may be public (e.g. governments or administrative bodies), 'civil' (e.g. parties, NGOs, interest groups, social partners, media, knowledge actors, etcetera) and private (e.g. businesses). The typology distinguishes between four governance modes: (1) Horizontal governance, (2) Top-down governance, (3) Multiple level governance and (4) Multi-level governance. Theoretically, all four might or might not involve actors at the EU level. Since this chapter specifically centres on the EU level, the typology presented in Table 6.2 is slightly different compared to that used in project reports and Chap. 5.

Horizontal governance is characterised by engagement and participation among actors at *one single institutional level*. In this chapter, this translates as a formal and/or informal engagement by actors at the EU level. *Top-down governance* is characterised by a hierarchical relationship in which the highest level involved (in this case the EU level) controls the actions of actors on other involved levels. A governance setting is only to be regarded as top-down governance if the EU level can impose solutions on the lower levels involved. In *multiple-level governance* the EU and actors on other levels enjoy a close to equal relationship. As shown by Table 6.2, no more than three levels can be involved in this third type. If all four levels are involved, the governance is a case of *multi-level governance.* In multilevel

Table 6.2 Modes of EU governance of intra EU mobility (Source: Modified version of typology in Chap. 5)

1. Horizontal governance					EU	EU	EU	EU		
2. Top-down governance								**3. Multiple level governance**		
								EU		National
EU	EU	EU	EU	EU	EU	EU		EU		Regional
National	National	National	National	Regional	Regional	Local		EU		Local
	Regional	Local	Regional	Local				EU	National	Regional
			Local					EU	Regional	Local
								EU	National	Local
4. Multilevel governance				EU	National	Regional	Local			

governance, there is a more or less equal engagement, participation and prerogative among all four governance levels. The data collection and analysis include formal as well as informal processes of governance.

6.2.1 Results

Formal EU institutions, member states, organised interests as well as EU citizens participate in governance of free movement at the European level. At a rough estimate, these processes involve about 33,000 employees in the European Commission, almost as many lobbyists, diplomats at 28 permanent representations and a staff of approximately 8000 in the European Parliament (European Commission 2015f; Traynor 2014). The involvement of various institutions and players also varies throughout the process.

To begin with, the European Commission has the prerogative of formulating the political priorities of the EU. Independently of whether one considers the European Commission to be simply at the service of the member states or able to pursue its own agenda, the EC indisputably has an important role in the management and enforcement of EU law (for a comprehensive discussion see Chap. 9 by Balch). When taking office, the new President-elect of the Commission presents the priorities for the years to come and provides each Commissioner with a mission letter. The political priorities of the two most recent Commissions constitute a point of departure for the forthcoming analysis. These, as the priorities of the Commission, form the overarching setting within which European bureaucrats and diplomats operate.[3]

Similar themes have dominated the free movement agenda under the two recent European Commissions: the need for increased intra-EU mobility of workers, regulated professions and students, the social and economic implications of that mobility and the implementation of the Posted Workers Directive.

The second Barroso Commission took office in 2009. The free movement of persons was evoked under the wider goals of ‘Developing new sources of sustainable growth and social cohesion’ and ‘Advancing a people’s Europe’. The first mainly referred to facilitating consumers, but mentions social progress and solidarity. The second area, including efforts to advance a people’s Europe, establishes that: ‘Citizens today should not find that they still face obstacles when they move across borders within the EU’ and adds that mobility for young people is a special priority. Barroso also called for ‘a new, much stronger focus on the social dimension in Europe, at all levels of government’ (Barroso 2009). In the portfolio specific mission statements, Barroso is more concrete and identifies a number of priorities.

The subsequent European Commission took office in 2014, headed by President Juncker. Free movement was discussed within the political priorities presented to the EP under the headline ‘An Agenda for Jobs, Growth, Fairness and Democratic

[3] Since 2009, the year of the second Barroso Commission.

Change'. A specific section of the statement was dedicated to 'A Deeper and Fairer Internal Market with a Strengthened Industrial Base' and the free movement of workers explicitly mentioned. Juncker also promised to 'ensure that the Posting of Workers Directive is strictly implemented and I will initiate a targeted review of this Directive to ensure that social dumping has no place in the European Union'. The right of national governments to fight fraud was also acknowledged in the speech (Juncker 2014).

There are some noteworthy differences. President Juncker's political programme explicitly mentions the free movement of citizens and workers as well as fair labour markets. Unlike Barroso, Juncker's agenda highlights the right of member states to fight abuse and fraud in welfare systems and labour markets. The Juncker Commission further announced an upcoming 'Mobility package' in 2015. The package consisted of a communication on labour mobility, a targeted revision of the posted workers directive and a revision of regulations on social security coordination (European Commission 2015a).

The various issues evoked by the European Commission are managed cooperatively within the institutional structure of the EU. Depending on the character of the issue at hand, different tools and mechanisms are available. This empirical section has described selected governance modes available to stakeholders. The following section goes on to categorise governance relating to the free movement of persons, by form and theme.

6.2.2 *By Governance Form*

6.2.2.1 Primary and Secondary Law

EU law provides the legislative structure of the European project, divided into 'primary' and 'secondary' law. Primary law refers in particular to the Treaties and is the basis for all EU action. Secondary law derives from the Treaties and includes regulations, directives and decisions. The most common way to legislate in the EU is via the so called 'ordinary decision-making procedure', a legislative process where the European Parliament approves EU legislation together with the Council of the European Union (Europa.eu 2015). All of these measures can rather straightforwardly be classified as top-down governance. The criteria for top-down governance set out earlier are fulfilled in the implementation of both primary and secondary law. The EU has the ultimate responsibility and authority to enforce the measures decided. It is equally true that the formulation of legislative acts includes elements of multiple level governance too, namely through the co-legislative role of the Council of Ministers, representing the member states. Although we will see later that there are relationships between the local and the European level, the law primarily concerns the EU institutions and national governments (who in turn might communicate with lower institutional levels). This is illustrated in Table 6.3.

Table 6.3 EU primary and secondary law

Implementation *Top - down governance*		Legislative process *Multiple level governance*	
EU	↓	EU	↕
National		National	

Table 6.4 EU 'soft law'

Multiple level governance	
EU	↕
National	

6.2.2.2 Soft Law

In contrast, so called 'soft law' is based on the mutual trust between member states. The Social Dialogue and Open method of Coordination are both examples of such soft law mechanisms. The Open method of Coordination (OMC) is a form of intergovernmental policy-making that does not result in binding EU legislative measures and it does not require EU countries to introduce or amend their laws (EUR-Lex 2015). As expressed in the White paper on governance from 2001, the OMC is 'a way of encouraging cooperation, the exchange of best practice and adding value at a European level where there is little scope for legislative solutions' (European Commission 2001). The Social Dialogue was developed as a way of ensuring that the single market would have a 'social dimension' and brings together EU institutions and the social partners (European Commission 2015h). Two advisory policy committees are linked to the soft law cooperation: the Social protection committee (SPC) and the Employment committee (EMCO) (European Commission 2015b, i). These modes of steering are best classified as multiple level governance, as shown in Table 6.4.

6.2.2.3 EU Pilot

Another mechanism used to solve issues without formal court procedures is EU Pilot. Based on a website, the Commission and Member States may share information on particular cases and in this way give member states a chance to comply voluntarily (European Commission 2015c). The first step in a formal process is a letter of formal notice, followed by a reasoned opinion. As a last resort, the Commission initiates an action against the member state before the court (Interview with DG Internal Market and Services, 2015). The resolution rate is 75% (cases closed, following national governments' satisfactory responses, as a percentage of all cases). Issues relating to the Internal Market make up 12 per cent of all errands

Table 6.5 EU Pilot

Top - down governance
EU ↓
National

(European Commission 2015c). EU Pilot is interesting in terms of governance typologies. The sharing of information and the focus on non-judiciary conflict solutions hints at regarding this as a multiple governance mode. However, the fact that the EU level owns the initiative, as well as the power to play the trump card of going to court, means that it technically qualifies as a top-down mode of governance (Table 6.5).

6.2.3 *By Governance Theme*

There now follows a categorisation of governance in areas that respondents highlighted as important themes within free movement governance: free movement of persons and workers, posting of workers and social security coordination.

6.2.3.1 Free Movement of Persons and Workers

Within the Commission, labour mobility is primarily handled within the portfolio of employment and social security coordination, monitoring the application of EU law in member states. As put by one of the respondents, the problem facing a well-functioning free movement of labour is not so much inefficient regulations, as the matter of implementation (Interview with DG Employment, Social Affairs and Inclusion, 2015). Respondents from the Commission, as well as diplomats at the permanent representations, stressed the need to address implementation gaps, rather than circumvent free movement:

> ...we see it (free movement) as a core value; we see also, however, that there are issues concerning abuse and with social systems and we want them to be discussed. We really want no taboos here, but to have an open exchange and ask that problems are addressed as far as possible
>
> Interview with Permanent Representation, 2015

The legislation confers every EU citizen with the right to go to another member state for work purposes, to stay in this member state, to stay after the end of the work relationship, to bring his or her family with him or her and to have equal access to social tax and balances. A recent alteration to the free movement framework came into being in 2014 and addressed information deficits in the labour mar-

Table 6.6 Governance modes of free movement of persons and workers

Secondary Law (Directive 2004/28/EC)		European Citizens' Initiative	Statutory committees
Top-down governance	*Multiple level governance*	*Top-Down governance*	*Multiple level governance*
EU	EU ↑	EU	EU ↑
National ↓	National ↓	European Public ↓	National level ↓

ket. The reality is that employers, public authorities and sometimes also EU workers themselves, are simply not aware of the content of EU laws.

There are two statutory committees under Regulation 492/2011: the Advisory Committee and the Technical Committee. The Advisory Committee on Free Movement of Workers is made up of representatives of member states and social partners, while the Technical Committee includes representatives from the member states. These committees meet approximately twice a year. In addition, DG JUST operates an expert group in which people from competent ministries, i.e. those dealing with free movement, meet regularly in Brussels, 3–4 times a year. This group is not written into the treaties but emerged in response to the court ruling of Metock (Interview with DG Justice and Consumers: Union Citizenship Rights and Free movement, 2015; European Commission 2014a).

Since the Treaty of Lisbon came into force, it is also possible for citizens to mobilise in order to raise awareness about a specific issue at the European level by means of the European Citizens' Initiative. As of the time of the data collection, an example relating to the free movement of labour was entitled, Fair Transport Europe – equal treatment for all transport workers. As the title suggests, the initiative demands action to guarantee equal working conditions in the transport sector, a business exposed to intra-EU competition (Fair Transport Europe 2015).

On the practical, operational level of free movement of workers, EURES is important. EURES is a free of charge online portal providing information on living and working conditions in all participating countries in 25 languages, and registers 4 million visits per month (Becker 2015) (Table 6.6).

6.2.3.2 Posting of Workers

In the interviews, respondents working with postings within the EU repeatedly brought up Directive 96/71/EC concerning the posting of workers in the framework of the provision of services as the central piece of legislation. The directive specifies

Table 6.7 Posting of workers

Directive 96/71/EC
Top-down governance
EU ↓
National

which employment conditions apply to workers temporarily posted in a member state other than the one where they are residing. The Court of Justice of the European Union (CJEU) has interpreted the directive in four rulings, known as 'the Laval quartet'. Together, the cases have set the European framework for the practice of collective bargaining. In a briefing about the consequences of the Laval quartet, the European Parliament summarises the judgements as follows: (1) Collective action may be a restriction of economic freedoms. (2) Collective action is a fundamental right. (3) The Posting of Workers Directive is a ceiling (not a minimum) (Malmberg 2010). The directive has been discussed since 2004 but has become even more salient since the Juncker Commission announced a planned revision. Member states have since mobilised to influence the work of the Commission. During the course of 2015, the Commission received two letters concerning the posting of workers in the internal market. The groups of signatures represented both receiving member states and sending member states (Table 6.7).

In what might be seen as a reaction to the lack of sensitie ear that traditional top-down governance signals, member states organised to make the European Commission listen to their objections. In June 2015, seven countries (Sweden, Netherlands, Germany, Austria, France, Luxemburg and Belgium) addressed Commissioner Thyssen with regards to the planned review of the posted workers directive. The aim was to 'to stop the race to the bottom in social protection for workers' (Hundstoffer et al. 2015). The Dutch government initiated the call and declared fair worker mobility one of the political priorities during the presidency in 2016 (Ministry of Social Affairs and Employment 2015). Also in 2015, a group of new member states (Latvia, Romania, Poland, Slovak Republic, Lithuania, Hungary, Estonia, Bulgaria and the Czech Republic) in the CEE region also wrote to the Commissioner. They expressed their concerns about the attempts to alter the free movement regime:

> It is important to emphasise that pay rate differences existing among Member States do not constitute an unfair competition where the freedom to provide services is concerned and there should be no obstacle for service providers to profit from a competitive advantage resulting from the differences between the national rates of pay, an advantage which was safeguarded so far by EU law, including especially case law developed by the Court of Justice of the European Union.
>
> Letter to Commissioner Thyssen from Kalfin et al. 2015

During the interviews, it became clear that the posting of workers was a political priority of the permanent representations, most explicitly so for Sweden and the Netherlands.

> To be active on the EU level and push for good working conditions in the internal market is a priority for the current government in particular. (…) I mean, that is a very clear priority: to avoid social dumping.
>
> Interview with Permanent Representation, 2015

6.2.3.3 Social Security Coordination

Social security coordination within the EU is a rather complex matter, as social security systems remain a national competence and vary widely across the EU. To manage the coordination, member states have agreed on four basic principles to guide implementation:

1) EU citizens are covered by the legislation of one country at a time and national authorities decide which one.
2) The principle of equal treatment or non-discrimination applies, meaning that EU citizens have the same rights and obligations as the nationals of the country in which they are covered.
3) Previous periods of insurance, work or residence in other countries are taken into account when claiming a benefit.
4) A 'principle of exportability' guarantees that cash benefits from one country can be received also by beneficiaries living abroad (European Commission 2015d).

The Juncker 'mobility package' includes a revision of the existing regulations on social security coordination and the outcome of that revision it not yet known. What we do know is that social security coordination is a politically delicate issue. As put by one of the national bureaucrats:

> This issue of social tourism always…, it's always there, smouldering under the surface.
>
> Interview with Permanent Representation, 2015

The Administrative Commission for the Coordination of Social Security Systems gathers member state representatives, to meet a number of times per year. The Commission is responsible for dealing with administrative matters, questions of interpretation arising from the provisions of regulations on social security coordination and for promoting and developing collaboration between EU countries (Interview with DG Employment, Social Affairs, and Inclusion, 2015; European Commission 2015e). There is FreSsco (Free movement of workers and Social security coordination) – a network of independent experts funded by the European Commission and a third group of statistical experts working to improve the available data on stocks and flows of EU citizens residing and/or working in another EU Member State/EFTA country (European Commission 2015g) (Table 6.8).

The categorisation of governance modes per form and theme indicates a pattern. Areas where the EU enjoys formal competence are mostly managed by means of

Table 6.8 Social security coordination

Administrative Commission		FreSsco		Expert group on statistics	
Multiple level governance		*Horizontal governance*		*Horizontal governance*	
EU	↕	EU	⟷	EU	⟷
National					

top-down governance, whereas multiple and horizontal level governance dominate in policy areas where the EU lacks such formal competence. Several modes of governance thus coexist in free movement management at the EU level. The next step in the analysis takes a close-up look at the interactions taking place within the existing governance structures.

6.2.4 Governance Interactions

The interaction between the Commission and member states looks different depending on which issue is being discussed. Some matters are solved by means of soft law, some through SOLVIT, while others might generate a legislative initiative. This section describes the interactions taking place within the three modes of governance identified in the previous section.

Member states and European institutions interact at the European level within horizontal and multiple models of governance. Interaction also takes place within top-down governance. A hierarchical structure does not exclude interaction between levels. It simply implies an unequal distribution of power.

The interviews revealed how preferences and agendas varied between governance stakeholders. Respondents within the European Commission expressed an overarching ambition to 'make the free movement work'. Representatives of national, regional and local governments in Brussels worked with the explicit aim to influence developments in the preferred direction of their principals. As a result, the EC and representatives of national, regional and local governments operate in a context of shifting alliances. Agendas would sometimes conflict, and sometimes coincide.

6.2.4.1 Regions and Municipalities at the EU Level

Free movement in general and labour mobility in particular, have been increasingly salient in national and European debates about the long-term sustainability of intra-EU mobility. Member states impatient for reform have repeatedly turned directly to the European Commission to insist on certain measures instead of following standard procedures within the Council structures. Several respondents mentioned 'the letter' during the interviews. This referred to an open letter from the Ministers of the Interior in Austria, Germany, Netherlands and the UK, sent to the president of the European Council for Justice and Home Affairs, Mr. Shatter (IE). The governments called for increased attention to the local consequences of free movement (Interview with DG Justice and Consumers: Union Citizenship Rights and Free movement, 2015; Interview with Permanent Representation, 2015). In response, the Commission published several reports to address the issues raised, and also organised the 'Conference of mayors on the impact of intra-EU mobility of EU citizens at local level' together with the Committee of the Regions (CoR). Over 200 participants attended the conference, where local and regional authorities were invited to make their concerns heard and discuss possible solutions (e.g. European Committee of the Regions 2014). The CoR has stressed the role of local and regional authorities in the everyday governance of free movement and practical implementation of EU citizenship on several occasions (Centre for Strategy and Evaluation Services (CSES) 2012). The overarching legal framework of free movement has not been altered as a consequence of the protests. However, the horizontal relations engendered have resulted in some improvements in the communication between the European Commission, member states and local authorities regarding the implementation of existing rules. In addition to arranging the conference, the Commission has issued handbooks and encouraged intensified exchange of information in general (Interview with Permanent Representation, 2015). Commission respondents acknowledged such initiatives were necessary, as intra-EU mobility often has more tangible implications at the local rather than at the national level:

> It's not really the member states that are being confronted with urban problems, it is the cities. So, we show them that we take interest in what the people on the ground actually do and try to see how we can accommodate them, rather than those complaining member states, you know, who are not the real persons taking care of the problems on the ground.
>
> Interview with DG Justice and Consumers: Union Citizenship Rights and Free Movement 2015.

Another strategy was to participate in the 'Open Days'; an annual four-day conference hosted by the CoR. In 2015, the Commission experienced high interest in and positive feedback to a workshop on inclusion of mobile EU citizens and the EU funds that can be used for those purposes (Interview DG Justice and Consumers: Union Citizenship Rights and Free movement, 2015; European Committee of the Regions 2015b).

According to the Commission, it is sometimes hard to find the optimal way of interaction between the European and local level. Nevertheless, the European Commission meets regularly with the Committee of the Regions at desk officer level. Recently, the Committee communicated its position to the Commission in the process leading up to the launching of the labour mobility package (European Committee of the Regions 2015a). Within the CoR, the Commission coordinates the work relating to the movement for Social Policy, Education, Employment, Research and Culture (SEDEC).

In terms of governance modes, the CoR operates at the European level, while at the same time representing lower levels of government, insinuating a multiple level component. However, as the organisation is active on the European level and cannot be assigned to a single specific local or regional context, the governance mode is better thought of as horizontal.

6.2.4.2 The Role of Permanent Representations to the EU

Interview respondents representing the European Commission and the permanent representations (PR) are in regular contact with each other. Both clusters differentiated between formal and informal relations between member state representations and the EC.

The formal relationships include various expert committees organised by the Commission and formal questions from the Commission regarding implementation of EU law. Various forms of informal interactions overlap and complement these formal platforms. Interactions between the permanent representations and the European Commission (EC) served one or several of the following purposes.

- To get information from the EC
- To pass on information about the preferences and positions of their own member state to the EC
- To circumvent initiation of a formal infringement procedure, i.e. by informing about practices or planned reforms.
- To form alliances with like-minded member states

Three of these relate to communication between the European Commission and the PRs. The fourth purpose concerns instead bilateral relations between like-minded member states.

Retrieval of information from the European Commission emerged as the dominant task of PRs. The quote below describes this:

> The most common game in Brussels is trying to figure out what the Commission will do and when.
>
> Interview with Permanent Representation, 2015

At the other end of the relationship, EU bureaucrats explained that they are in touch with member states on a daily basis and regularly receive e-mails from national representatives (Interview with DG Internal Market and Services, 2015). The task of keeping up communication seems to be more central to permanent representations than to the Commission. Most officials within the Commission mentioned other Directorate Generals (DGs) as their main point of contact. Nevertheless, information flows in both directions as explained by one member state representative:

> (…) the Commission is interested in listening to our input in order for their proposals to be well received, they don't want to present a proposal that no one wants on the table.
>
> Interview with Permanent Representation, 2015

Another interview respondent said it was very much up to the PRs to keep themselves informed about what the European Commission is doing (Interview with Permanent Representation, 2015). There were many ways of doing so, and these varied from individual to individual. Personal networks were considered an advantage. As an example, some respondents mentioned how former experience in the Commission could be a way to get access to information.

> As a [nationality of respondent] in the Commission, after a while I felt that I was expected to, like, be the link to [member state of origin] and provide [member state of origin] with information from the Commission. In a similar way, I am now expected to kind of use [staff of same nationality] or whoever it might be to provide me and, in the long run the Ministry back home, with information.
>
> Interview with Permanent Representation, 2015

The informality of those relations contributes to making information access unpredictable. The informal nature also contributes to the perception that the kind of information accessible is rather ad hoc. The two quotes below illustrate this view:

> Yes. I mean, I could definitely call them, or if there are questions I will write them an e- mail and ask 'Could you tell me?'. Of course, that depends if there are any new developments within the Commission, … if these are not yet decided, then they probably wouldn't tell me, (It depends) if it's still part of discussions and if they are, anyway, open issues.
>
> Interview with Permanent Representation, 2015

> It is not obvious that they [the Commission] are happy to share proposals and these things before they have passed through their hierarchy and it [the hierarchy] is after all rather strict. (…) with sharing drafts and these things, but the Commission also has an interest in presenting things that the member states want.
>
> Interview with Permanent Representation, 2015.

Another factor mentioned as influencing access to information is the length of EU membership. Member states with longer experience in Brussels were considered better at extracting information from the Commission. One respondent said that:

> I still think we [member state] have more to learn from those member states that really always know what is going to come, [that] are at the forefront.
>
> Interview with Permanent Representation, 2015

A second objective of the interaction between the European Commission and the national embassies is to communicate national priorities regarding specific matters to the EC. This is considered particularly important in the consultation phase leading up to a proposal from the Commission. At the time of the interviews (2015), the announced Junker mobility package was in that phase. One respondent used it to exemplify how the permanent representations might go about their work during the phase of consultation:

> When it [the announcement of the mobility package] is approaching we will try to meet with the Commission and say 'these are the things we have in mind' and so on. And meet with other member states we know have the same agenda.
>
> Interview with Permanent Representation, 2015

Similar to interactions designed to retrieve information, interactions aiming to convene national preference are characterised by informality. The quotes below confirm that both sides share that view:

> It's really very easy, very informal. They [ministry in capital of MS] might call me and say 'Hey, could you ask either the Commission, or could you probably ask other member states how they are doing different things?'
>
> Interview with Permanent Representation, 2015

> Then member states, individually of course, approach the Commission on different levels. There is the Commissioner, the presidents and then the services, to discuss these issues in more detail. And yes, there are some member states, of course, where this is a more pressing issue, which require more meetings, more information and which send us more comments.
>
> Interview with DG Employment, Social Affairs, and Inclusion, 2015

Several respondents mentioned how the European Commission is not always open to absorb information about member state preferences. Although invited to comment on the agenda of an expert committee for example, permanent representations perceive that the possibility of them influencing the outcome is limited. This was explained by reference to the diverging interests of PRs and the EC. Issues relating to the implementation of the free movement directive are likely to be highly relevant for member states. On such issues, member states naturally ask for access and influence. At the same time, as one respondent said, the Commission has little interest in acknowledging problems relating to implementation:

> If you are the player watching over the treaties, as the Commission is; the motor of integration and everything, of course you try to keep it low key, while the others will ask to put these issues on the agenda more often and to discuss them. So, it's always of course, a pool of negotiation and a bit of strategy as well. It's natural.
>
> Interview with Permanent Representation, 2015

This disinterest naturally causes frustration on behalf of member states. Sometimes, it even seemed to trigger more proactive behaviour vis-à-vis the EC. Both the European Commission respondents and the national diplomats mentioned an open letter signed by five member states that was sent to the Commission in 2013. The letter was a consequence of a situation where the Commission was perceived as ignoring member state preferences for too long. As one respondent said, the letter was sent after years of raising concerns about the local consequences of free movement:

> (…) the letter then raised huge political concerns and, you know, caused many reactions by the media and the press that went probably much further than the intention of the letter. Because the intention of the letter was simply to say "Look, we have issues and we want to address them, we want to talk about them and it's definitely not directed against any specific groups, it's not directed against free movement".
>
> Interview with Permanent Representation 7, 2015

European Commission respondents also brought up the aforementioned letter when asked if member states actively try to influence the actions and priorities of the EC:

> Like the letter. It can happen. It was a blunt way to do it. But of course, you get lobbied by member states for this or that but it's not our day to day experience.
>
> Interview with DG Justice and Consumers: Union Citizenship Rights and Free movement, 2015

A third type of interaction between national representations to the EU and the European Commission is contact designed to circumvent the initiation of a formal infringement procedure against individual member states. Permanent representations do so by, for example, informing Commissioners about practices and planned reforms in the domestic arena. Notably, there was a shared preference across institutions for solving problems informally, or at least, outside formal infringement procedures.

The preference for avoiding costly court proceedings has been institutionalised in the mechanism of SOLVIT. SOLVIT is managed from within the Commission and operated via an online database with national centres in each of the member states. The overarching purpose is to help 'people who move around Europe for work, study, business, etc. and encounter problems with public authorities which may not apply EU legislation correctly' (European Commission 2015j). SOLVIT works on the basis of mutual trust and the common willingness to solve problems resulting from cross border activity. Consequently, SOLVIT experts provide advice and mediate between parties that are willing to solve the matter without initiating a formal infringement procedure. As explained below, there are cases where such common ground is missing and a mechanism like SOLVIT reaches its limits:

> When something is politically sensitive, then it also starts to become much more difficult to have an informal solution. (…) For example, we had a Danish- Dutch case; it was on sailing licenses in the sea and was already at the level of Ambassadors talking to each other. The Ambassador in Denmark and the Ambassador in the Netherlands would go to the ministries, so the ministers would already have discussed it. The complainant also complained to SOLVIT, but the thing was already in the newspapers etcetera and then the SOLVIT centre just said 'I can't do anything here, because it's already at such a high level'. And then the authority will only change if he gets the instruction from the minister or whatever.
>
> Interview with DG Internal Market and Services, 2015.

Other, less institutionalised ways of solving problems outside the court room were also mentioned. Similar to the respondent quoted, several respondents discussed this:

> Before you get a formal notice, normally you have informal proceedings (…) Sometimes you also meet and ... It depends. In some areas, also sometimes some commission representative would ask you as well, also at my level, they would come and say 'How is it done?' and 'Are you sure this completely corresponds?' But there is always this before [a formal notice].
>
> Interview with Permanent Representation, 2015

Both the European Commission and PRs used informal contacts to avoid formal infringement processes. They do so either by explaining the reason for a specific practice or informing the Commission about upcoming changes in a criticised practice. This kind of contact could emerge as a response to a direct question from the Commission or as a proactive response on behalf of the PRs.

> The Commission might have raised an issue about the implementation of a Directive in [member state] and indicated that this might come up and become an infringement procedure, but then you try to solve a lot by explaining how this is done and what is in the pipeline within the [national] legislative process to see whether this really has to become an infringement procedure.
>
> Interview with Permanent Representation, 2015

> In some areas, also sometimes some Commission representative would ask you as well, also at my level, they would come and say 'How is it done?' and 'Are you sure this completely corresponds?'. And then you become aware that there might be some internal investigation or whatever. But there is always this before.
>
> Interview with Permanent Representation, 2015

> Prior to [an EU pilot] it is in our interest to provide the Commission with as much information as possible …'all this work is coming up in [member state] and might change the legislation, making the issue that you are raising a non-issue in a years' time, is it then really relevant to initiate an infringement procedure that will require a lot of work and resources?…'
>
> Interview with Permanent Representation, 2015

Respondents within the European Commission also confirmed that this could be the purpose of information exchanges between themselves and member states:

> So first we ask them to explain their system and then we show the problems. We ask them also to change it.
>
> Interview with DG Internal Market and Services, 2015

> I mean, if there is a practical problem, we do not act. If we have 50 cases which concern the same aspect, we could ask the member state 'what are you doing?'
>
> Interview with DG Employment, Social Affairs and Inclusion, 2015

Fourth, the permanent representations emphasised the strategic benefit of meeting with like-minded member states before meeting in consultative bodies or in the Council working groups. They explained that while constellations may shift between issues they remained quite stable once established. As an example, the UK and Sweden were known to often represent opposite positions in aspects relating to the exportability of social benefits but shared the same position in discussions about how to facilitate the mobility of regulated professions (Interview with DG Internal Market and Services, 2015; Interview with Permanent Representation, 2015) According to one of the respondents:

> I think it's an interesting development anyway at the EU level, that you have these kinds of like-minded member states meeting, like-minded groups (…). I think during my time, it has become probably more frequent, more regular, in a way.
>
> Interview with Permanent Representation, 2015

Connections with individual members of the European Parliament (MEP) may also serve as a way to channel national preferences. In addition to revising legislation and authoring reports, individual parliamentarians (MEPs), have the opportunity to ask the President of the European Council, the Council, the Commission or the Vice-President of the Commission /High Representative of the Union for Foreign Affairs and Security Policy written or oral questions. Each Member may submit a maximum of five questions per month (European Parliament, 2015). Among the Commission staff, parliamentary questions appeared as the most frequent form of interaction with the European parliament (e.g. interview with DG Employment, Social Affairs and Inclusion, 2015). The permanent representations stated that they had more regular contact with MEPs of their own member state than with other parliamentarians. Sweden has a way of keeping in touch with Swedish MEPs by means of regular, organised breakfast meetings with the objective of mutual exchange of information between Swedes working with EU affairs in Brussels (Interview with Permanent Representation, 2015). Rather than being central, influencing via individual MEPs is considered a complement to other ways of communicating national preferences.

In conclusion, the everyday governance of Brussels stakeholders seems dominated by horizontal and multiple level governance. In the context of the EU, the distinction between the two types is sometimes difficult to discern. The most clear-cut example of horizontal governance is when European institutions, for example, the European Parliament and the European Commission work together. When the Committee of the Regions, permanent representations and social partner organisations are involved, the distinction between the multiple and horizontal governance modes gets blurred. More specifically, this is the case when organisations representing various sub-European levels work together with EU institutions at the European level. The Committee of the Regions and the Permanent Representations are both examples of such hybrids.

Within governance structures stakeholders interact by means of formal and informal communication. Respondents emphasised informal interactions as being extremely important. It also became evident that the European Commission has an informational advantage vis-à-vis the permanent representations. The PRs have to influence or get access to the European Commission through informal relations, rather than the other way around. The European Commission relies more on formal means to pass on information, for example through the Council working groups.

6.3 Conclusion

Within the IMAGINATION project, results show that that while CEE migration has the potential to involve governance actions at all administrative and political levels, the EU level is often absent on the ground. The areas of prevention of human trafficking, crime and to some extent employment and labour mobility via EURES were noteworthy exceptions (See project report Zelano et al. 2016). The findings presented in this chapter substantiate those claims. Free movement governance is primarily an affair of top-down, multiple level and horizontal modes of governance. The top-down mode of governance has been challenged by member states, most dramatically when frustrated member states have let their discontent be known by means of open letters to the Commission. This rather unconventional way of protest signals a bottom-up demand for more inclusive governance. This was also something that respondents within the European Commission openly acknowledged.

Overall, the European Commission was aware of the importance of acknowledging and addressing the needs of local and regional stakeholders in order to safeguard the functioning of the free movement of labour and people. The IMAGINATION case studies however, indicate that this awareness does not trickle down to the local and regional levels.

According to European Commission respondents, there are few established ways of working directly with lower levels of government. The EC tries to address this gap by edited handbooks or interactive databases. But such initiatives alone cannot solve the multitude of implications resulting from intra-EU mobility.

Theoretically, the Committee of the Regions (CoR) is the primary tool for interaction between local and regional governments and the European Commission. The CoR was mentioned in this respect by stakeholders at the national level as well as higher ranked bureaucrats in the urban regions. In contrast, barely any street level bureaucrats, for example, outreach social workers, mentioned the CoR as an actor with a potential role in solving the challenges at hand. This indicates the distance between the local level bureaucrat and the CoR offices in Brussels negotiations.

The results reveal the gap between European and local levels in free movement governance. The gap should theoretically be addressed and minimised by the representative mechanism of the CoR. This does not seem to be the case empirically. Instead, complementary, direct links are emerging between the local level and the European Commission. Similarly, the work by the national representations does not seem to trickle down to the local level back home. The interactions between the national and the European level in Brussels seem to be well established and effective, as does the reporting back to national governments. However, the information flow appears to stop there and does not result in any domestic ripples at sub-national levels of government.

Provided that the EU wants to encourage multilevel governance, cooperation and the exchange of best practice, there are reasons for the European Commission to continue on the path chosen, more specifically to develop tools and platforms for interaction and cooperation with local and regional levels of governance. Such initiatives should exist alongside existing structures and serve as a complement rather than a substitute. Such complementary interaction may possibly have a better chance of addressing urgent matters relating to, for example, practical implementation and interpretation of specific paragraphs in EU law. By the same token, it is recommendable that the European Commission open up ways in which regional and local levels may interact directly with them. To some extent such mechanisms are already in place through European Social Fund (ESF) project grants and conferences at the EU level. However, this could be developed through more long-term interactions with local stakeholders and improved information exchange. Such a strategy would also offer a way for regional and local entities to move forward in cases where their preferences and political priorities differs or even clash with those at the national level.

6.4 Final Remarks

The findings in this chapter offer theoretical as well as empirical insights. Theoretically, the data may be used to inform the typology of governance modes. To start with, *multilevel governance* is unlikely in a governance setting as complex and diverse as the EU of today. In some areas, such as the inner market, conflicting interests seem to have generated top-down modes of governance out of necessity. In other cases, where politicisation is high or where member states share competence with the EC, multiple level governance seems to be more common. The involvement of multiple levels takes place in Brussels, at the European level. This intertwined and overlapping system, where, as an example, local governments are represented in the Committee of the Regions, makes it hard to discern a strict line between multiple level and horizontal governance.

The results also offer empirical insight. Political, legislative and bureaucratic processes run parallel in the governance of free movement. Focus and measures at the European level are influenced by increasing political concerns in local and national contexts. These, in turn, are predominantly communicated via the national permanent representations to the EC. The European Parliament, individual MEPs, the European Committee of the Regions and social partners also serve as channels for information to the EU level. To some extent, member states and local authorities have been successful in their efforts to make the European Commission address gaps in free movement governance. The announced revisions in the areas of posting and social security coordination, as well as the innovative formats developed, for example, e-learning tools, databases, facilitating information exchange and grants, indicates that the European Commission realises the need for all levels to strive towards the same goal.

The results give free movement advocates some reason for optimism. Both the member states and other key actors seem to be in favour of the free movement of people, at least in theory. The challenge for those convinced that the advantages of free movement surpass the downsides is to turn that support into well-functioning practices on the ground.

References

Barroso, J M. (2009, Sept 3). Political guidelines for the next Commission. Brussels.

Becker, H. K. (2015). Report on the proposal for a regulation of the European Parliament and of the council on a European network of employment services, workers' access to mobility services and the further integration of labour markets. A8–0224/2015. European Parliament.

Centre for Strategy and Evaluation Services (CSES). (2012). *Study on the role of local and regional authorities in promoting EU citizenship and citizens Rights*. Brussels: European Union.

Council of the European Union. (2015, Oct 14). Fair labour mobility in the EU. Retrieved from www.consilium.europa.eu

Doyle, N., Hughes, G. and Wadensjö, E. (2006). *Freedom of movement for workers from Central and Eastern Europe- Experiences in Ireland and Sweden*. Report 2006:5. Stockholm: Swedish Institute for European Policy Studies (SIEPS).
EUR- Lex. (2015). Glossary of Summaries: Open method of coordination. Retrieved from www.eur-lex.europa.eu
Europa.eu., (2015, Dec 18). *EU Law*. Retrieved from http://europa.eu/eu-law
European Commission. (2001). *European governance: A white paper*. Brussels: European Commission.
European Commission. (2010). EU CITIZENSHIP REPORT 2010: Dismantling the obstacles to EU citizens' rights.
European Commission. (2014a, May 26). Expert Group on the right to free movement of persons (Directive 2004/38/European Commission) (E02397). Retrieved from: www.ec.europa.eu/transparency
European Commission (2014b). Study on mobility, Migration and Destitution in the European Union.
European Parliament (2015). Rules of Procedure of the European Parliament. Published online: www.europarl.europa.eu
European Commission. (2015a). Annex to the communication from the Commission to the European Parliament, the Council, the European Economic and Social Committee and the Committee of the Regions Commission. Work Programme 2016 No time for business as usual.
European Commission. (2015b). Employment Committee. Retrieved from www.ec.europa.eu/social
European Commission. (2015c). EU Pilot. Retrieved from www.ec.europa.eu/internal_market
European Commission. (2015d). EU Social Security Coordination. Retrieved from www.ec.europa.eu/social
European Commission. (2015e). FAQ – Regulations. Retrieved from www.ec.europa.eu/social
European Commission. (2015f). Key figures: Staff Members. Retrieved from: www.ec.europa.eu/civil_service
European Commission. (2015g). Network of experts on statistics. Retrieved from www.ec.europa.eu/social
European Commission. (2015h). Social Dialogue. Retrieved from: www.ec.europa.eu/social
European Commission. (2015i). Social Protection Committee. Retrieved from: http://ec.europa.eu/social
European Commission. (2015j, Oct 7). SOLVIT. Retrieved from: www.ec.europa.eu/internal_market
European Commission (2016). Enlargement – transitional provisions. Retrieved from: www.ec.europa.eu
European Committee of the Regions. (2014). Conference of mayors on the impact of intra- EU mobility of EU citizens at local level: Proceedings. Brussels: Committee of the Regions and the European Commission.
European Committee of the Regions. (2015a). Free movement and migration- Factsheet. Retrieved from: www.cor.europa.eu
European Committee of the Regions. (2015b). What are the OPEN DAYS? Retrieved from: www.ec.europa.eu
Fair Transport Europe (2015). *Fair Transport Europe – equal treatment for all transport workers*. Retrieved from: www.ec.europa.eu/citizens-initiative
Hundstoffer, R., Peeters, K., Rebsamen, F., Nahles, A., Schmit, N., Asscher, L. and Johansson, Y. (2015, June 18). Posting of Workers Directive. (Letter).
Juncker, J.-C. (2014, July 15). *A new start for Europe: My agenda for jobs, growth, fairness and democratic change*. Strasbourg: Political Guidelines for the next European Commission.
Kalfin, I., Marksová, M, Vassiljev, R., Czomba, S., Augulis, U., Pabedinskiene, A., Kosiniak-Kamysz, W., Plumb, R. and Richter, J. (2015). Letter to Commissioner Thyssen.

Lynn, L. (2012). The many faces of governance: Adaptation? Transformation? Both? Neither? In D. Levi-Faur (Ed.), *Oxford handbook of governance*. Oxford: Oxford University Press.
Malmberg, J. (2010). The impact of the ECJ judgments on Viking, Laval, Rûffert and Luxembourg on the practice of collective bargaining and the effectiveness of social action (IP/A/EMPL/ST/2009–11 PE 440.275), Brussels: Directorate General for Internal Policies, Policy Department A: Economic and Scientific Policy. Employment And Social Affairs.
Ministry of Social Affairs and Employment. (2015). Seven countries want fair rules for posted workers in EU [Press release]. Retrieved from: www.government.nl
Reeger, U & Enengel, MM-L. (2015). Implications of CEE migration in European urban regions: The socioeconomic, socio-cultural and legal-political implications in comparison. IMAGINATION Project Report. Vienna Academy of Sciences: Vienna.
Svetlozar, A. A. (2009). The unbearable lightness of membership: Bulgaria and Romania after the 2007 EU accession. *Communist and Post-Communist Studies, 42*, 375–393.
Traynor, I. (2014, May 8). 30,000 lobbyists and counting: Is Brussels under corporate sway? *the Guardian*. Retrieved from: www.theguardian.com
van den Brande, L. (2014). *Multilevel Governance and Partnership- The Van den Brande Report.* Prepared at the request of the commissioner for regional and urban policy Johannes Hahn. Brussels: Committee of the Regions.
Your Europe. (2015, Nov 11). Cross-border commuters. Retrieved from: www.europa.eu/youreurope.
Zelano, K., Bucken-Knapp, G., Hinnfors, J., & Spehar, A. (2016). Urban governance of CEE mobility in European urban regions. In *WP3 comparative report*. Gothenburg: IMAGINATION Project.

Chapter 7
The Multi-Level Governance of Intra EU Movement

Gregg Bucken-Knapp, Jonas Hinnfors, Andrea Spehar, and Karin Zelano

7.1 Introduction

Free movement management is a challenge that emerged in a multi-level context, with policies developed at one level having unclear implications for actors working at other levels, and with questions of authority and competencies remaining highly uncertain. Broader issues of national and local contexts, as well as traditional institutional practices, all lay the groundwork for the need of clearly articulated governance solutions. As is clear from previous chapters, the flows of CEE migrants, as well as the social consequences of their presence in urban regions that are often unequipped in both policy and administrative terms, has led to substantial challenges for actors at all levels of government, both public and private, when it comes to free movement management.

In this chapter, we identify the specific governance patterns that have emerged in terms of free movement management. Our argument is that while free movement management may have emerged in a multi-level context, there is a surprising lack of multi-level governance when it comes to policy and administrative responses. Put bluntly, the governance measures that have been opted for in each of the four nations and eight cities display strikingly little in the way of multi-level governance. Rather, for the policy domains that have been most salient in each setting, we see that the governance solutions that have been institutionalized primarily represent either horizontal, top-down, or multiple-level modes of governance. Quite simply, with rare exceptions, the governance modes that have been adopted are not governance modes that meaningfully involve the EU. These empirical findings suggest that a political challenge that would have all the hallmarks of an opportunity for vertical governance networks to emerge is, at the end of the day, largely being resolved by actors at local levels.

G. Bucken-Knapp (✉) · J. Hinnfors · A. Spehar · K. Zelano
University of Gothenburg, Gothenburg, Sweden
e-mail: gregg.bucken-knapp@spa.gu.se

P. Scholten, M. van Ostaijen (eds.), *Between Mobility and Migration*, IMISCOE Research Series, https://doi.org/10.1007/978-3-319-77991-1_7

7.2 Mapping Free Movement Management: From the Multi-Level Governance Literature to Modes of Governance

On one level, it is unsurprising to consider the case of free movement management in urban regions against the backdrop of the broad multi-level governance approach. In general, the broad multi-level governance literature posits that there is a multiplicity of actors present from the EU, national, regional and local levels, who engage in what can be regarded as a process of negotiation, deliberation and implementation that is more or less continuous (Schmitter and Kim 2005). The relationship among actors at these four levels is one where there is substantive engagement of those involved, not merely presence, and where engagement allows for the possibility of genuine mutual influence, but also facilitates and mutual dependency as various policy-making activities become intertwined with one another (Stephenson 2013).

After all, the challenge associated with developing and implementing the tools to successfully manage free movement can be thought of as occurring in a clear-multi-level context. In a stylized nutshell, the principle of free movement of people within the EU often creates substantial challenges for urban actors (both public and private) who find their efforts to "solve" the issue difficult by a lack of clear policies at both the national and local level for addressing the issue. Coupled to this, CEE migrant integration within EU member states is regularly characterized by ambiguous lines of authority as to which actors have (or even want) responsibility for formulating and implementing policies. As such, given the multi-level context of the challenges associated with free movement management, one might suspect that it is a prime candidate for a governance solution that is fittingly multi-level in response. Indeed, some authors within the multi-level governance literature, as well as actors in the public sphere – in particular the EU itself – have worked from an assumption that multi-level governance is, by default, a desirable outcome where the problem context can be framed as multi-level in nature. Such excessively positive portrayals of multi-level governance have been called into question by scholars over the past decades, with arguments being made that multi-level governance has the potential to compromise democracy (Guy Peters and Pierre 2004), in essence undermining the principles of traditional government through facilitating for the establishment of self-organizing and self-regulating networks apart from traditional governing institutions (Harlow & Rawlings 2007).

However, as a number of studies focusing on urban administrative responses to the challenges of immigration have shown, the complexity of a multi-level system entailing many policy processes might not result in effective multi-level coordination at all. Rather, a broad variety of governance responses are possible, with the possibility that actors at any one level could play the decisive role in formulating and coordinating policy and administrative measures, or even, that no patterns of coordination might emerge. (Bowen 2007; Joppke 2007; Ostaijen et al. 2016; Duyvendak and Scholten 2012; Scholten 2012).

Clearly then, a response of multi-level governance to the challenge of free movement management is one possible outcome, but it should not be assumed to be the only or most likely governance result, solely because of the multi-level context in which actors find themselves embedded. What then are the other possible alternatives that might emerge?

In this chapter, we employ a typology of governance approaches that capture the full range of possible responses from the various public and private actors who are faced with developing responses to the challenges of free movement management. This typology of governance responses is comprised of the following four modes: horizontal governance, top-down governance and multiple-level governance and multi-level governance. We envision an overall governance setting comprised of four possible levels: the EU, national, regional and local. The actors inhabiting these levels may be either public (governments or administrative bodies) or those from the broader polity (parties, NGOs, interest groups, social partners, media, knowledge actors, etc.). This typology is more fully developed in the introductory chapter of this book, but we provide readers who might make use of this chapter in isolation from the others with a sufficiently detailed overview.

Horizontal governance is characterized by an engagement and participation among actors at only one level seeking to resolve free movement management challenges. While these actors may need to work within the confines of formal policy established at another governance level (most notably in the case of horizontal governance at either the local or regional level, who often must coordinate their activities against the backdrop of certain national policy mandates), formal and informal engagement is solely limited to one level of actors.

Top-down governance is characterized by a hierarchical relationship in which the highest level involved steers the overall governance response for actors from all other involved layers. In order for there to be a top-down governance response to the challenge of free movement management, there must be at least two levels involved, though these levels do not necessarily need to be adjacent. For example, in a setting where only actors at the national and local level are involved in developing free movement management measures, it can only be regarded as top-down governance if the national level has the ability impose solutions on local actors who are also involved in the deliberation process.

By contrast, *bottom-up governance* is characterized by a hierarchical relationship in which the lowest level involved steers the overall governance response for actors from all other involved layers. In order for there to be a bottom-up governance response to the challenge of free movement management, there must be at least two levels involved, though these levels do not necessarily need to be adjacent. For example, we witness bottom-up governance if the local level has the ability to impose solutions on regional or national – level actors who are also involved in the deliberation process.

However, it is imperative to stress that central to either top-down or bottom-up governance is the presence of a mutual collaborate relationship among actors at different levels, which is a necessary condition of governance. Lacking such a collaborative relationship, what may appear at first glance to be either top-down or bottom-up modes of governance is, in fact, a form of policy learning, in which actors at various levels simply adopt the governance solution developed horizontally at some other level, without any substantive engagement among these levels in constructing the specific governance response. We return to this point in the conclusion, highlighting the manner in which the repeated presence of horizontal governance at the local level across our cases ought not to be misinterpreted as evidence in support of bottom-up governance.

Multiple-level governance is characterized by a more or less equal relationship in terms of engagement and participation for actors at those levels involved in the process of responding to the challenges of free movement management. In order for there to be multiple-level governance, there must be at least two levels involved, though these levels do not necessarily need to be adjacent. However, as will be explained shortly, no more than three levels can be involved. For example, a setting where actors from national, regional and local levels are involved in developing free movement management measures can be regarded as multiple-level governance if there is a more or less equal relationship among actors from these different levels.

Lastly, there is *multi-level governance* in the traditional way that is understood in the literature: a situation where there is a more or less equal relationship in terms of engagements and participation among all four levels – including the EU level - as they seek to formulate responses to the challenges of free movement management.

As we turn to the major policy areas that have been the focus of free movement management responses in each of our four cases, we will see that multi-level governance, the one that has received the most attention in the literature, is that which is primarily lacking. Rather, the governance modes that are opted for in each of the major policy areas have exclusively been top-down, multiple, or horizontal in nature. It is only when we look beyond the key components addressed in each case responses that we see clear evidence of a multi-level governance response.

Following this, we intend to shift the theoretical discussion to matters of governance approaches more broadly, calling attention to the explanatory utility associated with network approaches (Curry 2015), as well as to horizontal, vertical and diagonal approaches (Torfing et al. 2012). We will stress the manner in which this combined literature highlights the importance of governance approaches as venues for interaction among actors at a variety of levels and within a variety of organizations – both state and civil society. The aim is to set the stage for a characterization of governance approaches that we regard as analytically straightforward for capturing the full range of possible governance relationships that can exist among and across levels: multi-level governance in the standard sense of the term within the literature: a largely equal relationship in terms of engagement and participation among actors at all four levels; top down governance, in which there is a hierarchical relationship steered by the highest involved level and directed downwards; a multiple level governance, in which there is an equal relationship in terms of engagement and participation among only those levels involved; and a horizontal governance approach, in which engagement and participation among actors at the same level can be observed (Zelano et al. 2016a, b).

The analysis that follows maps the policy measures taken in the different policy domains for which CEE migration have implications (socio-economic, socio-cultural and legal-political), characterizing them in accordance with the typology presented above. In order to reconstruct urban governance approaches, we have first mapped the relevant stakeholders. This was done by each country team for the two selected urban regions per country. Following the identification of relevant actors, a reconstruction was made of (a) their practices and measures with regard to CEE migrants and (b) the rationale behind these practices and measures. This was achieved through interviews as well as both primary and secondary document analysis. As such, the methodological strategy has allowed us to capture both formal policy responses as found in texts and the governance approaches that can be witnessed in actual practice.

7.3 Austria: Mostly Multiple-Level Governance, but Also Horizontal[1]

The predominant area in terms of the Austrian case and specific areas focused on developing policy instruments for free movement management at the urban level is that of the labour market. While a variety of instruments are evident in this sphere, they are united by the fact that they by and large do not consist of measures consisting of multi-level governance type responses. In general, these responses can be characterized as instances of *multiple-level governance*, reflecting the degree to which there has been a strong presence of the national level in those cases where legislation has been central to the response, and also the degree to which national responses have been mirrored by related activity at the local level.

The 2011 Anti-Wage Dumping Law, introduced by the Federal Ministry of Labour, Social affairs and Consumer Protection (BMASK) represents a multiple-level approach response to the integration of CEE migrants. This legislation, stemmed from concerns over the wage gap between the Austrian labour market and that of new EU member countries. In 2015, the law was amended so that violations were dealt with as matters of administrative and not civil law, with the result being the emergence of new networks to manage and make sense of the law's requirements. Such networks took shape at the local level, for example in Vienna, where the Chamber of Labour serves as a source of information and a point of coordination for the various units in the city administration whose work with the law on a regular basis.

Multiple-level governance responses also tend to be characteristic for the variety of measures intended to deal with the phenomenon of CEE migrant de-qualification upon relocating to Austria and seeking opportunities on the labour market. Similar to the measures dealing with the prevention of wage-dumping, the efforts targeting

[1] Please note that the empirical data for this and the following country sections is based on the IMAGINATION projects country reports regarding Urban Governance.

migrant de-qualification see BMASK assuming a central role. One example of this are the four Contact Points for the Recognition and Assessment of Qualifications Obtained Abroad (AST), established in 2013. These contacts points serve as regional centres that offer guidance and counselling in a variety of languages, free of charge, for those seeking to have the foreign qualifications validated. Yet, what makes these regional contact points examples of a multiple-level governance response is not their location across various regions of Austria, but rather the actors who are charged with running the centres themselves. Rather than this being under the direct auspices of BMASK, these four contact points are managed by both NGOs and local administrative actors, resulting in an initiative that has seen state, civil society and local public actors collaborate to deliver services to CEE migrants requiring help with validation of foreign qualifications. A similar multiple-level governance response addressing CEE migrant de-qualification is the Network for the Recognition of Qualifications, established by the Austrian Integration Fund, which brings together social partners and professionals to discuss specific measures that could be introduced to improve the process of validating foreign qualifications, and also providing an information platform for cities and regions seeking relevant information about the validation process.

Taken jointly, these examples hammer home the prevalence of a clear pattern: in devising solutions to address the labour market challenges associated with free movement management, there exists primarily close working relationship between national and local level – initiatives developed at one level find mirrored counterparts at the others, and there is substantial interaction between the two levels in addressing how labour market challenges are to be resolved within urban areas.

By contrast, the other key area of free movement management in Austria – housing – is characterized exclusively by *horizontal governance*, taking place primarily at the local level. Yet, this difference from the area of labour market is not simply in terms of the mode of governance. Rather, the focus on housing at the local level in Austria is characterized by measures that are not policy-specific in nature, nor are they exclusively targeted at CEE migrants. For example, in the Austrian capital, the housing situation for migrants, especially those who might be characterized as economically vulnerable, is made challenging by the fact that social housing is only available to those who have been permanently resident in Vienna for two years and who are in possession of a registration certificate. Horizontal governance measures at the local level that seek to respond to this challenge more generally include the "Immigrant Fund" which can quickly provides low-threshold housing for migrants, assuming they possess the requisite security deposit, or the short-term housing measure KuWo, which provides the homeless ill with a place to recover following being discharged from the hospital. In both instances, the actors involved in these measures represent may of the key organizational players at the local level, including social partners, NGOs, and the city of Vienna itself. When it comes to measures that are EU-migrant specific, two in particular stand out: the Centre for Homeless EU Citizens (*Zweite Gruft*) and the night shelter for male EU citizens "VinziPort". While both represent horizontal-level responses to deal with the problem of housing for vulnerable EU migrants, the NGO Zweite Gruft has an even broader mandate, with activities not just cantered around housing, but also providing mediation for EU migrants who need assistance when engaging with various public authorities.

As such, the governance network that has taken shape in this other primary area of free movement management is circumscribed to actors at the local level. A rich illustration of programs and policy initiatives all serve to underscore that, while there is substantial policy activity, it does not involve engagement among actors from different levels. Housing is acted upon solely in local terms.

7.4 The Netherlands: Business as Usual: Local Level Horizontal and Multiple Level Governance Approaches

In the absence of any multilevel governance approaches in the Dutch case, what do we find? Primarily, free movement management has been met with horizontal and multiple level governance approaches. Housing issues, labour market considerations and question about civic registration were the three primary policy areas which triggered extensive governance responses by Dutch policymakers. Moreover, these were soon defined as 'CEE issues' in the sense that administrators and politicians regarded them as meriting special treatment compared to how housing, labour market and registration were normally dealt with. Governance actors have defined housing, labour market and registration as areas where CEE migration has created new challenges as parts of it tends to be temporary and circular. The approach taken by the officials was in many cases that of trying to minimize problems that Dutch citizens expressed about CEE immigrants. To some extent this particular angle was a result of the long established Dutch type of corporatism, which is built on active inclusion of all recognized and organized communities in society. As CEE migrants have not developed any strong communities the Dutch institutional logic contributed to excluding them.

Other issue areas never seem to have evolved into CEE issues as such but have rather been funnelled by the administrative-political actors into already existing general policies. Examples of these were health care and education.

While the overall governance responses in the two Dutch case regions have been remarkably similar, there are still substantial variations inside each region. To some extent these differences have had to do with differences regarding different social consequences in different geographical areas.

A general observation is the fact that several policies and approaches began as municipality projects. In most instances, issues regarding CEE migration became evident at the local level, in the sense that immigrants literally encountered housing and employment problems in a certain city or village rather than in a government Ministry. Local level officials simply had to deal with issues arising at their doorstep. Later, local officials developed horizontal approaches by involving various local stakeholders – such as civil society, other Dutch municipalities and cities in neighbouring countries. In some cases regional and national level officials have stepped in as well.

A key aspect is whether policymakers have been able to fit CEE issues into existing local, regional or national level governance structures. Housing is normally dealt with at the local municipal level. Thus, a range of city policies ensued including a gradual development of horizontal cooperation between cities and other local level actors. However, since the Dutch Ministry of Internal Affairs and Social Affairs is responsible for overseeing the housing, labour market and registration areas some policies were developed at the national level as well. As a consequence, the governance responses have had elements of both local horizontal and multiple level features.

Housing remains an exceptionally pressing issue. Both the selected Dutch regions have been very active to combat various forms of housing problems such as abusive and non-compliant landlords. One particular concern has been to prevent two kinds of overcrowding: in flats and in neighbourhoods. A flurry of city initiatives have followed and in some cases elements of the local solutions have been picked up nationally and made into national law. However, these processes have rarely developed into mutually reciprocal systems of cooperation but there are exceptions, e.g. the 'Approach to attack slum landlords' (an agreement between municipalities and the Ministry of Internal Affairs). Thus, the overall governance approach in this regard has been local level horizontal with some elements of multiple level governance.

Dutch governance responses regarding labour market aspects have had a strong horizontal governance character. Rotterdam and the Hague have developed ties with each other and with other local level institutions such as by signing special agreements ('Covenants') to control fraud and mala fide employment arrangements.

To a lesser extent, an element of multiple level governance exists as well. Indeed, municipalities have collaborated to put labour migration on the national level agenda. The national government has increasingly been involved in issuing work permits and has introduced new legislation aimed at combatting wage dumping and at improving working conditions. Moreover, the national government has tried to coordinate actions against social dumping and other negative labour market aspects. While government ministers have been quite active, their efforts have mostly resulted in an element of coordinated agenda setting actions in a number of EU countries. Open letters have been written, op-ed articles have been published and conferences have been organized but little in terms of horizontal national level policies as such has been developed.

The general pattern of the Dutch case then, is that while local level responses may dominate, there are also clear instances of multiple-level strategies intended to assist in the management of free movement challenges. In the areas considered most salient for devising governance responses, networks and actions that are multi-level in nature are, by and large, lacking.

7.5 The Case of Turkey: Top Down

The governance approach in Turkey regarding CEE migration can best be summarized as top down. However, while Turkey is a unified state with a strongly state centred structure a multitude of laws and legislations contribute to inconsistent policies. Immigration policies are covered by jurisdictionally complex and fragmented legal orders. Due to this non established character, central authorities begin to develop their own policies, which sometimes clash with those of other central authorities. The result is an ad hoc, vague governance approach within an overall top down setting. Primarily immigration policies have been focusing on labour market and registration issues, while social security, health care access and housing issues have been more peripheral.

Within the overarching format, some differences exist between Edirne and Istanbul. Primarily these differences are down to differences regarding two aspects: the character of the migrants and the situation of the cities in a wider Turkish context. The bulk of Edirne's migrants are in fact well established CEE migrants (most of Turkish ethnic descent) of high socio-economic status. Istanbul on the other hand has become a major centre for Syrian refugees. Moreover, migration policies regarding Edirne are influenced by special border security considerations. As a consequence few specific CEE migrant policies have been developed in Edirne. Giant Istanbul attracts many immigrants. The various labour market regulations developed for immigrants do not differ between different migrant types. As with most policies policy coordination between different parts of the central authority structure has proved to be difficult although some data indicate efforts to strengthen and streamline central authority.

Some policy domains are absent or almost absent. For instance, very few policies have been developed regarding housing apart from some shelter provision in Edirne and some facilities regarding children in Istanbul. This absence reflects a traditional attention on labour market and registration aspects in relation to immigration. However, there appears to be a growing awareness among policymakers and other stakeholders that education, social security, healthcare and integration need more attention. To some extent the policy vacuum may disappear as a result of the heavy increase in Syrian migration. Since most of the existing policies so far have not differed between immigrant groups any development may well then affect CEE migrants as well.

Future developments will probably rely on which party or coalition of parties will hold the national majority. So far, the governance of migration has been clearly dependent on politics. The governance approaches have not been solidly institutionalised and have been subject to frequent changes. Moreover, although registration has been a primary domain on which policies have been developed this has not meant that a well-coordinated and systematic system has emerged. A bewildering array of rules, legislations and concept exist. Moreover, due to political and other tensions among policymakers even basic concepts such as 'asylum seeker', 'refugee' and 'migrant' have not become unequivocally defined even inside the top state level.

As such, given the nature of Turkish political institutions, it is perhaps the easiest case in which governance patters can be identified. Even the most cursory review of policies and networks suggests that there is an exceptionally close correspondence between, on the one hand, the institutional logic of the Turkish political system and the resulting top-down manner in which all aspects of managing migrant integration are constructed.

7.6 Sweden: Horizontal and Top-Down Predominate

Comparing the governance responses across the urban regions in Gothenburg and Stockholm, the group of destitute, often unregistered CEE citizens and beggars were at the centre of debates and governance responses. Homelessness of CEE citizens, most of them beggars from Bulgaria and Rumania, was one of the critical issues that required local governance responses. An institutional obstacle encountered by homeless EU citizens is their exclusion from the 'shelter guarantee' normally offered by Swedish municipalities. Since EU citizens are excluded from the shelter guarantee a *local horizontal governance* approach emerged to deal with the issue. The help and support for homeless EU/CEE citizens is offered through churches and charities, through formalized partnership with municipalities. The development of tighter and more frequent relations between the municipal level and the voluntary sector is a sign of new governance patterns set in motion by the novel social implications. Recent developments have also seen central authorities evicting homeless people who have set up temporary tent camps on private property. When faced with an increasing number of cases concerning illegal settlements, the Swedish Enforcement Agency ordered the regional units to contribute to a central, statistical record and initiated a project to harmonize local practices. Thus, while the governance approach regarding homeless CEE citizens is more or less local and horizontal there are some elements of *top down* activities as well.

Issues related to social security/help and registration of CEE EU citizens were also highly relevant for particular governance responses. These are two policy areas characterised by inconsistent practices, and bureaucratic uncertainty. Relevant documents and interviews show that Swedish municipalities seem to be at a loss about how to treat EU citizens who are living in Sweden and who are in need of social support. The municipal administrations find it difficult to decide whether an EU individual should be granted right of residence, which is in turn related to whether the individual can be granted social support on the same terms as Swedish citizens. A recurring theme has thus been for municipalities to call for clearer national guidelines regarding administrative procedure. In this area, we can observe development towards *multiple governance approach*. In an attempt to meet the demands of confused and uncoordinated local authorities, the Swedish Association of Local Authorities and Regions (SALAR) put together a handbook, including among other things, guidelines on how to assess applications for economic assistance by EU citizens. The National Board of Health and Welfare has also published a handbook, about how the national and the EU rules are to be interpreted by municipalities. In January 2015 the government appointed a national coordinator to improve the situation for the many EU migrants who are begging on the streets in Sweden. The role of the national coordinator is to work closely with, and gather information from, different national and international voluntary organisations and municipalities in order to improve the way they work together.

Similarly to the issue of social support, the registration procedure of EU citizens was subject to inconsistencies. In Sweden, EU citizens on short term contracts (or self-employed) can apply for a so-called Co-ordination Number (*Samordningsnummer*). In 2010 the Swedish Unemployment Insurance Board (a Government audit agency) highlighted inadequacies concerning the Jobseeking Agencies' EU citizen Co-ordination Number procedures. These citizens were unable to receive jobseeker-employer matching support from the Jobseeking Agencies on equal terms with Swedish citizens. However, it was not until spring 2013, when the issue was brought to the agenda by Swedish media that Swedish Jobseeking agencies promised to act in order to deal with the irregularities. To deal with this specific problem a *national horizontal governance* approach was established. The Swedish Tax Agency cooperates with other major national public agencies, e.g. the Employment Agency, and the Social Insurance Agency. Twice a year, and when needed, the Tax Agency and the Migration Board organise coordinating meetings, and keep in touch on a regular basis between the meetings. The Tax Agency also meets the National Board of Trade, the Social Insurance Agency, the Employment Agency and the Swedish Council for Higher Education about twice a year.

The blurred line between formal and informal employment create challenges in the receiving urban regions with informal work showing consequences such as wage related discrimination, exploitation, inferior working conditions and marginalisation. Here we can observe a governance mixture with some *top down* features and an element of *national horizontal governance* involving trade union and business sector cooperation. An issue addressed outside the reach of local public administrations, is the issue of posted workers from the CEE. Employers and trade unions disagree about the scope, and the implications posting brings to the Swedish labour market. Both have contact with public authorities at the national level. The four committees commissioned by the government to deal with various aspects of the posting of workers, are also an example of a top down approach. The presence of CEE workers has changed the context in which trade unions operate. They call for tighter regulations, better control and a revision of Lex Laval. Stockholm is also home to "the union centre for undocumented workers" a meeting point where undocumented migrant workers can get information and help they are in a conflict with employers. The centre is managed on a voluntary basis by the three major trade union confederations: Swedish Confederation of Trade Unions (LO), The Swedish Confederation of Professional Employees (TCO) and Swedish Confederation of Professional Associations (SACO). Similar to their Stockholm equivalent, the Building Workers Union in Gothenburg has adjusted to the new context: they now have a Polish speaking ombudsman, and occasionally offer evening courses in trade union history in Polish, and have added courses to their education program specifically aiming to reduce xenophobic attitudes and racism among members. Another example is how the local branch have facilitated enrolment for non-residents, by e.g. accepting cash payments.

On balance then, Sweden proves to be yet another case where multi-level governance is largely lacking when it comes to the primary issues areas in which actors seek to manage the effects of free movement. No single response dominates, as in the other EU-member state cases, and the policies show that various forms of horizontal governance are central to the management efforts. Yet, such a characterization needs to be tempered by an awareness of those responses that suggest both multiple-level and top down forms of governance.

7.7 Multilevel Governance

It is abundantly clear that CEE free movement is a policy field with multilevel political system repercussions. The effective implementation of the EU free movement law in the EU Member States and exercising EU free movement rights have not been straightforward. The complexity of a free movement challenge has meant that many policy processes did not involve effective multilevel coordination which would indicate a relationship or participation of all three or four levels of government (European, national, regional and local) in the development of policies, laws or legislation on CEE migration. Instead, traditional models of top-down coordination and localist models have been the most common governance response.

There are however some specific issues that have been handled by applying multi-level governance approach. One such issue is the governance of human trafficking prevention in Sweden and Austria where EU citizens recruited for prostitution come primarily from the CEE countries. There is formal, institutionalised interaction, horizontally and vertically, within an identified, specific policy area. The cooperation ranges from the international organ Interpol, to the operating units in the urban regions, via Europol, police authorities in CEE member states, the National Support Against Prostitution and Human Trafficking, and the regional coordinators. There is a clear regulatory setting and policies are jointly formulated. Another example is the multi-level governance approach to deal with Roma CEE free movers. In Sweden the Network for Roma EU citizens was established. The network connects stakeholders from all over Sweden, public and private as well as nongovernmental, and is well established in both the CEE region and the EU institutions. Based on the EU Framework for National Roma Integration Strategies up to 2020, the Federal Chancellery has adopted an Austrian version in order to ensure Roma inclusion in various domains. From 2012 until 2015, a total of 13 network meetings have taken place including various actors from national and local governments to NGOs and Roma organisations (ATAT-2-3). These meetings aim to encourage an institutionalised dialogue in order to establish Roma specific objectives on the administrative level and to enhance cooperation.

The fact that the free movement is a policy field where the competences are shared in the multilevel setting showed more in the concrete policy processes than in the established governance approaches. The complexity of the free movement implies that the policy authority is located at different levels, and leaving open the possibility of unclear chains of command and a lack of audit leading to the situation where actors expect other actors to take the lead. For example, in the Swedish case the local policy makers required national (or EU) directives in order to handle issues such as registration, begging and homelessness. In the Dutch case, the Minister of Social Affairs and Employment (Asscher) published an opinion article entitled: 'Code Orange for free labour mobility within the EU' to raise European awareness on this topic. He put priority on bilateral collaboration with Poland, Romania, Bulgaria and Croatia (and also on EU lobbying), raising issues like irregular labour contracts and mala fide temporary labour agencies, the adequate provision of information to and equal treatment of border workers. In Sweden, government representatives initiated collaboration between Romanian and Bulgarian politicians, civil servants and civil society representatives in order to discuss the challenges related to Roma beggars in Sweden. The focus was to ensure that these persons would have other solutions than to come to Sweden to beg. Beside horizontal engagement with other member states, the lobbying related to the free movement of CEE citizens was also directed towards the EU itself. For example, in April 2013, four Ministers – representing Austria, Germany, the Netherlands and the United Kingdom – wrote a joint letter to the European Commission. In that letter they asked for attention to the need for EU citizens to undergo civic integration, and to consider tightening free movers' rights to social security and to fight fraud and systematic abuse in connection with the freedom of movement more effectively.

7.8 Conclusions

In spite of a multilevel setting, not much has emerged in terms of multilevel governance approaches. The EU level is more or less absent. Curry suggests in his contribution to this volume that it can be seen as troubling that little awareness exists among actors involved in free movement management as to why genuine multilevel governance could accomplish, were it to be implemented. Indeed, not just from a policy standpoint, but also from a scholarly perspective, it would be illuminating to hear from those with formal competencies in this issue why the normative preference for multi-level governance represents an actual virtue. Yet, before we can ask – either normatively or theoretically – "why multi-level governance", we need to hammer home that, in this instance, there is essentially *no* multi-level governance, and then lay the groundwork for understanding why this is this case. Instead, what stands out is that many of the issues connected with CEE migration appear at the local level and are dealt with at the local level. Although local level municipalities and cities may sometimes seek for financial or legal support from the national level a more immediate governance response has been to develop horizontal ties and networks at the local level. As such, the local level responses in this chapter should not be interpreted as representing a bottom-up model of governance. While local horizontal governance networks have taken the lead in structuring governance responses to free movement management, the governance networks have chiefly been that – horizontal. While coordinated responses are indeed also characteristic of the responses in in several of our cases – most notably in the form of multiple-level governance, these cannot be characterized as instances wherein the "bottom" level was decisive. As Curry notes in Chap. 8 of this book, the relationship between local and national levels can best be defined as complex. Hands on solutions involving local actors are rife. However, a distinct feature of the comparison between different cases is that different traditions about constitutional logics set their marks on CEE governance responses as well. Among the selected cases, Turkey is the odd one out in the sense that Turkey is not an EU member and does not apply any regulation about free movement. In Turkey CEE migration governance does not seem to differ much from what is to be expected given normal Turkish top down procedures. Austrian officials resort to regular Austrian corporatism involving tripartite arrangement whereas Sweden and the Netherlands are mixed cases.

CEE migration concerns a number of policy domains but primarily issues that have to do with basic needs dominate: housing, employment, social security. These can be found in all our cases but the governance responses differ to some extent. Inside each domain a number of policy areas dwell and policymakers sometimes differ regarding on which policy areas they have put their attention. While housing is a concern everywhere, Swedish governance actors have been more focused on homelessness than on other housing concerns. The opposite focus can be found among Dutch policymakers. While policies for shelters exist the main concern has been about abusive landlords and about neighbourhood disturbances and to prevent figures of immigrants to exceed certain levels on particular housing estates. Similar differences exist regarding labour market policies. Austrian authorities have put a lot of emphasis on how to avoid nostrification and to help migrants gain necessary educational diplomas. This has not been a major concern in neither the Netherlands nor in Sweden. At this juncture, we will not speculate on why these governance approach differences occur, as within the scope of this project, there is not sufficient data to reach conclusive statements as to causality. This however, does not preclude us from engaging in the time-honoured pastime of academics: informed speculation with the intent of suggesting possible causal relationships that can be more closely examined with supplemental data in the future. It is clear that depending on the policy area, different institutional logics apply in different countries (and sometimes in different regions within the same country), and different historical traits regarding the relationship between government and migration have also developed. Moreover, the character of the CEE migration flows may differ. For instance, the Netherlands have a huge agricultural sector, which attracts large numbers of seasonal workers. Vienna in Austria attracts large number of commuters from neighbouring countries with which there are historical ties as well. This suggests to us that a fruitful strategy for grappling with issues of causality would be one that continues to be multi-disciplinary in nature. Indeed, as historical institutionalists, we argue for – if not the primacy of institutional relationships in shaping governance outcomes – then at least that they will rank among the most important factors. However, the cases examined here suggest that the historical experience of the local and national communities with migration also have much to tell us, and we would consider it beneficial for subsequent analysis to factor in the manner in which collective memories regarding migration are articulated in manners that are often path dependent – at both the organizational level within the public sector, but also outside of the public sector, most notable from the media.

Finally, our emphasis on variation in flows and types of CEE migrants suggests that not only does continued work need to be done on mapping flows of CEE migrants – and especially ensuring comparable data – but that scholars with an interest in free movement management consider how flows and types are made salient in various societal discourses, and how such discourses are then invoked when policy and administrative measures are adopted. Such analyses might also consider the way in which CEE migrants were problematized during the debates over the implementation of transitional arrangements in the early 2000s. As Sweden is the only one of the three not to have made use of transitional arrangements, and as the Swedish responses do not vary substantially from those of Austria or the Netherlands, there is little to suggest that the presence of transitional arrangements exercised causal influence on subsequent governance responses. Yet, this does not exclude the possibility that debates over transitional arrangements left their mark on the way in which governance actors have continued to formulate the challenges associated with free movement management and the related policy, programmatic and administrative tools that have been adopted.

The question remains as to whether an institutional effect is that CEE migration is treated much as any form of migration or as a separate 'EU mobility' case. Obviously, the fact that CEE migrants are EU citizens affects any governance response. Still, a number of Austrian governance responses do not seem to separate between CEE migrants and other migrants, this is particularly evident regarding labour market policies. Swedish officials on the other hand have a wide range of well-established policies that apply to third country nationals while the governance of CEE migrants often seems to fall between two stools.

For decision makers, we conclude with following observation: If those with broad discretion over free movement management – whether at the EU level or among the member states – wish to see the EU involved more via multi-level governance approaches or otherwise, a number of institutional changes will be necessary to consider. One route to go about this would be to create strong policy tools at the EU level concerning housing, labour market and social security. When applied, these tools would create incentives for governance approaches that would involve the EU level; thus multi-level governance responses might develop.

Along an alternative route, some kind of powerful EU legislation would have to emerge. This legislation would have to set clear and unequivocal steering standards, including strong audit institutions, regarding how the member states treat CEE migrants, or indeed EU migrants generally.

Both alternative routes would entail a stronger supranational approach.

References

Bowen, J. (2007). A view from France on the internal complexity of national models. *Journal of Ethnic and Migration Studies, 33*(6), 1003–1016.

Curry, D. (2015). *Network approaches to multi-level governance structures, relations and understanding power between levels*. London: Palgrave.

Duyvendak, J. W., & Scholten, P. (2012). Deconstructing the Dutch multicultural model: A frame perspective on Dutch immigrant integration policymaking. *Comparative European Politics, 10*(3), 266–282.

Guy Peters, B., & Pierre, J. (2004). Multi-level governance and democracy: A Faustian bargain? In I. Bache & M. Flinders (Eds.), *Multi-level governance*. Oxford: Oxford University Press.

Harlow, C., & Rawlings, R. (2007). Promoting accountability in multilevel governance: A network approach. *European Law Journal, 13*(4), 542–562.

Joppke, C. (2007). Beyond national models: Civic integration policies for immigrants in Western Europe. *West European Politics, 30*(1), 1–22.

Ostaijen, M. Scholten, P. Engbersen, G. (2016). *Mapping the multilevel governance context*. IMAGINATION Country report, The Netherlands.

Schmitter, P., & Kim, S. (2005). The experience of European integration and the potential for Northeast Asian integration. *East-West Center Working Papers, 10*, 1–23.

Scholten, P. (2012). Beyond national models of integration? Rethinking interconnectedness and fragmentation in Dutch and French migrant integration policies. In Fenger & Bekkers (Eds.), *Beyond fragmentation and interconnectivity: Public governance and the search for public connectivity*. Amsterdam: IOS Press.

Stephenson, P. (2013). Twenty years of multi-level governance: 'Where does it come from? What is it? Where is it going?'. *Journal of European Public Policy, 20*(6), 817–837.

Torfing, J., Peters, B. G., Pierre, J., & Sørensen, E. (2012). *Interactive governance: Advancing the paradigm*. Oxford: Oxford University Press.

Zelano, K, Bucken- Knapp, G., Hinnfors, J., Spehar A. (2016a). *Urban governance of CEE mobility in European urban regions*. WP3 comparative report.

Zelano, K. Bucken-Knapp, G. Hinnfors, J., Spehar, A. (2016b). *Urban governance of CEE mobility in Gothenburg and Stockholm*. Country report Sweden.

Chapter 8
Intra-European Movement: Multi-Level or Mismatched Governance?

Dion Curry

8.1 Introduction

The case of intra-European movement raises significant debate about multi-level governance (MLG). In analytical terms, it asks how *multi-level* governance of intra-European movement actually is, what actors are involved and how? In normative terms, it considers whether intra-European movement can be seen as 'successful' multi-level governance. Intra-European movement is an area that faces both *issue complexity* and *institutional complexity* (Stephenson 2013, pp. 817) and as such, the governance arrangements are often correspondingly complex. This chapter will attempt to locate the case of intra-European movement within the broader literature on multi-level governance and try to draw out lessons for understanding MLG as a practical, analytical and normative concept. This is relevant to both the understanding of intra-European movement and the understanding of MLG. On the one hand, additional cases help to support or refute the robustness of our conceptualisation of multi-level governance; on the other hand, MLG as a concept can help us to understand the entanglement of a complex issue that cuts across political and policy bounds. The chapter will first develop a framework of multi-level governance that can be applied to intra-European movement. Then, the structural, relational and policy factors that affect MLG will be explored in the context of this specific case. The final section will try to craft some answers about what intra-European movement policy can tell us about multi-level governance, and vice versa.

D. Curry (✉)
Swansea University, Swansea, UK
e-mail: d.s.d.curry@swansea.ac.uk

P. Scholten, M. van Ostaijen (eds.), *Between Mobility and Migration*, IMISCOE Research Series, https://doi.org/10.1007/978-3-319-77991-1_8

8.2 MLG as a Concept

As discussed in the introductory chapter, intra-European movement faces difficulties in conceptualising the ideas of both mobility and migration. However, this difficulty also extends to the concept of governance between and within political levels. Multi-level governance was first coined by Gary Marks as a way of explaining structural funding processes in the European Union (Marks 1993). Originally, MLG aimed to provide an alternative and somewhat middle-ground theory to European integration that avoided both the state-centric nature of intergovernmentalism and the federalism (or federalism light) espoused by supranationalism and neofunctionalism. MLG was conceived as a means of explaining how actors at different political levels work together to create and implement policies in areas with less clear-cut jurisdictional bounds than traditional policy. Two different types of MLG were identified. *Type I* MLG systems resemble federal-type structures, with non-intersecting, general purpose jurisdictions, clear spheres of authority and well-defined levels. In contrast, Type II MLG, a somewhat 'newer' governance form, is distinguished by overlapping, policy-focussed jurisdictions operating at shifting numbers of levels that are more flexible and inevitably messier than traditional federal-type multi-level structures.

While MLG was initially used as a way of analysing EU-level processes, it has since broadened out to include regional (e.g. Bache and Andreou 2011) and state-level analyses both within and outside the EU (e.g. Horak and Young 2012) as well as bottom-up examinations of the roles of local and urban governments (Grisel and van de Waart 2011; Zapata-Barrero et al. 2017; Zerbinati 2012). This includes expansion into functional uses, where the concept was applied in new policy areas or country studies (Stephenson 2013, p. 822) and even development of the concept as a way of identifying a normative 'good' form of governance (European Commission 2001; Committee of the Regions 2009). This creates the danger of conceptual stretching (Sartori 1970) or the creation of a 'container concept' that tries to be everything to everyone (Van Geertsom 2011, p. 169), but new research attempts to 'travel' the concept without reducing its precision or clarity. This has resulted in competing visions of how to study and explain multi-level governance (see, among others, Bache and Flinders 2004; Conzelmann and Smith 2008; Curry 2015; Hooghe and Marks 2003; Jordan 2001; Kohler-Koch and Larat 2009; Littoz-Monnet 2010; Piattoni 2010; Scharpf 1997). These refinements of the concept also raise new issues regarding MLG and its practical effects, including questions of scope (can MLG be applied outside of Europe, or to international relations?), academic rigour (is MLG a theory or just an organising framework?) and legitimacy and accountability (who is ultimately responsible when multiple elected and unelected actors at different levels are involved in crafting and delivering policy?).

The broadening and deepening of the concept in turn led to new attempts to categorise different modes of governance (see, for example, Grisel and van de Waart 2011; Howlett et al. 2009; Curry 2015; March and Olsen 1996; Offe 2006; Scharpf 1991; Treib et al. 2007; Weaver and Rockman 1993). These all offer their own strengths and weaknesses, trying to strike a balance between comprehensiveness and elegance, general applicability and specific nuance. This chapter takes a slightly different approach and focuses on the factors that go into assessing the nature of multi-level governance. When governance plays out at multiple levels, attempts at coordination can face several difficulties that manifest themselves in structural, relational and policy ways. Complex institutional structures can lead to fragmentary policy-making. Relationally, hierarchy may make coordination difficult as actors compete for power. Finally, different actors may have competing, conflicting or shifting policy interests and goals (Taşan-Kok and Vranken 2011, pp. 16–17). These structural, relational and policy processes map onto Hooghe and Marks' typology of MLG, but provide a more granular way of analysing the factors influencing MLG.

The three categories of processes can be mutually reinforcing, contradictory or separate. Institutional structures and actor relations will have an impact on what policy options are open. The realities of policy-making and specific policy areas will, in turn, affect how actors work together and use institutional structures to develop policy. If these three factors are mutually reinforcing, structures that are supportive of MLG-type processes will develop. This will give actors more room to manoeuvre in shaping policy outcomes in a multi-level manner, actors may utilise structures in a way that supports multi-level solutions, and/or policies may lend themselves to solutions that make use of structures and relations in a multi-level way. If these processes are not mutually reinforcing, they can result in governance mismatch, which can take two forms. When these processes operate in contradictory fashion, *disjointed* governance can result, where actors, institutions and policies operate at cross purposes (Curry 2015). When these processes operate separately, you find cases of *decoupled* governance, where there is little coordination between actors, institutions and processes (Scholten 2013). Structures, relations and policy can be further broken down into 6 sub-categories (see Table 8.1).

It is important to remember that these factors are not binary and operate on a spectrum. In addition, they do not operate discretely, and often complement or amplify each other. Structural/institutional factors that affect the nature of multi-level governance can be grouped into two categories. First, there may be a rigid or flexible institutional structure in which actors operate. Rigid structures may be binding on the actors involved, which is often, but not always, tied to the threat (or not) of sanctions for inaction (or negative action). Conversely, these structures may take a flexible, non-binding, 'soft law' form that is more responsive to contextual and policy-specific factors. Second, the jurisdictions that make up the 'multi-levelness' of the policy area may be general purpose (normally geographical or cultural entities that exist across policy areas) or specific to that particular policy, an increasingly common configuration in EU settings. These two broad categories combine to create the institutional milieu in which governance exists, a spectrum where there can be clear lines of authority (in rigidly structure, general purpose jurisdictions), or one with indistinct lines of authority (flexible, policy specific approaches), and any variation in between.

Relational factors are ones that affect how actors – whether governmental, quasi-governmental or non-governmental - interact with each other both within and between levels. Again, there are two broad categories of relational factors. First,

Table 8.1 Multi-Level Governance Processes in Intra-European movement

Type I multi-level governance		**Structural factors**		Type II multi-level governance
	Rigid institutional structure	↔	Flexible institutional structure	
	Multi-purpose jurisdictions	↔	Policy-specific jurisdictions	
		Relational factors		
	Hierarchical relations	↔	Heterarchical relations	
	Formalised relations	↔	Informal relations	
		Policy factors		
	Discrete policy responses	↔	Holistic policy responses	
	Uniform policy issue	↔	Complex policy issue	

relations may either be hierarchical with a clear chain of command, or be more heterarchical networks in which actors work more collaboratively. In areas where higher governmental levels have binding power, processes will be more likely to operate in a hierarchical manner, whereas heterarchical processes can originate where strong urban/local levels exist, or where urban/local levels assert themselves in areas left undeveloped by higher levels. In hierarchical, top down relationships, policy decisions are downloaded by decision makers at higher levels of government to be implemented by lower levels of government. Heterarchical relations allow for more two-way permeation of policy ideas, where processes may originate at lower levels and permeate upwards. Somewhere in between the two, lower levels of government may 'upload' information to decision-makers at higher levels of government (Güntner 2011). While not a truly heterarchical process, as decision-making is not shared between all actors, uploading does allow for more input from actors at lower levels. Second, these relations may be highly formalised and standardised or may take a more fluid, informal or ad hoc approach. This stability or fluidity can operate in terms of context, policy response, actors involved or other factors. The spectrum of relations can vary from a highly inclusive one marked by heterarchy and fluid, informal policy responses, to an exclusive one marked by hierarchy and stable, formal relations between actors.

Finally, policy factors affecting MLG can be grouped into two categories. First, policy responses may be discrete and compartmentalised, where issues are treated separately with clear lines of demarcation. Conversely, a holistic approach treats each issue as part of a larger whole covering a broader policy area. Coordination is required for both approaches, but for different reasons. Discrete policy responses require coordination in order to clarify and delegate roles and responsibilities within specific issues, whereas holistic responses require coordination to ensure harmonisation across disparate issues. A lack of coordination can develop either between levels (for instance, with different governmental levels having different policies on an issue), within levels (where, for example, governmental and non-governmental actors may have different roles, policy goals and approaches) or over time. The level of coordination may also be tied to whether competence over that policy issue is exclusive or shared, and whether those creating the policy are the same as those implementing the policy. Finally, uncoordinated responses may develop when the policy issue is contested, either through new or unclear jurisdictional bounds or through attempts by actors to either take over or relinquish ownership and control of the policy. Second, the policy itself may be complex and cross-cutting or uniform, discrete and straightforward. Complex policies are ones that may deal with cross-cutting policy problems, have incomplete, contradictory or changing solutions, or have many possible options with no clear-cut 'best'. Policy approaches are then found on a spectrum from chaotic (uncoordinated, contested, complex and non-state controlled), to controlled (coordinated, uncontested, straightforward, state-controlled policy).

To relate this back to Hooghe and Marks' initial typology, governance that mainly hews to the left side of Table 8.1 can be seen as mutually reinforcing in a way indicative of Type I MLG, whereas governance that fits on the right side is mutually reinforcing in a way closer to Type II MLG. Governance responses may in turn target structural, relational or policy factors. This can result in various governance outcomes depending on how complete the change is in the three identified factors. There is little question that intra-European movement policy operates (and has operated for some time) at multiple levels, but this can still take several different forms. For example, shifts in the locus of power, such as to urban levels, may not actually improve the policy's 'multi-levelness' in a governance sense. In other words, EU-level principles of free movement may not necessarily result in true *multi-level governance* and instead be an incomplete solution where a new EU-level policy approach is bolted onto an existing state- or urban/local-level governance solution. If there is no change in structural, relational or policy factors, the status quo will obviously ensue. If there is a change in only some of the factors, it may result in governance mismatch – either decoupled governance, where the levels operate more or less independently, or disjointed governance, where different levels may operate at cross purposes. A true *multi-level governance* response therefore must encompass complementary, mutually supporting shifts in all three factors. This results in three possibilities for the EU and member states' policy responses to intra-European movement:

P1: Structural, relational and policy factors are clearly demarcated and distinct across and within levels, indicating no multi-level governance.

P2: Structural, relational and policy factors are misaligned across and within levels, thus indicating there is *governance mismatch*, which may take two forms. Contradictory governance responses on the three spectrums indicate *disjointed governance*, while independent, non-reinforcing responses indicate *decoupled governance*.

P3: Structural, relational and policy factors are interdependent, mutually reinforcing and complementary across and within levels, resulting in *multi-level governance*.

The chapter now explores these governance possibilities more thoroughly by turning to an examination of the multi-level governance processes at play in intra-European movement, drawing on the cases examined in this book. In addition, the case of Turkey is used as a comparison and counterpoint to look at how third-country migration is treated within EU countries, its relation to intra-European movement and its effects on governance.

8.3 Structural Processes

8.3.1 Rigid Versus Flexible Institutional Structures

As a policy issue, intra-European movement is subject to EU-level directives, with member states required to abide by the EU's free movement rules. In addition, once clear jurisdiction over migration is established within member states, these arrangements remain relatively stable over time (see the chapter by Zelano). However, intra-European movement is inextricably linked to issues of migrant integration. This issue is largely non-binding and flexible in nature and often takes place at the urban/local level, which plays a significant role in many of the case countries, at times even without significant member-state support. Overall, there was mainly evidence of a flexible and fluid structural approach to dealing with migrant issues, in a way that corresponds to Hooghe and Marks' Type II MLG. This is largely due to the nature of intra-European movement and the temporary nature of much of the movement. The EU's free movement requirement, coupled with the Schengen agreement, only seems to have an effect on rigidity in terms of the legally binding macro-policy considerations of migration. The day-to-day policy approaches were more left up to the member states, who in turn often involved or delegated certain responsibilities to urban/local and regional levels, which created a more flexible approach.

An example of this flexibility is the agreements between Polish and Dutch governmental and non-governmental bodies to facilitate movement of labour between the two countries and reasonable treatment of these migrants. Central governmental bodies such as the Polish National Labour Inspectorate and the Dutch Arbeidsinspectie work together on employment regulation and worker complaints with NGOs such as FairWork, who aim to protect migrant workers' rights (see Kindler's chapter). However, this institutional flexibility has not necessarily increased responsiveness, as many of the case countries still struggle in providing services to short-term migrants. In addition, flexible structures can have a deleterious effect on coordination. This flexibility was also evident external to the EU in Turkey, where migration as a policy concern is less institutionalised, with a comprehensive *Law of Foreigners and*

International Protection only coming into force in 2015 (see Chap. 11 in this book by Korci Korfali and Acar). Indeed, the need to institutionalise governance processes to improve coordination is noted elsewhere in this book (see Zelano et al.).

8.3.2 Multi-Purpose Versus Policy-Specific Jurisdictions

The issue of jurisdiction is a complicated one for European movement. While traditional governmental levels are clearly evident in establishing the bounds of the policy, the ways in which these levels operate are more specific to the policy area alone, with fluidity and policy specificity in how migrant integration is addressed. Requirements for free movement of labour are binding on EU member states and follow traditional, general purpose jurisdictional lines emanating down from the EU to member states. However, those member states then take different approaches to developing more policy-specific structures to meet the needs of migrants. Therefore, policy specificity largely depends on what aspect of the policy one is considering. While intra-European movement follows more multi-purpose jurisdictional lines, migrant *integration* is largely carried out in a more policy-specific jurisdictional capacity, often at the urban/local level.

The interplay between intra-European movement requirements and subsequent questions of integration has created some governance tensions between the inherently multi-level nature of international migration and the nation state-specific issues of labour markets. These difficulties are different for receiving countries that face an overabundance of labour supply and sending countries that may face a brain drain and a decline in the labour force. The problem of sending countries is particularly evident in Poland, where a large proportion of the population has emigrated from Poland to other EU countries. Poland then requires specific responses to deal with job shortages in regions hard hit by this emigration. This involved, ironically, opening up in-migration from Eastern Partnership countries such as Ukraine (see the chapter by Kindler). While general intra-European movement requirements are undertaken at an EU level, the high variability in member state responses to these requirements marks this case as one that has many policy-specific jurisdictional aspects. It is an area where member states have ceded power over their (intra-European) migration policies to the higher EU governmental level, but its close connection to migrant integration issues, which mostly takes place at the urban/local level, gives this high policy specificity.

8.4 Relational Processes

8.4.1 Hierarchical Versus Heterarchical Relations

Both hierarchical and heterarchical processes are evident in the case of intra-European movement. The EU must contend with a complex and contingent vertical structure of governance in all policy areas. This may take the form of (1) administrative regionalisation where regions are subordinate to the central government, such as in Greece and Portugal; (2) regionalisation through existing urban/local authorities, such as in the Netherlands and Ireland; (3) regional decentralisation in countries such as the United Kingdom, Sweden and the Czech Republic; (4) regional autonomy in Spain and Italy; or (5) federal cases such as Austria, Germany and Belgium (ESPON 2005, p. 296). However, these categories are contested and may change over time (ESPON 2005, p. 285; Tosics 2011a, p. 28). In addition to different national-regional governance structures, nation states may also deal with local governments and urban conurbations in different ways. This can be affected by the rate of growth of urban areas, structural differences between countries and whether countries have explicit urban policies or not (Tosics 2011b, pp. 36–39).

Given the wide variety of both national-regional and national-urban/local (or regional-urban/local) structures in place, any study of vertical governance structures must take into account (1) how many intermediary levels exist; (2) how strong these levels are; and (3) to what extent the levels are integrated (Tosics 2011a, p. 27). The case of intra-European movement displays both numerous and strong levels involved in the policy, with EU directives providing a clear hierarchical structure in which both urban/local governments and member states must operate according to those directives. Whereas migration displays clear hierarchy, with the EU controlling the process, integration, housing and often social policy are treated more heterarchically, involving multiple actors with little to no hierarchical control from higher governmental levels. Within nation states, there was also variance on how hierarchically controlled integration was and how much it involved other levels – mainly the urban/local actors –in delivering policies related to migration. It was often unclear who had control over migrant integration, and which level might wish to take on such a responsibility. Accordingly, in many countries, infrastructure for supporting integration was seen as somewhat lacking (see chapter by Zelano et al.).

While the overarching policy on migration may be hierarchical and top down, urban levels have still been able to craft bottom-up solutions to issues of integration where there has been a gap in policy-making from higher levels. Restrictions placed on new member states, as seen in Austria and the Netherlands for 2004 and 2007 accession countries, represent a clearly hierarchical process in regard to intra-European movement. These restrictions had some initial effects on mobility and migration patterns, temporarily limiting formal employment, although not necessarily stemming the flow of CEE citizens. The effects of these restrictions on the number of migrants in the long term (especially after the transitional period lapsed) were minimal, but one of the biggest effects was in legalising pre-existing migration corridors and formalising labour positions and social security. Countries such as the United Kingdom and Sweden did not exercise this hierarchical control over migration and instead waived transition periods for 2004 accession countries. Initially, this had some effect on patterns of movement in the UK, with an influx of Polish immigrants following the 2004 accession, but Sweden saw no visible impact on the number of Polish migrants (see Kindler's chapter). However, the lack of hierarchical control in imposing migration restrictions ended up placing more of the onus for action on lower levels of government (see Chap. 2 by Sert) and resulted in a somewhat more bottom-up approach to addressing migration issues. The Dutch case also provides an example of a more heterarchical approach to developing policy options, albeit in a slightly more limited fashion than in Sweden. In the Netherlands, city initiatives such as the 'approach to attack slum landlords' were initially developed at the urban level. In a process that is perhaps more akin to uploading or policy learning than true multi-level governance, the national level then adopted this policy for broader usage (see Zelano et al. in this book). This did not necessarily involve true MLG in terms of a partnership between levels, but it did indicate policy diffusion upwards.

Both Sweden and the Netherlands have precedents in other policy areas for utilising more heterarchical approaches to developing multi-level policy responses. Green investment programmes in Sweden provide an example of this. The central government provided funding for green initiatives, but it was the urban/local levels that developed the programmes and strategies for improving ecologically sustainable development and reducing emissions. This also required the urban/local levels of government to work horizontally with other actors in order to deliver effective policies, as an explicit goal of these programmes was the development of local networks involving governmental and non-governmental actors (Kelder 2011, pp. 150–156). The policy approach had significant multi-level components, although it did not involve the EU. It did, however, involved numerous state and non-state actors at local, regional and national levels.

Other policy case studies in the Netherlands also point to a complex relationship between urban/local and national levels. For instance, an initiative to create healthier neighbourhoods in disadvantaged areas was undertaken jointly by urban/local and national levels starting in 2007. The former Ministry for Housing, Planning and the Environment, along with municipalities, housing corporations and other ministries created a Wijkenaanpak (neighbourhood policy) to address health issues in the areas. The project was truly multi-level, drawing on (limited) European Social Funds but mainly spearheaded by national and urban/local levels. Activities were coordinated centrally but undertaken locally, with most of the funding also originating from local sources. Semi-public, non-governmental and private actors were involved, as were citizens of the neighbourhoods in question. The actual concrete plans were largely bottom-up processes driven by the municipality, as they were expected to set their own goals and approaches. These arrangements also had a cross-regional components, with major urban conurbations (Amsterdam, the Hague, Rotterdam and Utrecht) banding together to establish a regional agreement to address health inequalities (van de Waart 2011, pp. 130–136). This initiative was seen as successful for two main reasons. First, the role of leadership was key, with the Ministry of Public Health, Welfare and Sports playing a central role in both persuading the central government to develop this initiative and in convincing urban/local levels to take part. Second, local levels were given significant autonomy in how they implemented this policy, allowing them to tailor the policy to meet specific neighbourhood needs. Some parallels can be seen in the migrant integration case, particularly in regard to the central role played by urban authorities.

8.4.2 Formal Versus Informal Relations

Some types of formal, institutionalised relationships between actors usually exist in both hierarchical and heterarchical actor networks. Intra-European movement initiatives that originated from the top down often had in-built mechanisms for ensuring adequate communication and coordination of urban-level responses as well. For example, the Swedish Enforcement Agency centralised statistical capacity and initiatives to harmonise urban/local practices in terms of illegal migrant settlements (see Zelano et al.). There were political apparatuses in place to ensure communication between levels, although these were not always used effectively by all actors and more fluid, informal contacts seemed to be used more regularly. In fact, formalised conduits for interaction between the EU (Commission) and urban levels were identified as being lacking (see Zelano's chapter). Looking from the EU level, communication between EU and member states on migration issues was seen as strong (often daily) in general terms, but members of the Commission were more likely to interact most with other DGs within the Commission, rather than member state representatives. Likewise, interaction between member states was more likely to occur first outside of traditional EU structures before moving to consultative bodies or council working groups, with evidence that this trend was increasing over time (see Zelano). These indicate a general lack of formalised connections between levels.

More positively, this informality in relations extended to ways of developing consensus, at least in the early policy development stages. Actors were less likely to rely on overly formal procedures such as court challenges and instead focus on less structured ways to come to agreement on policy approaches. However, this informality also required a focus on lower-level policy action; once issues became too high up the political ladder, the efficacy of these informal relational solutions was greatly reduced (see Zelano). This difficulty when issues travel further up the governance levels is evident in research in other policy areas. While urban/local levels may participate in various governance processes in a wide variety of policy areas, there is a difference between participation or involvement and true influence or governance (see, for example, Blom-Hansen 2005; Stephenson 2013, p. 822; Bache 2008; Curry 2015, p. 181).

This also appears to be true in the case of intra-European movement, where there was strong urban *involvement* in the policy but less indication that policies around free movement were *changed* as a result of such initiatives involving the urban level (see Zelano). However, again there was more evidence of urban government effects on migrant integration. There, the prominent role of the urban level had an effect on the shape and formality of relations between levels. As mentioned above, many decisions about integration of migrants and their associated housing, social and welfare needs take place at the urban level, sometimes even without significant member state support. This creates dynamic responses to address policy problems while also bypassing or disrupting more stable, formalised relational networks between levels. In fact, intra-European movement policy shows signs of disintermediation - 'level-skipping' or cutting out the middleman – with the increasing role of local levels, especially urban areas, in shaping migration policy. Within member states, regional levels are sometimes passed over with local and national levels working together on policy solutions. Austrian policies illustrate a clear case of this type of disintermediation, with many policies involving national and urban/local levels whilst skipping the Länder (see Zelano et al.).

National levels themselves may also be informally skipped. The 'Conference of mayors on the impact of intra-European movement of EU citizens at local level' is a strong example of this type of disintermediation. The conference was organised at the EU level and brought together local actors to discuss the impact of migration and policy options available in the area while mainly bypassing the nation state level. The conference provided a forum separate from the national level where these issues could be discussed. However, in general there was not clear coordination between urban/local levels and the EU level, with the EU failing to engage significantly with the urban/local levels in integrating migrants. This disintermediation and the flexible approach to policy solutions identified above do not necessarily restrict the true multi-levelness of a policy area and may in fact aid it. However, the flexibility afforded by disintermediation does not extend to all aspects of migration policy. This flexibility is especially necessary for seasonal and circular forms of migration, where governance networks might need to be more flexible than in situations of permanent migration. However, this flexibility in which levels are involved is not always evident in practice. The relative stability of actor networks dealing with the broad issues of migration somewhat reduced the responsiveness of policy approaches to targeting specific migrant groups.

8.5 Policy Factors Affecting MLG in Migration Policy

8.5.1 Discrete Versus Holistic Policy Responses

Structural and relational factors come together to create a policy setting that either addresses broad policy issues in a holistic manner, or divides them into discrete sub-issues. In most if not all the case countries there was a clear divide between a) intra-European movement as a legal requirement, which was mainly addressed at the EU level; b) intra-European movement as a labour-market and social policy issue, which mainly took place at the member state level; and c) intra-European movement as a question of integration, which often took place at the urban/local or regional level. This is a clear indication of the broad policy issue of intra-European movement being treated as a group of responses to smaller, discrete policy issues. The issue then becomes a question of how these discrete policy issues were coordinated.

Most cases examined in this book were marked by a lack of vertical coordination between governance levels, but there were clearer examples of horizontal coordination between actors within levels. While migration policy is a central state concern, it does involve non-state actors in delivering services to migrant communities. The Austrian case shows clear coordination between state and non-state actors. In that case, horizontal integration is more evident in housing policy, centred on the local level and involving non-state actors in a significant way (see Zelano et al.). In policy areas such as home care, horizontal coordination is evidenced by the role played by private actors in delivering services, with agencies occupying a central position in placing EU migrant care workers with Austrian families. These migrants play a key role in this policy area, as few Austrians work in 24-hour care. At the same time, in order to ensure coordination this service is highly regulated from the centre and the agencies themselves guarantee (at least in some cases) that working conditions are met (see the chapter by Drbohlav and Pavelková). This horizontal coordination of state regulation and protection and non-state provision through agencies was similar in the case of Polish migrants to Sweden (see Kindler). In both cases, non-state actors play a key role but still operate within the confines set by the state, thus increasing horizontal coordination.

In the Netherlands, urban actors have coordinated horizontally within their level to develop policies to address issues related to free movement. As in Austria, this has taken the form of including non-state actors in the policy process and in developing initiatives across regions, such as the partnership between Rotterdam and The Hague in creating arrangements to control fraud and mala fide employment arrangements (see Zelano et al.). Sweden provides a third case of horizontal coordination, as urban levels bring in non-public sector actors (in this case, religious institutions and charities) to address gaps in national policy with regard to housing (see Zelano et al.). Horizontal coordination is increasingly necessary in the Swedish case, especially where urban/local levels play a central role in addressing migration issues, which creates the need for more horizontal coordination between local levels of government who often face similar pressures and opportunities with regard to migration.

This horizontality is not limited to the local levels and also takes place to a more limited extent across member states. For instance, the Dutch government has worked in coordinating with other member states to set the agenda on migration issues and bring action in the area of wage dumping and other negative labour market practices (see Zelano et al.). However, despite the Dutch efforts this agenda-setting has not always resulted in coordinated national-level policies between member states. Looking outside of the EU, Turkey was in many ways an outlier to this tendency towards horizontal rather than vertical coordination. Turkish policy was exemplified by its top-down nature on specific policy issues, but this was not matched by horizontal coordination to bring the disparate strands of migration policy together. The lack of coordination at the urban/local level hampered the effectiveness of Turkey's migration policies and created the danger of mismatch between the actions of the central government and the urban/local levels (see Korci Korfali and Acar).

8.5.2 *Complex Versus Uniform Policy Issues*

Migration policy is also a complex policy as it is an essentially contested issue with often contradictory satisficing options. In addition, as has previously been shown in this chapter, different levels may not always work closely together and policy responses may conflict or misalign. These factors create a complex environment that cuts across numerous policy areas, has multiple policy options and solutions, and has a constantly shifting policy context. Despite the EU's binding power over issues of intra-European movement, the issue remains significantly contested with multiple 'solutions' and no clear cut answer. Recent negotiations with the United Kingdom about migration and free movement post-Brexit are illustrative of its contested nature. The attempted renegotiation of UK membership revolved (inter alia) around issues related to EU migration, such as limiting EU migrants' claims to benefits (European Council 2016), and the ongoing Brexit negotiations paint intra-European movement as a key source of disagreement (Mason and Duval Smith 2016). In addition, although intra-EU and external migration are treated separately, they are inextricably linked in many of the policy debates, as well as being held together in issues such as migrant integration.

The cross-cutting nature of intra-European movement creates additional dangers of governance mismatch, with the most noticeable cross-cutting issue being the interplay between migration and integration. While EU-level processes are on firmer, more binding footing in regard to the economic aspects of migration, the social issues that are part of migrant integration remain more member state-driven (see Zelano). In addition, the focus of the issue may shift depending on the stage of the policy process, with different aspects (and actor configurations) being more important during policy design than during implementation (see Zelano). As well as the danger of mismatch between levels, this raises the likelihood of mismatch within the policy area itself, for instance between social and economic issues. Related to this, EU movement contains both new policy issues that need to be addressed – in the form of, for example, specific integration issues that have developed since the 2004 accession – and pre-existing policies where new migration pressures need to be incorporated, such as health and education (see Zelano et al.). Migration patterns can exacerbate existing social, demographic, employment and other issues, which in turn create separate governance issues that may only be tangentially related to the governance of migration itself. And, in some cases, instead of developing true cross-cutting policies, the approach may be more fragmentary. For instance, outside of the EU in Turkey, while migration-orientated approaches may be evident in certain policy issues such as labour market controls and registration, there is less development in other related areas such as housing (see Zelano et al.).

8.6 Intra-European Movement: Multi-Level or Mismatched Governance?

While governance processes always operate on a spectrum and no policy area will fit perfectly into one or the other types of MLG, certain tendencies in structure, relations and policy can be identified for intra-European movement. In terms of structure, intra-European movement most closely resembled Type II MLG, with flexible institutional structures and policy-specific jurisdictions to address the issue. The situation is more complex in terms of relational and policy factors. Relationally, clear hierarchies exist in intra-European movement, with the EU having clear legal authority. While issues of migrant integration may be more heterarchical in that urban/local levels are more centrally involved, this participation is either at the behest of the central member state government or due to a gap created by policy inaction at higher levels, thus operating in a 'shadow of hierarchy' (Héritier and Lehmkuhl 2008). At the same time, these relationships are not highly formalised, with more informal and fluid relationships often taking precedence. In terms of policy factors, intra-European movement is clearly regarded as a collection of discrete policy issues, with 'integration' treated differently from other migration issues such as labour market controls. However, it is also a complex policy issue with multiple facets and degrees of contestation.

To put this in perspective of the possibilities outlined at the beginning of this chapter, intra-European movement has, to a large extent, required some augmentation of governance processes to a) recognise the central legal role played by the EU in this area; and b) accommodate the multi-faceted and inter-related social and labour policies affected by migration. This has resulted in some shift of structural, relational or policy factors, meaning the status quo of traditional governance processes (P1) is not simply maintained. At the same time, there has been an uneven shift in how structures, relations and policy processes have adapted to the specific realities of intra-European movement, meaning that true MLG (P3) has also not been attained. The combination of hierarchical, often informal relations and a complex policy environment that nonetheless treats sub-issues as discrete silos creates *governance mismatch* in the nature of MLG in intra-European movement, affirming P2, as shown in Table 8.2.

Table 8.2 Multi-Level Governance Processes in intra-European movement

Type I multi-level governance		**Structural factors**		Type II multi-level governance
	Rigid institutional structure	↔	**Flexible institutional structure**	
	Multi-purpose jurisdictions	↔	**Policy-specific jurisdictions**	
		Relational factors		
	Hierarchical relations	↔	Heterarchical relations	
	Formalised relations	↔	**Informal relations**	
		Policy factors		
	Discrete policy responses	↔	Holistic policy responses	
	Uniform policy issue	↔	**Complex policy issue**	

The cases examined in this book reveals migration and mobility policies to undoubtedly take place across multiple levels, even if all levels are not involved at all times. In terms of governance processes, relational factors appear to play a more predominant role in shaping migration policy than structural factors. In fact, the lack of institutional capacity was identified as an impediment in some cases. In the Netherlands, these relational factors allowed for innovative policy approaches, such as a bottom-up approach to integration driven by the urban/local level. This approach falls more in line with a true multi-level approach, as policy actions permeated upwards instead of simply travelling downwards, although it was still ultimately driven by a willingness at the central (national) level to adopt urban/local policy initiatives more broadly. The evolving nature of this approach highlights the need for more and wider research to build on existing literature examining governance networks over time (see, for example, Kapucu and Garayev 2012; Lowndes and Skelcher 2002; Jack et al. 2008). The strong presence of the urban/local level in this policy area further emphasises the need to consider MLG from two angles - both from the perspective of the decision-makers and from the perspective of the implementers by utilising a backward-mapping approach (Lipsky 1980). This approach starts from the perspective of the implementer and works back to the top to see whether the implementers' outcomes match with the initial goals of the policy (Elmore 1979–1980, p. 604). This can highlight any governance mismatch that is evident between the actors involved at various stages of the policy process.

Governance mismatch can have a significant impact on the efficacy of multi-level arrangements and was evident in the case of intra-European movement. While there are some successful examples of intra-European movement governance processes that approach true multi-levelness, significant parts of the policy display either *decoupled* or *disjointed governance*. The relative lack of EU-level coordination indicates governance decoupling between EU and member state levels. Again, this is partly the result of the unique supra-national powers of the EU, but it also creates the risk of a clear split between EU and member state goals. In a related case to this, that tension is already evident in the rifts between the EU-level response to Syrian refugees and member states that are firmly opposed to quotas imposed at the EU level. Within member states, there were clear cases of *disjointed governance*. Urban/local levels often drove policy initiatives, but these bottom-up responses lacked the coordinating powers of higher governmental levels, again limiting the true multi-levelness of these approaches and creating a misalignment of policy goals between levels.

Partly, this governance mismatch may result from the unique nature of intra-European movement policy. While many policy issues are contested as different actors and levels try to gain (or maintain) control over issues, migration also contains policy problems that are contested in terms of actors trying to *give up* control over these issues. Movement flows are controlled by the EU (for intra-EU 'mobility') or nation states (for non-EU migration). In contrast, issues of migrant integration are often ignored or left to urban/local levels to address. The split between decision-making and implementation has created often leaderless policy approaches, and while true MLG supports and indeed often calls for a networked, heterarchical approach to governance, in reality the lack of leadership can create deadlock or inaction. Chapters 6 and 7 point to a surprising lack of EU involvement on migration issues, despite the free movement directive coming from that level. This results in a fragmented and uncoordinated policy approach that creates governance mismatch between urban/local and regional approaches as well as between member states. In many ways these processes can be seen as incomplete MLG (with only some levels involved) or 'MLG-light'. These variations display many characteristics of MLG – multiple levels are involved, non-governmental actors can play a key role and policies may be relatively fluid and responsive – but remain incomplete in either the number of levels included or the structural, relational and policy processes that can support a multi-level governance frame.

8.7 Conclusions

This chapter provides a thorough study of a policy case that highlights the fine-grained capacity of the concept of multi-level governance to analyse policy processes. In addition, it increases the robustness of MLG as a concept by travelling it into a new policy area with its own unique governance framework. Analytically, this research points to the need for a more nuanced understanding of the various structural, relational and policy factors that shape multi-level governance. Practically, intra-European movement provides a deep and rich case to test the robustness of MLG as a way of understanding real-world processes. In particular, the work raises questions about the need to consider partial multi-levelness, where only certain levels are included in the policy process, and partial governance, where policies may operate over several levels but maintain traditional structures of power and decision-making. Finally, the case of intra-European movement shows the importance of context in determining the mode of multi-level governance that best fits a particular situation. Some examples in the case countries do point to relatively successful or 'true' MLG that encompasses both the multi-level and governance components of the term. However, in general the distinct lack of EU involvement beyond the directives on free movement point to an incomplete or mismatched case of MLG that does not fit neatly into Hooghe and Marks' typology.

In many ways, intra-European movement represents both the promise and the disappointment of multi-level governance as a normative ideal. Different examples presented in this book highlight the flexibility and responsiveness of some policy initiatives, innovative ways of including non-governmental actors and the possibility of bottom-up initiatives permeating upwards. However, this is often welded on to a more traditional, state-centric structural system that can create governance mismatch where actors are not always able to respond in a way that fully meets policy needs. Ultimately, the range of initiatives presented herein highlight the reality that there is no 'right' answer to dealing with complex, multi-level policy issues. While different permutations of structural, relational and policy factors can result in successful or unsuccessful cases of MLG, all three broad factors must be mutually complementary to avoid governance mismatch. Importantly, variations in any of these factors also require a concurrent shift in the other two in order to avoid disjointed or decoupled governance. However, the exact shift necessary in the other two areas is not always readily apparent.

Several characteristics of the type of MLG present in intra-European movement are worth highlighting in conclusion. First, *disintermediation*, where certain government levels may be skipped, was relatively common in the policy area, especially in terms of migrant integration, with urban/local levels addressing the issue directly without national-level input. Second, coordination *between* political levels was noticeably absent in many of the case countries. Instead, policy actors (mainly at the urban/local level) were more likely to coordinate horizontally within their level, developing new and less formal relations with non-typical actors, such as NGOs, housing associations and charities. Perhaps the most interesting addition to the understanding of multi-level governance presented by the case of intra-European movement is the need to separate out multi-level *contexts* from multi-level *governance*. There is no doubt that intra-European movement operates in a multi-level context, as multiple levels are necessarily involved. However, this does not necessarily equate with multi-level *governance*, as shown in this chapter and others (see Hinnfors). Care must be taken in the study of MLG to distinguish between policies that merely operate in a multi-level context and those that operate as multi-level governance, and the indicators developed in this chapter can hopefully act as a starting point for assessing MLG.

Intra-European movement policy also highlights several possible ways forward for MLG literature. First, it illustrates the importance of a bottom-up understanding of policy in explaining governance processes, one that takes into account implementation as well as decision-making. There is great flexibility in how multi-levelness is manifested, with bottom-up processes often equal to, or even superseding, top-down policy responses. In the case of migration, this was evident in the actors themselves and the central role played by the urban/local level in dealing with a policy that is ostensibly international by nature. The relationship between levels also extended both ways, at least in a limited fashion. Central governments shaped what urban and other local governments were and were not able to do, and in turn urban/local governments uploaded new policy options to the centre. While this power was ‘soft’ in nature, as local levels could not force higher levels to act, it is an important finding nonetheless as it illustrates the strength of persuasive policy approaches and policy uploading. Related to this, the change in context and situations related to intra-European movement in countries such as Sweden, the UK and Poland illustrate the need for greater and more systematic examination of multi-level governance processes over time.

Several final lessons on MLG can be drawn from this research. Other works have highlighted the importance of common and shared objectives between actors, coordinated strategies and actions and clear monitoring and evaluation of processes in ensuring that MLG is truly ‘multi-level governance’ (Van Geertsom 2011, p. 170). In dealing with international policy issues such as migration, cross-national (instead of, or in addition to, supranational) approaches to policy problems are often necessary. Cases examined in this book, such as the Czech-Austrian, Polish-Dutch and (involving migration from outside the EU) Bulgarian-Turkish migration corridors, show that migration still often has a significant geographical component, with migrants moving to different countries but remaining relatively close to home. This could lead to the development of bilateral agreements at a regional level to facilitate easier and more effective migrant integration across shared borders. While improving coordination, common objectives and policy responses from all levels represent some good practice examples of achieving true multi-level governance, these are often easier said than done and do not represent overly helpful or concrete strategies for developing or changing specific MLG processes. By breaking the issue down into relational, structural and policy factors, this research shows the centrality of actor relations in crafting policy solutions, and also the necessity of having structural factors to protect these relations. More troublingly, there does not seem to be as much consideration of what multi-level governance processes are attempting to accomplish at a policy level. Successful MLG requires more consideration of what the point of these multi-level processes is intended to be and how it relates to a specific policy context. Even more importantly, careful consideration must be given to the interplay between the structural, relational and policy considerations at play. Whether these multi-level governance processes are intended as an indicator of power relations, a tool of coordination, a tool of participation and influence, or something else will have an effect on what form the governance processes should take, and how successful they are in meeting those goals.

References

Bache, I. (2008). *Europeanization and multilevel governance: Cohesion policy in the European Union and Britain*. Lanham: Rowman and Littlefield.

Bache, I., & Andreou, G. (Eds.). (2011). *Cohesion policy and multi-level governance in South East Europe*. Oxford: Routledge.

Bache, I., & Flinders, M. (2004). *Multi-Level governance*. Oxford: Oxford University Press.

Blom-Hansen, J. (2005). Principals, agents, and the implementation of EU cohesion policy. *Journal of European Public Policy, 6*(2), 624–648.

Committee of the Regions (2009). *The White Paper on Multi-Level Governance*. Available at http://cor.europa.eu/en/activities/governance/Documents/mlg-white-paper/0387_inside-en-last.pdf. Accessed 28 Feb 2016.

Conzelmann, T., & Smith, R. (Eds.). (2008). *Multi-level governance in the European Union: Taking stock and looking ahead*. Baden Baden: Nomos.

Curry, D. (2015). *Network approaches to multi-level governance: Structures, relations and understanding power between levels*. Basingstoke: Palgrave Macmillan.

Elmore, R. (1979-1980). Backward mapping: Implementation research and policy decisions. *Political Sciences Quarterly, 94*, 601–616.

ESPON. (2005). *Project 3.2: Spatial Scenarios and Orientations in Relation to the ESDP and Cohesion Policy – Second Interim Report, Part 1*. Available at http://www.espon.eu/export/sites/default/Documents/Projects/ESPON2006Projects/CoordinatingCrossThematicProjects/Scenarios/2.ir_3.2-full.pdf. Accessed 29 Feb 2016.

European Commission (2001). *European governance: A white paper*. COM (2001) 428, Brussels: European Commission.

European Council. (2016). European Council meeting (18 and 19 February 2016) – Conclusions. Available at http://docs.dpaq.de/10395-0216-euco-conclusions.pdf. Accessed 04 May 2016.

Grisel, M., & van de Waart, F. (2011). *Multilevel urban governance or the art of working together*. Amsterdam: European Urban Knowledge Network.

Güntner, S. (2011). Urban development and European forms of MLG. In M. Grisel & F. van de Waart (Eds.), *Multilevel urban governance or the art of working together* (pp. 17–25). Amsterdam: European Urban Knowledge Network.

Héritier, A., & Lehmkuhl, D. (2008). The shadow of hierarchy and new modes of governance. *Journal of Public Policy, 28*(1), 1–17.

Hooghe, L., & Marks, G. (2003). Unraveling the central state, but how? Types of multi-level governance. *American Political Science Review, 97*, 233–243.

Horak, M., & Young, R. (Eds.). (2012). *Sites of governance: Multilevel governance and policy making in Canada's big cities*. Montreal & Kingston: McGill-Queen's University Press.

Howlett, M., Rayner, J., & Tollefson, C. (2009). From government to governance in Forest planning? Lessons from the case of the British great bear rainforest initiative. *Forest Policy and Economics, 11*, 383–391.

Jack, S., Drakopoulou Dodd, S., & Anderson, A. (2008). Change and the development of entrepreneurial networks over time: A processual perspective. *Entrepreneurship & Regional Development, 20*(2), 125–159.

Jordan, A. (2001). The European Union: An evolving system of multi-level governance…or government? *Policy and Politics, 29*(2), 193–208.

Kapucu, N., & Garayev, V. (2012). Designing, managing, and sustaining functionally collaborative emergency management networks. *American Review of Public Administration, 43*(3), 312–330.

Kelder, T. (2011). Green investment programmes in Sweden: 1+1 can be 3. In M. Grisel & F. van de Waart (Eds.), *Multilevel urban governance or the art of working together* (pp. 150–156). Amsterdam: European Urban Knowledge Network.

Kohler-Koch, B., & Larat, F. (Eds.). (2009). *European multi-level governance: Contrasting images in national research*. Cheltenham: Edward Elgar.

Lipsky, M. (1980). *Street-level bureaucracy: Dilemmas of the individual in public services*. Madison: University of Wisconsin Press.

Littoz-Monnet, A. (2010). Dynamic multi-level governance – bringing the study of multi-level interactions into the theorising of European integration, available at http://eiop.or.at/eiop/pdf/2010-001.pdf. Accessed 28 Feb 2016.

Lowndes, V., & Skelcher, C. (2002). The dynamics of multi-organizational partnerships: An analysis of changing modes of governance. *Public Administration, 76*(2), 313–333.

March, J., & Olsen, J. (1996). Institutional perspectives on political institutions. *Governance, 9*, 247–264.

Marks, G. (1993). Structural policy and multi-level governance in the EC. In A. Cafruny & G. Rosenthal (Eds.), *The state of the European Community: The Maastricht debate and beyond* (pp. 391–411). Lynne Rienner: Boulder.

Mason, R. and Duval Smith, A. (2016). Theresa May takes Brexit's immigration message to eastern Europe, *The Guardian*, 28 July, available at http://www.theguardian.com/politics/2016/jul/28/theresa-may-on-brexit-tour-of-eastern-europe. Accessed 01 Aug 2016.

Offe, C. (2006). Political institutions and social power: Conceptual explorations. In I. Shapiro, S. Skowronek, & D. Galvin (Eds.), *Rethinking political institutions: The art of the state* (pp. 9–31). New York: New York University Press.

Piattoni, S. (2010). *The theory of multi-level governance: Conceptual, empirical and normative challenges*. Oxford: Oxford University Press.

Sartori, G. (1970). Concept misinformation in comparative politics. *American Political Science Review, 64*, 21.

Scharpf, F. (1991). Political institutions, decision styles, and policy choices. In R. Czada & A. Windhoff-Heritier (Eds.), *Political choice: Institutions, rules and the limits of rationality* (pp. 53–86). Frankfurt: Campus Verlag.

Scharpf, F. (1997). Introduction: The problem-solving capacity of multi-level governance. *Journal of European Public Policy, 4*(4), 520–538.

Scholten, P. (2013). Agenda dynamics and the multi-level governance of intractable policy controversies: The case of migrant integration policies in the Netherlands. *Policy Sciences, 46*, 217–236.

Stephenson, P. (2013). Twenty years of multi-level governance: "Where does it come from? What is it? Where is it going?". *Journal of European Public Policy, 20*, 817–837.

Taşan-Kok, T., & Vranken, J. (2011). *Handbook for multilevel urban governance in Europe*. Amsterdam: European Urban Knowledge Network.

Tosics, I. (2011a). Multilevel government systems in urban areas. In M. Grisels & F. van de Waart (Eds.), *Multilevel governance or the art of working together* (pp. 26–35). Amsterdam: European Urban Knowledge Network.

Tosics, I. (2011b). Urban development and urban policies in EU member states. In M. Grisels & F. van de Waart (Eds.), *Multilevel governance or the art of working together* (pp. 36–44). Amsterdam: European Urban Knowledge Network.

Treib, O., Bähr, H., & Falkner, G. (2007). Modes of governance – Towards a conceptual clarification. *Journal of European Public Policy, 14*, 1–20.

van de Waart, F. (2011). The healthy Neighbourhood experiment: A multilevel venture. In M. Grisels & F. van de Waart (Eds.), *Multilevel governance or the art of working together* (pp. 130–136). Amsterdam: European Urban Knowledge Network.

Van Geertsom, J. (2011). Postscript: The need for a common European method of multilevel urban governance. In M. Grisel & F. van de Waart (Eds.), *Multilevel urban governance or the art of working together* (pp. 169–170). Amsterdam: European Urban Knowledge Network.

Weaver, R., & Rockman, B. (Eds.). (1993). *Do institutions matter? Government capabilities in the United States and abroad*. Washington: Brookings Institute.

Zapata-Barrero, R., Caponio, T., & Scholten, P. (2017). Theorizing the "Local Turn" in a multilevel governance framework of analysis: A case study in immigrant policies. *International Review of Administrative Sciences, 83*(2), 241–246.

Zerbinati, S. (2012). Multi-Leve governance and EU structural funds: An entrepreneurial local government perspective. *Local Government Studies, 38*(5), 577–597.

Chapter 9
The Politics of Intra-European Movement

Alex Balch

9.1 Introduction: Intra-European Movement in an Era of Crisis

One need only consider the referendum that took place in Switzerland in 2014 on 'mass-immigration' and the referendum on membership of the EU in the United Kingdom (UK) in 2016 to understand the significance of free movement. The topic stalks the present and future of European integration and has become central to relations between European states. It is no exaggeration to state that the context surrounding the European politics of mobility in the twenty-first century is one of heightened tension and a gathering sense of uncertainty and crisis surrounding the future prospects for freedom of movement (Guild et al. 2015). This might perhaps have surprised those drafting the early treaties who saw free movement as a necessary and relatively unproblematic cornerstone of regional integration. This chapter will explore and analyse the politicisation of free movement, offering a conceptualisation of these politics as an interaction, or dialectical conversation, between two competing languages or 'frames' through which intra-European movement is conceptualised: solidarity and hospitality.

Aside from the theatrics of European Council meetings, and high stakes of national referenda, a key indicator of an increasing politicisation is the sensitivity and importance attached to what kind of language one uses to describe the international movement of persons within the European Union (see van Ostaijen 2016). The apparently pedantic insistence of the EU institutions to use the terms 'mobile EU citizen' and 'mobility' rather than migrant or migration is in fact an essential part of policy. It relates directly to the privileged status of European citizens within a formal system that guarantees free movement – they are supposed to be spared the

A. Balch (✉)
University of Liverpool, Liverpool, UK
e-mail: A.R.Balch@liverpool.ac.uk

P. Scholten, M. van Ostaijen (eds.), *Between Mobility and Migration*, IMISCOE Research Series, https://doi.org/10.1007/978-3-319-77991-1_9

label of 'immigrant'. By contrast, the continued use of the language of immigration, alongside reference to (Eastern) European migrant or migration – particularly by older EU Member States – is revealing of political pressures to limit, dismantle or weaken the institution of free movement. The implications of this discursive battle over intra-European movement are thus much more than simply in terms of the choice of words. They reflect a competition between different political philosophies over intra-European movement that have inevitably influenced EU-level law and policy and have concrete impacts.

Although one can point to a gradual extension of rights to free movement along the course of European integration, the politics of intra-European movement have led to a series of decisions that are associated with negative short and long-term socio-economic impacts for certain Europeans. For example, transitional restrictions targeting the citizens of new member states in the first decade of the twenty-first century have had particular affects on these groups and their position in the European labour market (Currie 2007; Recchi 2015: 18). Despite the language of equality there is a distinct possibility that the EU's free movement regime has created denizens alongside permanent legacies, structures, inequalities and hierarchies within European citizenship. In addition to this there have been important ramifications from what could be described as an accelerated politicisation – or 'rollback' - from the principle of free movement following the 2004 and 2007 enlargements. There is also the noticeable shift in the direction of travel with respect to the EU's political economy away from 'social Europe' and towards a more neoliberal settlement. This can be traced to the Laval ruling in 2007 which was seen as a setback to the principle of equal treatment for workers, in favour of the rights of businesses and employers (to pay wages to workers from the newer Member States at a lower rate). There are now numerous and prominent examples where free movement has become central to some of the core dilemmas in European politics. Perhaps the best example is the case of France's expulsion of European citizens on the basis of racial profiling in 2010 which brought direct confrontation between a founding Member State and the European Commission as 'Guardian of the Treaties'. The affair brought under close scrutiny the basis upon which there could be any truth to the claims that integration was creating a 'Europe of rights and values' (Balch et al. 2014).

9.2 Explaining the Politics of Free Movement

Can existing theories of immigration politics or European integration offer an explanation for this politicisation of free movement? As with the topic of immigration more generally (Hollifield and Wong 2015), the politics of intra-European movement has only recently garnered significant interest from political studies scholars. Before that research tended to focus on efforts to develop a common immigration and asylum policy for non-EU citizens. Scholars largely internalised the EU's conceptual separation of intra-European movement from extra-EU migration - something reflected in the institutional set-up of the EU. The increasing relevance of the

EU in matters of immigration (of non-EU citizens) post the treaties of Amsterdam, and particularly Lisbon, generated a number of interesting areas of research around immigration and Europeanisation (Faist and Ette 2007), and the emerging political economy of migration in the EU (Menz 2010). Studies have looked at how policy-making over immigration in Europe has changed since 2000 in a more 'liberal' or economic-interests basis, through, for example, the role of experts and expertise (Balch 2010), the significance of 'strange bedfellows', and 'unholy alliances' between political parties (Berga and Spehara 2013).

Considering the variation in the experiences of intra-European movement - and the national interests at play - across the North, South, East and West of the EU, it would theoretically be possible to generalise about different camps likely to be for or against further integration in this area. However, crude divisions into 'sending' and 'receiving' states are unlikely to remain permanent, as we have seen previously in the cases of Spain, Italy and Greece. A more fruitful approach might be to consider the relative fundamental ways in which intra-European movement is conceptualised by different actors in the European space, i.e. not reading off solely on the basis of national economic interests. This recognises the fact that narrow economic interests are likely to oscillate considerably depending upon a host of factors. For example, alliances between Member States and with the EU institutions over the issue and over time are likely to be dynamic and involve shifting coalitions of convenience. At any given time intra-European movement can be used by in an expanding economy to balance the books (Balch 2010) or in an instrumental way to reconfigure national policy systems (Paul 2013). The role of urban areas in this developing politics is also likely to vary. Europe is home to cities with greater and lesser influence both within and outside their national borders. While only relatively few are placed in the league of 'global cities' (Sassen 2005), many still feature the polarisation of primary and secondary labour markets, a growing dependency upon mobile workers, and reliance on cross-border, city-to-city, networks and transactions partly catalysed by Europeanisation (Favell 2008).

One way to understand the politics of intra-European movement might be to link the different positions of national/EU actors on free movement with broader understandings around the process of integration – represented by the 'ideal-type' theories of neofunctionalism or liberal intergovernmentalism. This line of thinking might predict that supranational institutions will seek ever-deeper integration over free movement, while national/intergovernmental fora would be more cautious, seeing cooperation as contingent upon the higher priority of national interests (see, e.g. Wiener and Diez 2009). While this might be a somewhat out-dated conceptual division, it does map neatly on the migration/mobility distinction as it has developed institutionally. There is evidence that free movement of European citizens is seen as primarily driven by neo-functional/supranational forces while immigration (of third-country nationals) is characterised as something more intergovernmental. According to Boswell and Geddes, thinking on mobility in the EU is informed by two rival 'paradigms': "a liberal, free-trade-oriented paradigm emphasising the economic benefits of free movement; and a more state-centric, restrictive paradigm premised on concerns about the impact of migration and mobility on the state's capacity to allocate socio-economic and political resources" (2011: 191).

Such a division provides a useful starting point or meta-narrative but it side-steps the previous point that states should logically be expected to swing between more expansive and more restrictive phases vis-à-vis intra-European movement. It could also be accused of betraying a normative slant, or bias against restrictive/communitarian arguments. One side is presented as relying upon a rational, economically beneficial, project (to further freedom of movement) while the suggestion is that the other is driven (less rationally) by ideology – populism, or nationalism – or perhaps more charitably, an 'interior ministry logic' pre-conditioned to resist the expansion of transnational rights (Bresso 2014). It is certainly the case that the principle of free movement is often defended in terms of economic efficiency and increasing productivity (e.g. the importance of increased mobility in the 'Europe 2020' strategy), but this in turn can be traced to an ideological framework. The next sections briefly sketch out the ways in which the ideas of solidarity and hospitality operate to construct and deconstruct arguments over free movement in the European space, before using these ideas to analyse the politicisation of intra-European movement in the twenty-first century.

9.3 Solidarity and Free Movement as Foundational

The importance of different frames for understanding a political issue become increasingly salient when a policy field is more contested (Schoen and Rein 1994). They help political actors to 'define problems', 'diagnose causes', 'make moral judgements' and 'suggest remedies' (Entman 1993). They are not always visible or recognised; they can be somewhat hidden – underlying and pre-conditioning our response to contemporary issues - pushing 'particular definitions and interpretations of political issues' in public debates (Shah et al. 2002). For the first of these, much as in the mythical story of Europa the virginal Phoenician princess, the 'founding principle' of free movement, and associated elements (non-discrimination, the Schengen area) is presented as something pure and beautiful, but fragile and vulnerable. Thus the deep concerns when Member States apparently prioritize national border control over 'solidarity' with other Member States, or betray the 'spirit' of Schengen (Carrera et al. 2011). From this perspective protecting the system of free movement has become synonymous with sustaining the European project or even the very 'idea' of Europe; its existence constantly under threat from populist and Euro-sceptic politicians and publics; the purity of the founding principles at risk of compromise and erosion via the illiberal forces that they wish to unleash (e.g. Bresso 2014).

This way of thinking effectively raises the stakes by entangling free movement with the whole question of the European project - the politics of free movement framed as a 'bell-weather' for the wider politics of European integration. This presents the issue as somehow connected at the affective or emotional level to the very construction of the EU. Accounts of the development of EU free movement are framed within the narrative of the wider story of the development of European integration. So, these might point to a long history of obstacles and hurdles overcome, accomplishments made and rights won with the vision of frictionless mobility as an end-point, each step towards this end-point celebrated or marked as a moment of achievement.

The Treaty of Rome and the inclusion of the free movement of workers as one of the four 'freedoms' is the fundamental reference point, and the year 1968 emerges as an important watershed in the narrative (see, e.g. McMahon 2015). This was the point signifying an end to the first phase of the work post-Rome to actually establish free movement. It was at this point that the developing European polity had removed many of the restrictions on the movement of workers (through Regulation 1612/68). It also coincidentally came at the end of the first 'golden age' of European integration; after which, as we know, stagnation and intergovernmentalism came to dominate the European project in the 1970s. Neo-functionalism no longer appeared to explain the dynamics of European integration, but the return to a more cooperative phase in the 1980s demonstrated a kind of 'dialectical functionalism' where stagnation eventually acted as a spur to further integration (Corbey 1995).

The considerable political capital invested in completing the single market in the late 1980s led to further moves to enhance freedom of movement within the EU. This effort opened up the next 'golden age' in European integration, and various extensions to rights of free movement in the 1990s. The timing of these extensions, and the associated creation of European citizenship, took place at the same time as Europe was faced with new political challenges following the fall of the Berlin Wall. Undoubtedly the high-point of this second golden-age (or at least the beginning of the end) is signified by the milestone Directive 2004/38 which provided permanent residence rights for long-term EU movers and formalised what had been hitherto established through ECJ case-law. However, despite the apparent inevitability of 2004/38, there are plenty of examples of obstacles and hurdles along the way meaning that 'true' free movement is still far from the reality (Zelano – this book Chap. 4). These include significant resistance in the 1990s when attempts following Maastricht to go further on freedom of movement were thwarted by countries such as Britain and Denmark – e.g. Portugal's doomed 'European Citizens Charter'. The Amsterdam Treaty also contributed little to the expansion of free movement rights.

So, on closer inspection of the history of freedom of movement reveals that it has actually been a case of one step forward, one step back. Another example is with the introduction of more 'supranational' forms of decisionmaking in this area following the Treaties of Nice (2001) and Lisbon (2007). It could be argued that this means greater accountability and legitimacy for policymaking in the EU (e.g. Kaunert et al. 2013), but this needs to be weighed against the French and Dutch rejection of EU constitutionalism and the limited reforms of Lisbon. This can hardly be said to have ushered in a third 'golden age' even if the incremental institutional changes might have lessened the iron grip of the EU's intergovernmental institutions who prefer policies affecting migrant rights be made 'behind gilded doors' (Guiraudon 1997).

9.4 The Enduring Metaphor of Hospitality

Competing with this is an alternative liberal communitarian frame of social justice where control of non-citizens is closely associated with the maintenance of the nation-state (Walzer 1983). This is the idea of immigration as hospitality: a paradigm that requires that the welcome of the other is always conditional; a metaphor that has become so embedded that we often forget it is a metaphor (Rosello 2002). From the very first immigration systems the idea of hospitality has endured and allowed states to make sense and justify the expansion of controls on international movement (Balch 2016). In the context of liberal democratic states, the presence of non-citizens creates dilemmas around community, membership and principles such as equality and universality (Dauvergne 1999). This situation has led to the development of a range of different arguments within the liberal tradition to 'resolve' these dilemmas - justifying or accounting for the priority of citizens, and the exclusion of non-citizens – e.g. on the basis of economic, security or cultural well-being of the state (Bader 2005). The success of these kinds of arguments has been based on the ability for state actors to equate the arrival of newcomers with threats to the state as nation or community. Talking about immigration, as Sayad puts it, means thinking about the state and that it is 'the state that is thinking about itself when it is thinking about immigration'" (Sayad 2010: 166)

Ideas about hospitality, while referring to the state, have a deeply transnational resonance, travelling across Europe from receiving to sending states, West to East, North to South. The same arguments justifying controls on any international movement - including intra-European movement and refugees - are shared, copied and repeated across the region (Balabanova and Balch 2010). One of the most potent examples is in the notion that immigration should be controlled on the basis of domestic social justice. This argues that immigration threatens the state because immigrants will naturally deplete scarce welfare resources and must therefore be controlled for the public good. A debate which emerged in the US in the 1990s. Milton Friedman (1997) famously remarked in an interview that 'it's just obvious that you can't have free immigration and a welfare state'. The US economist Borjas also argued that 'welfare programs will probably attract persons who qualify for subsidies and repel persons who have to pay for them. A strong magnet effect, combined with an ineffective border control policy, can literally break the bank' Borjas (1999: 114). The connection between these arguments and the enlargement of the EU into countries with much lower income levels in the 2000s led to similar arguments about the 'end of the welfare state' for Europe (Sinn 2002).

This, it is argued creates a 'progressive dilemma' for those on the left, because while they might be in favour of universal rights and equal treatment, the spectre of immigration threatens all the protections and support previously established via the welfare state (Goodhart 2004). However, these arguments are based on a series of myths about the impacts of immigration. They rest upon an underlying assumption that immigration is partly driven by a desire to take advantage of generous welfare systems in destination countries. Research into the behaviour of intra-EU migrants has challenged this ‘welfare magnet’ hypothesis. The evidence would suggest that newcomers from other EU member states tend to be less likely (than host-country nationals) to avail themselves of welfare benefits and public services (Eurofound 2015). Indeed, this suggests a need for additional support for EU mobile citizens who often find themselves at a disadvantage both in the job market and in terms of societal integration.

The metaphor of hospitality allows states to frame European citizenship and free movement not only as undermining domestic social justice, but as an opportunity to launch political attacks that work in the interests of those seeking to assert the power and identity of the state. This is one of the reasons why hospitality has remained the dominant frame within which discussions of immigration take place (Balch 2016). As Doty (2003) points out, the positioning of politicians regarding the restriction immigration can be linked logically with state-building strategies. The focus, and insistence on, immigration control as a central task of government, is itself an act of statecraft, produces further demands for a (national) centralisation and extension of governmental powers (Ibid). In stark contrast with this restrictive impulse, it is through the aggressive removal of restrictions and greater levels of free movement that the EU gains some of its scarce and valuable sources of popular support, especially from younger European citizens (Recchi 2015). Central to both sides is the struggle over nothing less than the legitimate exercise of political power: the risks and rewards are therefore high.

Solidarity and hospitality emerge as very useful and powerful ideational weapons. They underpin the politics, and the language, that frame intra-European movement, but neither is entirely consistent with either the history of integration in this area, or the actual experience and governance of European mobility. On the one hand, the achievement of freedom of movement through European integration is radical - it demands states recognize the ‘rightful presence’ of other European citizens in their territory. As such it actively challenges the ubiquitous conceptualisation of immigration as ‘hospitality’ (for a local example of this, see Squire and Darling 2013). Yet on the other, notwithstanding the discourse of rights there are serious doubts over the EU’s cosmopolitan credentials (Brown 2014). Concerns include the treatment of certain (‘new’ or Central/Eastern) European citizens when they choose to exercise free movement. While the right to move is considered the main benefit of European citizenship the lived reality of workers from the ex-Communist regimes has not always been a positive experience (IOM 1998; EPRS 2014). Also, despite the progressive removal of physical and bureaucratic barriers to movement for certain groups of persons, countervailing restrictions and obstacles to movement remain remarkably resilient (and tend to be extended) when it comes to the movement of other, non-EU, citizens.

9.5 The Politicisation of Intra-European Movement in the Twenty-First Century

How have these competing ideas featured in the developing political story around intra-European movement? One paradox is that the local level has emerged as central to arguments about impacts even though city-regions have found that 'their role in European policy-making is limited if not irrelevant' (Perulli 2012). Research into the political economy of managed migration tends to ignore the urban level, preferring to consider the role of non-state actors or organised interests such as employers' groups (Freeman 2006, Menz 2010). This next section explores the politicisation of this topic, and how the urban level has featured, by focusing on the key contemporary battles over the 'prize' of free movement – both real and symbolic – in the twenty-first century, looking at the instruments and strategies of the EU and its Member States.

The power and penetration of ideas about hospitality become apparent when we consider how political conflicts over intra-European movement have developed. In discussions around internal movement within the EU by European citizens, connections with other forms of international movement constantly emerge. This is because free movement is applicable to parts of Europe's periphery (e.g. Norway, Switzerland), highly relevant to others (e.g. new and aspiring members) and non-EU migration is simply impossible to separate in the debate – it represents the wider migratory environment in which such discussions take place. The political changes that took place in North Africa in 2010/2011 and the ensuing conflicts in Syria/Iraq provide a backdrop of pressure and crisis that politicians can present as existential threat. They raise the prospect of large-scale immigration from outside Europe and put pressure on the trust and solidarity between states that have reduced border checks. One response has been a wave of states threatening Schengen suspensions which directly affects freedom of movement for all European citizens. In 2011 the Franco-Italian affair saw France re-introduce border checks in response to Italy's deal with Tunisia that resulted in the issuance of residence permits to people who had arrived previously. Then, weeks later, there was the reaction of Denmark, reinstating controls on its border with Germany and Sweden, citing a rise in 'trans-border crime'. This prompted serious concerns about an absence of solidarity between Member States, the threat to freedom of movement, and a 'race' away from 'the principles of proportionality, solidarity, accountability and fundamental rights' (Carrera et al. 2011).

These concerns proved to be accurate when in 2015–2016 the migrant crisis was blamed by a long list of states for temporarily reintroducing border checks (via the invocation of Article 25 of the Schengen Borders Code[1]). Coupled with the actions by Hungary to raise its borders with Croatia and Serbia, and the launching of infringement proceedings against the same country over its asylum arrangements

[1] Allows Schengen states to 'exceptionally and immediately reintroduce border control[s] at internal borders' when 'urgent action' is needed

(EC 2015), the sense of crisis at the EU level became palpable. This was well articulated in the 'State of the Union' speech given in Strasbourg by the European Commission president, Jean-Claude Juncker. He complained about the behaviour of the Member States to restrict freedom of movement within the EU and appealed emotionally for this to be reversed, referring to memories of the Second World War and arguing that 'walls and fences have no place in an EU Member State' (Juncker 2015).

It is interesting to note that in 2016 national politicians such as Austria's then-Chancellor Werner Faymann justified the reintroduction of external border controls as the only way to save Schengen, and by extension, the EU. One analysis could be that the system as a whole has demonstrated its flexibility, and that despite the developments since 2010 intra-European movement of European citizens is relatively unaffected. The actions of the Member States mostly followed the rules set out in the Schengen Borders Code (SBC) and so one could argue that reports of Schengen's demise are somewhat exaggerated (Guild et al. 2015). There is an assumption that the aim is to restrict extra-EU migration rather than intra-European movement. However, it is in this context of uncertainty and fear over migration flows from outside the EU that certain Member States have been making the argument that intra-European movement is adding to the 'burden' at the local level, in certain parts of the EU. The long Schengen crisis of 2010–2016 was a period when transitional restrictions for some Eastern Europeans were being lifted across the Union. There is also the issue of the highly public attempts by Switzerland and the UK to re-negotiate free movement rules in favour of enhanced national autonomy. The Swiss case took two years to resolve, but in late 2016 an agreement was reached by a joint committee. It demonstrated that by withholding some of the benefits attached to Switzerland's relationship with the EU (participation in EU programmes such as Horizon 2020 and Erasmus) pressure could be applied to maintain free movement (Maurice 2016).

As part of preparations for the UK's referendum on EU membership that country's government made explicit moves to revisit and potentially reconfigure intra-European movement and modify some of the core elements of freedom of movement. The UK's demands echoed those outlined in a letter sent to the Council presidency by four countries in 2013 and revolve around access to welfare and public services by other European citizens. This restrictive tone regarding intra-European movement has been coupled with an increased eagerness on the part of the same Member States to identify and punish those who 'abuse' the system (Eurofound 2015).

The deal eventually struck by the UK with its European partners in early 2016 proved insufficient to win the referendum for Cameron, but in the process it opened up the possibility for changes to the EU citizens' Directive, the EU Regulation on free movement of workers, and the Regulation on social security (Peers 2016). The referendum debate also saw the issue of Turkey's prospective membership of the EU raised, taking advantage of the ongoing negotiations with that country around the relocation of refugees. A 'Leave' campaign poster warned that 76 million Turkish citizens would soon enjoy free movement, despite the slim prospects of Turkey's membership.

While the UK's referendum result meant that changes to intra-European movement were no longer guaranteed to go ahead they have been placed on the negotiating table in any future political wrangling over free movement. They may not have represented a wholesale revision, and they would not have required treaty amendment, but they did represent a perceptible shift in the politics of intra-European movement. They effectively offered up the possibility that a greater level of conditionality could be re-inserted into the rules on freedom of movement. They emphasised one more time that the welcome of other European citizens remains fundamentally conditional, and ultimately that the principle of free movement would always be trumped by the powers of states to restrict and intervene in order to control intra-European movement.

Post the financial crash there have been a series of cases where Schengen States have re-introduced border checks, EU states have increased border controls, and demands have been made for greater recognition and mitigation of the impacts of intra-European movement. These moves have gained considerable media attention because the stakes have been perceived as heightened due to the context of a general crisis of legitimacy faced by the EU (Longo and Murray 2015). They are also qualitatively different from other examples since the 1990s where increased checks were regularly brought in by Member States, e.g. during significant political meetings or large sporting events (see EC 2010b: Annex I).

As one of the core tenets of integration, the EU has developed a number of instruments, methods or 'weapons' to embed, protect, strengthen and even encourage free movement and intra-European movement. Recchi (2015) draws on Lowi to categorise these into three main types. The first are 'constituent' and include the construction of European citizenship and monetary union which aim to dissolve barriers through the fabric of treaties and institutional arrangements. The second are 'regulatory' and include directives on free movement and other practical steps such as the mutual recognition of qualifications between member states. Finally there are 'distributive' policies which include the creation of mobility grants and schemes such as Erasmus that encourage greater intra-European movement.

Of these strategies it is probably the first, backed up by a doctrine of the primacy of EU law and the interpretation of the treaties (where there are of course expansive declarations on the principle of free movement) that has been most successful in enabling the idea of free movement to be pushed forward, via judgements of the ECJ. The key principles established through ECJ case-law up to 2004/38 include (a) non-discrimination and equality of treatment; (b) recognition of all insurance periods independently of the country of employment; (c) exportability of acquired rights; and (d) application of the law of the country of employment (lex loci laboris) (Ferrera 2005, 100–4). However, it is notable that the ECJ 'won' these rights for individuals rather than them being established via a more recognizable democratic process. Boswell and Geddes argue that this top-down process of establishing rules on free movement, notwithstanding the 'high-flown' rhetoric on citizenship from the Commission, has resulted in less penetration among the EU's residents – hardly impacting upon the conception of political membership as something national (Geddes and Boswell 2011: 190). Plus the public appeal of free movement has been somewhat damaged following rulings such as the Laval case[2] where the politics of judicialisation have taken a decidedly neoliberal turn. These and other judgments have led some to accuse the court of prioritizing market freedoms over the protection of workers rights (Dølvik and Visser 2009).

Turning to the Member States, what have been the main options in terms of responding to the EU's developing rules on free movement? How have they been able to claim 'ownership' and victory for their citizens? How successfully have different Member States pushed their interests? How well have they been able to react or adjust? Although the principles underpinning free movement are a sine qua non of EU membership, the Member States actually have significant scope and latitude. This is because the EU is neither able or willing to opt for a strongly supranational system of governance in this area. Not only would such an approach be politically impossible, it runs contrary to the concept of subsidiarity.

For those aspiring and new member states where the possibility of exercising the right of free movement is popular, the EU emerges as a powerful actor: a gatekeeper to membership and a system that imposes (but also limits the effect and duration of) transitional arrangements and other obstacles. Of course the EU institutions only develop policies in areas where a competence is established or agreed. The only possibility of seriously altering this balance would be through treaty change, which seems unlikely but not out of the question. More feasible is the option of reaching some kind of EU-wide agreement to restrict or limit the application of free movement and thereby control intra-European movement, which would naturally mean negotiation via the Council. This was the kind of settlement arrived at over the 2004/2007 enlargements, with the imposition of transitional arrangements for citizens of those new member states. This emerged as a compromise in the negotiations around the 2003 Act of Accession when the language used to justify restrictions referred to the 'potential to seriously disturb the labour markets in the Member States' (EC 2001: (2). This was a decision taken against available research that suggested such arrangements would have little long-term impact on migration patterns, leading most observers to argue that the issue was made on the basis of a political rather than social or economic logic (Lang 2007). The inability for the UK and others to secure significant limitations on free movement rights after the 2004/2007 enlargements could reflect the shifting balance of negotiating power within the Council, where studies have shown that smaller states can be surprisingly effective (Golub 2012).

In terms of post-hoc reactions, when there is an apparent clash or conflict between national arrangements and ECJ judgements, there are a number of options beyond straightforward compliance/non-compliance. These include the more difficult tactic of trying to shift the future direction of integration at the EU level or the more pragmatic method of re-regulating at the national level in order to 'contain' domestic impacts (Blauberger 2012). In addition, there is considerable scope for 'grey' compliance – even where there is apparently clear guidance for Member States about how they should treat mobile EU citizens, there is the question of interpretation. For

[2] C-341/05, December 2007

example, the language inserted in the Directive 2004/38 creates a distinction between 'genuine' free movement as opposed to its 'abuse' without offering any concrete definitions of what would constitute either. This matters because the Directive requires the provision of social welfare and protection only for those who 'genuinely' make use of free movement, and allows for Member States to put in place safeguards against 'abuse' and the prospect of 'unreasonable burdens' on their welfare systems. All of this can naturally be defined and decided upon in the national interest, however narrowly the government of the day chooses to understand that, and notwithstanding the prospect of a future ECJ judgement that policies are incompatible with EU law.

Outside the Commission, Council and ECJ there are of course other venues in the EU sphere that have become battlegrounds for the politics of free movement. The European Parliament has tended to echo the Commission's fierce defence of the principle of free movement – issuing statements against national political leaders calling for the right to be changed or restricted (EP 2014), or questioning the continued imposition of checks in the Schengen zone (EP 2017). The increase in the powers of the EP post-Lisbon and the widespread success of Eurosceptic parties in the 2014 elections opens up the possibility that this normative position could be challenged. However, the new populist MEPs initially failed to create formal groupings within the parliament, although they have since attempted to change attitudes, put pressure on mainstream parties, and obstruct parliamentary proceedings (Grabbe and Groot 2014: 38).

9.6 Impacts and the Role of Local and Urban Spaces

The local level – urban areas, cities, city-regions – has emerged as an important terrain for all sides in the political struggles over free movement (Nicholls and Uitermark 2016). This is because, as Bucken-Knapp et al. (2018) demonstrate, there has been a general absence of policies at either national or local levels to manage the impacts of free movement. This policy vacuum has eventually led to multiple actors jumping in to promote their own preferred solution. In the case of certain national governments, it opened the way for local impacts to serve wider arguments against the principle of free movement. Notable in this context was the intervention of April 2013 with a joint letter to the European Council Presidency from Austria, Germany, the Netherlands and the United Kingdom. This underlined their belief that freedom of movement was not an unconditional right, and claimed that 'a number of municipalities, towns and cities in various Member States are under a considerable strain' and that intra-European movement 'burdens the host societies with considerable additional costs, in particular caused by the provision of schooling, health care and adequate accommodation.' The letter also went on to assert that 'a significant number of new immigrants draw social assistance in the host countries, frequently without a genuine entitlement, burdening the host countries' social welfare systems.'

(Mikl-Leitner et al. 2013 The letter then demanded a veritable array of legal and non-legal actions to be drawn up including EU funding and sanctions (Ibid).

The immediate response of European Parliament and European Commission was both defensive and dismissive. Hannes Svoboda (from the Progressive Alliance of Socialist and Democrats in the European Parliament) opposed the proposals and Cecilia Malmström (then-Home Affairs Commissioner) complained of the equation of immigration with mobility which she declared like comparing 'apples and oranges' (see Hansen 2015). The eventual, rather more measured, formal response from the Commission was a Communication conceding increasing mobility caused 'challenges for local communities' (EC 2013: (3). In contrast to the escalatory language of the joint letter, proposals to address the absence of policies or clear priorities for governance at the local level consisted of a series of concrete actions. There were attempts to limit and and clarify definitions for social security 'abuse' and 'fraud' and also discussion of 'errors' by officials and citizens in making and processing claims (EC 2013: 9). The help offered to local authorities to meet these challenges came in the shape of training and exchange of best practice, with funding for social inclusion through the European Social Fund (ESF) for 'marginalised communities, in particular Roma' (ibid. 11). However, the Communication emphasised the joint responsibility of the EU and Member States to counter negative public perceptions of intra-European movement that were 'not based on facts' (EC 2013: 13). Perhaps unsurprisingly considering the 'top-down' way in which it has been constructed (Geddes and Boswell 2011: 190) a survey of sub-national authorities found little awareness of the rules around European Citizenship at the local level (CSES 2012). There is little evidence that any special measures have been put in place by Member States to improve social inclusion at the local level. Inclusion policies towards European citizens, such as they exist, tend to rely on services or institutions dedicated to all foreign citizens (Ernst and Young 2014). For the European Commission here is a problem of not enough Europe, or of obstacles to freedom of movement - a situation where the benefits of European citizenship need to be better communicated or implemented.

The Commission strategy has been to concede as little as possible with regards to conditions or changes to the core principles of freedom of movement. The response to the 2013 letter was technical in character – much of the communication was dedicated to clarifying and re-stating the rules – followed by the commissioning of expertise and consultations to produce additional knowledge and support to counter the Member States' claims. A 2010 EU Citizenship Report identified a 'gap' between the 'rules and the reality' faced by European citizens 'particularly in cross-border situations', and called on local authorities to promote European citizenship (EC 2010a). The Committee of the Regions (Europe's assembly of local and regional representatives) suggested that local and regional authorities could place pressure on their national governments to remove obstacles to implementation, and as a means of 'eliminating the EU's democratic deficit' (CoR 2011). The EU's other consultative bodies such as the European Economic and Social Committee (EESC) likewise are better set up to feed in problems of non-integration, where published opinions match closely with Commission priorities to expand free movement, rather than as a conduit for concerns over that movement's impacts.

A study carried out for the European Commission on the local impacts of free movement concluded that 'the overall evidence' on the impacts of intra-European movement 'suggests that this situation is not placing major issues and burdens on the local communities or local public services' (Ernst and Young 2014: (4). The research looked at how six European cities (Barcelona, Dublin, Hamburg, Lille, Prague and Turin) dealt with the issue and among its key findings were that more should be done to facilitate intra-European movement because 'practical and legal obstacles continue to limit the effective exercise of free movement rights' (Ibid: 6).

Notwithstanding the publication of such research backing up the Commission position on intra-European movement and 'welfare tourism', the gap between the positions outlined in the 2013 letter and its response persists and continues to resurface. A good example is provided by the long negotiation carried out by the UK government in preparation for its 2016 referendum on membership of the EU. One of Prime Minister Cameron's four demands for a 're-negotiated' settlement included provisions to limit access to in-work welfare benefits for European citizens exercising their right to freedom of movement. Cameron pointedly ignored the plea made by the Commission in its Communication and exaggerated both the problems of mobile EU citizens abusing the benefits system, and the idea that welfare acted as a 'magnet' for further migration. His meetings with other European leaders provided a useful snapshot of the European politics around freedom of movement. They certainly proved that the letter of 2013 was not indicative of a gathering consensus over 'welfare tourism'. Instead, the negotiations were instructive of the complexity of political negotiation around intra-European movement. Cameron's tour of Europe confirmed that every Member State has its own interests and concerns vis-à-vis European free movement its challenges. Germany's Merkel was happy to join with UK complaints about welfare 'abuses' but was keen to defend the principle of free movement and non-discrimination against Cameron's wider demands (Mason and Oltermann 2014). For sending countries like Poland there was the obvious interest in protecting large numbers of their citizens working abroad (Krajewski and James 2016). Ultimately, the eventual deal, complete with a 'safeguard' for 'exceptional inflows' of European citizens and further declarations on welfare 'abuse' (EUCO 2016) proved insufficient for the UK government to secure its favoured result in the 2016 referendum. Subsequent statements regarding the 'Brexit' negotiations have indicated that UK politicians are willing to relinquish membership of the Single Market to escape any obligations regarding free movement (May 2017).

9.7 Analysis and Conclusions

The topic of intra-European movement can be connected to an increasingly long-term crisis of political legitimacy in the EU and among European liberal democracies. Politics is a battle of ideas, and in conflicts over intra-European movement each side will naturally seek to use the topic to maximise their legitimacy and symbolic resources. As we have seen, the principle of free movement and increased levels of intra-European movement shifts patterns of legitimacy and support for political authority at different levels, albeit by alternative routes. In the case of nation-states this can be via in the form of resistance to supranational rule-making and demands for conditionality on the part of those receiving newcomers, or alternatively for the protection of rights already won for those whose nationals reside elsewhere in the EU. For the former, the battle over free movement has become a convenient way to assert national identity and the right to welcome through the language of hospitality. This speaks to populist demands for a re-assertion national political control and acts as a proxy for age-old arguments about state sovereignty. For those seeking to enlarge support for European integration, free movement can become central to demonstrating common European values and the politico-cultural benefits of European integration (ibid: 188) (see Pioneur Project - Rother and Nebe 2009).

This chapter has demonstrated how the contemporary struggles over this topic in the European space presents puzzles for all sides. One of these revolves around the obvious difficulties, tensions and/or incongruity in creating and sustaining a parallel regional politics of intra-European movement (based on one of the 'four freedoms' of the 1957 Treat of Rome) alongside one of immigration (the 'common immigration policy' promised by the Lisbon Treaty). This conceptual separation has clearly not been entirely absorbed at all levels. The very idea of a policy framework targeting intra-EU 'mobility' rests on a set of assumptions regarding the ability of political actors at the sub-EU level to successfully separate one kind of international movement from, inter alia, non-EU, irregular, asylum-seeking, or family-related migration. This raises the question of whether, and to what extent, the politics of intra-European movement can - at the EU, national and sub-national levels - really be characterised as something distinct or 'new' when compared with the usual business of (national) immigration politics and policy-making.

Another puzzle is at the local level – where the outcomes and consequences of intra-European movement are actually experienced. A key benefit of the project of which this book is an output is its focus on the urban setting and the specificities of CEE migration. This chapter problematized the assumption that politics around free movement can ever be 'resolved'. The topic reveals the limits and boundaries of European integration, the way in which international movement remains a key battle-ground for competing interests and ideas in the European political space. One of the observations has been that, despite the apparent 'flattening' of difference through transnational rights, structure and hierarchy can become re-imposed at the nation-state level because of the dominance of a paradigm of hospitality, e.g. through transitional arrangements and the discourse of welfare chauvinism. This is crucial because we know that notions of fairness and justice remain central to the struggle for legitimacy by political actors. As Zelano (2018) points out, the Commission has more recently demonstrated a greater willingness to talk of fraud around free movement, implicitly moving towards the language of hospitality. This concession to the language of fairness, implying an abuse of states 'generous' benefits, has been adopted in the absence of evidence that such a problem is significant.

The local has become the site of tensions between a purportedly progressive establishment and expansion of principles and rights for European citizens to move, live and work in other EU countries (e.g. through the ECJ) and arguments about impacts that result from mobility – the people and places that experience or 'deal' with it. Sub-national political units have become the battleground where this plays out, while they are often emasculated in terms of a lack of policy tools to govern and manage free movement. A key question is then how the urban implications can become incorporated into the politics of intra-European movement. As is explained elsewhere in this book, there are consequences that can be traced to a relative absence of a prominent or coherent policy agenda at the EU level which incorporates a narrative of impacts, or the urban implications of mobility. These consequences include the development of ad-hoc arrangements that for some have failed to address the consequences of the 'big-bang' enlargements of 2004/2007. These characteristics are especially notable if we pause to consider the central role which the urban environment plays in immigration patterns, where cities are known to be 'a major factor in shaping the trajectories and effects of immigration' (Nicholls and Uitermark 2016: 878). As scholars have demonstrated, there is a politics of venue-shopping where the EU is convenient for actors to avoid national constraints (Guiraudon 2000), but it is also convenient for governments to apportion blame where there is policy failure.

The case of intra-European movement demonstrates the complex, and sometimes unequal, outcomes of subsidiarity. The absence of a supranational governance system emphasises the central role that national governments maintain in European decision-making and in the interpretation and implementation of European rules. In this context we find that references and claims about the local and urban level from all sides are more instrumental than based on evidence - or on any genuine reflection of sub-national claims. Indeed, the discussion as it has developed at the European level tells us relatively little about the actual impacts of intra-European movement at the local level; rather it says more about the politics underlying the articulation of deliberative processes in the EU. These politics have real effects for European citizens. The result of conflicts and compromise over intra-European movement has been to construct a kind of social denizenship for mobile European citizens by those Member States that have been the main receivers of this kind of movement. The problems with the political claims based on ideas of solidarity or hospitality is they simply serve as convenient conceptual short-cuts in the debate over free movement, enlargement and labour market effects. They have political consequences and may not accurately reflect the migratory reality of intra-European movement - deliberately exaggerating some features while obscuring others. The balance reflects the continued dominance of the national paradigm, with myths such as the Polish plumber or Romanian strawberry picker tending to operate in the service of national interests (Sobis et al. 2015).

Returning to the opening point in this chapter about language, the vocabulary used to discuss these issues - 'migration' as opposed to 'mobility' - can be clearly linked to competing paradigms for understanding freedom of movement, its impacts, sustainability and future in policy terms. We should be aware in discussions of uncritically following the divisions set by state actors and be fully conscious of the ways that policy decisions affect EU and non-EU citizens, and their subjection to regimes of mobility and migration respectively. Otherwise we risk creating the spurious impression that, at least at the EU level, the question of who should be allowed to move between EU states, and on what basis, is – or can ever be – finally settled in political terms.

References

Bader, V. (2005). The ethics of immigration. *Constellations, 12*(3), 331–361.

Balabanova, E., & Balch, A. (2010). Sending and receiving: The ethical framing of intra-EU migration in the European press. *European Journal of Communication, 25*(4), 382–397.

Balch, A. (2010). *Managing labour migration in Europe: Ideas, knowledge and policy change*. Manchester: Manchester University Press.

Balch, A. (2016). *Immigration and the state: Fear, Greed and Hospitality*. Basingstoke: Palgrave MacMillan.

Balch, A., Balabanova, E., & Trandafoiu, R. (2014). A Europe of rights and values? Public debates on Sarkozy's Roma affair in France, Bulgaria and Romania. *Journal of Ethnic and Migration Studies, 40*(8), 1154–1174.

Berga, L and Spehara, A (2013). Swimming against the tide: Why Sweden supports increased labour mobility within and from outside the EU, *34,* Issue 2, 2013 *(Special Issue: Migration, Mobility and Rights Regulation in the EU).*

Blauberger, M. (2012). With Luxembourg in mind ... The remaking of national policies in the face of ECJ jurisprudence. *Journal of European Public Policy, 19*(1), 109–126.

Borjas, G. (1999). *Heaven's door: Immigration policy and the American economy*. Princeton: Princeton University Press.

Bresso, M. (2014). *Address to the conference of mayors on the impact of intra-EU mobility of EU citizens at the local level* (1st vice-president Committee of the Regions), Brussels, 11 February 2014, http://ec.europa.eu/justice/citizen/files/bresso.pdf

Brown, G. W. (2014). The European Union and Kant's idea of cosmopolitan right: Why the EU is not cosmopolitan. *European Journal of International Relations, 20*(3), 671–693.

Bucken-Knapp, G, Hinnfors, J. Spehar, A. and Zelano, K. (2018) The multi-level governance of intra EU mobility, in Scholten, P. and van Ostaijen, M. (Eds) (2018) *Between Mobility and Migration The Urban Consequences of Intra-EU Movement.*

Carrera, S., Merlino, M., & Parkin, J. (2011, June). *A race against solidarity: The Schengen regime and the Franco-Italian affair*. Brussels: CEPS Paper in Liberty and Security in Europe, Centre for European Policy Studies.

CoR (2011). Opinion of the Committee of the Regions on the "EU Citizenship Report 2010", Committee of the Regions, 2011/C 166/02, 2011.

Corbeye, D. (1995). Dialectical functionalism: Stagnation as a booster of European integration. *International Organisation, 49*(2), 253–284.

CSES. (2012). *Study on the role of local and regional authorities in promoting EU citizenship and citizens' rights*. Brussels: Centre for Strategy and Evaluation Services (CSES).

Currie, S. (2007). De-skilled and devalued: The labour market experience of polish migrants in the UK following EU enlargement. *International Journal of Comparative Labour Law and Industrial Relations, 23*(1), 83–116.

Dauvergne, C. (1999). Ammorality and humanitarianism in immigration law. *Osgoode Hall Law Journal, 37*(3), 598–609.
Dølvik, J., & Visser, J. (2009). Free movement, equal treatment and workers' rights: Can the European Union solve its trilemma of fundamental principles? *Industrial Relations Journal, 40*(6), 491–509.
Doty, R. L. (2003). *Anti-Immigrantism in western democracies*. London: Routledge.
Entman, R. (1993). Framing: Toward a clarification of a fractured paradigm. *Journal of Communication, 43*(4), 51–58.
EPRS (2014). The problem of human trafficking in the European Union, European Parliamentary Research Service, briefing 09/04/2014. http://www.europarl.europa.eu/RegData/bibliotheque/briefing/2014/140780/LDM_BRI(2014)140780_REV1_EN.pdf.
Ernst & Young (2014). 'Evaluation of the impact of the free movement of EU citizens at local level: An inventory of best practice' EY - Ernst & Young Global Limited (European Commission DG Justice) http://ec.europa.eu/justice/citizen/files/best_practices.pdf
EUCO (2016). Conclusions: European Council meeting (18 and 19 February 2016), General Secretariat of the Council (1/16) http://docs.dpaq.de/10395-0216-euco-conclusions.pdf
Eurofound (2015). Social dimension of intra-EU mobility: Impact on public services, publications Office of the European Union, Luxembourg (author: Klára Fóti).
European Commission (2001). 'The free movement of Workers in the Context of enlargement' information note, European Commission, Brussels, 6 March 2001.
European Commission (2010a). EU citizenship report 2010: Dismantling the obstacles to EU citizens' rights, European Commission, COM(2010) 603 final, 2010.
European Commission (2010b). Report on the application of title III (internal Borders) of regulation (EC) No. 562/2006 establishing a Community Code on the rules governing the movement of persons across borders (Schengen Borders Code), COM(2010) 554 final, Brussels, 13 October 2010.
European Commission (2013). Free movement of EU citizens and their families: Five actions to make a difference, COM(2013) 837 final, Brussels.
European Commission (2015). 'Press release: Commission opens infringement procedure against Hungary concerning its asylum law', Brussels, 10 December 2015, http://europa.eu/rapid/press-release_IP-15-6228_en.htm
European Parliament (EP) (2014). 'EU countries must respect the right to free movement, say MEPs', Press release - Employment policy – 15-01-2014, REF: 20140110IPR32337.
European Parliament (EP) (2017). 'Schengen: Civil liberties MEPs to debate new extension of internal border checks' Press release - Schengen – 08-02-2017, REF: 20170207IPR61521.
Faist, T., & Ette, A. (2007). *The Europeanization of National Policies and politics of immigration: Between autonomy and the European Union*. Basingstoke: Palgrave.
Favell, A. (2008) Eurostars and Eurocities: Free movement and mobility in an integrating Europe, Wiley.
Ferrera, M. (2005). *The boundaries of welfare: European integration and the new spatial politics of social protection*. Oxford: Oxford University Press.
Freeman, G. P. (2006). National models, policy types, and the politics of immigration in liberal democracies. *West European Politics 29*(2), 227–247.
Friedman, M. (1997) Interview with Peter Brimelow ('Milton Friedman, Soothsayer'), Forbes Magazine, December 29, 1997.
Geddes, A., & Boswell, C. (2011). *Migration and mobility in the European Union*. Houndmills: Palgrave Macmillan.
Golub, J. (2012). How the European Union does not work: National bargaining success in the Council of Ministers. *Journal of European Public Policy, 19*(9), 1294–1315.
Goodhart, D. (2004). 'Too diverse?', Prospect Magazine, February 2004 issue.
Grabbe, H., & Groot, N. (2014). Populism in the European Parliament: What implications for the open society? *The International Spectator, 49*(4), 33–46.

Guild, E., Brouwer, E., Groenendijk, K., and Carrera, S., (2015) What is happening to the Schengen borders? CEPS Paper in Liberty and Security in Europe No. 86.

Guiraudon, V. (1997). Policy change behind gilded doors: Explaining the evolution of Aliens' rights in contemporary Western Europe, 1974–1994, PhD Dissertation, Harvard University.

Guiraudon, V. (2000). European integration and migration policy: Vertical policy- making as venue shopping. *Journal of Common Market Studies, 38*(2), 251–271.

Hansen, P (2015). Undermining free movement: Migration in an age of austerity, Eurozine, http://www.eurozine.com/articles/2015-02-06-hansenp-en.html

Hollifield, J., and Wong, T., (2015) The politics of international migration in Brettell, C. and Hollifield, J. (eds) (2015) *Migration theory: talking across disciplines*. New York: Routledge.

IOM (1998). Trafficking and Prostitution: The Growing Exploitation of Migrant Women from Central and Eastern Europe, (Migration Information Programme) Trends In Organized Crime, 3 (4) (International Organization for Migration, Budapest).

Juncker, Jean-Claude (2015). 'State of the Union 2015: Time for honesty, Unity and Solidarity', speech by president of the European Commission, Strasbourg, 9 September 2015, http://europa.eu/rapid/press-release_SPEECH-15-5614_en.htm

Kaunert, C., Leonard, S., & Occhipinti, J. (2013). Agency governance in the area of freedom, security and Justice. *Perspectives on European Politics and Society, 14*(3), 273–284.

Krajewski, A., and James, W., (2016, 5 February). Poland's Kaczynski backs deal with Cameron to keep Britain in EU, Reuters, http://uk.reuters.com/article/uk-britain-eu-poll-idUKKCN0VE0IE

Lang, I. (2007). Transitional arrangements in the Enlarged European Union: How free is the free movement of workers? *Croatian Yearbook of European Law & Policy, 3*, 241–271.

Longo, M., & Murray, P. B. (2015). *Europe's legitimacy crisis: From causes to solutions*. Basingstoke: Palgrave Pivot.

Mason, R., and Oltermann, P., (2014). 'EU freedom of movement non-negotiable, says Germany', The Guardian Newspaper, Monday 3 November, http://www.theguardian.com/world/2014/nov/03/eu-freedom-of-movement-non-negotiable-germany

Maurice, E. (2016). 'EU and Switzerland agree on free movement' EU Observer: Brussels 22 December 2016 https://euobserver.com/justice/136398

May, Theresa (2017). 'The government's negotiating objectives for exiting the EU' (Speech of the UK Prime Minister), 17 January 2017 Lancaster House: London https://www.gov.uk/government/speeches/the-governments-negotiating-objectives-for-exiting-the-eu-pm-speech

McMahon, S. (2015). Regional integration and migration in the European Union. In Talani & McMahon (Eds.), *Handbook of the International Political Economy of Migration*. Elgar.

Menz, G. (2010). *The political economy of managed migration: Nonstate actors, Europeanization, and the politics of designing migration policies*. Oxford: Oxford University Press.

Mikl-Leitner, J., Friedrich, H. P., Teeven, F., and May, T. (2013). Letter to the President of the European Council http://docs.dpaq.de/3604-130415_letter_to_presidency_final_1_2.pdf

Nicholls, W. J., & Uitermark, J. (2016). Migrant cities: Place, power, and voice in the era of super diversity. *Journal of Ethnic and Migration Studies, 42*(6), 877–892.

Paul, R. (2013). Strategic contextualisation: Free movement, labour migration policies and the governance of foreign workers in Europe. *Policy Studies, 34*(2.) Special Issue: Migration, Mobility and Rights Regulation in the EU.

Peers, S. (2016). 'The final UK renegotiation deal: Immigration issues', EU Law Analysis blog 'Expert insight into EU law developments', http://eulawanalysis.blogspot.co.uk/2016/02/the-final-uk-renegotiation-deal.html

Perulli, P. (2012). The ontology of Global City-region: A critique of statehood. *GaWC Research Bulletin, 415*.

Recchi, E. (2015). *Mobile Europe: The theory and practice of free movement in the EU*. Palgrave: MacMillan.

Rosello, M. (2002). *Postcolonial hospitality: The immigrant as guest*. Stanford University Press.

Rother, N., & Nebe, T. (2009). More mobile, more European? Free movement and EU identity. In E. Recchi & A. Favell (Eds.), *Pioneers of European integration: Citizenship and mobility in the EU*. Cheltenham: Elgar.

Sassen, S. (2005). The Global City: Introducing a Concept. *Brown Journal of World Affairs, XI*(2., Winter/Spring 2005, p. 27. Ibid. Ibid.), 28–29.

Sayad, A (2010) Immigration and state thought In Martiniello, M., Rath, J. (Eds) (2010) Selected studies in international migration and immigration incorporation, Amsterdam: Amsterdam University Press.

Schoen, D., & Rein, M. (1994). *Frame reflection: Toward the resolution of intractable policy controversies*. New York: Basic Books.

Shah, D., Watts, M., Domke, D., & Fan, D. P. (2002). News framing and cueing of issue regimes: Explaining Clinton's public approval in spite of scandal. *Public Opinion Quarterly, 66*, 339–370.

Sinn, H.,–W. (2002). EU enlargement and the future of the welfare state, Scottish Journal of Political Economy, 49 (1), p 104–116.

Sobis, I., Junjan, V., and de Vries, M., (2015). 'Polish plumbers and Romanian strawberry pickers: How the populist framing of EU migration impacts national policies' Migration and Development, online June 2015.

Squire, V., & Darling, J. (2013). The "minor" politics of rightful presence: Justice and relationality in City of sanctuary. *International Political Sociology, 7*(1), 59–74.

van Ostaijen, M. (2016). Between migration and mobility discourses: The performative potential within 'intra-European movement. *Critical Policy Studies*. https://doi.org/10.1080/19460171.2015.1102751.

Walzer, M. (1983). *Spheres of justice: A defense of pluralism and equality*. New York: Basic Books.

Wiener, A., & Diez, T. (Eds.). (2009). *European Integration Theory*. Oxford: Oxford University Press.

Zelano, K. (2018). Free movement governance at the European level – An animal that lives in Brussels In Scholten, P. and van Ostaijen, M. (Eds) (2018) *Between mobility and migration the Urban Consequences of Intra-EU movement.*

Part III
Perspectives from Sending and Receiving Regions

Chapter 10
Poland's Perspective on the Intra-European Movement of Poles. Implications and Governance Responses

Marta Kindler

10.1 Introduction

To understand the consequences of intra-European movement for Poland we have to be aware of several political and socio-economic developments, which have shaped its scale and character. The main (geo)political occurrences, the falling apart of the Soviet Union and the end of the Cold War, allowed Poland to transform from a communist to a democratic system. It has changed from a country with strictly controlled outflows to one with borders open to migration. The possibility of free movement for Poles has increased even further with Poland joining the European Union (EU) and the Schengen Area (Anacka and Okólski 2014). As a result, Poles in the EU turned from so-called 'third-country nationals', whose movement is controlled, to freely moving EU citizens. The UK, followed by Ireland and Sweden, declared that they would not apply transitional arrangements and provided Poles with full access to their labour markets immediately after Poland's EU accession in 2004. By 2011 the last EU countries (Germany and Austria) opened up their labour markets to Poles. This means that Poles can work officially in all of the countries in the Schengen Area. According to the European Commission's terminology they are no longer 'labour migrants', but 'mobile workers'. The absence of these 'mobile workers' is for Poland a governance concern. *Poland's Migration Policy,*[1] approved by the Polish government in 2012, is a strategic document that sets out the general direction of activities that aim to 'minimize negative effects of emigration' by focusing on systemic solutions, especially concerning assistance to returnees, and monitoring the impact of emigration on Poland (in particular its social consequences) (MI 2012).

[1] The current Polish government has rejected this document in March 2017, calling for a new migration policy doctrine. No new document has been delivered by May 2018.

M. Kindler (✉)
Center of Migration Research, University of Warsaw, Warsaw, Poland
e-mail: marta.kindler@uw.edu.pl

P. Scholten, M. van Ostaijen (eds.), *Between Mobility and Migration*, IMISCOE Research Series, https://doi.org/10.1007/978-3-319-77991-1_10

The key economic and social developments, which have shaped the character of the intra-European movement of Poles, are a result of Poland's change from a centralised economy to a capitalist market economy. Since the early 1990s the country has witnessed structural unemployment, growing discrepancies in wages and unstable working conditions. Social aspects, such as a growing number of youth with higher education and more intense participation of women in the labour market (Augustyn 2010) increased the dynamics of labour market changes. Of crucial importance here are the different paste and level of economic development of Poland's regions, resulting in a growing polarisation – with some regions flourishing, while others being close to economic recession and the rate of unemployment being very diversified across the country (Anacka and Okólski 2014).[2] Overall, the average monthly salary in Poland is considerably lower than in other EU member states.[3] The significant differences between wage levels in Poland and other EU member states, combined with access to relatively cheap transport, a better knowledge of English than 20 years ago, and awareness of a large group of Poles 'out there' (potentially to fall back in case of need), made moving from a small town in Poland to London more attractive as a destination than moving to Warsaw, Poland's capital.[4]

Finally, we need to underline that the consequences of intra-European movement are not limited to EU countries. The possibility of intra-European movement for Poles, was accompanied by restrictions for migrants wanting to enter Poland. The liberal approach to foreigners entering Poland since the 1990s has slowly been curtailed with Poland's process of joining the EU. Visas for third country-nationals, among them Ukrainians, the main migrant group in Poland, were introduced in 2003, just before Poland's accession to the EU, and a more complex visa system was introduced upon Poland's joining the Schengen Area in 2007.[5]

The aim of this chapter is to provide, as part of the European research project 'IMAGINATION', the perspective of the migrant sending countries on intra-European movement. The chapter characterizes the migration corridors between Poland and urban regions in countries, which are the focus of this book, Austria, the

[2] In 2014, the overall unemployment rate for Poland was 11.7 per cent, but in the Warmia-Masuria region, for example, it was 18.4 percent, while in Warsaw, the capital it was 4.6 per cent. Apart from the few "winners of transformation", majority experienced ambivalent changes, with the situation of many people worsened. 7.4 per cent of the Polish population, around 2.8 million, lives below the subsistence minimum (CSO 2015).

[3] Equivalent to approximately 887 Euro net (3783.46 PLN) in 2014. http://stat.gov.pl/sygnalne/komunikaty-i-obwieszczenia/18,2015,kategoria.html

[4] In the 1990s Poland experienced a decline in internal migration from rural to urban areas due to labour market restrictions, increase in costs of living (rise in real estate prices and rental rates). In the year 2000 those moving from cities to rural areas outnumbered rural to urban migrants (Zborowski et al. 2012).

[5] Since June 2017, Ukrainian citizens can enter the EU for tourist purposes without a visa, on the basis of a bio-metric passport (in April 2017 approx. 3 million Ukrainians owned such passports). This visa-free migration does not affect regular labour migrants, however it may have an impact on irregular migration flows.

Netherlands and Sweden.[6] It concentrates on the Dutch-Polish corridor for three main reasons. First, the post-2004 movement of Poles was the largest to the Netherlands from the three respective countries. Second, the sending regions represent those with the highest intensity of outflow from Poland and are the places of origin of Poles who engaged in pre- and/or post-2004 movement. Third, it provides important examples of regional and trans-national migration governance. The chapter analyses the implications of intra-European movement of Poles for Poland, and in particular for sending urban regions to the Netherlands. It also reflects upon the link between the EU freedom of movement and the migration of third-country nationals to Poland.

10.2 "Let's go West!" CEE Migration Corridors from Poland: Characteristics and Institutional Context

10.2.1 Scale and Regions of Origin

Poland has had a long history of emigration and a significant track of increased temporary migration after its systemic transition in 1989. However, the post-EU accession brought an increase in scale difficult to ignore. While, according to 2002 census data, 2 percent of Poland's population were emigrants (786, 000 persons), the 2011 census data shows a 154 percent (sic!) (over 1.2 million) increase (for comparison of pre- and post-enlargement data see Chap. 2). Over 80 percent of these migrants stayed in European Union countries (CSO 2013).[7] Annual CSO estimates show that the stock of temporary migrants abroad has stabilized at 2 million people (6.6 percent of the total population), which is a significant number of absentees in particular regions. There is little evidence of returns of post-EU accession migrants. The substantial return migration to Poland, which was especially felt during the economic crisis of 2008–09, consisted mainly of migrants who have left Poland before 2004 and who returned to regions "with relatively long traditions of emigration and not necessarily the ones with strong pull factors" (Kaczmarczyk & Lesińska 2012:30).

According to the 2011 population census, Poles involved in intra-European movement originated mainly from Śląskie, Małopolskie, Dolnośląskie and Podkarpackie region (South-Western and Southern Poland) (see Fig. 10.1). The leading regions for intensity of outflows as compared to the number of inhabitants were Opolskie in Southern, Podlaskie in Eastern and Podkarpackie in South-Eastern

[6] Regarding the case of Turkey as a CEE migrants destination in the IMAGINATION project, apart from pre-1989 migration of Poles, contemporary migration is of incidental character.

[7] Among the "traditional" emigration destination countries for Poles are the United States, Canada and Australia. The United States, with the inflow of 255 thousand Polish emigrants between 1990 and 2005, was for a long time the main destination country. However, it has lost its position after 2004 to the UK and Germany (Fiń 2014; Kaczmarczyk 2010).

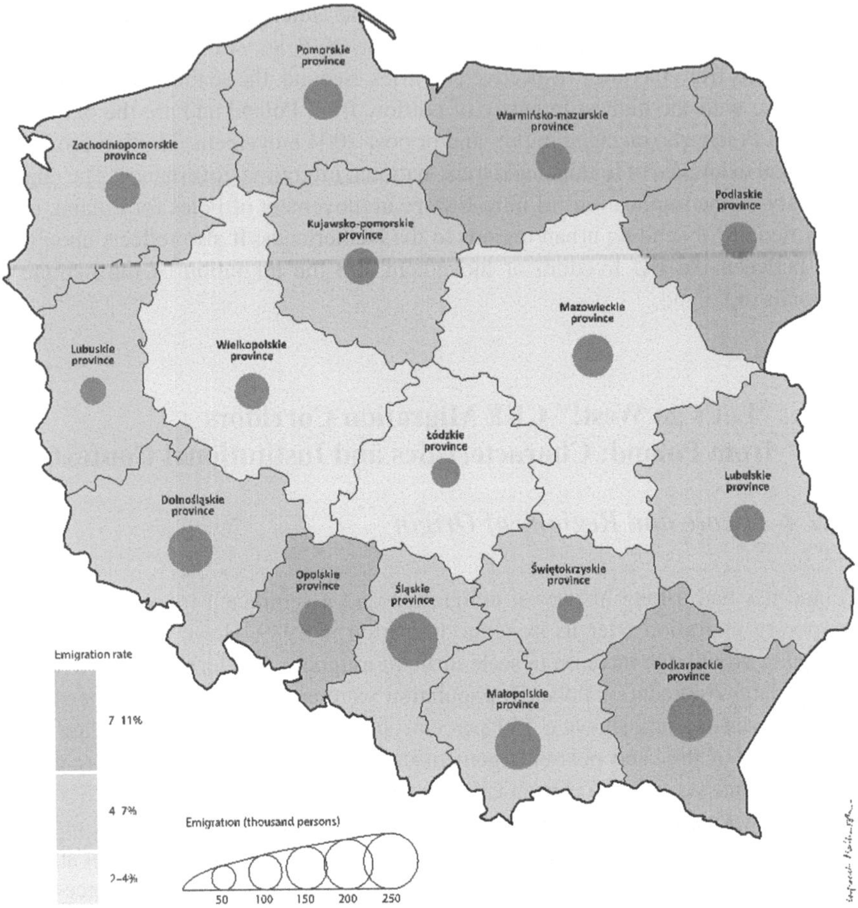

Fig. 10.1 Emigration from provinces in Poland, 2011

Poland (see Fig. 10.1, emigration rate). In terms of pre- and post-enlargement changes we can note that Dolnośląskie region has outnumbered Małopolskie in terms of people leaving. In addition, while for years the Opolskie region was in the lead and it continues to be among significant sending regions, migration from this region decreased (Grabowska-Lusińska & Okólski 2009).[8] In light of implications to be discussed, it is important to keep in mind that Opolskie and Podlaskie regions have the lowest number of inhabitants in Poland. Małopolskie and Podkarpackie regions are also no demographic strongholds. Opolskie, Podlaskie and Podkarpackie regions are for the most part economically underdeveloped areas with large agricultural sectors and declining industrial sectors (Kaczmarczyk 2012). Śląskie, Opolskie and Dolnośląskie regions, which are set near Poland's western border, also repre-

[8] The long history of international migration from Poland is among others present in the region of Małopolska, which has an over 100 years' long tradition of emigration to the United States.

sent the 'traditional' pattern of Polish migration based on ethnic ties and kinship, primarily to Germany (CSO 2013; Kaczmarczyk 2014). However, the intra-European movement involved also the participation of regions, which before 2004 played a marginal role as regions of migrants origin. It meant that the differences between the intensity of out-migration from particular regions in Poland has decreased (Grabowska-Lusińska & Okólski 2009, see Fig. 10.1).

It is worth noting that Poland is slowly transforming into a net immigration country. From the 1990s to 2005 the registered permanent emigration exceeded immigration, reaching its peak in 2006. Emigration remained high in the subsequent two years due to the already mentioned rapid growth of out-migration connected with EU accession. However, a visible increase in immigration is visible since 2007 and combined with a decrease in emigration, both flows equalised (Grzymała-Kazłowska 2013).

10.2.2 Intra-European Movement Corridors and Characteristics of Migrants

According to the 2011 population census, the four main EU destination countries for Poles were: the United Kingdom, Ireland, Germany and the Netherlands.[9] Table 10.1 shows the dynamics and changing patterns of the movement of Poles. We can trace the significant change occurred with the mass migration to the British Iles. 2007 was the peak year, with 2.3 million persons (6.6 percent of the population) abroad. Much smaller increases than those observed in the early post-accession years were recorded in the years 2011 to 2013. These changes were mostly due to an increase in the number of emigrants to Germany and the United Kingdom.

From the countries, which are the focus of the book, apart from the already mentioned Netherlands, which is among the main destination countries, in the case of Austria the most significant increase occurs between 2004 and 2007, with a substantial decrease due to the economic crisis in 2008. Fluctuations occur between 2011 and 2012, but the scale of migration in general is not that high. Sweden shows a steady increase, with no decrease due to the economic crisis (for comparison of data for Austria, the Netherlands and Sweden see Chap. 2).

Analysing the estimates of 'temporary migrants' from the perspective of the opening of labour markets to Polish nationals, there is a clear impact caused by the lack of transitional arrangements in accessing the labour market by Poles in the case of the UK, Ireland (access in 2004) and the Netherlands (access in 2007) and no visible impact in the case of Sweden (access in 2004) and in the case of Austria (access in 2011) (see also Chap. 2; for an in-depth analysis of the role of transitional

[9]According to the Polish 2011 Census data, the United States had the third highest number of Polish residents who stayed abroad for over three months (219 thousand). Among the other "traditional" destination countries, 48 thousand Polish residents stayed in Canada and 14 thousand in Australia.

Table 10.1 Estimates of Polish citizen staying abroad for longer than two months (three months since 2007) (thousands), and percentage changes as compared with previous year, 2002–14 (data for UK, Germany, Ireland, the Netherlands, Sweden and Austria)

Destination	Population census May 2002	2004[a]	2005[a]	2006[a]	2007[a]	2008[a]	2009[a]	2010[a]	2011[a]	2012[a]	2013	2014
	Thousands											
Total	786	1000	1450	1950	2270	2210	2100	2000	2060	2130	2196	2320
Europe	461	770	1200	1610	1925	1887	1765	1685	1754	1816	1891	2013
EU 27	451	750	1170	1550	1860	1820	1690	1607	1670	1720	1789	1901
United Kingdom	24	150	340	580	690	650	595	580	625	637	642	685
Germany	294	385	430	450	490	490	465	440	470	500	560	614
Ireland	2	15	76	120	200	180	140	133	120	113	115	113
Netherlands	10	23	43	55	98	108	98	92	95	97	103	109
Sweden	6	11	17	25	27	29	31	33	36	33	40	43
Austria	11	15	25	34	39	40	39	29	25	23	31	34
	Percentage change as compared with previous year[b]											
Total	.	.	45.0	34.5	16.4	−2.6	−5.0	−4.8	3.0	3.4	3.1	5.6
Europe	.	.	55.8	34.2	19.6	−2.0	−6.5	−4.5	4.1	3.5	4.2	6.4
EU 27	.	.	56.0	32.5	20.5	−2.2	−7.1	−4.9	3.9	3.0	4.0	6.3
United Kingdom	.	.	126.7	70.6	19.0	−5.8	−8.5	−2.5	7.8	1.9	0.8	7.5
Germany	.	.	11.7	4.7	8.9	0.0	−5.1	−5.4	6.8	6.4	12	9.6
Ireland	.	.	406.7	57.9	66.7	−10.0	−22.2	−6.4	−8.4	−1.7	−2.5	−1.7
Netherlands	.	.	87.0	27.9	78.2	10.2	−9.3	−6.1	3.3	2.1	6.2	5.8
Sweden	.	.	54.5	47.1	8.0	7.4	6.9	6.5	9.1	5.6	5.3	7.5
Austria	.	.	66.7	36.0	14.7	2.6	−10.0	−19.4	−13.8	12.0	10.7	9.7

Source: CSO (2015).

[a]as for the end of a given year

[b]2002–04 changes not reported due to lack of full data comparability

arrangements see (Fihel et al. 2015). As Fihel and co-authors write (2015) the primary drivers of migration were labour demand and such factors as migration networks and socio-cultural factors (including language). The impact of transitional arrangements (or their lack), although, as noted above, visible in the case of some countries, was less important. For example, the stable increase of Poles staying temporarily abroad in the Netherlands between 2004 and 2006, as well as the increase in 2007, apart from the impact of transitional arrangements, could be explained as a combination of the characteristics of migration from the Opolskie region (traditional sending region), the structure of the Dutch labour market and the role of recruitment (employment) agencies. The stable increase in the case of Austria between 2004 and 2006 may be due to the existence of migrant networks. Meanwhile, the lack of drastic increase in Sweden may be due to the low demand for foreign workers as a result of 'social control' mechanisms (trade unions and employer agreements), where wages are fixed at a high level, which may make employing a foreigner less profitable. Here the employment agencies direct the flows of qualified manpower to specific industries where migrant workers are in demand. In addition, in the case of Sweden and other Scandinavian countries 'posted worker' arrangements[10] are common. Another barrier to a sudden increase in the case of Sweden are socio-cultural factors, such as language.

As mentioned, the employment (recruitment) agencies play an important role in forming the migration corridor between Poland and some of the EU countries. The fact that they match employer and employee, and prepare prospective employees to take up work abroad is mostly relevant to non-English speaking countries (Napierała & Fiałkowska 2013). For example, agencies from Sweden organise language courses for new employees, often sharing the costs with employers. Research shows that courses were offered in French, German, English, Swedish, Dutch or Norwegian (Napierała & Fiałkowska 2013). Employers anticipate that investments made in future employees will pay off when they start working. It is also an opportunity for workers to improve their skills and employability.

Who were those Poles who engaged in mobility after 2004? According to the CMR/BAEL database from 2004–2006 almost two-thirds of post-accession migrants are men. Four regions, among them Opolskie and Śląskie, are an exception to this masculinisation of migration. Meanwhile, 2011 Census data shows already a 54% share of women among all emigrants (CSO 2013). Migrants involved in intra-European movement are also younger (on average below 30 years old) when compared to pre-2004 migrants. Here again four regions, among them Opolskie, are exceptions, with the migrants being older (Grabowska-Lusińska & Okólski 2009). The 2011 Census data shows that women migrate at a younger age then men. However, an important share constitute also women over 60 years old (possibly elderly-care workers or grandmothers proving care for their grandchildren) (Ślusarczyk & Slany 2016). Post-accession migrants are also relatively well educated, with the share of those with higher education having increased and those with

[10] A posted worker is employed in one EU Member State but sent by his/her employer on a temporary basis to carry out his work in another Member State.

primary education – decreased. According to the 2011 Census data women engaged in the post-2004 movement were better educated than men, with also a smaller share of women then men with primary vocational education. The share of migrants originating from towns with over 100 thousand inhabitants has increased. However, still the majority of migrants originated from villages (Grabowska-Lusińska & Okólski 2009). Unfortunately the available data tells us little about the socio-economic status of these migrants. From regional studies we know that many of those young migrants were graduates with no labour market experience. They were also rather childless. However, the proportion of accompanying dependents (under 14) has been growing over the past few years, which may be a sign of temporary migration changing into more long-term or even settlement migration (Kaczmarczyk 2013; CSO 2013). No mass migration of highly qualified labour was noted at that time, although in some professions, such as anaesthetists, the outflow was significant (Wiśniewski & Duszczyk 2007) (for information on types of Central and Eastern European migrants see Chap. 3). However, the socio-demographic diversity of this group points to high selectivity and suggests heterogeneity in terms of socio-economic status of Poles engaged in intra-European movement (see Chap. 1 in this volume).

As the CMR/BAEL data-base from 2004–2006 shows, the United Kingdom and Ireland are the main recipients of a large share of the young (not exceeding 28 years), relatively well educated post-accession migrants, who originate often from urban areas and frequently from regions which previously were not sending migrants abroad. 26 percent in Ireland and 22.5 percent in the UK of Poles had tertiary education. Meanwhile, intra-European movement from Poland to Germany and the Netherlands is characterised by the participation of a different type of migrant: over 40 years old, with vocational education and originating from rural areas (Grabowska-Lusińska & Okólski 2009, Kaczmarczyk 2010). Among migrants to the Netherlands only 4 percent had tertiary education. The two types of migrants in EU destination countries were present before 2004, however accession to the EU has changed the proportion of these in favour of younger, better educated, male migrants.

It is worth shortly outlining the particularities of the migration corridors, which are the focus of this book, these are: Austria, Sweden and the Netherlands (see also Chap. 2). The main regions of origin of Poles migrating to Austria are Małopolskie, Dolnośląskie and Podkarpackie, closely followed by the Śląskie and Mazowieckie regions. The first four regions of migrant origin are geographically concentrated, all located in the south, spatially the closest for travel to Austria. In Małopolskie, in the case of migrants going to Austria urban areas dominated as places of migrant origin (Bieńkowska et al. 2010b). The average length of stay abroad of Dolnośląskie region inhabitants was two years. 57 percent of migrants from Małopolskie region stayed 25 months or longer in Austria. However, the Małopolskie region study shows also that over 28 percent of those who stayed in Austria were short-term migrants (between 3 and 12 months) (Bieńkowska et al. 2009, 2010b). Thus, the general trend is rather long-term migration, although the scale of short-term migrants should not be ignored.

In the case of Sweden, the majority of Poles originated from the Zachodniopomorskie, Pomorskie and Mazowieckie regions (see Fig. 10.1). The first two regions are located in the north, neighbouring with Sweden across the Baltic Sea. When looking at the share of migrants to Sweden as compared to the total number of migrants from the region, Zachodniopomorskie, Mazowieckie and Dolnośląskie have the most (CSO 2013). As in the case of Austria, Poland's EU accession has not significantly impacted migration from Poland to Sweden. Migrant networks play a role, with Sweden having already had a large Polish diaspora before 2004 (Gerdes & Wadensjö 2013). The role of recruitment agencies is also significant, as is the demand for highly skilled migrants originating mainly from urban regions. The recruitment agencies are to a large extent responsible also for the selectivity of migration, with a predominance of young women in post-accession migration to Sweden.

As we will later on focus also on the regional implications of the Poland-Netherlands corridor, the description of this corridor is more detailed. In case of the Netherlands, Poles have migrated there long before Poland's accession to the European Union. The autochthon population (having German roots) from the Opolskie region has a long history of labour migration primarily based on dual Polish-German citizenship (Walaszek 2007, Jończy 2014, CSO 2013, Kaczmarczyk 2013, Chap 2). The 2002 population census showed 10,000 Poles staying temporarily in the Netherlands. The scale of post-2004 migration from Poland has completely taken by surprise Netherland's policy-makers, who were expecting approximately 20,000 persons arriving. The 2011 census shows a ten-fold increase to the data from 2002, with over 105, 000 Poles staying there temporarily.

The migrants to the Netherlands originate mainly from Southwestern Poland (see Fig. 10.1). The Opolskie region borders with the Czech Republic. It is known both for its history of emigration and the intensity of outflows. According to Jończy (2014) approximately 9 thousand persons are permanently absent for already several years from the Opolskie region, which he coins as a new type of post-accession "suspended migration" (the total estimate for the region of those suspended migrants – i.e. those who have emigrated, but did not deregister - is 100,000). Estimates of unregistered emigration (permanent and labour) in the population of Opolskie region (total of 1013 thousand) were equal to 200 thousand persons by the end of 2011 (Jończy 2014). The informal channel of recruitment that developed in the past between Opolskie and the Netherlands was cemented and further developed by recruitment agencies in the 1990s, providing access to the non-autochthon population of the region, which dominated post-accession migration.[11]

Apart from the already mentioned Opolskie, also Śląskie and Dolnośląskie dominate as sending regions (see Fig. 10.1). The Śląskie region borders with the Czech

[11] In a study of labour demand based on the activity of private intermediary (placement) agencies in the Opolskie region, 57 per cent of the 67 agencies surveyed (a total of 71 agencies were as identified as functioning in the region) were companies with Dutch capital (Duczmal et al. 2008). Over 40 per cent of these agencies were based in the city of Opole, 28 per cent in the opolskie county and 15 per cent in the kędzierzyn-koźle county.

Republic and Slovakia and is a traditional emigration region like Opolskie. This spatial closeness and existence of migrant networks are important explanations for the reasons for migration from this area, as in terms of economic indicators the region is doing well.[12] At least one member of over 7 percent (120,931) of households went abroad for over three months between 2004 and 2011. From these, approximately 10 percent (12093) chose the Netherlands as their destination (Bieńkowska et al. 2011).

The Dolnośląskie region is placed at the border with Germany and the Czech Republic. In Dolnośląskie there is a great internal discrepancy in regard to unemployment rates with the highest rate equal to 25.9 percent (wałbrzyski poviat) and the lowest to 4.2 percent (wrocławski poviat).[13] These differences meant that the region was at the bottom end among regions in Poland in regard to the stability of the functioning of the labour market. However, thanks to the EU accession it became one of the fastest developing regions. Still the systemic transformations were so dramatic that the level of employment has not reached yet the levels from 1999.[14] Between 2004 and 2007, 6 percent (12012) of all 182,000 migrants from the Dolnośląskie region headed for the Netherlands (Bieńkowska et al. 2009).

Almost 90 percent of Poles staying in the Netherlands fall into the category of labour migrant and a significant share constitute short-term migrants (3–12 months) (CSO 2013). The 2011 population census data also shows that short-term migration (3–12 months) is certainly more significant in the case of the Netherlands, than it is for Sweden or Austria. This is linked to both the larger scale and the more seasonal character of labour migration to this country. Migration to the Netherlands was feminized until Poland's EU accession and the post-accession migration brought an increase of male migrants (Kaczmarczyk et al. 2012).

10.3 Implications of Post-2004 Migration for Poland

Post-enlargement migration from Poland is characterised by a greater variety of forms then post 1989 migration, including the tendency to stay longer and even settle abroad (see also Chap. 2). The population outflow due to intra-European movement has already had enormous consequences for the intensification of depopulation[15] at regional and local level, especially for cities (Zborowski et al. 2012; Spórna et al. 2016). This is due to the fact that particular regions in Poland are clearly 'migrant-sending regions' and due to the selectivity of migration, with particular

[12] http://www.mg.gov.pl/files/upload/8436/RoG20150820_ost.pdf

[13] http://wroclaw.stat.gov.pl/publikacje-i-foldery/inne-opracowania/raport-o-sytuacji-spoleczno-gospodarczej-wojewodztwa-dolnoslaskiego-w-2014-r-,1,3.html

[14] http://www.umwd.dolnyslask.pl/fileadmin/user_upload/Rozwoj_regionalny/SRWD/poprawionySWOTwtorek1.pdf

[15] Depopulation is understood as the phenomenon of statistical long-term population loss (Spórna et al. 2016)

groups more inclined to migrate. As a result of migration population, ageing intensifies. The young age of migrants has caused the birth rate to fall in Poland by approximately 10 percent (Fihel & Solga 2014). This, together with the number of children born abroad, influences the changing population structure of Poland as a whole and of particular regions. Assuming no return of post-accession migration, the birth rate will fall by another 10 percent and by 2035 the population structure will be a challenge to the labour market with a decrease in those of working age (KBM PAN 2014).

Focusing on the migrant sending regions to the Netherlands, Śląskie and Opolskie (traditional emigration regions) have to cope with consequences of depopulation (accompanied by low birth rates and an ageing population) (KBM PAN 2014; for information on consequences for receiving regions see Chap. 3). A number of towns in these regions can be classified as "shrinking cities", among them in the Katowice conurbation (total of 33 cities) in Śląskie and small urban centres in Opolskie (Zborowski et al. 2012; Spórna et al. 2016). The most difficult situation is in the Opolskie region. As was already mentioned, according to estimates approximately one-third of the regions' population have left the region over the past 35 years (Jończy 2014). The rate of emigration for this region is 10 times higher than the average rate for Poland, and the region's birth rate is the lowest in the country. Depopulation has had a negative impact on development in over 70 percent of the Opolskie region's counties. This is primarily due to the migration of young and entrepreneurial inhabitants. One in every five people aged 20–30 has left the region (Jończy 2014; Solga 2013). Jończy (2014) writes that emigration abroad is accompanied by the internal exodus of young people to large urban centres, especially to the city of Wrocław, both to study and to find work. As a result of all of these factors population ageing in this region is especially acute, with the regional government having established a special demographic area.[16]

The depopulation of the region, particularly visible in rural areas and in smaller cities, is accompanied by the reduction of infrastructure. Schools, kindergartens, and nurseries are being closed down, the number of local associations, sports clubs and voluntary fire brigades decreases, bus and train connections cease to exist (Jończy 2014, Solga 2013). This is not only the result of emigration, but it also becomes its additional cause, decreasing the region's attractiveness as a place to live and thus making it even more prone to depopulation and emigration (Jończy 2014).

Since 1990s, the process of depopulation affected all cities of the Śląsk region. In the years 1990–2013, the Katowice conurbation depopulation process concerned 32 out of 37 municipalities, characterised by urban shrinkage of some cities, with a large number of young people under 35 migrating to other cities and abroad. For example, the city of Bytom has lost practically all of its economic base - it has currently only one coal mine operating (out of 6 mines in the 1980s) and companies related to the fuel and clothing industries have been closed or moved to other cities. Approximately 8 percent of flats are uninhabited (Spórna et al. 2016).

[16] http://ssd.opolskie.pl/page/

Researchers analysing the impact of the post-accession migration on families in the Opolskie region, using a normative and blaming phraseology, claim that non-autochthon (Silesian) population is less masculinised and thus causes more often what has been called 'full euro-orphanage' (both parents working abroad and children remaining in Poland) (Jończy 2014).[17] Authorities point out the substantial financial strain caused by the combination of migrant workers paying taxes abroad and not contributing to the local budget, while at the same time expecting local institutions to educate their children and to care for their elderly parents. As Solga notes (2013) after 2004 there has been a clear increase in expenditure on elderly care for migrant families in 39 percent of the counties in the Opolskie region. The counties have to cover the full costs of home-based care or social assistance provided to elderly members of migrant families, as it is often difficult to find evidence of the real income of those working abroad (Solga 2013).

Depopulation is linked also to lack of labour force at the regional labour markets. 25 percent of the gminas (administrative communities) in Opolskie experience a deficit of labour supply due to the migration of specialists and qualified workers (Solga 2013). The potential impact of post-2004 returnees on the regional labour markets is not yet known, as was noted earlier it seems that those who have returned are pre- enlargement migrants. However, the post-2004 migrants may not fill the gaps. As was stated before post-accession migrants to the Netherlands are predominantly temporary labour migrants, who are rather older and with vocational education. Thus, these are not the type of returnees that local and regional authorities wish for (Solga 2013). Also among the returnees to Śląskie region in the period 2004–2011, the majority did not have a proof for the new qualifications and skills they gained abroad (Bieńkowska et al. 2011). As a result the unemployment rate can actually rise.

When it comes to the macro-economic implications, the post-2004 migration resulted in a decrease in the unemployment rate in Poland to below 10 per cent in 2007 and a general improvement in economic indexes. However, these can be attributed also to other factors such as a better economic climate or wider structural changes. Has migration had a positive impact on the level of unemployment in the regional labour markets as claimed in the "crowding-out" hypothesis (Grabowska-Lusińska & Okólski 2009)? The hypothesis states that the people from peripheral regions with low financial capital an oversupply of labour move. In Opolskie the decrease of the unemployment rate in the years 2004–2008 is clearly visible. The Western part of the region was much more affected by a decrease of unemployment due to migration, as it was until the enlargement characterised by 2–3 times higher rates of unemployment then in the rest of the region (Jończy 2014). Similarly, migration abroad played one of the key roles as drivers of unemployment decrease in cities in the Katowice conurbation (Śląsk province) (Spórna et al. 2016). However,

[17] As Walczak (2014) rightly notes, although there may be negative consequences to leaving the socialisation and upbringing of one's child to a (non-parent) family member, such a state cannot be equated with the condition of an orphan, since the parents are very much present via phone or other means of communication.

since 2008 the impact has declined, with a number of migrants deciding to settle abroad and the purchasing power and the possibility for investments (due to the strengthening of the Polish currency) of the returnees having declined. A number of autochthons decided to return, which on the one hand resulted in partial economic revival, while on the other hand (combined with the macro-economic crisis) meant an increase in unemployment rates.

Also what should be noted from macro-economic implications is that for the past 20 years remittances have played a growing role in the Polish economy, increasing from 0.5 to 1.5 per cent of GDP in the years 1995–2011, with a peak of 2.5 per cent of GDP in 2006–07. Remittances have contributed to the growth of real disposable income and to an increase in household consumption contributing a further 0.1 percentage points to GDP from 4.3 to 4.4 per cent (Barbone et al. 2012). As Luca Barbone and other authors write: 'The value and share of remittances in GDP increased considerably after Poland joined the EU and most European labour markets opened their doors to Poles. Remittances were also larger than EU transfers until 2008.' Remittances have an enormous effect on macroeconomic aggregates (consumption and income). At the level of household budgets, Barbone and other authors (2012) showed that: 1) remittances are sent to a relatively small number of households in Poland (2.5 percent in 2008) and represent a sizeable portion of their incomes; and 2) recipients of remittances are mainly from small towns and rural areas rather than large cities.

Focusing on the Poland-Netherlands corridor remittances in the Opolskie region were appraised at PLN 6 billion in 2010 (approx. € 1,5 billion). This huge sum accounted for half of the Opolskie inhabitants' annual disposable income and as a result has led the rankings of disposable income among all the regions in Poland (Jończy 2014). Data on other regions show that approximately one fourth of migrants has sent remittances in a regular fashion. According to data from a study (2004–2011) carried out among returnees in Śląsk, 27 percent of returnees have sent regular remittances while abroad (the majority a monthly amount between PLN 1000 and PLN 2500, approx. €250–625). 19 percent sent remittances occasionally. What is also of great importance is that among households receiving remittances, they were the main source of income for 41 percent and in addition an important source of income for 32 percent (Bieńkowska et al. 2011). In general remittances were spent on consumption, renovations and buying property (evidence among others from Śląskie and Opolskie region) (Bieńkowska et al. 2011; Solga 2013).

It is difficult to find support in data on social remittances, which actually are a more long-term effect of migration. This difficulty stems partly from the newness of post-accession migration. According to research results from Dolnośląskie and Śląskie, return migrants were more open, tolerant and self-assured than before migration (Bieńkowska et al. 2010a, 2011). The studies mainly referred to cultural capital in the form of learned language and work experience that was regarded as valuable (i.e. helped them to find work back in Poland.) Kaczmarczyk (2012:11), who analyses Social Diagnosis data, writes that: 'persons with migration experiences assess their chances on the Polish labour market in a more positive way than non-migrants, are more self-confident, open-minded and ready to accept different lifestyles, while at the same time are relatively critical of religious or political authorities'. However, he also points to the fact that overall the return migrants do share roughly the same characteristics as non-migrants. However, Gawlewicz (2015a), who studied how migrants and non-migrants influence each other's ideas regarding sameness and difference in terms of gender, ethnicity, religion and sexuality, shows that although there is a multi-sidedness to the circulation of ideas, migrants as 'experts in migration' are more often seen by non-migrants as 'being correct'. This circulation of ideas is not determined by the migrants', but occurs also during migration, due to regular contact via Internet and phone. Among the social transfers is also a particular language of difference, either that of respect (inclusive or 'politically correct') or of stigma (essentialist and orientalist understanding of difference), with the latter being more often transferred than the former (Gawlewicz 2015b). The sending regions with a large share of seasonal migrants and temporary workers are characterised by a particular migration culture, affecting the rhythm of life of local inhabitants. Yet another important aspect is the transformation of attitudes toward 'traditional' gender and family roles of post-EU enlargement migrants with a belief that more balance in household responsibility is needed. At the same time there is resistance towards these changes, with the public discourse on emigration characterised by a normative and blaming phraseology[18] (Grabowska & Engbersen 2016).

Summarising, financial remittances have a powerful impact on the overall poverty rate and result in a slight decrease in income disparities (Barbone et al. 2012). For example, studies from the Opolskie region shows that the opportunity to work abroad has improved standards of living (better housing, providing education for children) in social groups which before migration were socio-economically marginalised (Jończy 2014). Although, the opportunity to earn well relatively quickly allowed numerous families to escape social marginalisation, regional authorities in general see rather the negative consequences of migration predominating. For regional authorities trans-European movement translates into demographic change and challenges related to regional development. Even within those regional authorities that, due to long emigration experience, seem to be better prepared for dealing with the challenges and facilitating migrants' return, new counties start to send migrants, and demand a response to the consequences from the local authorities. Some representatives of the authorities claim the migration of those who belong to a labour oversupply (young graduates) and the return of migrants with new skills and capital as positive implications. Even the positive aspect of remittances with increased consumption and overall improvement of living standards of migrant families has another side results in polarised development of regions. The outflow of the most entrepreneurial and relatively well educated has demographic, social and economic consequences and intensifies this polarisation. Apart from the Opolskie region, hardly any of the regional development strategies respond to international migration issues.

[18] For a more detailed discussion see Kindler 2015.

10.4 EU Mobility and Third-Country Nationals Migration as two Sides of the Coin: Poland's Governance Responses

In general, contemporary migration, meaning actually intra-European movement, was not until recently among the Polish state's priorities. The authorities saw their obligations as being primarily towards Polonia – to those who had long been settled abroad, but especially to Polish ethnic minorities in the countries of the former Soviet Union. The Poles abroad who are of greatest interest to representatives of the state are those who can 'stand for Poland': those working in international organisations, Polonia leaders, etc. The more challenging migrants – those who are exploited, are victims of trafficking or have failed to integrate abroad – were for a long time seen as having to bear the burdens of their own migration decisions. However, the scale of post-accession migration, its consequences for particular regions in Poland in terms of labour shortages and a change in institutional competencies[19] resulted in the inclusion of post-accession migrants as one of the groups addressed by the diaspora policy. The Ministry of Foreign Affairs (MFA), which has taken over responsibilities for Poles abroad, provides funds to civil society in Poland and abroad, supporting both Polonia and contemporary migrants with top-down activities (administrative determinants of governance). This funding programme also forces the professionalisation of Polonia organisations and a change from state-centric to civil society-centric in terms of implementation of activities (although financed from the national budget).

In regard to the protection of Poles rights abroad, there is a scarcity of bilateral and transnational forms of governance. The migration corridor between Poland and the Netherlands is a rare case that provides some examples. The transnational co-operation takes place at different levels. When it comes to the country level, such institutions as the Polish Social Insurance Institution (ZUS) and the National Labour Inspectorate (PIP) send their representatives abroad to organise meetings with Polish migrants and opening liaison offices abroad. In addition, in November 2006 the Polish National Labour Inspectorate (PIP) and its Dutch counterpart (*Arbeidsinspectie*) signed an agreement on co-operation and data exchange that covers existing legal regulations, placed workers and workers' complaints. It is clear that those migrants using intermediary agencies get most of their information from these agencies, and if inaccurate, or deliberately false, information is provided to the potential migrant, they are at increased risk of becoming victims of human trafficking. In 2014 the Netherlands' Embassy in Poland began to develop a regional network on labour migration, funded by various authorities in the Netherlands. Its principal mission is to engage with local networks, experts and civil society in Poland, and to provide pre-departure information for potential migrants. Regarding

[19] Until 2007 the Polish Senate was responsible for Polonia issues and the notion of 'caring for the diaspora' was present in the discourse. With the MFA taking over responsibilities for Poles abroad the discourse shifted to treating the diaspora as a partner.

multi-level governance, many bottom-up activities are funded or co-funded nationally. There are examples of projects carried out between Polish and Dutch regulatory bodies, civil society, local, regional and national authorities aimed at preventing exploitation of Polish migrant workers.[20] Among the organisations involved in such projects are La Strada Poland, the NGO FairWork,[21] the Association of Polish Women in the Netherlands[22] and the Foundation Barka NL.[23]

Returning to the country-level of governance, in 2008 an Interdepartmental Working Group on Return Migration was appointed which developed a programme that assumed the government should not try to influence individual migrants' decisions to return, but rather should provide migrants with necessary information enabling them to make an informed decision (Duszczyk et al. 2009). The programme was quite ambitious and consisted of several packages. The main flagship however was the information portal POWROTY (returns) launched in 2009. The most systematic examples from the local (urban) level of governance are regional policy solutions concerned with the outcomes of migration in the Opolskie province. In 2007 the local authority launched the 'Opolskie – I'm staying here' project to promote employment and professional development within the region and thus decrease the number of migrants. The programme is also aimed at potential students and migrant returnees. Regional office representatives took part in employment fairs in numerous European countries to promote returning to the Opolskie region among Polish migrants. Information meetings about unemployment benefit and business start-up funds were held in countries where Poles were working and planning to return. The 'Opolskie – I'm going to live here' programme, in place since 2009, aims to ameliorate the effects of migration from the region and the resulting depopulation, and to encourage people from other regions by promoting sales of land. The demographic impact of migration is regarded as the most significant obstacle to the regional development strategy for the years 2012–20.[24]

However, the absence of a significant number of Poles, combined with a very low fertility rate and accelerated ageing of the population (CSO 2013, European Migration Network and European Policy Committee, 2011), meant that the share of economically active population decreased and the share of economically passive population of Poland increased. Counting on returnees did not seem to be sufficient. In 2006 the Ministry of Labour and Social Policy stated that labour shortages were becoming a serious issue and the government needs to elaborate a 'method of ensuring a decent amount of highly qualified workers to address the current state of affairs within the Polish and the international labour market" (Sejm RP 2006 cited in Duszczyk et al. 2010: 69). As a result of these declarations Poland introduced already in 2006 a simplified employment scheme for short-term workers from countries of the Eastern Partnership, including Ukraine. This scheme allowed citizens' of

[20] For a more detailed discussion on the different forms of governance see Kindler 2015.

[21] http://www.fairwork.nu/polska.html

[22] http://www.topolki.nl/

[23] http://www.barkanl.org/

[24] For a more detailed discussion see Kindler 2015.

Poland's neighbouring countries to take up employment in agriculture and horticulture without a work permit for a period of three months within six months. It enabled farmers to employ foreign workers already in the harvest period of 2006. This regulation was further liberalised in 2009, with today citizens of five countries allowed to work for up to six months within a twelve month period without a work permit. Although the declarations concerned highly qualified workers, this ordinance attracted mainly low skilled workers. Over 1.3 million (96 per cent of all declarations) employer's declarations was issued to Ukrainian nationals in 2016,, while in the first half of 2017 there were 947,917declarations registered to Ukrainian nationals showing the significant demand for foreign workforce.[25] Since 2009 employers, who have employed a foreigner who entered on the basis of the mentioned declaration and work for at least 3 months, can apply for a work permit without the labour market test.[26] From 2012 to 2014 the regional (voivodship) administrative offices issued 12,984 work permits without the labour market test. This constituted 11.14 per cent of all work permits issued in that period. Further liberalisation of access to Poland's labour market is visible in changes in the procedure for granting work permits to foreigners, which was time-consuming and expensive for employers until 2007. The legal changes starting in 2007 regarding the labour market and promotion of employment simplified the process and speeded it up, as well as considerably reducing the fees paid by employers when applying for a work permit or for an extension of a work permit.

The character of immigration is "island-like" – concerning only certain regions in Poland (mainly well prospering and eastern border regions), while in others migrants are practically nonexistent. Ukrainian migrants are mainly concentrated in large towns and urban centres, with a clear predominance of the Mazowieckie region, with the capital, Warsaw (Fihel 2006; Górny and Toruńczyk-Ruiz 2014). The Mazowieckie region has the lowest unemployment rate and the highest number of those economically active in Poland. The Ukrainian labour migrants, similarly to Poles migrating abroad, are on average relatively young (below 40 years old). The majority of Ukrainians are relatively well educated, with the greater part having at least secondary vocational education (Kaczmarczyk 2015), however the agreement on mutual recognition of education (2005) is not *de facto* applicable, as a lion's share end up in low-skilled or unskilled jobs.

Important to mention is the presence of a segmented labour market, with Poles being less and less willing to work in the secondary sector of the labour market for a low remuneration. This makes the Ukrainian migrants a complementary labour force, with most migrants engaged in seasonal work in agriculture, but also in construction and domestic work, including elderly and child-care. The implications of the presence of Ukrainian labour force is especially important for those regions where labour market sectors, such as agriculture (for the Mazowieckie, Lubelskie, Podkarpackie and Małopolskie regions), play a dominant role. The presence of

[25] Data from the Ministry of Family, Labour and Social Policy https://www.mpips.gov.pl/analizy-i-raporty/cudzoziemcy-pracujacy-w-polsce-statystyki/

[26] A labour market test proves that no Polish worker can perform the duties offered.

Ukrainian women in the domestic works sector translates also in the possibility for Polish women to enter the labour market, and fill-out an important institutional care-gap. However, at the same time a petrification of domestic work as 'women's work' occurs, with Polish men not engaged (Kindler et al. 2016). Ukrainian migrants are also visible in education – as either foreign language teachers working in provincial schools or as teachers of Russian or Ukrainian language in private language schools. In the former case they have a very positive impact on the respective town, where it is usually difficult to find Polish teachers for the position (Bieniecki & Pawlak 2008).

As some scholars claim budget losses occur due to the unofficial character of work (no taxes) and little spending by Ukrainian migrants in Poland (mainly spending in Ukraine) (Brunarska et al. 2012). However, these budget losses are disputable. As a recent study considering different scenarios of the fiscal impact of Ukrainian migration shows there might not be any, rather the opposite. As Kaczmarczyk writes (2015:28), "Ukrainian immigrants not only do make a positive contribution to the Polish public finances but it is higher than in case of the native-born". As the author explains this is a result of the particular forms of labour market incorporation, rather than a function of the socio-demographic characteristics of Ukrainians migrants. However, at the same time, a complete legalisation of migrants from Ukraine in Poland is expected to translate into a significant increase of the tax base and extension of the revenue side (Kaczmarczyk 2015). The Polish migration policy points among the future needs and recommendations of further action to provide novel legal channels for managing labour migration, thus reducing the scope for irregular migration and to create a welcoming environment for the settlement of migrants who are perceived to improve significantly the competitiveness of the Polish economy. Still, the Polish authorities show no political will to adopt a migrant integration policy, with a strategic document prepared by a few dedicated administrative officials and experts waiting "in the drawer". In general, having a large group of irregular migrants may mean a marginalised and exploited group that the state will have at some point to take responsibility for.

10.5 Conclusions

During the communist era emigration from Poland was closely controlled by the state, restricted and politicized, which is reflected in the great value placed by Poles on freedom of movement within the EU. This freedom as such is an important factor in triggering migration from Poland.

The character of pre- accession migration and intra-European movement did not change substantially in the case of Poles. What has changed significantly is the scale of temporary labour migration – with a significant increase in the stock of migrants in the United Kingdom, Ireland and the Netherlands and gradual but highly selective increase (with young women dominating) of the migrant stock in the case of Sweden. What is also important, there are signs of temporary migration changing into more long-term or even settlement migration. It seems that transitional arrangements as to the opening of labour markets were not of key importance, and social factors, such as existing networks and recruitment agencies, as well as cultural factors, such as language, did play important roles in the formation of the migration corridors from Poland.

As at length presented in this chapter, the implications for Poland's main sending regions, range from outright negative such as depopulation, in some cases characterised by the shrinkage of cities, decrease of labour force and increase in intra-regional inequalities, to a few positive (among others improved the lot of individual families). When it comes to governance responses to those implications we can point at the country-level to three main changes in state policies (1) the redefinition of policy towards the diaspora by identifying the post-accession migrants as one of the addressees, as well as providing support for organisations representing *Polonia* and Poles abroad, (2) liberalisation of access to the labour market for third-country nationals, (3) activities facilitating return (both at state and at regional level). The Ministry of Foreign Affairs' (MFA) governance towards Poles abroad is clearly 'in the making'. They are attempting to harmonise the very different interests of the diverse Polish community abroad. We need to note the changes that occurred after the 2015 elections, with the party Law and Justice in power. The current Minister of Foreign Affairs has already announced that the Polish Senate will again receive the competencies for the Polish diaspora and the emphasis will be yet again on "Polonia in the East". At the local (urban) governance level, bottom-up activities are much more ad hoc, but also seem to be more responsive to the specific needs of migrants and overall migration implications. However, examples of a systemic form of migration governance can be found in the case of Opolskie province.

Poland is - similarly to the Czech Republic (see Chap. 6) and to Turkey (see Chap. 8) – a special case in the 'IMAGINATION' research analysis. It is both a sending and a receiving country. Poland's responses towards the entry and work of Ukrainian migrants provide evidence how the consequences of free movement are not limited to EU territory. Intra-European mobility and migration of third country nationals, while treated often as two separate phenomena by policy-makers, are two sides of the same coin. For Poland this means a double governance challenge. Apart from informing its citizens abroad on the possibilities of return to Poland, they responded to the labour demand created partly by Poles leaving by simplifying the access to the labour market by Ukrainians. The question remains whether the facilitated access to labour markets for Ukrainians really was an answer to the consequences of Poles leaving. Probably to a small extent. It rather was an answer to the changes within Polish society and labour market, making the complementarity (in the terms of competence) of Ukrainian labour force debatable. Ukrainians take over those jobs that Poles are able to do (in terms of competence), but are not willing to do due to unfavourable working conditions. Whether these who have previously worked in jobs currently occupied by Ukrainians is not clear. Looking at the regions from which Poles have emigrated and which experience depopulation do not have, most, apart from Opolskie region, a policy actively attracting immigrants (both internal and external) to settle. Thus, regional governments do not as of yet use the emigration-immigration nexus for their benefit. Time will tell whether the governance of third-country nationals will contribute to solving the challenges related to consequences of intra-European mobility in Poland.

References

Anacka, M., & Okólski, M. (2014). Migracja z Polski po akcesji do Unii Europejskiej. In M. Lesińska, M. Okólski, K. Slany, & B. Solga (Eds.), *Dekada członkostwa Polski w UE. Społeczne skutki emigracji Polaków po 2004 roku* (pp. 45–70). Warszawa: Wydawnictwa Uniwersytetu Warszawskiego.

Augustyn, M. (2010). Opieka długoterminowa w Polsce. Opis, diagnoza, rekomendacje. 9 Availabe at: http://rszarf.ips.uw.edu.pl/kierunki/ODzielona.pdf

Barbone, L., Piętka-Kosińska, K. & Topińska, I. (2012). "The Impact of Remittances on Poland's Economy" CASE Network E-briefs. Available at: http://www.case-research.eu/sites/default/files/publications/2012-12_Barbone.pdf

Bieniecki, M., & Pawlak, M. (2008). *Wpływ integracji migrantów na lokalne społeczności.* Warszawa: Instytut Spraw Publicznych.

Bieńkowska, D., C. Ulasiński, J. Szymańska (2009). Migracja powrotna w województwie Dolnośląskim. Skala zjawiska, potencjał oraz pogłębiona charakterystyka powracających (Return migration in the Dolnośląskie region). Opracowanie w ramach projektu Kierunek Śląsk. Centrum Doradztwa Strategicznego: Kraków.

Bieńkowska, D., Ulasiński, C., & Szymańska, J. (2010). Warto Wracać? Strategie zachowań reemigrantów i rozwiązania służące wykorzystaniu ich potencjału. Opracowanie w ramach projektu Kierunek Dolny Śląsk. Kraków: Centrum Doradztwa Strategicznego.

Bieńkowska, D., Ulasiński, C., & Szymańska, J. (2010b). *Powroty z migracji zagranicznych do Małopolski. Opracowanie w ramach projektu Kierunek Małopolska.* Kraków: Centrum Doradztwa Strategicznego.

Bieńkowska, D., Szymańska, J., Ulasiński, C., Gruszka, M., Majka, M., Chodacz, W., Trzaskalski, B., & Nowak-Trojnar, N. (2011). *Wyjazdy i powroty z emigracji mieszkańców województwa śląskiego (Migration and return of the śląskie region inhabitants).* Kraków: Wyniki badań. Opracowanie w ramach projektu Kierunek Śląsk. Centrum Doradztwa Strategicznego.

Brunarska, Z., M. Grotte & M. Lesińska (2012). Migracje obywateli Ukrainy do Polski w kontekście rozwoju społeczno-gospodarczego: stan obecny, polityka, transfery pieniężne. CMR WP 60/118. Migration Research Centre, University of Warsaw. Available at: http://www.migracje.uw.edu.pl/publ/2017/

CSO (2013). Migracje zagraniczne ludności. Narodowy Spis Powszechny Ludności i Mieszkań 2011 (Population migration abroad. National Population Census 2011).Warsaw: Central Statistical Office. Available at: http://old.stat.gov.pl/gus/5840_14782_PLK_HTML.htm

CSO (2015). Concise statistical yearbook of Poland 2015, GUS/CSO. Available at: http://stat.gov.pl/obszary-tematyczne/roczniki-statystyczne/roczniki-statystyczne/maly-rocznik-statystyczny-polski-2015,1,16.html.

Duszczyk, M., Kaczmarczyk, P. & Rusielewicz, A. (2009). Raport z działania grupy roboczej ds. migracji powrotnych Polaków (Report of workinggroup on return migration of Poles), Kancelaria Prezesa Rady Ministrów. Warszawa.

Duszczyk M., Lesińska, M., Stefańska, R., Szczepański, M., & Szulecka, M (2010). Polityka migracyjna w Polsce oraz jej wpływ na napływ i osiedlanie się imigrantów. W: Górny A, I. Grabowska-Lusińska, M. Lesinska, M. Okólski. Transformacja nieoczywista. Polska jako kraj imigracji, pp. 69–124. Wydawnictwa Uniwersytetu Warszawskiego. Warszawa.

European Migration Network, European Policy Committee (2011). The 2012 Ageing report: Underlying assumptions and projections methodologies, European Economy Series

Np. 4/2011, Brussels. Available at: http://ec.europa.eu/economy_finance/publications/european_economy/2011/pdf/ee-2011-4_en.pdf
Fihel, A. (2006). Przestrzenny wzorzec osiedlania się cudzoziemców w Polsce. *Studia Demograficzne, 2*, 49–67.
Fihel, A. and Solga, B. (2014). Demograficzne konsekwencje emigracji poakcesyjnej. W: Lesińska M., M. Okólski, K. Slany, B. Solga (red.). Dekada członkostwa Polski w UE. Społeczne skutki emigracji Polaków po 2004 roku, pp. 87–108. Wydawnictwa Uniwersytetu Warszawskiego. Warszawa.
Fihel, A., Janicka, A., Kaczmarczyk, P. & Nestorowicz, J. (2015) Free movement of workers and transnational arrangements: Lessons from the 2004 and 2007 enlargements". European Commission. Available at: http://ec.europa.eu/social/main.jsp?langId=en&catId=89&newsId=2223&furtherNews=yes
Fiń, A. (2014). Współczesna emigracja polska w Stanach Zjednoczonych: liczebność, rozmieszczenie przestrzenne, przyczyny wyjazdów. *Studia Migracyjne – Przegląd Polonijny, nr, 2*, 105–130.
Gawlewicz, A. (2015a). 'We inspire each other, subconsciously': The circulation of attitudes towards difference between Polish migrants in the UK and their significant others in the sending society. *Journal of Ethnic and Migration Studies, 41*(13), 2215–2234. https://doi.org/10.1080/1369183X.2015.1045463.
Gawlewicz, A. (2015b, December). Production and Transnational Transfer of the Language of Difference: The Effects of Polish Migrants' Encounters with Superdiversity. *Central and Eastern European Migration Review, 4*(2), 25–42.
Gerdes, Ch. & Wadensjö, E. (2013). Immigration to Sweden from the new EU member states. Swedish Institute for European Policy Studies.
Górny, A., & Toruńczyk-Ruiz, S. (2014). Neighbourhood attachment in ethnically diverse areas: The role of Interetnic ties. *Urban Studies, 51*(5), 1000–1018.
Grabowska-Lusińska, I. & Okólski, M. (2009). Emigracja ostatnia? Wydawnictwo Naukowe Scholar. Warszawa.
Grzymała-Kazłowska, A. (2013). Migration and socio-demographic processes in central and Eastern Europe: Characteristics, specificity and internal differences. *Central and Eastern European Migration Review, 2*(1), 2013. http://www.ceemr.uw.edu.pl/vol-2-no-1-june-2013/editorial/migration-and-socio-demographic-processes-central-and-eastern-europe.
Jończy, R. (2014). *Ekonomiczno-społeczne skutki współczesnych migracji na przykładzie region opolskiego*. Warszawa: Komitet Badań nad Migracjami Polskiej Akademii Nauk.
Kaczmarczyk, P. (2010). Poakcesyjne migracje Polaków. *Próba bilansu, Studia Migracyjne – Przegląd Polonijny, nr, 4*, 5–36.
Kaczmarczyk, P. (2012). Matching return migrants' competencies and labour market needs – the case of Polish returnees. Paper prepared for the OECD conference 'The Economic Impact of Emigration in Latvia and the other Baltic Countries: Challenges and Policy Implications', 17 December 2012.
Kaczmarczyk, P. & Lesińska, M. (2012). Return Migration, State Policy and Integration of Returnees – The case of Poland. In: Isabell Zwania-Rößler & Vanya Ivanova (eds) Welcome Home. Challenges and Chances of Return Migration. Transatlantic Forum on Migration and Integration. Available at: www.gmfus.org/file/2876/download
Kaczmarczyk (2013) Are immigrants a burden for the state budget? Review paper. European University Institute. Italy. Available at:http://cadmus.eui.eu/bitstream/handle/1814/28637/RSCAS_2013_79.pdf?sequence=1.
Kaczmarczyk, P. (2014) Recent Trends in International Migration to Poland. The 2012 SOPEMI Report. Available at: http://www.migracje.uw.edu.pl/publ/2373/
Kaczmarczyk, P. (2015) Burden or Relief? Fiscal Impacts of Recent Ukrainian Migration to Poland. IZA, Discussion Paper No. 8779. Bonn. Access at http://ftp.iza.org/dp8779.pdf
Kaczmarczyk, P., Lesińska, M., & Stefańska, R. (2012). *Polacy przebywający czasowo w Królestwie Niderlandów*. Warszawa: Opracowanie. Fundacja Ośrodek Badań nad Migracjami.

KBM PAN (2014). Społeczne skutki poakcesyjnych migracji ludności Polski. Raport Komitetu Badań nad Migracjami Polskiej Akademii Nauk.Warszawa.

Kindler, M. (2015) "A closer look at the mobility of poles. Post-accession migration to Austria, the Netherlands and Sweden – Its character, its impact on Poland and its governance" Country report – Poland. IMAGINATION working paper. Available at: http://project-imagination.net/publications/country-reports/294-country-report-poland

Kindler, M., Kordasiewicz A. & Szulecka, M. (2016). Care needs and migration for domestic work: Ukraine-Poland. International Labour Organization. Geneva. (report).

MI (2012). Polityka migracyjna Polski. Stan obecny i postulowane działania. Warsaw: Ministry of Interior.

Napierała, J. & K. Fiałkowska (2013). Mapping the market for employment agencies in Poland. In: Jon Horgen Friberg& Line Eldring (eds) Labour migrants from central and Eastern Europe in the Nordic countries patterns of migration, working conditions and recruitment practices. Nordic Council of Ministers. Denmark. Online: http://norden.diva-portal.org/smash/get/diva2:702572/FULLTEXT01.pdf

Ślusarczyk, M. & Slany, K. (2016) „Demograficzne i socjologiczne implikacje wyjazdów z Polski. Dyskusja na bazie wyników narodowego spisu powszechnego 2011 roku". *Studia Migracyjne-Przegląd Polonijny* z.1 (159), pp.127–150.

Solga, B. (2013). *Miejsce i znaczenie migracji zagranicznych w rozwoju regionalnym (the place and meaning of migration abroad for regional development).* Opole: Politechnika Opolska.

Spórna T., Kantor-Pietraga, I. & Krzysztofik, R. (2016) „Trajectories of depopulation and urban shrinkage in the Katowice conurbation, Poland", Espace populations societies, 2015/3–2016/1 DOI: https://doi.org/10.4000/eps.6102.

Walaszek, A. (2007). Migracje Europejczyków 1650 – 1990. Wydawnictwo Uniwersytetu Jagiellońskiego. Kraków.

Walczak B. (2014). Dziecko, rodzina i szkoła wobec migracji rodzicielskich: 10 lat po akcesji do Unii Europejskiej. Rzecznik Praw Dziecka. Warsaw: Pedagogium. Available at: http://brpd.gov.pl/sites/default/files/raport_-_dziecko_rodzina_i_szkola_wobec_migracji_rodzicielskich_-_10_lat_po_akcesji_do_unii_europejskiej.pdf

Wiśniewski, J. & Duszczyk, M. (2007). Migracje zarobkowe Polaków po 1 maja 2004. In: L. Kolarska-Bobińska (ed.) Emigrować i wracać. Migracje zarobkowe Polaków a polityka państwa. Instytut Spraw Publicznych. Warszawa.

Zborowski, Andrzej, Soja, Maria and Anna Łobodzińska (2012) Population trends in Polish cities-stagnation, depopulation or shrinkage? Prace Geograficzne, zeszyt 130. Doi….

Chapter 11
Intra-European Movement of Czechs with Special Regard to Austria and Care Givers (The "MICO" Type - Between MIgration and COmmuting)

Dušan Drbohlav and Lenka Pavelková

11.1 Introduction

A new era in the field of European migration came in the late 1980s and the very beginning of the 1990s when CEE countries freed themselves from communism and started to build their new democratic future. Deep societal (political and economic) transition and transformation processes in this region were crowned in 2004 when 8 CEE countries joined the European Union (EU). New migratory patterns typically showed increasing flows correlating with the date of joining the EU however, these patterns started to evolve only step by step over time.[1] In any case, the intensity of international migration of CEE citizens both within and outside the EU depends on many various factors related to both macro and micro level characteristics of the given country of origin – be it socioeconomic conditions, working opportunities, living standard, mentality, age, life satisfaction but also experience of migration movements and their historical context, existing social networks abroad and the "strength" and activities of respective diasporas. On the other hand, conditions in countries of destination matter too (e.g. Fassmann et al. 2014a).

Our goal is to contribute to the topic of intra-European migration while elaborating more on emigration of Czechs or rather on intra-European migration mobility of Czech citizens in general and their migration movements to Austria in particular. The emigration or long-term migration of Czechs (by contrast to immigration) and related patterns were almost ignored by the academic sphere (see exceptions to this trend – Nešpor 2002; Brouček et al. 2001; Hrubý, Brouček 2000; Filípek 1999;

[1] There are various studies informing us about migration and mobility to the EU, within the EU generally, between individual European regions or even between EU member states (see e. g. Okolski 2012; Verwiebe et al. 2014; Kahanec et al. 2014; Fassmann et al. 2014; Favell 2013, 2008; O'Reilly 2007; Engbersen et al. 2013; Bahna 2015; Verwiebe et al. 2015).

D. Drbohlav (✉) · L. Pavelková
GEOMIGRACE, Department of Social Geography and Regional Development, Faculty of Science, Charles University, Prague, Czech Republic

P. Scholten, M. van Ostaijen (eds.), *Between Mobility and Migration*, IMISCOE Research Series, https://doi.org/10.1007/978-3-319-77991-1_11

Brouček, Grulich 2014; Pařízková 2011; Vavrečková, Hantak 2008; Vavrečková et al. 2000; 2008; Drbohlav, Rákoczyová 2012; Kuchyňková, Ezzeddine 2015). Therefore there is not much information we can rely on.

The chapter is structured into four sections. Following this introduction, selected available information about emigration and long-term migration of Czechs is presented. Some of the migratory/mobility flow and stock data for Czechs to/in Austria are also highlighted. Furthermore, our empirical study on Czech care givers in Austria, the topic which has not been much tackled so far, is introduced. The conclusion summarizes the most important results. Comments on how the given migratory patterns of Czech care givers fit other migratory types known among intra-European CEEc migrants are also made.

11.1.1 Emigration and Labour Migration from Czechia Abroad – Basic Parametres and Patterns

When dealing with the Czech international migration data, one has to mention that the flow as well as the stock emigration data is incomplete. Obviously, data on emigration of Czech citizens from Czechia is underestimated because, although citizens are obliged to declare a change of their permanent residence when emigrating abroad (leaving the country for a longer period or forever), they often do not follow this obligation (Kupiszewska, Nowok 2006, see also Fassmann et al. 2014a, b). In fact, the same fact is typical of many other EU countries and their intra-European migrations – very often they are not recorded and reported to respective authorities (see e.g. Verwiebe et al. 2014).

Despite logical expectations for more intensive international migration movements of Czechs after the Velvet Revolution, Czechs have always been rather reluctant to move. A summary of the most important factors which stand behind the low level of emigration (and long-term international migration) from a 1994 quotation is still relevant today: "Czechs seem to be firmly rooted in their own country. Although there is a tradition of emigration there are factors curbing the numbers of those leaving the country. First, there is the not completely unrealistic hope of a better tomorrow. Secondly, people always were and more so are tied to their own country (strong emotional ties to their properties and home than in many other countries). Thirdly, there is a heritage of the last forty years during which nearly all aspects of "personal activities" (a very important factor to emigration) were subjugated (… this is valid especially for middle-aged and older individuals who also often suffer from the lack of knowledge of foreign languages … - new remark). Fourthly, it is typical of the Czech mentality in particular not to solve a situation directly and drastically" (Drbohlav 1994: 102; see also Drbohlav, Rákoczyová 2012; Hampl et al. 1999 – some of the above aspects can also explain low intensity of internal migration in Czechia). Moreover, "fascination with the West" has diminished whilst

Table 11.1 Immigration to and emigration from Czechia, (flows) 2009–2014

	2009	2010	2011	2012	2013	2014
Immigration	39,973	30,515	22,590	30,298	29,579	41,625
Citizins of Czechia	1,174	2,469	1,917	1,691	1,736	3,135
Emigration	11,629	14,867	5,701	20,005	30,876	19,964
Citizens of Czechia	2,279	2,386	3,233	3,331	3,724	3,910
Overall net migration	28,344	15,648	16,889	10,293	−1,297	21,661

Source: Czech Statistical Office (n.d.)

being transformed into short or very short visits focusing on education, tourism, recreation or shopping. In addition, living standards in Czechia vis-à-vis old member states have been, albeit slowly, increasing while more working opportunities have started to appear.[2] Overall, regardless of the gradually less restrictive (intra-EU) policies of the old member states as potential destinations, the estimated emigration flow out of Czechia has been perceived as rather low so far (see Vavrečková et al. 2000) and its impacts on the society as a whole have been rather small (except for a very specific issue of Roma emigration and border zone circular labour migration at the beginning of the 1990s). Simply expressed, immigration rather than emigration has become an issue in Czechia.[3]

As Table 11.1 demonstrates Czechia, except for 2013, has recently been gaining population via the international migration. The overall immigration has been increasing after a drop in 2011 (due to the global crisis) whereas the overall emigration oscillates between around 6,000 people emigrating in 2011 and 31,000 people emigrating in 2013. The emigration of Czechs according to the official statistics represents numbers between 2,000 and 4,000[4] for a period 2009–2014. The problem is that this data is unreliable and many of those who had left the country are not taken into account, including migrants moving to other EU countries.

[2]Very good economic performance in Czechia was interrupted by the global economic crisis in 2008, nevertheless, the current economic development of the country measured via GDP growth is among the highest in the whole EU (as of the third quarter of 2015 – 4.5%) and is accompanied by low inflation rate (0.4% in 2014) and very low unemployment rate (as of October 2015 – 4.8%), too - see https://www.czso.cz/.

[3]The booming economy (especially in the mid of the 1990s, between 2000 and 2008 and since 2014 onwards) created strong "pulls" and in some of these periods brought increasing numbers of foreign labour force to Czechia: number of immigrants residing in Czechia grew from 78,000 in 1993 to 254,000 in 2004 and to the current 451,923 (as of December 2014 – see http://www.mvcr.cz/clanek/cizinci-s-povolenym-pobytem.aspx?q=Y2hudW09MQ%3d%3d)

[4]Between 1994 and 2000 registered emigration figures did not exceed 1,300 persons a year (this figure includes both foreigners and Czech citizens). After 2000, registered outmigration increased mainly due to foreign nationals leaving Czechia while the number of Czech citizens emigrating according to official statistics remained very low during the 2000s. Recently (2005–2009) this number has been around 2,000 persons (regardless of the change of emigration intensity as a whole).

Some of the information about Czech emigrants abroad can be taken from the EUROSTAT databases about Czech citizens living in other EU member states[5] (stock data). According to this source, the most numerous Czech minorities living abroad long-term (data for 2014 or 2013) are in Germany (43,000), Slovakia (12,000) Austria (10,000), Spain (9,000) and Switzerland, Italy and Ireland (between 5,000 and 6,000). As the data proves, there has been a significant increase of the given numbers from the 2000s onwards. On the other hand, in comparative perspective (Czechia vis-à-vis other "emigration countries") increasing of Czech intra-EU migratory mobility is in relative terms rather moderate (see Fassmann et al. 2014a, b). If the most recent data is summarized for the EU countries (although using the incomplete database, e.g. not including data for France or the United Kingdom) there were around 93,000 Czech citizens living in other EU member states in 2014. Whereas there is no specific and "robust" data about their reasons for migration, we can deduce that economic motives clearly predominate (see also Vavrečková et al. 2000, 2008; Vavrečková 2014).

Table 11.2 (see annex) brings another stock data – data from different sources put together by the Ministry of Labour and Social Affairs. This kind of data gives a very rough estimate of the Czech citizens employed in the EU and Switzerland between 2006 and 2014. These estimates indicate that numbers of Czech citizens abroad had increased significantly over time reaching around 112,000 in 2014. Since 2008, the estimated figures of Czechs employed in Austria have been significantly increasing too, with almost 13,000 Czechs in 2014. According to this data source, Austria ranks third among the given countries after the United Kindom and Germany where some 37,000 and 32,000 (respectively) Czechs might have worked in 2014.

11.1.2 Czechs in Austria

Because of many historical ties, Austria has been a traditional destination for CEE migrants for a long time. More specifically, in 2013 Czechs ranked the fourth most numerous immigrant (foreign-born) group in Austria among CEE with around 42,000 people (14.1%)[6] (many of them however, had already lived in Austria for many decades – see also Fassmann et al. 2014a, b; Reeger, Enengel 2015). Migrants from Czechia were also part of temporary, mostly circular and often cross-border movements just after the Velvet Revolution, i.e. in the early 1990s (see also sources in Verwiebe et al. 2014). This flow continues although it has been diminishing. The data from the latest Czech Census 2011 shows that 5,109 Czechs[7] acknowledged their regular cross-border commuting to Austria. Majority of them were eco-

[5] The data sources are administrative records or national surveys. For some datasets statistical estimation methods are applied, mostly based on census, migration and vital statistics data – see more: http://appsso.eurostat.ec.europa.eu/nui/submitViewTableAction.do

[6] After Romanians, Poles and Hungarians (Fassmann et al. 2014a, b).

[7] 0.5 million people however, did not answer the respective Census questions at all.

nomically active people commuting for work, with 46% commuting daily and 26% weekly.

As indicated above, between 10,000 and 13,000 "new Czechs" may be currently living and/or working in Austria. This is further supported by the data from The Public Employment Service Austria ("Arbeitsmarktservice" - www.ams.at) that shows that 12,742 Czechs worked in Austria at the end of 2014 (data based on social security payments). These numbers have been growing over time – e.g. in 2009 it was only 5,136 migrants. It seems that some of these migrants commute (see above) which is why most of them work in federal states bordering with Czechia – Lower Austria (4,296) and Upper Austria (2,770). The third most important hub of working Czechs is in the capital city of Vienna (2,248).

Overall, Austria represents quite an important destination for Czechs. Nevertheless, the intensity of migration and commuting of Czechs is, in a comparative perspective, rather low. Based on the above and generally limited information which would enable to break down the data by important sociodemographic and geographical characteristics, one can only speculate or deduce. There is probably no dominating "migration corridor" from Czechia to Austria in terms of migratory types, destinations, occupational structure, age and so on. There are rather smaller, fragmented "migration/mobility corridors" that respect diversity patterns even among one migratory group of Czechs within the intra-EU migration/mobility from Czechia to Austria. One may deduce that different Czech migrants and commuters move to Austria staying for shorter or longer periods or circulating back and forth. Vienna will be the destination for both highly-skilled Czechs often working for multinational or international companies (– these will not be as numerous), and medium or low-skilled blue-collar workers and small self-employed entrepreneurs operating mainly in services, construction, some industrial branches or private households. The latter migratory type will also be typical of Austrian regions, towns and villages that border or are located close to Czechia where, in addition, seasonal migrants and commuters will also be very active. As mentioned above the impact of the migration/mobility of Czechs upon Austrian cities and society is rather moderate due to a "dispersed character" of the given phenomena. Accordingly, the same moderate effect is apparent in Czechia. Work experience in Austria, be it long or short term, now brings additional financial sources for the Czech migrant/commuter and their families (via financial remittances) and in some cases an "added value" from social remittances. In any case, because of a growing living standard this has become a pleasant bonus rather than a necessity for Czech families involved in the given migration/mobility. On the same note, the overall impact of Czech activities performed in Austria is moderate and does not fundamentally influence economy and any sphere of the society.

Respecting the context outlined above we have decided to shed some light on the migration of Czech female care givers to Austria. There are several reasons behind this strategy: (1) This migratory type has been selected as one of the prominent ones within the studied intra-EU mobility, more specifically between the CEE and selected old EU member states (see Chap. 2 - by Denis Sert). (2) Through the research of this flow, we want to publish an important message about feminization of the migration as pointed out throughout the whole book. Moreover, this type of migration deserves a special attention since what we currently know about this phenomenon lags behind due to "blurred realities" that accompany often informal organisation, on top of that, encapsulated in a private, family environment. Hence, we also contribute to demonstrate the complexity and diversity which are typical for the current CEE intra-EU mobility (see e.g. Ostaijen, Scholten – Chap. 13). (3) Though not so robust in quantitative terms now, the given flow has a potential to grow since there is an increasing demand on the Austrian side (related to ageing of Austrian population – see below). At the same time, it will probably be advantageous for Czech women to make use of these opportunities in Austria in the future (higher income). Furthermore, both sides can benefit from historical, cultural and geographical proximities.

11.1.3 Czech Care Givers in Austria

Like most European countries, Austria is an ageing country which means that the number of elderly people who are often in need of special assistance is increasing. This intensive ageing process seems to be a permanent feature of the today's Austrian society (see also UN 2015). Similarly to other European countries, for example Italy and Spain, Austria relies on foreign workforce. Unlike Italy and Spain however, care workers in Austria usually come from the EU countries (Österle, Bauer 2015). Similarly again vis-à-vis to Italy and Spain, taking care of the elderly is percieved as a family issue and families tend to care for their elderly at home instead of using institutional care (European Commission 2012; Riedel, Kraus 2010). This broadly used system resides in employing migrant care workers (predominantly women) in the 24-hour caring system (24-Stunden-Betreuung). It is based on rotation of two workers, normally after two weeks. Workers usually live with their client/patient for two weeks and are with them round the clock whilst having only a short break during the day. After two weeks, they switch with their colleague and go home for two weeks. This way, the patient is cared for constantly but workers also get some spare time and are free to go to be with their own family (Österle, Bauer 2012).

The system started to be used in Austria at the beginning of the 1990s but was practiced illegally or semi-legally for a long time. The application of this system has also been supported by cash-for-care benefits introduced in 1993. Using such benefits, people in need would get certain financial support without having to prove how it was spent (it could be given to family members or to an employed worker) (Österle, Bauer 2015; Bahna 2014). Thanks to this system, Austrian families could get benefits without having to show any employment contract of their care giver. The use of this system had become a widely spread phenomenon and an accepted option for Austrian families whilst the government did not proceed with any regulations. It was not until 2006 when several cases of irregular employment of migrant care workers were reported (including families of some political leaders[8]). Hence, care work became a political issue and was part of the election campaign in 2006 (Österle, Bauer 2012; Riedel, Kraus 2010). As a result, the new government introduced a legal framework for care work in 2007 (in force since 1st January 2008). The main law, the Home Care Act (Hausbetreuungsgesetz), was applied. It introduced a new profession - personal care workers/givers in private households. Apart from this law, foreign care workers in Austria were also exempted from the labour market restrictions for workers from the new EU member states. These restrictions were in force between 2004 and 2011 (Österle, Bauer 2015). The new legislation specified the rules of employment of care workers, giving the list of tasks that should be performed, including medical tasks (which must be delegated by a doctor). To make the system affordable, the option of self-employment (instead of employment contract) was introduced (today, a vast majority of the care workers in Austria are self-employed). The legislation also changed the benefit scheme – currently, benefits are means-tested and the care workers have to prove their training (minimum of 200 hours) and work experience otherwise the family will not receive, according to the law, any financial aid.

Currently, according to available data, most women employed in care work in Austria are from Slovakia (56% in 2013) and Romania (30% in 2013) (Österle, Bauer 2015). It seems that women from Czechia constitute a less important group of care givers in Austria now (see in Bahna 2014). By contrast, in the 1990s, Czech women were probably the most numerous group working in the care sector there. With improving economic situation of Czechia, however, the care work in Austria is for Czechs not such an attractive option anymore and there are fewer women taking this path now. It does not mean, nevertheless, that it is not worth studying. Despite the decrease, this migration flow does not seem to stop. It is rather getting stabilised as an option for women working in care work and health care who need to earn more money. Differences in wages and prices between Czechia and Austria have been diminishing, nevertheless, in the field of care work, the gap still remains substantial. According to the OECD statistics, the average annual wage in Austria was 5.7 times higher than in Czechia in 2000, whereas it was still 3.4 times higher in 2014 (OECD n.d.).[9] Therefore, for nurses and care givers, especially from regions bordering on Austria (if necessary, they can return quickly back home), or originating in poorer Czech regions and for those with a good knowledge of German language a care giver job in Austria remains attractive. Moreover, similar culture and long-term good relations between Czechia and Austria makes Czech care givers acceptable in Austrian families, thus also supporting sector that to large extent must relay on foreign labour force. And, due to the ageing it will need even more such support.[10]

[8] For instance, mother-in-law of the then prime minister, Wolfgang Schüssel, was cared for by an irregular migrant (van Hooren 2008).

[9] In 2000, the average annual earnings in Austria were 27,935 € whereas in Czechia 4,830 €. In 2014, it was 39,988 € and 11,472 €, respectively (OECD n.d.).

[10] Interestingly, unlike in many other EU countries, the ageing process in Austria has so far been more of an issue for rural or less urban areas than urban areas (Goll 2010).

Moreover, just care/domestic workers who are identified within the IMAGINATION project as one part of "persons working in private households", are one of the current important migratory types through which CEE migrants operate in old member states and which also has become a target subpopulation to be explored (Scholten, van Ostaijen – Introduction).

11.2 Research and Methodology

Our qualitative approach using semi-structured interviews (see e.g. Vargas-Silva 2012) enables us to describe but also to understand migrants´ behaviour in their internally structured richness (Hitchings 2012). Such research activity, when properly applied, contributes to a more nuanced understanding how migrants experience life (in harmony with the concept of everydayness – e.g. Bennett, Watson 2002, in general, and "the relevance of studying migration from the perspective of everyday matters" - Ho, Hatfield 2011, 707, in particular).

Specifically, to research the care givers´ issue in Austria, we conducted seven interviews with Czech women who work in Austria as care workers. Of course, since we applied a qualitative research, we cannot make generalizing statements based on these seven interviews. Nevertheless, as mentioned above, these interviews give us insight into important types of migration and informants' migration strategies. The findings are, indeed, also supported by other research results (see for example Kuchyňková, Ezzeddine 2015; Rodrigues et al. 2012).

The interviews were conducted between August and October 2015. Four of the interviews were held via Skype with a webcam (in one case, the informant was at her home in Vienna, in other cases, the informants were at homes of their patients). Three interviews were held in person – one at a Czech home of the informant close to Lipno, one in a café in Brno and one in a restaurant in Otrokovice. The informants were found through advertisements, Facebook groups, church, Czech schools and agencies (partly in Vienna). The agencies turned out to be the most effective way to reach care workers. The search for informants was quite difficult – due to the nature of the work and constant moving between Czechia and Austria, the care workers do not have many ties among themselves. The interviews were designed as semi-structured, i.e. with a given structure, but room was left open to informants' own narratives and order in which they answered the questions. The main topics of the interviews were structured into the following thematic sections: motivation to start and keep working in Austria, working environment, social interaction with families where they work and future plans.

All the interviews were held in a very friendly atmosphere and the informants seemed to be relatively open about their work. The only exception was Valerie. She was worried that somebody will recognise her by her personal data. One of the other respondents, Lilia, asked to stop the recording since she realized she will talk about her irregular work in Austria before 2008.

Table 11.3 shows personal characteristics of the informants. Their age oscillates between 31 and 64, with more respondents being older than 50. This is in harmony with overall picture where 65% of the care workers in 24-hour care in Austria are between 41 and 60 years of age (Österle, Bauer 2015). Their length of work in Austria also varies a lot, with the longest period of 21 years. Only one of the informants, Saša, works outside the scheme of 24-hour care. She did such work for a shorter period of time and, then, she moved to work in a retirement home. Another informant, Martina, does not currently work directly in the 24-hour care system either. Martina has worked as a care giver in families for 2 years. Then, she was asked by her agency to coordinate other workers. Now she is employed in the office of the same agency. Therefore, during the interview, she also shared with us pieces of information about the organisation of the system, role of agencies and experience of agency's nurses. The informants work all around Austria. Due to the character of the 24-hour care, they change their location in Austria quite often. The only person who has not been moving around Austria is again Saša, she is based in Vienna.

11.3 Results of Own Empirical Study

The results are summarized in six main areas: motivation to work in Austria as a care giver, working environment, career, social interaction with families, future plans and decisive moments. Such structuring can show us why people actually decide for a career of a care giver in Austria, what makes them continue such work and what are the crucial points and events in this decision making. After going through these topics, the comparative perspective is added to the results.

11.3.1 Motivation to Work in Austria as a Care Giver

A poor financial situation of almost all of the informants was behind the motivation to start working in the care sector in Austria. Specific reasons vary: three informants were at that time alone in Czechia with one or more children, some of them had mortgage that they were not able to pay off (either alone or even with a husband). Other could not cope with their Czech pension.

"... My motivation to leave was purely financial – we had a mortgage to pay off."(Jana)

"So I decided to come here and do the same, but for better money." (Johana)

Only one respondent, Saša, did not leave because of her bad financial situation. She left first to Germany and later to Austria because she was upset with conditions in Czech hospitals and retirement homes (both for patients and for employees). Many times during the interview, she gave examples, as is the following one:

Table 11.3 Informants´ personal characteristics

Name (pseudonym)	Age	Family situation	Number of children	Years of work in Austria	Number of patients up to now
Saša	36	long-term relationship	0	11	x (works in a senior home)
Jana	59	married	3	15	15
Johana	54	single	3	6	5
Lilia	57	divorced	2	1,5[a]	3
Valerie	64	married	2	21	49
Martina	60	married	2	16	x (works more as a manager of an agency)
Diana	31	divorced	1	2	4

Notes:[a]*Lilia had worked in Austria also before without proper contract, but she did not want to talk about it*
Therefore, her irregular experience is not included in the length of work in Austria

> *"... at night, some patients sleep and some not, not like in Czechia, where when you don't sleep, they give you a pill to fall asleep, that is something that doesn't exist here, it's our work to be here for the people, we are paid for that, that's something everybody should realize." (Saša)*

Moreover, she was young and wanted to gain new experience abroad (she was 25 at the moment of departure). Currently, Saša is moving to Prague to a new retirement home that is being open by her Austrian company. Therefore, she might find a solution how to be back in Czechia while having "Austrian working environment" and the type of care she wants to give to her patients. At the same time, her life partner is Austrian – which is also the reason why she does not have far-reaching plans for the future.

11.3.2 Working Environment

As it was described above, the informants mostly work in the system of 24-hour care. In the system, there is a crucial role of agencies which mediate work and which also check working conditions that are listed in the Home Care Act. Hence, there is a clear list of duties that the care workers are supposed to do – the focus is naturally on the patient. Thus, besides direct taking care of the patient duties may also include cooking for the patient or other basic domestic work. The extent to which domestic chores are done depends on the situation – if the patient needs continuous care, care workers have to focus exclusively on him/her and they do not do other things around the house.

> *"This is not my own experience, but I know from my colleagues that in the beginning, it was terrible, that the relatives really thought that the nurses would do everything, but not now, if a patient is in a really serious condition, someone else in the family has to cook, because the nurse wouldn't have time for it." (Johana)*

Sometimes, the care workers do something extra if they have time. It seems that they manage to get extra money for such work. In case of Diana, such work includes gardening because her client is doing very well and Diana likes gardening. In any case, nobody forces her into it.

> *"Well, for example, I do some gardening for the lady, I don't have to, but as I say, I pass time like this, because I have to be here anyway. .... as I say, she is almost independent by now." (Diana)* (Diana currently takes care of a woman after operation who is getting better and she will not need Diana's assistance soon.)

Naturally, there are families that try to use the workers as maids who do everything, but from what the informants said, the agencies manage to solve such situations quickly and if they are not able to do so, they exclude these families from their services. It seems, as some informants indicated, that such a nice, almost ideal, situation is typical of Czech and (most) Slovak workers rather than that of workers from Romania. Apparently, there are agencies which do not follow the rules so much and there are workers from Eastern Slovakia, Romania and some other Eastern Europen countries who are, because of their worse economic situation, willing to work in worse conditions for much less money, which is, however, not in harmony with generally stipulated rules. All the informants seemed to be satisfied with the arrangement of two week non-stop stays in Austria. It gives them time to often go back home to see their family (some expressed that they even enjoy a model with these short-term separations). At some points, the informants mentioned that something in their job is not exactly like it should be, but all more serious issues seemed to be solved either by their agencies or by changing the patient, without any big conflict.

> *"... last time I was for one and half year in one place, but there was a terrible draught, so the granny had two rooms, but in one she slept and in the other she was sitting the whole time, as we are sitting, TV in front of her, but the TV was on only for news and love stories in the afternoon, otherwise nothing, and there was the draught, there was a balcony, when I was there, I didn't even have a bed, so her son came only after three weeks with it, the granny would let me lie down in her bed in the afternoon, such conditions I had. And I am supposed to have a room and a bed, right." (Valerie)*

> *"... well, if you have a "lying patient", the family doesn't come, then you don't have your two-hour break you should have, you don't get to go anywhere." (Diana)*

11.3.3 Career

Domestic work is often seen as work without any career possible: be it cleaning or caring, it is usually considered as a dead-end job without many prospectives of improvement (see, for example, discussion in Triandafyllidou 2013). To some extent, findings springing from our interviews supported the fact that care work is rather stable over time. At the same time, however, the life stories of our informants showed certain improvement over time. The first improvement is definitely legalization and stable position of the job compared to the beginning of their careers. The second, and somehow more important for our study, is the improvement of the position within the whole care givers sector: the informants mentioned a more stable financial situation and more possibilities to choose a location of their next place of employment. In the case of Martina, the career moved even further as she started working as a manager of other care workers. Saša, who is the only one not working in the 24-hour care, got a good job in an Austrian care home that was about to open in Czechia. Before that, Saša was in charge of Czech and Slovak staff in her company. The possibilities of career in care work might be limited, but they are, nevertheless, existing and the position of the informants has been improving over time. (Of course, one has to keep in mind that this conclusion is based on our rather limited sample of informants.)

"So I am at this company, I did management here as well; I was in charge of the care workers in the 24-hour care. Czech and Slovak care workers. Also some workers from Romania and Hungary, but minimum... I went to help them, to control their work, I went to the families. I had around 80 care workers under me." (Saša)

11.3.4 Social Interaction with Families Where They Work

Obviously, in the system of 24-hour care, it is hard to fully integrate into the family because the workers switch, the patient often lives alone or he/she needs a lot of care. Therefore, it is complicated for the nurses to do anything else than being with the patient. There are usually some relationships established with the relatives. Except for Saša who only worked in a family for a short time, all the informants spoke about some families that they stay in touch with or some they particularly liked. From their stories, it is clear that sometimes, the care worker does not fit completely in the family, whereas in other cases, care workers are treated as family members and after leaving the family (mostly because their patient dies), they stay in touch. Sometimes, they stay in contact via sending each other a card at Christmas, birthday, etc.… They even keep meeting sometimes. Martina talked about some Slovak nurses that had "their" Austrian families over for a visit in Slovakia.

"Oh yes, I stayed in touch with them, via e-mail, especially those in Sölden, even though I was there just for a short time, I stayed in touch with the daughter-in-aw, also from Aurach. I also have a phone number of the lady from Upper Austria, where I was, but I don't have time… simply, to call them, but if it's Christmas or something, I remember all of them, this way, I don't ask too much, but I send a postcard or an SMS, e-mail. That's all." (Johana)

Diana then spoke about the intimacy within the family, that she treats the patient and the relatives almost as her own family. She also feels that she is taken as a family member. Nevertheless, Diana points out the need to stay little distant, especially from the emotions of the relatives of dying patients who, then, might behave badly towards the care worker.

"(The daughter of the patient)... *shouted at me, she was so upset, but it wasn't because of me, she just couldn't bear the situation. .... it is harder to deal with the family and their emotions, because working with the patient who is dying, that's my profession, I do that automatically." (Diana)*

In some cases, relatives of the patient tried to tell the nurse how to take care of the patient, especially in the beginning of their stay. It mostly seemed to work out well after some time when relatives could see that the care worker knew what she was doing. Sometimes, however, the agency had to intervene. On the other hand, there were also some cases mentioned when the care worker could not reach agreement with the family and she left.

11.3.5 Future Plans

Apart from Saša, who is now moving to Prague with her Austrian company (see above), all other informants plan to keep working in Austria at least for some time. Financial motives remain strong but it is not any more the most important reason. In some cases, informants' children are already grown up and they do not need that much financial support any more and the mortgages have been paid off. Therefore, a need to gain extra money is not too urgent. All the informants seem to like their work now even though they mention negative sides, too, namely loneliness and difficulties of the job. Only Jana seems to be quite sad about her job, pointing out how lonely she gets, also due to the fact that many of her patients cannot even talk to her. She states it quite clearly:

"If I didn't have to be here, I wouldn't." (Jana)

But other respondents appear to enjoy work with elderly and also the 24-hour care system:

"... you need to like this work and people, I really like old people... and... I really like helping them, so for me, this is no problem." (Johana)

"...you know this is also good that you work for two weeks, but then you have two weeks off – there is no other occupation where you can have this. And in these two weeks, you really have time to have some rest, to organize what you need to organize." (Diana)

Overall, informants seem to be motivated to stay longer at their current occupation (see also Vavrečková 2014), more times they mention their age and a retirement threshold until which they want to keep working as care givers. Some of them, for example Jana, also mention that by now, it would be hard for them to find work in Czechia because of their age. Therefore, it is better to keep working in Austria until they are retired.

11.3.6 "Decisive Moments"

As the interviews tell us, it seems that there are some crucial moments that led to the decision to work as a care worker in Austria. These are important, turning changes in one's life, such as divorce, mortgage or loss of work, that have left the respondents in financial problems which could not be easily solved via participation in the Czech labour market. Therefore, a common reason standing behind the start of working in Austria as a care worker is a serious financial situation.[11] At the same time, the 24-hour care system offers the workers to earn better salaries in Austria, but it does not force them to move there completely – they can still spend time at home with their families.

> *"... it's because I have high expenses and for the house, I was left with a mortgage after the divorce. If I was alone, without a child, I would rather work in a hospital, maybe I would move here completely, I wouldn't choose home care."* (Diana)

Secondly, during the time of work in Austria, there is probably one, not explicit, moment that is also important. It is resolving the initial financial problems, be it a debt or supporting younger children. In more interviews the informants proclaimed that currently, the original reason for such work had disappeared – children had grown up, the mortgage was paid off, but they still keep working in Austria as they did before.

The last common moment is reaching a retirement threshold. Except for Diana and Saša, who are in their thirties, the informants talked about retirement as an important turning point. Some of them wanted to keep working in Austria until their retirement age. Some others had already got Czech pension and keep working because they still want to earn more money and save little more for the time when they will not be able to work anymore. But even for those who keep working the retirement is significant. They know they have some basic income and, therefore, they can, for example, work little less, can have longer breaks between patients etc. Their retirement gives them extra sense of security despite the fact that the Czech pension is not really high.

11.4 Comparative Perspective, "Proving Robust Regularities"?

Austria is one of the typical countries benefiting from the work of migrant care givers. If we compare it with other countries, we can find some similarities but also important differences. Austria is comparable to other countries in the sense that its ageing society is in need of care. At the same time, Austrians themselves do not want to do such work – there is just around 1% of Austrians working in the

[11] Similarly, Kuchyňková and Ezzeddine (2015) found out that such important moment was a loss of work in advanced age and subsequent financial and social difficulties.

24-hour care system (Österle, Bauer 2015). Therefore, the country relies on migrant workers.

The difference from other countries is especially the high degree of regulation and also, as mentioned above, the fact that most care workers are from the EU countries, mostly from Slovakia, Romania, Bulgaria and Hungary. Furthermore, what is different from many other countries is that there is a significant role of agencies organizing the whole system in Austria (including non-profit organisations). They mediate care work and make arrangements for care workers. All these facts were clearly indicated in our interviews. Most of our informants (similarly to other care workers) have found their work just through agencies and currently, they seem to rely on them in all their working arrangements. It seems that from the perspective of Czech workers the existence of agencies helps prevent irregular activities in the sector.[12] The agencies seem to be reliable, stable and well-organized. They also seem to provide good means of control of the working environment and treatment of their workers. On the other hand, it seems quite possible that those agencies that our respondents made use of are those situated higher on the ladder of quality. There may be many other agencies which are far from providing such good services. As already touched above, conditions might be quite different (worse) for workers coming from Romania. But also in their case, the role of agencies will be probably rather important. This is something different from other European countries where the role of individual workers and his/her social networks prevail in the process of finding a job (see e.g. Ungerson 2010; Lutz 2012).

Another issue that is different from the experience of the given field in other countries is the problem of discrimination. As studies from some other regions show us,[13] we can find long stories of discrimination, often connected to ethnic differences among employers and employees. In this study, only one respondent, Diana, mentioned that some of her colleagues were treated badly and that they were told they are just *"... stupid Czechs who will do what we say"*. Apparently, no other demonstrations of discrimination were detected. This can be also due to ethnic and cultural similarities between Czechs/Slovaks and Austrians which might prevent such discrimination. Nevertheless, it is again worth noting that the situation can be quite different for care givers coming from countries further to East, and it would definitely deserve more attention.

On the other hand, what resonates with research experience in this field in many other countries is an important role of emotions (see for example Hondagneu-Sotelo 2007; Lutz 2011). All the respondents agreed that care work is highly demanding, not so much physically (but also) emotionally. Especially Diana developed her thoughts around difficulties of work with family members who might firstly try to tell nurses how they should do their work, but who can be often in stress because of their mother or father dying and therefore behaving disrespectfully or nervously towards their employees. On the other hand, the informants also talked about the

---

[12] On the other hand, one can deduce that among 29,000 who are estimated in the care sector in irregular position in Austria (see in Reeger, Enengel 2015) Czech females will appear too.

[13] See for example Hondagneu-Sotelo 2007 and Lutz 2011.

fact that they like to work with elderly, that it is a rewarding work and it gives them satisfaction. Therefore, they realize that the emotions also get back to them, that they are there to help somebody in need.

11.5 Concluding Remarks

The intra-European migration currently represents more or less a free migratory field. A very simplified proposition is that during the last decade in harmony with dominating economic motivations (see e.g. Fassmann et al. 2014a, b; Kahanec et al. 2014) CEE´ migrants started to move to the west within the continent while taking jobs at a secondary labour market – those jobs which are manually rather than intellectually demanding (see also in Scholten, van Ostaijen – Introduction; Favell 2013).

This fact is however too general and is ramified into many partial migratory modes and patterns (different in terms of quantity and also "quality" of the migratory flows and, consequently, stocks) whilst some of them can even go against the general proposition described above (e.g. the migration of highly qualified specialists). The emigration and long-term migration of Czechs in general and the migration of Czech care givers to Austria in particular seems to be a "strange type", standing somewhere on the borderline (see discussion on a large variety of the mobility/migration along with the overall feminization of the migratory process - see in Scholten, van Ostaijen - Introduction). Nevertheless, this type fully corresponds to newly identified trends in intra-European migrations (see e.g. Verwiebe et al. 2014), e.g. differentiation of the causes of and motivations for migration, different composition of migration populations as well as new forms of migration and, indeed, new sharply polarized roles on the primary versus secondary labour markets of immigrant societies (see Favell 2013) – see in this context also Kindler (Chap. 10).

As for Czechia, labour migration of Czech care workers to Austria has been - in accordance with the general patterns of migration - based primarily on economic motivation. Since the 1990s, when the economic differences between the two countries were big, Czech women started to migrate to Austria while finding their places mostly in an informal economy of care work. In fact, apart from the "pulls" on the Austrian side, factors such as historical relations, adequate knowledge of German language and shared culture eased the integration into the Austrian labour market. Moreover, after 2011, when Austria fully opened its labour market for Czech workers, new advantages appeared – namely no border controls and no need for special work permits. To summarize, the work of Czech women (supplemented by work of women from other countires, e.g. from Slovakia - Bahna 2014, 2015) has been an important pillar of the care for the elderly in Austria for a long time (Kraler et al. 2008), benefiting all the involved subjects. Despite the fact that the differences in living standards between Austria and Czechia have been diminishing, the wages in health care in Czechia remain fairly low. Hence, working in 2-week shifts in a rich nearby Austria still offers Czechs some advantages (e.g. decent money and a possibility to find another part-time job at home) and some of them permanently "settle within mobility" (Fassmann et al 2014a, b). It seems apparent (based on statistics and the interviews) however, that over time Czech (and Slovak) women in the care work sector in Austria are gradually being replaced by other female workers from poorer Eastern parts of Europe (namely Romania – see also Bahna 2014) who accept lower salaries and overall worse conditions. Consequently, although there is still a stable migration connection/corridor between Czechia and Austria its strength and character have been changing in the last two decades.

There are three main factors that contributed to creating a specific migratory type we called "**MICO**": geographical closeness (between migrants´ original home and destination where the care service is delivered), a repeated and stable short stay and return model (usually two weeks in Austria and two weeks in Czechia) and a very busy working scheme (not enabling to normally integrate to Austrian society). This model lies between **mi**gration and **co**mmuting and it has, albeit to only a limited extent, some transnational features related chiefly to economic domain/integration, namely a circulation and remittances. Other activities (taking place when migrants stay to work in Austria) within political and sociocultural domains which also belong to key forms of migrant transnationalim (e.g. Boccagni 2012) are almost non-existent. Importantly, there is a very limited existence of a new, Austrian identity among these migrants. Accordingly, there is none or a very limited "socialization pressure" (except for a micro-family level) put on these care givers in the destination country. On the other hand, there is no disruption or breakdown of social/family relations in their mother country (similarly Bahna 2015; Kuchyňková, Ezzeddine 2015). Moreover, based on our interviews it seems that unlike within many other migratory types, the position of these care givers (at least within the legal/formal labour market) is less vulnerable, exploitative and discriminatory as their position is stable and they are well protected by their agencies.

What seems to be obvious however, like within the transnationalism these female migrants are trapped in their "myth of return" (we mean a wish to stop the "**MICO**") and they "tend to settle within mobility" (Fassmann et al. 2014a). They know that once "on the move" their benefits are higher than losses. The consequences of the arrangements described are positive for them since they make use of the free movement in the Schengen area while benefiting from ongoing differences between Czechia and Austria in wages and pensions. The importance of the MICO type is even higher when realizing that besides Czech care givers there is also a much more numerous group of Slovak care givers who would probably fit in it as well (see Bahna 2014, 2015).

Due to harmonizing "push" and "pull" migratory factors between Czechia and Austria in this particular care work sector (springing from wider mainly socioeconomic, demographic, historical and geographical settings), we might predict that the given flow (creating the Czech-Austrian specific migration corridor) will very likely continue in the future whilst having an impact on both Austrian rural areas and Vienna and other big cities.

11.6 Annex

Table 11.2 Number of Czech citizens being employed in the EU/EEA and Switzerland, 2006–2014

Country/year	2006	2007	2008	2009	2010	2011	2012	2013	2014
Belgium	1,593	*	617	2,072	2,210	2,921	*	*	*
Bulgaria	*	*	*	186	10	187	*	*	221
Denmark	*	*	*	155	263	*	470	511	421
Estonia	*	*	7	85	106	121	153	110	*
Finland	11	11	*	135	175	358	408	444	505
France	82	72	96	*	1,163	*	*	*	*
Croatia	*	*	*	*	*	*	*	*	*
Ireland	4,524	12,000	10,230	12,900	12,700	11,960	11,358	10,121	4,256
Iceland	140	120	250	*	*	*	*	*	138
Italy	4,115	4,050	4,496	5,801	6,009	6,134	6,250	5,925	5,561
Cyprus	*	457	403	354	341	*	404	335	*
Liechtenstein	*	*	5	17	19	28	*	*	*
Lithuania	*	*	*	*	*	7	12	4	5
Latvia	*	35	*	125	*	*	*	*	*
Luxembourg	*	*	*	209	*	*	*	824	*
Hungary	118	110	285	261	250	*	*	*	*
Malta	61	66	63	56	77	*	*	*	219
Germany	12,404	13,579	13,931	14,013	14,341	22,372	23,500	26,893	31,753
The Netherlands	1,394	1,250	2,242	*	2,602	2,854	2,954	2,820	3,170
Norway	210	633	544	486	343	385	*	1,579	
Poland	205	164	134	176	1,089	1,183	1,247	1,285	1,950
Portugal	*	*	212	*	*	*	*	*	*
Austria	6,680	5,278	5,060	5,136	6,164	7,782	9,802	11,329	12,742
Romania	*	*	88	15	*	*	*	*	*
Greece	*	*	*	*	*	*	*	*	*
Slovakia	1,065	1,241	1,915	2,293	2,830	3,179	*	3,400	2,525
Slovenia	128	141	76	113	111	72	47	52	92
The United Kingdom	17,400	30,000	20,000	30,500	24,500	33,000	33,850	29,200	37,100
Spain	2,944	2,800	*	2,370	1,200	*	5,757	1,190	3,517
Sweden	140	232	73	*	1,212	1,249	*	1,320	*
Switzerland	1,440	4,157	1,098	4,809	5,570	*	*	*	6,219
Total number of Czech citizens	**54,654**	**76,396**	**61,825**	**82,267**	**83,285**	**93,792**	**96,212**	**97,342**	**112,408**

*Data not available

Source: Internal materials of the Ministry of Labour and Social Affairs of the Czech Republic

Data as of December, 31. Data represents only indicative numbers, while possibly putting side by side not compatible figures – e.g. on employees versus foreign citizens etc. To sum up, data is inaccurate and often incompatible; somewhere it suffers from not deregistration or, on the othe hand, registration of those who also represent second or third generations; some data was not available, somewhere it is only an expert estimate.

Table 11.4 Example of earnings of care givers in 24-hour care system in Austria (2015)

Type of service	Daily gross salary
Earnings	
Basic care for patients with care level between 0 and 3[a]	63 €
Care for patients with dementia with care level between 0 and 3	67 €
Highly qualified care for patients with care level between 0 and 3	70 €
Basic care for patients with care level between 4 and 7	68 €
Highly qualified care for patients with care level between 4 and 7	72 €
Presence of another person in the household	2 €
Care for another person in the household	7 €
Fees	
Initial fee to the agency for training and information seminar (in own language)	318 €
Annual fee to the agency	148 €
Taxes	
Income tax (for earnings between 11,000 € and 25,000 € annually)[b]	36.5%

[a]*The care level is determined by a doctor*

[b]*The earnings up to 11,000 € annually are tax free for self-employed workers. The tax is paid only for the earnings that exceed this amount – up to that sum, there is no taxation which makes the work even more profitable*

Source: based on one of the respective agencies´ documents

References

Bahna, M. (2014). Slovak care workers in Austria: How important is the context of the sending country? *Journal of Contemporary European Studies, 22*(4), 411–426.

Bahna, M. (2015). Victims of care drain and transnational partnering? Slovak female elder care workers in Austria. *European Societies*, on 20/07/2015, available online: http://www.tandfonline.com/10.1080/14616696.2015.1051074

Bennett, T., & Watson, D. (Eds.). (2002). *Understanding everyday life*. Oxford: Blackwell Publishers.

Boccagni, P. (2012). Even a transnational social field must have its boundaries: Methodological options, potentials and dilemmas for researching transnationalism. In C. Vargas-Silva (Ed.), *Handbook of research methods in migration* (pp. 295–318). Cheltenham: Edward Elgar.

Brouček, S., & Grulich, T. (Eds.). (2014). *Nová emigrace z České republiky po roce 1989 a návratová politika*. Praha: Etnologický ústav AV ČR.

Brouček, S., Hrubý, K., & Měšťan, A. (Eds.). (2001). *Konference zahraničních Čechů. Emigrace a exil jako způsob života*. Praha: Karolinum.

Czech Statistical Office. (n.d.). – www.czso.cz. Accesses on 14 Feb 2016.

Drbohlav, D. (1994). International migration in the Czech Republic and Slovakia and the Outlook for East Central Europe. *Czech Sociological Review, 2*(1), 89–106.

Drbohlav, D., Rákoczyová, M.. (2012). *Social impact of emigration and Rural-Urban migration in Central and Eastern Europe. Final Country Report – Czech Republic*. Prague: GVG and the EC – DG Employement, Social Affairs and Inclusion.

Engbersen, G., Leerkes, A., Grabowska-Lusinska, I., Snel, E., & Burgers, J. (2013). On the differential attachments of migrants from Central and Eastern Europe: A typology of labour migration. *Journal of Ethnic and Migration Studies, 39*(6), 959–981.

European Commission. (2012). Long-Term care for the elderly. Provisions and providers in 33 *European countries* Luxembourg: Publications Office of the European Union.

Fassmann, H., Kohlnbacher, J., & Reeger, U. (2014a). The Re-Emergence of European East-West migration – The Austrian example. *Central and Eastern European Migration Review, 3*(2), 39–59.

Fassmann, H., Musil, E., Gruber, K. (2014b). *Dynamic Historical Analysis of Longer Term Migratory, Labour Market and Human Capital Processes in the SEEMIG Region.* SEEMIG Working Papers, No. 3, Budapest, Hungarian Demographic Research Institute.

Favell, A. (2008). The new face of East-West migration in Europe. *Journal of Ethnic and Migration Studies, 34*(5), 701–716.

Favell, A. (2013). The changing face of 'Integration' in a mobile Europe. *Council For European Studies Newsletter, 43*(1), 53–58.

Filípek, J. (1999). *Odlesky dějin československého exilu.* Praha: Karolinum.

Goll, M.. (2010). Ageing in the European Union: Where exactly? Eurostat.

Hampl, M., et al. (1999). Geography of Societal transformation in the Czech Republic. In *Prague: Department of Social Geography and Regional Development.* Charles University: Faculty of Science.

Hitchings, R. (2012). People can talk about their practices. *Area, 44*(1), 61–67.

Ho, E., & Hatfield, M. E. (2011). Migration and everyday matters: Sociality and materiality. *Population, Space and Place, 17*, 707–713.

Hondagneu-Sotelo, P. (2007). *Doméstica* (p. 281). Los Angeles: University of California Press.

Hrubý, K., Brouček, S. (eds.), (2000). *Češi za hranicemi na přelomu 20. a 21. století: sympozium o českém vystěhovatelství, exulantství a vztazích zahraničních Čechů k domovu*, 29. – 30. června 1998. Praha: Karolinum. Internal materials of the Ministry of Labour and Social Affairs of the Czech Republic.

Kahanec, M., Pytliková, M., Zimmermann, K. F.. (2014). *The free movement of workers in an Enlarged European Union: Institutional Underpinnings of Economic Adjustment*, IZA Discussion Paper No. 8456, Bonn: IZA.

Kraler, A., Reichel, D., Hollomey, H.. (2008): *Clandestino Country Report: Austria. Unpublished Draft Report for the project Clandestino - Undocumented Migration: Counting the Uncountable.* Data and Trends Across Europe. Available at http://clandestino.eliamep.gr/wp-content/uploads/2009/10/clandestino_report_austria_final_2.pdf. Accessed Dec 1, 2015.

Kuchyňková, A., & Ezzeddine, P. (2015). "Ještě nepatřím do starého železa" aneb paradoxy migrace péče z ČR do Rakouska. *Gender, Rovné příležitosti, Výzkum, 16*(2), 30–41.

Kupiszewska, D., & Nowok, B. (2006). Country report Czech Republic. In M. Poulain, N. Perrin, & A. N. Singleton (Eds.), *THESIM: Towards Harmonised European Statistics on International Migration* (pp. 391–401). Louvain: Presses Universitaires de Louvain.

Lutz, H. (2011). *The new maids.* London: Zed Books.

Lutz, H. (2012). *Migration and Domestic Work – A European Perspective on a Global Theme.* Surrey: Ashgate.

Nešpor, Z. R. (2002). The disappointed and disgruntled: A study of the return in the 1990s of Czech emigrants from communist era. *Sociologický časopis/Czech Sociological Review, 38*(6), 78–808.

O'Reilly, K. (2007). Intra-European migration and the mobility-enclosure dialectic. *Sociology, 41*(2), 277–293.

OECD Statistics. (n.d.). https://stats.oecd.org/. Accessed 3 Dec 2015

Okolski, M. (Ed.). (2012). *European immigrations. Trends, Structures and Policy Implications, IMSCOE-AUP Research Series*. Amsterdam: Amsterdam University Press.

Österle, A., & Bauer, G. (2012). Home care in Austria: The interplay of family orientation, Cash-for-care and migrant care. *Health and Social Care in the Community, 20*(3), 265–273.

Österle, A., & Bauer, G. (2015). The legalization of rotational 24-hour care work in Austria: Implications for migrant care workers. *Social Politics*, 1–22.

Pařízková, A. (2011). *Pracovní migrace do Velké Británie v kontextu životních drah lidí z České republiky*. Doctoral Thesis. Plzeň, University of West Bohemia, Faculty of Philosophy and Arts, p 185.

Reeger, U., Enengel, M. L. (2015). Migration from Central and Eastern European EU-Member Countries to the Vienna Urban Region: Different Types and Recent Developments. IMAGINATION research report.

Riedel, M., Kraus, M. (2010). *The Long-term Care Sytem for the Elderly in Austria*. ENEPRI Research Project No. 69, Contribution to WP1 of the ANCIEN Project.

Rodrigues, R., Huber, M., Lamura, G. (2012). Facts and figures on healthy ageing and long-term care – Europe and North America. European Centre for Social Welfare Policy and Research. Available at http://www.euro.centre.org/data/LTC_Final.pdf. Accessed on 7 May 2016.

Triandafyllidou, A. (2013). *Irregular migrant domestic Workers in Europe – Who Cares?* Surrey: Ashgate.

UN. (2015). World population prospects. In *Key findings and advance tables (2015 revision)*. New York: United Nations.

Ungerson, C. (2010). Commodified care work in European labour markets. *European Societies, 5*(4), 377–396.

Van Hooren, F. (2008): *Bringing Policies Back in: How Social and Migration Policies Affect the Employment of Immigrants in Domestic Care for the Elderly in the EU-15*. Paper prepared forTransforming Elderly Care at Local, National and Transnational Levels – International Conference at the Danish National Centre for Social Research (SFI), Copenhagen, 26–28 June 2008. Available online at: http://www.sfi.dk/Files/Filer/transforming%20care/Franca-van-Hooren.pdf. Accessed 21 Nov 2015.

Vargas-Silva, C. (Ed.). (2012). *Handbook of research methods in migration*. Cheltenham: Edward Edgar Publishing Inc..

Vavřečková, J. (2014). Pracovní zkušenosti českých kvalifikovaných pracovních sil z pobytu v zahraničí a jejich postoje k návratu. In S. Brouček & T. Grulich (Eds.), *Nová emigrace z České republiky po roce 1989 a návratová politika* (pp. 101–109). Praha: Etnologický ústav AV ČR.

Vavrečková, J., & Hantak, N. (2008). *Pracovní zkušenosti českých kvalifikovaných pracovních sil z pobytu v zahraničí (zejména státech EU) a jejich postoje k návratu do ČR (výsledky empirických šetření)*. Praha: VÚPSV.

Vavrečková, J., Baštýř, I., Michalička, L., Drbohlav, D., Musil, J. (2008). *Riziko možného odlivu kvalifikovaných odborníků z České republiky do zahraničí*. Project Final Report 1J 019/04 DP2. Praha: VÚPSV.

Vavrečková, J., Fischlová, D., Janata, Z., & Michalička, L. (2000). *Důsledky vstupu ČR do EU na vztahy s Rakouskem se zaměřením na zaměstnanost, trh práce a migraci. Analytická část, svazek 1b. Migrační potenciál obyvatelstva České republiky – výsledky empirického šetření*. Praha: VÚPSV.

Verwiebe, R., Wiewboeck, L., & Teitzer, R. (2014). New forms of Intra-European migration, labour market dynamics and social inequality in Europe. *Migration Letters, 11*(2), 125–136.
Verwiebe, R., Reinprecht, C., Haindorfer, R., Wiesboeck, L. (2015): How to Succeed in a Transnational Labor Market: Job Search and Wages among Hungarian, Slovak, and Czech Commuters in Austria. *International Migration Review*, Fall 2015, pp. 1–36, published online: 16 JUL 2015 DOI: https://doi.org/10.1111/imre.12193.

Chapter 12
Migration from Central and Eastern Europe to Turkey

Deniz Karcı Korfalı and Tuğba Acar

12.1 Introduction

Until recently, despite the fact that the country had received many immigrants since the initial years of the Republic, migration literature treated Turkey as a country of emigration. Turkey's position in the international migration system, and thus, in the migration literature, has changed only recently to a country of transit and immigration. In this regard, the literature on international migration in Turkey is still very limited and either focused on mobility of specific groups,[1] or on general historical trends.[2] In this frame, focusing on current trends and implications of Central and Eastern European (CEE) migration in Turkey is a novel task. However, as the collection and distribution of international migration data have been generally neglected and a large portion of international migration in Turkey is on irregular basis, this is a challenging task. In addition to the limited data availability, the heavy internal and external migrant population also complicates migration research and blurs the distinction between the implications of CEE migration and migration in general.

The analysis of the newly established corridors between CEE and Turkey, the current migrant categories and finally, the implications of CEE migration require an overview of the background on CEE migration to Turkey.[3] Following a historical background, this chapter will first assess the regular CEE migration by employing residence and work permit data along with citizenship statistics. In this respect,

[1] See for example, Danış on Iraqi, 2007, Parla on Bulgarian, 2007, or Eder on Moldovan (2007) migrations

[2] See for example, İçduygu and Kirişci, 2009

[3] In this study, CEE is perceived as a geographical region that includes Bulgaria, Croatia, Czech Republic, Estonia, Hungary, Latvia, Lithuania, Poland, Romania, Slovakia and Slovenia, Albania, Belarus, Bosnia Herzegovina, Kosovo, Macedonia, Moldova, Montenegro, Serbia and Ukraine.

D. K. Korfalı (✉) · T. Acar
Özyeğin University, Oyzegin, Turkey
e-mail: dkorfali@ku.edu.tr

P. Scholten, M. van Ostaijen (eds.), *Between Mobility and Migration*, IMISCOE Research Series, https://doi.org/10.1007/978-3-319-77991-1_12

the limited data still brings to light the corridors of permanent, student and labor migration established between CEE countries and Turkey in addition to patterns of gender and education. Next, irregular CEE migration will be addressed. This will be followed by region-specific focus on Edirne, which has traditionally received CEE migrants and Istanbul, Turkey's migration hub that includes various types of migrants from across the world.[4] These two research areas reveal how different CEE migrant profiles lead to different implications of CEE migration. The final conclusion and discussion will shed light on the challenges of migration governance during Turkey's transformation to a migrant receiving country.

Within this framework, it should also be noted that the Turkish case can be received as a reference case. Unlike Austria, Netherlands and Sweden, here, CEE migrants are subject to the general terms for migrants in Turkey within an immigration regime established distinct from regulations on CEE migration applied by the EU members.

12.2 Background on CEE Migration into Turkey

Among the migration trends of the Early Republican Period, the course of CEE migration into Turkey, usually categorized as Balkan migrations, was the widest one and formed of four origin countries of the time: Bulgaria, Greece, Romania and Yugoslavia (Please see Chart 12.1). The Republic of Turkey, in need of human capital for a homogenous nation state, welcomed migrants of Sunni-Islam origin rather than Turkish ethnicity (Kirişci 2006). In 1935, out of an approximate population of 16 million citizens in Turkey, approximately 110,000 people were of CEE origin including Pomaks, Bosnians, Albanians, Bulgarians and Romanians (Çağatay 2007).

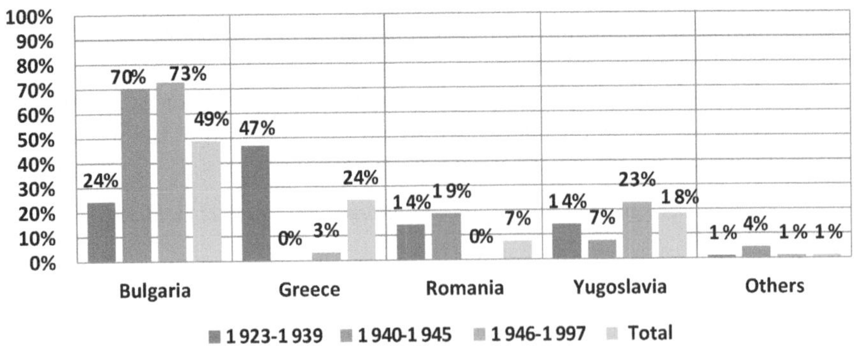

Chart 12.1 Immigration from Central and Eastern Europe to Turkey (1923 to 1997)

[4] These will be explained in further detail in the sections below.

According to the 1960 Census, Pomaks, Bosnians and Albanians formed the 2‰ of Turkey's population (Dündar 1999).

In the period following the foundation of the Republic of Turkey in 1923 until the start of the Second World War, more than 800,000 people migrated to Turkey from the Balkans. Close to half of the total migrant population constituted of Greek migrants (47 percent) followed by Bulgarian (24 percent), Romanian (14 percent) and Yugoslavian migrants (13 percent). Migration from the Balkans declined in the war years and remained limited to approximately 20,000 migrants most of whom were Bulgarians (70 percent) and in much smaller numbers, Romanians (19 percent). During the Cold War, Turkey welcomed a massive wave of 600,000 ethnically Turkish Bulgarians due to Bulgaria's negative policies against its minorities coupled with a population of 200,000 Yugoslavian migrants. In spite of this rich variety of movements across the border, Bulgarians' mass migration based on ethnic kin is the most studied pattern of CEE migration in Turkey.[5]

In the current period, ethnic kin migration and migration to find a safe haven from repressive communist regimes are replaced by various types of CEE migration. Turkey's neo-liberal economic policies after the year 1990 and the growing economy resulted in more diverse migration flows from this region to Turkey. Today, five main movements of CEE migration into Turkey are (1) high skilled migration of professionals, (2) low skilled migration of domestic workers –with both regular and irregular status, (3) marriage migration, (4) increasing numbers of student migration and finally, (5) trafficked persons –albeit the official numbers from CEE seem to be decreasing. Along with the already existing migration flows from Bulgaria, Romania and ex-Yugoslavian countries, wider migration corridors from countries like Moldova and Poland started becoming significant. Lastly, although the numbers of migrants from Baltic Countries are relatively smaller, in the last decade migrants from Estonia, Lithuania and Latvia increased four-fold, six-fold and ten-fold respectively. Based on the official data, these current trends of CEE migration can best be analyzed in two main categories of regular versus irregular migration.

12.2.1 Regular CEE Migration into Turkey

Official statistics on current and regular migrants in Turkey are based on residence permits and citizenship acquisition. Traditionally, CEE migrants have a large weight in the number of total regular migrants in Turkey. The data from the Ministry of Interior demonstrates that in the years from 2003 to 2007, around an average of 40 percent of all regular migrants came from this region (Please see Chart 12.2). In the year 2008, however, the CEE migrant population in Turkey dropped to 26 percent. Consequently, except a small uptrend in 2011 right after the Eurozone Crisis, the weight of regular CEE migrants is in a steady decline. The main reasons behind this

[5] See Parla 2003, 2006

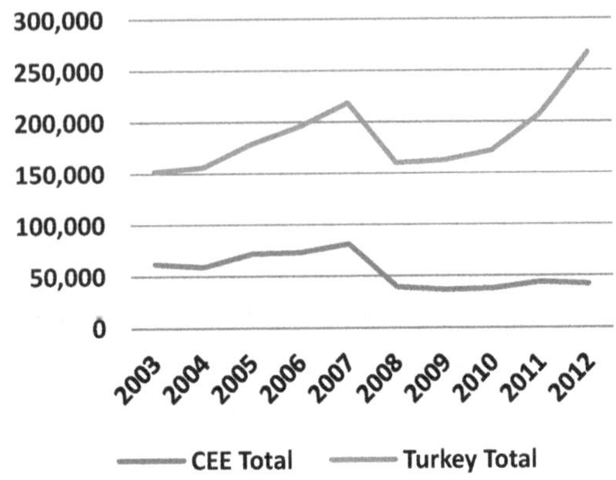

Chart 12.2 Comparison of number of migrants from CEE Countries and all countries

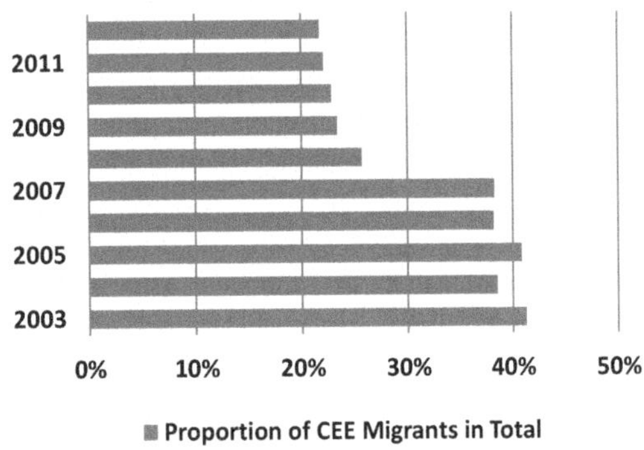

Chart 12.3 Change in CEE proportion at total migrants from 2003 to 2012

decline are the Eastern Enlargement of the EU in 2007 and more importantly, the faster increase of non-CEE migrants and the shrinking CEE proportion in the enlarging population of total migrants in Turkey. To illustrate, between 2008 and 2012, CEE population in Turkey increased by 2500 migrants, however, as the number of total regular migrants increased by 100,000, CEE nationals' proportion in the total migrants fell to its lowest levels since the Republic's foundation (Please see Chart 12.3).

Regarding the migration corridors with the CEE countries, the residence permit data from the Ministry of Interior demonstrates that Bulgaria has the steadiest migration corridor to Turkey while other migration corridors from Serbia and Montenegro, Ukraine, Romania and Moldova are also strongly established (Please see Figs 12.1 and 12.2). In the early 2000s, the number of regular migrants from Serbia and Montenegro, Ukraine, and Romania were lower compared to Bulgarians, but they still remained among the top three countries after Bulgaria. In more detail, statistics on residence permits that CEE migrants received between 2003 and 2012 highlight that the yearly residence permit approvals of Bulgarian migrants change between 55,000 and 15,000. Still following the second Eastern Enlargement of the EU in 2007, the number of regular Bulgarian migrants dropped by more than half.

Fig. 12.1 The proportion of stocks of CEE migrants in 2003

Fig. 12.2 The proportion of stocks of CEE migrants in 2008

In the period between 2009 and 2012, strong migration corridors were also established with Romania and Poland, following Ukraine and Moldova. Overall, Bulgaria, Ukraine, Moldova, Romania, Macedonia, Poland, Albania, Belarus and Kosovo are crucial actors in the CEE regular migration scene in Turkey (Please see Table 12.1).

A more in-depth analysis of residence permits reveals the complex gender patterns of CEE migration. In spite of the widespread belief that CEE migrants are always women, Ministry of Interior's residence permit data revealed that male

Table 12.1 Regular CEE Migration Corridors in 2012

Nationality	CEE Total	Bulgaria	Ukaraine	Moldova	Bulgaria (Turkish Ethnicity)	Romania	Macedonia	Poland	Albania	Belarus	Kosovo
Number	42.027	14.766	7.575	5.538	3.118	1.563	1.395	1.205	1.124	1.025	948
Proportion among CEE	100,00%	35,13%	18,02%	13,18%	7,42%	3,72%	3,32%	2,87%	2,67%	2,44%	2,26%
Nationality	Serbia	Czech Republic	Bosnia Herzegovina	Hungary	Lithuania	Slovakia	Montenegro	Latvia	Slovenia	Croatia	Estonia
Number	695	543	442	418	401	350	326	263	116	112	104
Proportion among CEE	1,65%	1,29%	1,05%	0,99%	0,95%	0,83%	0,78%	0,63%	0,28%	0,27%	0,25%

migrants reached as high as 75 percent of all regular CEE migrants in 2007. Still, even though male CEE migrants are usually the majority in the overall CEE community, an assessment of gender proportions based on origin country uncovers the fact that women from Latvia, Lithuania, Slovakia, Romania and Estonia are higher than men. Furthermore, although migrants from Moldova, Hungary, Poland and the Czech Republic display some mixed trends earlier; they also become female dominated after 2007. This contradiction between the overall male domination and the country specific female domination can be explained by the heavy weight of male migrants from Bulgaria. Since Bulgarian migrants have the largest share in the migration corridors between Turkey and the CEE, the male dominance of Bulgarian migrants has a balancing effect in terms of gender distribution against the female CEE migrants.

In the same data, residence permits based on education may provide some idea on CEE students excluding those whose residence is based on their parents' residence permits. Overall, approximately five percent of all CEE migrants have received residence permits based on education between 2003 and 2012. Along with this, CEE students represented 28 to 14 percent of all international students in a declining trend at the same period. In the year 2010, the proportion of non-CEE migrants in the international student community started increasing. To illustrate, in 2003, 6000 CEE migrants in this category constituted almost 28 percent of a total of 22,000 students. In 2012, however, the number of CEE migrants fell only to 4600, which now constituted close to 13 percent in a total of 35,000 international students in this category. Thus, similar to the residence permit patterns in general, the increase of non-CEE migrants and the slight fall in the CEE students decreased the CEE weight significantly. Regarding the migration corridors, students from Bulgaria, Albania, ex-Yugoslavia including migrants from Kosovo, Serbia and Montenegro and Macedonia have established strong student migration corridor with Turkey.

Next, employment statistics received from the Ministry of Interior demonstrate that CEE migrants, who hold work permits, changing between 2.700 to 5.300, represent 13 to 19 percent of all migrants who were issued work permits in the period between 2003 and 2012. In this population, although the number of female CEE migrants usually fell behind the number of males until 2008, their numbers were close to equal in 2009 and in 2012, female migrants almost doubled the male workers. Regarding origin countries, the largest labor migration corridor is established with Ukraine, followed by strong migration corridors with Bulgaria and Romania, and after 2008, with Moldova and Poland. Here, similar to the patterns of CEE student migration, CEE migrants with work permits only increased approximately by 2000 while total work permits increased from 17,000 to 33,000 from 2009 to 2012, creating a massive fall in the CEE proportion. Here, the proportion of increase in the CEE migrant community is higher than the total increase. Still, in the rapid expansion of the Turkish labor market, the CEE proportion remained limited.

Concerning citizenship acquisitions, as the final data available in relation to regular migrants, CEE migrants constitute over 40 percent of migrants who acquired citizenship in the period between 1989 and 2012. More specifically, in a total of more than 250,000 citizenship acquisitions, approximately 120,000 citizenship acquisitions belonged to CEE nationals. Among the citizenship acquisitions of this group, Bulgarians constitute approximately 90 percent of all citizenship acquisitions with slightly more than 104,000 citizens, followed by Romanians, Moldovans, Macedonians and Ukrainians. Furthermore, as the most common route to acquire citizenship is through ethnic kinship, citizenship through marriage with a Turkish citizen represents roughly ten percent of all acquisitions. Still, citizenship through marriage is widespread among Belarussians, Moldovans and Polish. However, the available citizenship statistics do not disclose more detailed information concerning the grounds migrants acquired their Turkish citizenship.

12.2.2 Irregular CEE Migration into Turkey

The data available on irregular migration in Turkey is limited to the number of apprehensions and human trafficking provided by the Ministry of Interior Affairs. To begin with, 30 percent of a total of 50,000 apprehensions based on irregular migration in 2003 were of CEE migrants. Almost half of these irregular CEE migrants were Moldovans, followed by Romanians (18 percent), Ukrainians (13 percent) and Bulgarians (six percent) in smaller numbers. With the Eastern Enlargements of the EU in 2004 and 2007, CEE apprehensions decreased to 7000 in 2005 and to 3000 in 2008 and the apprehension of CEE irregular migrants is on a general decline. Next, human trafficking statistics demonstrate that only a total of 1145 cases came to the attention of state authorities between the years 2004 and 2010. Accordingly, 29 percent of all human trafficking incidents included a CEE national with 288 Moldovans, 27 Romanians and 11 Bulgarians in this population. Based on these statistics, CEE human trafficking cases display a decreasing pattern in Turkey. However, neither the numbers on irregular migration nor human trafficking are realistic for several reasons. Due to its geographical situation, growing economy and widespread informal labor, Turkey is a major country of transit and destination for irregular migration flows. As these factors are coupled with the current mass migration of Syrians, the numbers of irregular migrants are visibly and substantially higher than the available statistics.

Following this background on regular and irregular CEE migration based on official statistics at the national level, an assessment of the diverse range of CEE migrant profiles in the specific urban regions Edirne and Istanbul will shed more light on this migration type. Due to the lack of statistics on the local level, the source of information here is limited to the non-governmental organizations, state authorities and consulate officials. Firstly, in Edirne, permanent, high-skilled CEE migrants settled during the Cold War period and CEE university students are the two most apparent migrant types. Additionally, while Edirne does not commonly host irregular CEE migrants, this province is associated with irregular migrants who aim to cross the borders to reach Europe. Therefore, it should be noted that CEE migration in Edirne is frequently overshadowed by tragic migrant deaths. Secondly, in Istanbul,

CEE migration is visible in many categories, including the high skilled migration of professionals, low skilled migration of domestic workers with both regular and irregular status, marriage migration, increasing numbers of student migration and finally, trafficked persons – even though the official numbers from CEE seem to be decreasing. Thus, the assessment of these two different CEE migration contexts offers a thorough and integral view of CEE migration in Turkey.

12.3 CEE Migration in Edirne and Istanbul

The two research areas under study in this book chapter, Edirne and Istanbul, constitute diverse settings for CEE migration in linkage to their distinct migration histories. Before highlighting the differences in the implications of CEE migration in these urban regions, however, it should be noted that migrants' experiences of integration in Turkey differ based on three main factors. First, CEE migrants from countries with long-established migration corridors usually join the regular labor force without much difficulty by using their connections with permanent migrants from their origin country. Second, the duration of residence in Turkey also has a direct effect on CEE migrants' integration level. In this study, residence in Turkey is categorized into four terms: Temporary, mid-term and permanent stayers and circular migrants.[6] The third factor influencing the level of integration is the migrant's category. While no statistics are available on the specific migrant categories, knowledge workers, entrepreneurs, manual workers, domestic workers, sex workers and trafficked persons, students and non-working spouses are known to be common migrant categories in Turkey and as will be discussed below, some migrant categories have less advantaged experiences of migration. Against this background, more in-depth information on the urban regions will shed light on the implications of CEE migration in Edirne and Istanbul.

12.3.1 CEE Migration in Edirne

To begin with, the largest community among the permanent migrant population in Edirne is the ethnically Turkish Bulgarians settled in this area during the Cold War period. Welcoming this migration wave on the grounds of ethnic kinship, Turkish state built migrant neighborhoods, namely Binevler area which today is the most upscale neighborhood in Edirne. Most members of this ethnic Turkish community received dual citizenship when Bulgaria's accession to Europe became evident and currently, enjoy a transnational life style with high mobility across the border and continuing connections to Bulgaria. Moreover, this permanent migrant population

[6] Temporary stay is shorter than one year, mid-term is between one and five years, permanent stay is five years or longer and circular stay is repeated migration.

is well integrated and perceived by the public as well educated, high skilled and hardworking. Permanent CEE migrants, according to the general opinion, have well employed the benefits of multiple citizenship and state services that allowed them easy access to housing and employment. Today, permanent and regular CEE migrants from Bulgaria, Albania, Bosnia Herzegovina, Hungary, Kosovo, Macedonia, Moldova, Romania and Ukraine form Edirne's highest socio-economic group and belong to the migrant categories of knowledge workers, entrepreneurs and less often, manual workers. Concurrently, these high CEE migration rates in the urban region generate the migrant category of non-working spouses and children.

Aside from the permanent CEE migrants, Edirne receives a large-scale student migration from Kosovo, Serbia, Montenegro, Croatia and Macedonia in connection to the University of Trakya, which has established the well-known Balkan Research Center and the Department of Balkan Languages and Translation. Aiming to draw students from Balkans, University of Trakya is shaping the student migration patterns in the province. To illustrate, CEE students enrolled in the university in 2013 are approximately 47 percent of the total foreign student population in the province. The largest CEE student communities are from Kosovo with 287 students, Bulgaria with 215 students, Macedonia with 103 students and Albania with 33 students, which are mostly gender balanced groups. Membership of student solidarity organizations based on nationality is very common among this well integrated population. It should be noted here that even though student migration can be categorized under temporary or mid-term migration, CEE students in Edirne often have long-term plans to reside in Turkey permanently after graduation. Unfortunately, no specific data is available on the number and backgrounds of the students who actually realize this plan.

12.3.2 CEE Migration in Istanbul

The second research area under study is Istanbul, known as Turkey's migration hub hosting a diverse range of CEE migrants. To begin with, since the 2000s, female domestic migrants, mostly caretakers from the CEE region have replaced the internal migrants from less developed regions in the care sector. In this category, irregular Moldovan and Bulgarian women are assumed to be the most numerous among the CEE migrants (Suter 2008).[7] Recent legal amendments concerning domestic labor have facilitated the acquisition of residence and work permits. However, employers' unwillingness to pay the high social security fees for the migrants, the lack of migrants' documents and migrants' fear of deportation once noticed by the authorities persist the widespread irregularity. As a high number of female migrants spend long periods in Turkey despite their irregular status, the line between temporary and permanent migration for this migrant type is blurred. Moreover, excluding

[7] Suter, B. (2008) 'The different perception of migration from Eastern Europe to Turkey: The case of Moldovan and Bulgarian domestic workers.'

the ethnically Turkish Bulgarians, the common prejudice that CEE women engage in prostitution creates even more adversity for irregular female CEE migrants in Turkey.

A second type of CEE migrant category in Istanbul is the high skilled migrants and entrepreneurs who consider Istanbul as an attractive destination to live and work due to the historic ties between Turkey and CEE. Apart from the CEE professionals employed in the highly competitive job market, small-scale Hungarian and Czech entrepreneurship through Turkish partnership–as required by the Turkish business laws, is common. As frequent among the Czech community, high skilled migrants often re-unite with their families in Istanbul. While most migrants in this group are career oriented, temporary stayers, some CEE migrants engaged in international trade can also be categorized as circular migrants.

Thirdly, in linkage to this last point, family unification and marriage migration are common patterns of CEE migration in Istanbul. A great majority of Hungarian and Czech migrants in Istanbul are women married to Turkish citizens. Furthermore, the number of dual citizens with Hungary is on the rise after Hungary's facilitation of dual citizenship for those married to citizens of Hungary as well as their children.[8] Therefore, although this group constitutes mostly of permanent stayers, those with dual citizenship often enjoy the trans-border life style and can be categorized as circular migrants.

A fourth type of frequent CEE migration in this urban region is student migration. However, the weight of exchange students involved in Erasmus, bilateral student exchange agreements, and other EU scheme characterizes CEE student migration in Istanbul more temporary compared to Edirne. Finally, a migration type that still remains partially in dark is human trafficking. The highest populations of human trafficking cases, according to the IOM, originate from Moldova and the Ukraine and involve women aged between 18 and 24 years.[9] Accordingly, Istanbul is a main port of human trafficking where women are brought into Turkey "legally" under the cover of tourist visas valid for 3 or 6 months.[10] However, the lack of data on this migrant category does not allow making further assumptions on these migrants' duration of residence.

12.4 Diversification of CEE Migrants: Temporality and Socio-Economic Status

Overall, temporality and socio-economic status seem be two key points of diversification for the major types of CEE migrants in Turkey. To illustrate the diversification based on temporality, first, the permanency of the most settled community of

[8] The information specific to Hungarian and Czech migrants is based on interviews with the Hungarian and Chech Consulates.

[9] http://www.turkey.iom.int/pa2.htm accessed on November 10, 2015

[10] http://www.turkey.iom.int/pa2.htm accessed on November 10, 2015

Bulgarians becomes questionable as they spend longer periods in Bulgaria compared to before Bulgaria's EU accession. Second, student migration and short-term exchange programs are being encouraged at a greater extent, which increases the weight of temporary stays among the CEE migration. Third, as qualitative findings demonstrate, professional migrants in Istanbul mostly regard employment in Istanbul as a temporary life-plan rather than seeing Turkey as their home. Finally, other types of CEE migration move towards more permanent migration. The increasing family unification and marriage migration patterns, migrants in the domestic sector who reside permanently despite their irregularity, and finally, CEE students enrolled in universities who often make long-term plans to reside in Turkey illustrate this tendency towards permanent residence. Thus, temporality is an element that sheds light on the diversity of CEE migrants in Turkey.

Another key point in the diversification of CEE migration is migrants' socio-economic status, which seems closely related with their migration type. In Edirne, first, ethnic Turks from Bulgaria are considered to enjoy higher living standards than the general population. As this community brought with them a certain level of social capital and artisanship when they settled in Edirne during the Cold War period, in time, they also acquired a socio-economically higher status. Second, CEE students generally seem in conformity with the university student profile in Edirne. Hence, even though the distinction between high/low socio-economic statuses may not always be crystal clear, CEE migrants in Edirne have either higher or similar socio-economic status compared to the general population. In Istanbul, the socio-economic status of CEE migrants is more diverse compared to Edirne. On the one hand, low skilled migrants employed in the domestic sector as caretakers, whether irregular or regular, generally earn less compared to Turks working in the same sector. On the other hand, high skilled migrants, such as Hungarians and Czechs regularly employed in the job market or those residing in Istanbul either as spouses seem to present a socio-economically high profile.[11] In parallel with the findings in Edirne, CEE students in Istanbul do not display a great variance from the general university student profile in terms of socio-economic status. Thus, along with temporality, the different levels of socio-economic status also prove the diversity of CEE migrant population.

12.5 Urban Implications of CEE Migration

Assessing the implications of CEE migration is a challenging task. First, the presence of a high number of non-CEE migrants overshadows the specific implications of CEE migration. Second, the expertise on CEE migration is immature in Turkey. In this regard, the fact that solely a handful of public institutions or non-governmental organizations only partially, concentrate on the topics concerning migration results

[11] The information specific to Hungarian and Czech migrants is based on interviews with the Hungarian and Chech Consulates.

in a major data constraint. Third, the implications on the domains concerning less heated issues such as social and political participation, housing and neighborhood consequences or education and language are outweighed by hotly debated domains of labor and registration of migrants in general. Within this frame, to shed light on the influences of CEE migration in Edirne and Istanbul, CEE specific data was collected through online surveys, expert interviews and a focus group organized with the participation of migration experts, stakeholders including public offices and NGOs. Based on this data, the following part will focus on five domains where CEE implications are visible: (1) labor market, (2) housing and neighborhood consequences, (3) registration, (4) social security and welfare, health, societal and political participation and finally, (5) education and language.

12.5.1 Urban Implications of CEE Migration in the Case of Edirne

A better comprehension of CEE implications requires a quick glance at Edirne's general character. This urban region offers only a limited job market due to its constrained industrial base and thus, most residents join the labor force as public servants, agricultural workers or entrepreneurs. CEE migrants enliven the small local economy and broaden the narrow employment profile by entering the job market as knowledge workers and entrepreneurs. In this context, manual workers are more infrequent than knowledge workers and entrepreneurs because the Roma population or the internal migrants from Eastern Turkey often take the low number of disqualified jobs in Edirne's labor market.

In more detail, to begin with the knowledge workers, time of migration is a key determinant of the challenge level in the ***labor market.*** To illustrate, permanent CEE migrants employed as **knowledge workers** experience fewer problems in comparison to newcomers due to their established networks, market experience and accredited diplomas. Today, qualified newcomer migrants face major challenges concerning diploma accreditation considering that many workplaces refuse to make preliminary contracts with migrants before their diplomas are formally recognized and in a vicious cycle, that Turkish authorities start the accreditation only once they receive a migrant's preliminary work contract.

Second**, entrepreneurs** who deal with trans-border trade or own small businesses are a frequent migrant category in Edirne. Following their mass migration, ethnically Turkish Bulgarians were provided business credits and benefitted from their bilingualism, which is a high asset due to Edirne's proximity with Bulgaria. Many CEE entrepreneurs join Edirne's labor market as entrepreneurs in small businesses ranging from restaurant management and the beauty sector to goldsmith. Overall, labor implications of CEE migration are widely considered as positive as CEE migrants have vitalized the economy and the labor market in the province.

Concerning ***housing and neighborhood consequences*** of CEE migration, permanent CEE migrants reside in the most expensive *Binevler* region state-built for the ethnic Turks from Bulgaria. Utilizing the facilitated mortgage options offered by the state, members of this community could afford buying housing and even renting their second housing to newcomers in the early 2000s. In-depth interviews with stakeholders demonstrate, however, that jealousy arose among the low socio-economic groups in Edirne living in Edirne's poorest neighborhoods with bad housing conditions. Meanwhile, in-depth interviews also reveal CEE migrants' skepticism against the internal migrants from Eastern Turkey. Aside from the positive experiences of permanent migrants, mid-term CEE **students** often share housing with crowded groups as rents have increased with the incoming student population. In response to this difficulty, several CEE investors started buying houses to transform into student accommodation and new public dormitories are being built for foreign students. Concerning neighborhood consequences, public's perception of students is generally positive and the students' preference for Edirne is considered as a source of pride for the locals.

Concerning ***registration***, at a first glance, most permanent CEE migrants employed as **knowledge workers, entrepreneurs** and **manual workers** in Edirne are registered as citizens and thus, face no problems in this domain. In terms of labor registration, Edirne's Chamber of Commerce introduced an electronic system for business registration to facilitate the process to encourage entrepreneurs and investors. Dissimilar to these positive experiences of CEE migrants, registration for **students** involves a long bureaucratic procedure between the Ministry of Education, their university and the police department. Once the Turkish Ministry of Education recognizes students' high school diploma and the university receives their recognition document, students will apply to the police department, which then issues a residence permit. Thus, being accepted to a Turkish University does not always guarantee registration. This registration duty has been transferred from the Foreigners' Police to the provincial organization of Directorate General of Migration Management in May 2015, however, the performance of the new registration model is not yet clear. Finally, concerning the migrant category of **non-working spouses**, CEE migrants in mixed marriages usually apply for Turkish citizenship, which takes between six months and three years, but is often a smoothly working process.

Regarding the domain of ***societal participation***, permanent CEE migrants are quite visible and well represented by numerous migrant NGO's. In-depth interviews reveal that politically, CEE migrants from ex-socialist countries often avoid the left-wing and instead, feel closer to migrant solidarity organizations advocating their national roots, e.g., "Organization of Turks from Bulgaria's Kardzhali" and "Turks from Bulgaria's Razgrad". Likewise, CEE **students** are active in organizations such as the Kosovan Students Club or Bosnian Students Club, which have networking activities with other CEE student organizations and migrant business people that sometimes financially support CEE students in Edirne. Apart from this, economic vulnerability sometimes drives CEE students to membership in Islamic organizations for scholarships, as widespread in Turkey with both Turkish and non-Turkish students.

Next, within the frame of reciprocity agreements and high public investments in Edirne's health sector, the domain of ***social security and health services*** is generally a settled area for permanent CEE migrants. For **students** with no scholarships, however, expensive health services and high social security fees are a major disadvantage. Aside from this, the well-known hospital under the University of Trakya has started health tourism by attracting high numbers of patients from Bulgaria, Romania and Greece.

The implications of CEE migration in ***education and language*** vary mostly in connection with duration of residence in Edirne. To begin with, the education level of the permanent CEE community is generally high and language does not seem to be a challenge for this migrant population as they mostly arrived in the Cold War period. However, except from the Turkish-speaking **students** from Kosovo, Gagauzia or Macedonia, newcomer students experience language difficulties as they are expected to follow classes in Turkish. Overall, language and language education, especially of Bulgarian and Greek, play a major role in Edirne's economy. For instance, CEE **knowledge workers** or **entrepreneurs**, who sometimes experience language problems in business negotiations or concerning legal contracts, employ bilingual CEE migrants as translators. At the same time, Bulgarian entrepreneurs often attend Turkish courses in Bulgaria to trade with Edirne. In this context, Turkish and Bulgarian governments agreed to facilitate the establishment of language institutions. Apart from the issue of Turkish, in-depth interviews demonstrate the concern of the Ukrainian community over the preservation of their language and culture as the second and third generations of Ukrainians in Edirne are now fully integrated into Turkey.

12.5.2 Urban Implications of CEE Migration in the Case of Istanbul

Implications of CEE migration in Istanbul are currently overshadowed by the Syrian mass migration. As the unforeseen, intensive flows of Syrians and their highly visible presence in Istanbul is a much-heated topic both with the public and state authorities, "migrant" has recently become synonym to "Syrian" in Istanbul. The arrival of unexpectedly high numbers of Syrian migrants into Istanbul has caused a sudden appearance and surfacing of extreme xenophobia, and a deteriorating public image of migrants and refugees. Due to the scapegoating against the Syrians and migrants in general, most locals typically adopt a totally negative stance against the presence of migrants in Istanbul, or for some of them, their negativity towards the Syrian migrants pushes them to consider the CEE migrants as "better migrants".

In spite of this adversity, as a huge center of trade and industry, Istanbul attracts migrants of various backgrounds from around the globe including knowledge workers, entrepreneurs and manual workers of both regular and irregular status. Coupled with the widespread informal labor in most labor areas, the lack of social policies concerning child and elderly care services also opens a vast employment area for domestic workers. Finally, both short and long-term international students are attracted to nine public and 40 private universities in Istanbul.

In this frame, Istanbul's vast ***labor market*** consists of various CEE migrant categories ranging from permanent **knowledge workers** and **entrepreneurs** from Albania, Bosnia Herzegovina, Bulgaria, Kosovo, Macedonia, Romania and Ukraine, **manual workers** from Moldova, Belarus, Croatia, Montenegro, Poland and Serbia, **domestic workers** from Moldova and Ukraine and in some cases, CEE **students** involved in the labor force irregularly. Until 2008, CEE **sex workers and trafficked persons**, mostly consisting of women from Romania and Moldova were the largest migrant community among all sex workers and trafficked persons in Istanbul. Since then, their numbers have decreased and fallen behind the Central Asian migrants. Information gathered from the in-depth interviews and a focus group study provides more detailed information on the implications of labor market in Istanbul.

Accordingly, the main challenge for high skilled CEE professionals is Istanbul's competitive labor market, which includes both local and international migrants and reduces the likelihood of finding permanent employment. As the second category, CEE entrepreneurs in Istanbul mostly focus on suitcase trade through which they sell Turkish goods and products in their home country and also transport goods to the families of irregular CEE migrants in their home countries. Due to the high demand for Turkish commodities in Bulgaria, Macedonia, Bosnia Herzegovina, Kosovo and Romania and the constant need of irregular migrants to send goods to their home countries, this entrepreneurship is very common, especially in the migrant populated areas.

Apart from these two migrant categories, the enormous labor market also hosts foreign manual workers. Although the Syrian, Afghan and Iraqi irregular migrants take the current disqualified jobs, Bulgarian migrants worked in the temporary, low-skilled jobs as irregular migrants in the 1990s. Today, many irregular CEE manual workers are employed in the textile sector; however, their irregularity leads to lack of information on their numbers, market conditions and profile. Here, it should be highlighted that there is no consensus on how the irregular labor force should be evaluated in Turkey. According to the one side of the debate, irregular workers should be registered to end their vulnerability against employers and to standardize better working and living conditions while according to the other side of the debate, state's registration or irregular migrants may first, increase unemployment and second, generate the risk of deportation for the irregular migrants.

Another migrant type that is partially in dark due to irregularity is the domestic workers most of whom are female CEE migrants who enter with tourist visa and overstay. Employed as caretakers or cleaners, most migrants in this category live in their employers' house to save enough to send remittances. Subject to employers some of whom seize migrants' passports, irregular domestic migrants often earn less than Turkish women employed in this sector. Similarly, CEE students also may become part of the irregular labor force in Istanbul due to the low number of scholarships and the insufficiency of existing scholarships' allowances. As the work hours allowed for foreign students is 24 hours per week and this right is not valid until a student completes the first academic year, many CEE students irregularly join the labor force in the areas of tourism and service sector as most speak Turkish, Russian and English. However, due to their irregularity, they are vulnerable against employers and they encounter the risk of losing scholarships.

In the domain of ***housing and neighborhood consequences***, CEE migrants are found dispersed across Istanbul where their experiences differ significantly based on their residence status. An analysis of the heavily migrant-populated *Beyoğlu*, *Fatih* and *Zeytinburnu* districts demonstrates this dissimilarity. For instance, **regular CEE migrants** from Albania, Bosnia Herzegovina, Bulgaria, Macedonia and Romania live in the middle class *Telsiz* neighborhood of *Zeytinburnu* which is home to a high number of well integrated and permanent CEE **entrepreneurs** and **manual workers** with good reputations as talented, disciplined and trustworthy migrants.

Irregular CEE migrants, however, are found in the poorer *Tarlabaşı* in *Beyoğlu* and *Aksaray* in *Fatih* all of which are also home to **manual workers** from Syria, Iraq, Uzbekistan and African Countries. Due to high rents for low quality housing, irregular CEE migrants in these areas often rent single rooms alone or share flats with other CEE migrants employed in textile shops that sell cheap leather products to foreigners in *Aksaray*. In the past, *Aksaray* was associated with CEE **sex workers** who now seem dispersed in the urban region. Still, it is common to label all CEE women in these neighborhoods as *Natashas* that is used as a synonym for sex workers from the Former Soviet Union and Eastern Europe. As another negative example concerning neighborhood consequences, Georgian manual workers in *Aksaray* are claimed to often dispute with the local residents and seem to be generally disliked because they are believed to engage in theft. In contrast, in the heavily migrant populated district of *Fatih*, CEE migrants seem to be more accepted compared to African and Syrian migrants. Apart from these, most Ukrainian and Moldovan **domestic workers** reside in their workplaces in Istanbul's most expensive neighbourhoods. While they face the risk of exploitation due to their irregularity, they live in better housing conditions compared to most irregular CEE migrants.

Regarding ***registration***, besides the widespread irregularity, CEE **knowledge workers** must undergo an exhausting bureaucratic process during the recognition or verification of their documents due to the phenomenon of purchased diplomas in their countries. Because most companies require a work permit from a job candidate and state authorities frequently refuse to issue a work permit if a foreigner does not have a job contract, knowledge workers' have difficulties in registration. Concerning the other categories, entrepreneurs are encouraged to make their monthly wage payments to their manual workers via Turkish banks as a means for the Ministry of Finance to monitor the registration of foreign workers and repress irregular employment. Irregular migrants, whether **manual workers** or female **domestic workers**, even if they wish to be registered, find it risky to approach the police authorities due to the fear of deportation and prefer to remain invisible. For the category of **sex workers and trafficked persons** from CEE countries, the domain of registration appears to be more problematic compared to the other migrant categories. In some cases, a very thin line separates domestic workers from sex workers or trafficked persons and the state authorities may deport migrant women without considering the possibility of human trafficking. Unlike most other CEE migrant categories, **non-working spouses,** typically women married to Turkish citizens; do not appear to encounter registration difficulties as they obtain citizenship through their marriage.

The domains of ***societal and political participation*** are mostly dependent on migrants' residence status. Regular and permanent CEE migrants have high rates of membership in migration organizations and are well integrated in their communities. Furthermore, their political ideologies appear to be of lesser importance compared to their group loyalty. Thus, when a community member joins a political party, others often support this party even if they do not share their political views. For the CEE **students**, despite their high number, the number of student organizations is lower than in Edirne in spite of the high number of CEE migrants. However, unlike Edirne where each community has its own student organization, NGO's in Istanbul, such as the Balkan Dialogue Groups bring together students from various Balkan countries. Apart from these, irregular migrants, even though they do not have formal membership in migrant NGO's, are very well connected in their communities. However, this connectedness is mostly related to sharing information on registration and security or the available job opportunities. Thus, political participation is not a concern for irregular migrants. Likewise, **non-working spouses** do not seem to be interested in political participation and instead, they have migrant solidarity organizations for their own community, e.g. Latvian wives.

Concerning the **educational backgrounds** and **language** proficiency, the heterogeneity of CEE migrants in Istanbul does not easily permit generalizations. Firstly, the regular and permanent CEE migrants settled in Istanbul during the Cold War period are generally high skilled, well educated and as they are fully integrated, they speak Turkish well. The language domain for the well-educated CEE **knowledge workers** seems primarily to depend on their employment area. Among the permanent or short-term CEE employees of international firms and universities, the motivation to learn Turkish is very low as English is often a valid working language in these circles. In similar, CEE **students** are mostly enrolled in short term university exchange programs for which they may not need to learn Turkish. As most universities offer programs in English, Turkish is not an obligatory language for university studies. While the entrepreneurs' education level in Istanbul is not well known, learning Turkish seems to be more crucial for this category. Likewise, less educated CEE **manual workers**, whether regular or irregular, often need to learn basic Turkish to get on by every day. However, there are no state efforts for the integration of foreign manual workers into the education system or provision of language courses for permanent or short-term migrants. In the category of **non-working spouses and children**, no information is available regarding the implications of spouses concerning education and language. However, children born in Turkey have the right to attend public schools, regardless of their residence status. For the **domestic workers** and **sex workers and trafficked persons,** migrant profiles seem to vary greatly but no concrete data exists on the educational backgrounds. However, in-depth interviews reveal that learning Turkish increases sex workers' chances for working as domestic workers or manual workers.

12.6 Conclusion and Discussion

The heart of the distinctions between the implications of CEE migration in Edirne and Istanbul is linked to their dissimilar characters. On the one hand, Edirne is a small, strictly controlled border city with a limited industrial base and mostly permanent migration. On the other hand, Istanbul is a large, less controlled province that is home to extensive flows of short and long-term internal and international migrants. This context shapes the implications of CEE migration in the domains of labor market, housing, neighborhood consequences, registration, social security, societal and political participation, education and language.

To outline the basic points, CEE migrant types in Edirne and Istanbul show variances. In Edirne, the most visible CEE migrant categories are knowledge workers, entrepreneurs and students well integrated into Edirne's urban fabric and is known to have enlivened the province through their education and skills. In Istanbul, the most frequent CEE migrant categories are knowledge workers, entrepreneurs, manual and domestic workers. However, the heterogeneous migrant profile does not easily permit general statements. In addition, the category of CEE sex workers and trafficked persons is known to exist even though little is known on this migration type. In both urban areas, knowledge workers, entrepreneurs and students receive most of the attention and overshadow the remaining categories of manual workers, non-working spouses and in the case of Istanbul, domestic workers, sex workers and trafficked persons.

Based on the stakeholder survey results, the most frequent trend in both urban regions is permanent CEE migration followed by circular migration. In the case of Edirne, the presence of dual citizens coupled with the strong role of trade with the CEE and in Istanbul, the substantial number of irregular domestic workers may lead to this weight of circular migration. Still, Istanbul holds more mid-term and short-term stayers compared to Edirne. Additionally, unlike Edirne, Istanbul is home to an irregular CEE population. Here, irregularity of long-term migrants is also possible, e.g. irregular domestic workers. Moreover, given the changing nature of migration systems, the established patterns also evolve. Even in the case of earlier migrations, where CEE migrants are considered as permanent migrants, their permanency may be questionable. For instance, with the accession of Bulgaria into the EU, many ethnically Turkish Bulgarians applied for Bulgarian citizenship to become dual citizens and have begun to lead more transnational lives. In this mode, their permanent migration becomes more transnational. Hence, as the old migration patterns are evolving, and new patterns are emerging, the task of mapping CEE migration on temporality and socio-economic status is becoming harder. Thus, in cases similar to the highly diverse CEE migration in Turkey, these two elements typically used to categorize international migrants may be insufficient.

In summary, against this background, in the domain of labor market, CEE migrants in Edirne appear to be generally more privileged in comparison to Istanbul as they are strongly supported by the local authorities, admired for their hard-work and high skills. In Istanbul, a much higher level of competition and the availability of both local and foreign knowledge workers complicate the labor market. Likewise, in the domain of housing, CEE migrants in Edirne appear to mostly have better standards of housing than those in Istanbul. Concerning neighborhood consequences, dissimilar to Edirne several CEE migrant types in Istanbul face discrimination (e.g. irregular female migrants). Regarding registration, majority of CEE migrants in Edirne have obtained citizenship while irregularity is frequent in Istanbul. The consequences of irregularity are the inability to benefit from the social security and welfare systems and difficulties in access to health services. Regarding the domain of societal and political participation, regular CEE migrants in both urban areas are represented by numerous migrant organizations except the less visible categories of domestic workers, sex workers and trafficked people in Edirne. The implications concerning education and language seem to vary mostly in connection with the migrant categories and their duration of residence. Still, education profiles are more heterogeneous in Istanbul compared to Edirne and language seems to be less required to live in Istanbul where learning Turkish is more widespread in Edirne due to the weight or permanent migrants.

Overall, research on migration corridors, migrant categories and urban implications of CEE migration is challenging due to the unavailability of basic statistics, lack of expertise, stakeholders' disinterest on some migrant categories and domains, invisibility of irregular CEE migrants and the dominance of Syrian mass migration in the public and state discourse. Still, the parallel and contrasting features of implications based on the existing information demonstrates how the dissimilar migration contexts shaped the outcomes for the CEE migrants and reflected on specific domains ranging from labor market to education. Thus, the diversity in the CEE migrant profiles in the two urban regions is remarkable.

As Turkey currently receives an increasing number of migrants with diverse backgrounds, the management of urban consequences of temporary and more permanent forms of migration is of key importance. However, in spite of the immigration since the 1980's policy makers only recently accepted that Turkey is a migrant receiving country. The fact that the first comprehensive legal instrument on managing international migration, the *Law No. 6458 of Foreigners and International Protection,* endorsed in May 2015, illustrates how international migration to Turkey has become a policy concern only very recently. Thus, Turkey is going through a time of major change in its migration management.

Due to this policy vacuum on international migration, the Turkish legal framework in relation to migrants typically consists of state centered legal orders fragmented into ad hoc, jurisdictionally complex and sometimes inconsistent arrangements. In this setting, the Law on Foreigners and International Protection aims to embrace a comprehensive approach to migration management, eliminate the excessive bureaucracy of registration and establish procedural standards in every migration related domain. In this direction, following the endorsement of the law, the *Directorate of Migration Management* was established under the Ministry of Interior in 2015. Seemingly contradictory to the aim of reducing the bureaucracy, another state institution, the Prime Ministry Head Advisory for Migration and Humanitarian Aid has entered the scene in 2016 as a new stakeholder in migration management with the aim of establishing a network and coordination between state institutions on the management of the Syrian mass migration. Moreover, the first days of 2016 also witnessed the enforcement of new regulations regarding the work permits of foreign nationals under temporary protection, tailored specifically for the Syrian migrants in Turkey. While the enforcement of regulations facilitating employment for Syrians may raise eyebrows due to the unfairness against non-Syrian migrants, it is not yet possible to imagine their reflections on the future of migrants in Turkey. The key question here is whether the expansion of Syrian migrants' rights will have positive repercussions on other migrants; however, it is still too early to make any predictions on the subject.

Furthermore, these progresses do not yet bring an end to the debates surrounding the governance approaches to migration. Despite the progress, the state-centered hierarchical order, the top-down understanding towards policy making and a security based approach still dominate the migration governance. The sharp shift from neglect to integration of millions of migrants requires an enormous change of mindset. The main fault line in this critical debate runs between those who believe migrants should be offered easy access to labor and extensive rights of social security and those who fear this would create an inequality between migrants and Turkish citizens who do not enjoy a high level of social security, especially if they are employed informally. This fault line, appearing in relation to almost all policy areas, runs deep because it is linked to most basic ideas on immigration, integration and naturalization. The common suggestion shared by all sides, however, is the need for more state focus on migrants' integration and the necessity to create a positive public opinion of migrants to facilitate this process.

References

Çağatay, S. (2007). Race, Assimilation and Kemalism: Turkish Nationalism and the Minorities in the 1930s. *Middle Eastern Studies, 40*(3), 86–101.

Kirişci, K. (2006). Disaggregating Turkish citizenship and immigration practices. *Middle Eastern Studies, 36*(3), 1–22.

Parla, A. (2003). Marking time along the Bulgarian-Turkish border. *Ethnography, 4*, 561–565.

Parla, A. (2006). Longing, belonging and locations of homeland among Turkish immigrants from Bulgaria. *Southeast European and Black Sea Studies, 6*(4), 543–557.

Suter, B. (2008) The different perception of migration from Eastern Europe to Turkey: The case of Moldovan and Bulgarian domestic workers.

Websites: IOM Turkey: http://www.turkey.iom.int/pa2.htm

Chapter 13
Conclusions and Reflection

Mark van Ostaijen and Peter Scholten

This book shows that intra-European movement not only raises various practical social and governance issues, but also deepens important theoretical and conceptual issues. This includes fundamental questions concerning the conceptualization within migration studies about its core object of analysis; when can something be considered as migration? In this book this concerns in particular whether to conceptualize intra-European movement as 'migration' or 'mobility'; can those who move in the EU be considered 'migrants' in a sociological sense or should they be conceptualized merely as mobile EU citizens making use of their right to free movement? The contestation of this very basic conceptualization reveals not only the political character of some of concepts used in this research field, but also the need for more cross-disciplinary work in the conceptualization of migration, here in particular between sociology and political sciences.

Furthermore, the book spurs theoretical thinking on intra-European movement; what are the implications, for whom, and why? Here the book builds on the existing body of knowledge on labour migration in particular. However, as Penninx amongst others in this volume shows, knowledge about the guest labour system of the last century cannot be simply extrapolated for understanding the contemporary intra-European labour movement system. In particular, it highlights that the political context in which current movements takes place does matter to understand its implications. Once again, the political setting of the EU has emerged as pertinent here. However, the book shows, based on empirical research in various countries,

M. van Ostaijen (✉)
Tilburg Institute of Governance, Tilburg University, Tilburg, The Netherlands
e-mail: m.vanostaijen@uvt.nl

P. Scholten
Erasmus University Rotterdam, Rotterdam, The Netherlands

P. Scholten, M. van Ostaijen (eds.), *Between Mobility and Migration*, IMISCOE Research Series, https://doi.org/10.1007/978-3-319-77991-1_13

that the implications of intra-European movement become especially visible on the local level, in urban settings where intra-European movers often settle, work and interact. In particular, the book reveals a high-degree of internal complexity and diversity in terms of various (urban) implications for different forms of intra-European movement. This clearly renounces simplified objectives of intra-European movement in terms of 'EU citizens' 'moving freely' for 'economic purposes'.

This speaks directly to a third theoretical contribution from this book, regarding the conceptualization and theorization of multi-level governance in this area. Adopting a critical lens on relations between various levels of governance, and bringing together sociological research on the implications of intra-European movement with a thorough analysis of governance on these levels, the book shows that multi-level governance is more an *ideal* than an *achievement* in this policy area. In fact, various chapters in this volume speak of decoupling or a mismatch between levels, with a variety of implications both for EU free movers, as well as for the places in which they settle. This speaks more broadly to the literature on multi-level governance, which has often focused primarily on EU-national relations and has presumed the existence of effective vertical channels for policy coordination between different levels (Hooghe and Marks 2001). However, our analysis shows that the local level is equally important to understanding multi-level governance, that vertical channels are difficult to achieve and to some extent even absent in this case, and that sometimes vertical relations between levels are initiated from below by local governments rather than top-down from the EU (Scholten et al. 2017).

A key issue running through these three theoretical contributions is the need for a reflexive use of categories and even theories to understand pertinent issues within the research-policy nexus. The book shows that in various ways, the political context is central to understanding the language scholars use to approach intra-European movement. This applies not only to the conceptual contestation on migration versus mobility, but for instance also on whether the implications of intra-European movement can be understood in terms of 'integration' and even on whether we should speak of 'multi-level governance' in this area. This political context should therefore be considered *endogenous* to our conceptual and theoretical understanding of intra-European movement. We need to be reflexive in the use of concepts and theories for understanding a phenomenon that is in itself politically constituted. Working across disciplines, bringing together disciplines and fields such as sociology, political science and governance studies, provides a strategy for enhancing this reflectivity.

In this concluding chapter we will bring together the key (analytical) findings from this book and elaborate on the main contributions to the literature that have already been briefly outlined above. This also involves confronting the empirical chapters on intra-European movement (based largely on the IMAGINATION project) with the theoretical chapters.

13.1 The Diversification of Intra-European Movement

The book started with a number of expectations based on previous studies of (European) migration. First of all, we expected that especially in terms of *time-span* and *socio-economic background*, free movement of people would result in a '*diversification of diversity*', a further diversification of migration types. This echoes findings from various studies that show that intra-European movement can be temporary or circular, but can sometimes also evolve into a more permanent form of settlement migration, as well as into 'in-between' categories that have been described as 'liquid mobility' (Engbersen 2012).

Indeed, various chapters in this volume confirm that 'CEE migrants' cannot be considered as a homogenous group based on their region of origin, culture or ethnicity. Instead it is a rather differentiated category with high and low skilled, as well as temporary and permanent migrants. The research confirms our expectation on the *diversification of diversity*, showing a wide range of types in terms of socio-economic status and duration of stay. It shows that the free movement of persons in Europe enables a wide range of Europeans to move outside their national-state borders and search for opportunities in other nation-states. This however does not imply that the status one has by leaving the origin region is the same status in the receiving region. The valuation of skills and the socio-economic position differs from both perspectives. And to put it more sharp, sometimes one starts as a manual worker and end up as homeless and sometimes one begins its trajectory in the agricultural industry but ends up in a blue-collar profession. This economic mobility within territorial mobility complexifies this diversification argument even more and illustrates the heterogeneous picture of this population. This is an important empirical observation that is not always reflected in societal or political debates and has important implications, also described in this book, which we will elaborate on in this chapter. Next to this diversification, it also reveals a *feminization* of migration, which is described here as an increasing number of female migrants in CEE migration, but we lack knowledge about gender relations or the changing profile and status of female migrants.

Next to this diversification of diversity, the previous chapters show some significant data on *migration corridors*, or on the historical path dependency of sending and receiving regions. The cases illustrate the importance of the historical context and the legacy of certain migration networks. For example, the Chaps. 10, 11 and 12 of Marta Kindler, Dusan Drbolav Lena Pavelkova and Deniz Korfali and Tugba Acar show that the migration corridors between Poland and the Netherlands, Czech Republic and Austria and Bulgaria and Turkey are quite substantive and transformed over time. In many ways, institutional regimes (such as the European framework of free movement) rather than geographical proximity (such as in the case of Bulgaria and Turkey and Poland and the Netherlands), have played a significant role in these transformations. In other cases, such as the Czech and Austrian commuting routes show the importance of even further diversifying the mobility argument towards a 'mico-type'; between migration and commuting.

The country cases, with all different transitional restrictions, also show some interesting findings. In those countries where transitional restrictions were exercised, it only had consequences for formal employment. Sometimes despite these transitional rules, deploying different tactics, such as self-employment, migrants from the CEE member states still arrived and worked in all these countries. However, it did show quite clearly the *labour market as governance tool,* since this type of movement is mainly characterized by socio-economic reasons, such as work. Not insignificantly, because the European framework is designed to make the 'Single Market' more flexible. While all EU citizens have the right to move, but this right can be better applied, when one has a position on the labour market. It shows the significance of the European and national labour market to regulate, legalize and penalize some of the newly moving EU citizens. Moreover, taking everything into account, we see a diversification of intra-European mobility, where historical path-dependency and political-institutional structures have contributed to specific migration corridors.

13.2 Consequences of Intra-European Movement

A second expectation that lay at the foundation of this book was that, given the '*uneven distribution*' of migrants in specific localities, the diversification of intra-European movement would also lead to a *diversification of local consequences*: not only in terms of labour market issues, but a wide range of issues that evolve from short-term (housing) to long-term implications (language and education) in the receiving and sending countries. We developed this expectation since there are huge differences between types of migrants in terms of access to and provision of local resources, the respective trajectories as well as barriers they are facing.

The Chap. 3 of Ursula Reeger also shows a nuanced perspective to intra-European movement, a perspective that proves that the *triple-win scenario* promoted by the EU does not entirely hold true (Favell 2008). Especially if we take the consequences on the labour market into consideration, as one of the most significant domains. Migrants may sometimes gain on their socio-economic circumstances, in terms of higher wages, but have to take in on their socio-cultural position and status, especially regarding their work and living circumstances. It reveals that individual implications are often interrelated with each other, resulting in a '*chain of implications*', or like '*the dominoes of dependency*' (Zelano et al. 2016). With a close look at these implications, despite that EU citizens have almost the same rights as nationals and being treated like them legally, does not necessarily result in equal outcomes (e.g. Favell 2008; Ciupijus 2011; MacKenzie and Forde 2009; Sabater 2015). EU citizens still face obstacles and are in need of help and guidance at least at the beginning of their stay, and this is where they do not differ much from third country nationals (TCN) (van Ostaijen et al. 2017). But contrary to TCN, EU citizens are, at least up to now, often not subject to integration policies due to the principle of non-discrimination of EU-citizens which could evolve into some unintended consequences as well.

Furthermore, the analyses in this book show significant variation in the implications for urban regions and cities. This involves both different types of implications, ranging from labour market issues to housing and social security, language and integration, as well as variation between cities. Here the type of movement that is involved as well as the history of intra-European movement to a specific city, matters significantly. For instance, whereas in Sweden there was a strong focus on the situation of homeless and beggars, in the Netherlands the focus was almost entirely on low-skilled manual workers, housing and labour market issues, whereas in Austria the focus was more on circular migration from household and manual workers.

What speaks from these findings is that implications of intra-European movement cannot simply be understood only by economic motives. In fact, this book shows that intra-European movement has broader social implications, often situated at the urban level. This includes implications that are described by stakeholders in terms of 'integration issues.' Although from a regulatory perspective the notion of integration would not apply to intra-European citizens, this study shows that from a more sociological perspective, integration issues do arise particularly at the local level. The extent to which this is problematized differs between cities, with the Dutch cities being most particularly focused on integration while Austrian cities, also because of proximity and the history of migration, were much less concerned about integration issues in relation to intra-European movement.

However, this also involves implications for intra-European movers themselves. Especially in the Dutch case, examples emerged of intra-European movers being put in situations of significant economic and social dependency. For example, some situations occurred where labour recruitment agencies developed integral packages for intra-European movers, which included next to a labour contract also housing, transport, security and health care. Combined with the fact that many intra-European movers do not register in the place where they live, have little knowledge and understanding of where and how to get services when required, and the fact that there has been significant malpractice in terms of housing facilities, this has led to clear cases where intra-European movers were exploited. The 'economic' freedom of movement within the EU can thus sometimes come at significant costs.

Finally, this book also shows that intra-European movement has consequences not only for the urban regions of arrival but also for the regions of origination. As Kindler observes (Chap. 10), this includes positive as well as negative consequences. Positively, financial remittances have been rather important for sending regions (such as Opolskie), as well as (more limited) social remittances. Negatively, depopulation but in particular the decline of the workforce in the sending region, is also indicated as an important effect. In fact, the Polish case shows a combination of policies facilitating labour migration in Europe, facilitating return migration, but also facilitating labour migration into Poland in order to replace the workforce that left for other parts of Europe. In this sense, sending regions can develop into central areas of chain migration, such as in the case of Poland sending labour migrants to other parts of the EU as well as receiving labour migration from Ukraine in particular.

13.3 Between 'Multilevel Governance' and 'Disjointed Governance'

A third expectation explored in this book was that to what extent the wide range of local consequences leads to *multi-level governance*: mutual collaborations between the European, national and local governmental levels resulting into a coordinated 'politics' of 'European free movement'. Despite this expectation, the Chaps. 6 and 7 of Zelano and Bucken-Knapp et al. show that in spite of a multilevel *setting*, not much has emerged in terms of multilevel *governance*. In other words: the EU level is more or less absent. Curry suggests in his Chap. 8 that it can be seen as *troubling* and indeed, what stands out is that many of the issues connected with CEE migration appear at the local level and are dealt with at the local or maybe national level, which is remarkable. Local level municipalities and cities sometimes seek for financial or legal support from the national level which result in some immediate horizontal ties and networks at the local level. But this does not always result into vertical collaborations between governments or institutional venues where problem definitions are met.

As such, we cannot confirm our expectation on multi-level *governance*, which is at least theoretically, surprising. When new laws, policies and legislations were developed, these mostly concerned the most primary issues such as housing, employment and registration. It is clear that depending on the policy area, different institutional logics applied in different countries (and sometimes in different regions within the same country). Moreover, different historical paths guided how governments reacted upon this EU migration. All the studied cases show large variety in their local-national approaches and focus areas, but the absence of the EU level is a comparative element observed in all cases.

In some cases active engagement of local municipalities was visible, pushing up this issue on the agenda not only of their local council but striving for national attention as well. This kind of *policy entrepreneurship* has not been observed in all cases, sometimes also because of a lack of political significance, social urgency or historical-institutional path dependency. But in the cases where this policy entrepreneurship worked, and levels of government felt responsible to act and collaborate, these levels surprisingly seemed to have the same ground. In terms of Durkheim, these actors did not only have an agreement in terms of *logical* but also *moral* conformity: they not only agreed on their *logical presuppositions and perceptions* but also agreed upon their *values*. However, in most cases this did not occur, and one important lesson is that in spite of its broad theoretical definition and application in the literature, multi-level governance is hard to achieve in practice and need to be seen as one of the varied ideal types of governance in a multi-level setting.

These findings speak to the broader literature of multi-level governance, raising attention to the agency of local, national and European governments in establishing horizontal and vertical governance configurations in a multi-level setting (Hooghe and Marks 2001; Bache and Flinders 2004; Piattoni 2010). The Chaps 8 and 9 of Curry and Balch also show *"the importance of a bottom-up understanding of policy in explaining governance processes, one that takes into account implementation as well as decision-making"* (Curry), sometimes even leading to *disintermediation.* It highlights the importance of the local level for governance in a multi-level setting, and the need to regard *local actors as strategic entrepreneurs* in moulding multi-level governance processes. This complements with a more bottom-up perspective to the typology of Hooghe and Marks (2003), having a rather top-down approach of Europeanization. This finding adds new insights how governance in multi-level settings work and argues that multi-level governance is not the only one but just one of the ideal types one could investigate. Rather than taking multi-level governance as a given, or as 'independent variable', our study shows why one cannot assume 'multi-level governance' but it has relevance to study this as one ideal typical configuration. It displays that a better understanding is required how and why multi-level governance evolves under specific circumstances, as a 'dependent variable.' This contributes to a more precise theoretical understanding and conceptualization of multi-level governance.

Moreover, in terms of governance in a multi-level setting, this book not only raises significance to the local level, it also gives substance to cases of *non-governance in a multi-level context*, which has institutional consequences. Not only did we observe cases of institutional non-collaboration, this eventually also resulted in dispersed, contested or even incongruent policies. One example also mentioned before, there was for instance a four-Minister-letter written to the Vivian Reding to ask attention for the consequences *"since this type of immigration burdens the host societies with considerable additional costs"* (Mikl-Leitner et al. 2013). This was complemented with a call from the Dutch Minister Asscher in the Netherlands signalling a 'Code Orange' considering free movement (Asscher and Goodhart 2013), while a Dutch aldermen earlier indicated free movement as a 'tsunami of Eastern-Europeans' (Zuidervaart 2010) and European cities developed a Memorandum of Understanding to address the 'complex manageable influx' of EU citizens (MoU 2011). As a response, the European Commission developed a meeting for mayors in which Vivian Reding concluded *"that there is not just simply one single perspective on free movement. There are a variety of experiences"* (Reding 2014: 1). Moreover, the then Home Affairs Commissioner, Cecilia Malmström, criticized this member-states letter since *"EU citizens who have the right to travel, live, work and study where ever they want in the Union are put on a par with immigrants from countries outside the EU. For instance, they are being called 'EU immigrants', a concept that does not exist"*. She even stated that: *"they are mixing apples and oranges"* by "*mixing up internal EU mobility and immigration*" (Hansen 2015). Also, Vivian Reding, the then Commissioner for Justice wanted *"to make it absolutely clear: free movement is a fundamental right, and it is not up for negotiation. Let language not betray us: European citizens exercising their right to free movement are not 'immigrants"'* (Reding 2013). It made clear that the different authorities involved do not hold a comparable perspective and have dispersed interests. Moreover, in a response to the local and national level concerns, the European Commission asked for an independent research to study the effect of free movement in cities. In this study they concluded that: "*the overall evidence suggests that this situation is not placing major issues and burdens on the local communities or local public services, whereas issues related to discrimination are being gradually overcome and positive attitudes towards migration and mobility are generally recorded*" (EY 2014: 2). This did not marked the end of the controversy, since after this, seven European Ministers wrote a letter to the EC to address 'the improper and abusive use' of the Posted Workers Directive (Hundstorfer et al. 2015). It gives an insight in the contestation and controversy of this issue between local municipalities, member-states and the European Commission.

Importantly, such controversy is not limited to statements only since such statements lead to different institutional practices and sometimes evolves into policy deadlocks or policy stalemates. Such contestation or controversies can also have consequences on for instance the efficacy of multi-level arrangements. In Chap. 8, Curry also observed that *"significant parts [...] display either decoupled or disjointed governance. The relative lack of EU-level coordination indicates governance decoupling between EU and member state levels. Again, this is partly the result of the unique supra-national powers of the EU, but it also creates the risk of a clear split between EU and member state goals"*. This gives again a different contribution to the multi-level governance literature, with some different substance around 'ideal' typical configurations.

13.4 Central and Eastern European Perspectives; Beyond a North-West European Bias

Various contributions in this book also show that a deeper understanding of intra-European movement requires migration studies to look beyond a North-Western European bias. Intra-European movement invokes issues in receiving as well as sending regions and countries. For instance, Kindler's contribution to this volume shows that intra-European movement also has various positive but also negative consequences for the sending regions in Poland, such as Opolskie. Especially this Polish case shows how the departure of labour force to other European countries is also creating a need for labour migration towards Poland. In what is described by Kindler as a 'double governance challenge', Polish regions try to organize and enhance the benefits from migration to other EU regions as well as liberalize labour migration towards Poland (especially from Ukraine). This shows how intra-European movement is connected to broader (labour) chain migration from East to West, which also involves migration from non-European countries. Once again, the observed social reality shows much more complexity than a simplified distinction between EU and non-EU migration could cover. The Chap. 11 by Drbohlav and Pavelkova shows that across the borders of European countries, a specific form of migration is emerging that they describe as the MICO type, combining elements of migration and commuting. CEE countries are also developing their own governance responses to intra-European movement. This includes efforts to organizing the diaspora across Europe as well as facilities to promote return migration. Moreover, Chap. 12 shows the specificity of Turkey. Apart from emigration from Turkey to various parts of Europe, especially the Edirne and Istanbul areas have seen a gradual increase of migration from especially Central and Eastern Europe. To some extent this involves ethnic Turks, but it also includes broader categories of labour migrants seeking for work (industries, services, household work) in the growing Turkish economy (as well as student migration). Although there are indications that this migration recently decreased and that Turkey itself is much more concerned about refugee migration than labour immigration, this does reinforce the conclusion that intra-European movement is not bound by EU borders and should be considered as part of a broader migration system.

13.5 Reflectivity Towards Idioms on the Research-Policy Nexus

A topic that runs throughout this book, is the key role of language or 'discourses' on intra-European movement. This applies, as we have seen above, both to the conceptualization of intra-European migration or mobility as well as to whether the implications of intra-European movement are framed in terms of 'integration.' What springs from the analyses in this book is the importance of the political context in which discourses on intra-European movement develop (van Ostaijen 2016). The language we use to understand intra-European movement is itself produced in intensive and sometimes contested research-policy dialogues. From an academic perspective it is not interested whether intra-European movers should or should not be considered migrants, but rather whether the concept of 'migration' helps us to understand the phenomenon of border movement better in ways that cannot be achieved with other concepts. Therefore, as this book has argued at various points, a more reflective use of idiom is required, especially when it comes to concepts that originate from broader research-policy dialogues.

This reflective use of idiom should involve a more critical use of concepts, based on a sound conceptualization as well as a sound empirical understanding of social reality, also when this may counteract specific institutional discourses. For instance, this volume brings insights by showing that European movement cannot solely be seen as just migration from a settlement perspective, but it can also not be seen as just mobility from a circular or liquid perspective (See also Chap. 4 of Engbersen). Furthermore, it shows that many stakeholders, including representatives from intra-European movers themselves, clearly recognize the importance of integration issues, while it also shows that traditional theories of assimilationism or even transnationalism are not always suited to understand these consequences. In fact, what the book shows is that the social (and political) reality of intra-European movement is characterized by much more complexity than implied in simplifying dichotomies such as migration versus mobility. Rather than reducing this complexity, migration research should aim at enriching its conceptual apparatus in order to grasp this complexity, to which this book has sought to contribute.

Furthermore, a more reflexive use of idiom should treat the political context in which migration discourses originate, as *endogenous* to our analyses. In the case of intra-European movement, this involves in particular a problematization of the European context in which key concepts emerge. Since the European Union plays a key role in defining citizenship, constructing a territory and managing a regulatory and legal framework, European movement displayed in different member-states need to be understood in this specific 'new' political and institutional context. And this context is unprecedented from a European point of view, but is also incomparable with the US context, as an immigrant country of 'united' states. It shows that scholars in the European context studying intra-European movement, need political-institutional sensitivity, not only to embed this case in its right legal context but also to refine and be reflexive of the vocabulary used. For instance, terms as migration and integration are commonly associated with nation-states, while the European Commission defines this phenomenon as 'EU movement' and the 'mobility' of 'EU citizens'. This is not just a linguistic difference, but a clash of discourses, representing different institutional consequences on this topic (van Ostaijen 2016). This volume displays that such a struggle cannot be met without a political sensitive lens of our conceptual tools to understand the topic of investigation.

Finally, we believe that a more reflective idiom on intra-European movement requires more cross-disciplinary cooperation. All key findings from this book originate from a confrontation between sociological research on the character of intra-European movement, its (social) implications and a more political science driven analysis of the governance of intra-European movement at various levels. It is this cross-disciplinary work that brought to light not only the discrepancies between concrete implications and the policies developed at the local level, but also the conceptual contestation to understand and address intra-European movement.

13.6 The Consequences of Failing Multi-Level Governance

Furthermore, speaking more broadly to the literature on governance studies, this book shows that contestation of intra-European movement is not without consequences. The contestation on discourses is not just some juggling with words, but is the epitome why multi-level governance fails. The conflicting discourses, the contested perspectives on this phenomenon, and the non-congruent positions consequentially sometimes have led to a *dialogue of the deaf*. It led to a deadlock situation in which certain governmental authorities did not met in terms of cooperation, concerted interventions and synchronized actions. Instead it led to a diversified palette of varied laws, policies and legislations active on 'EU migrants' and 'EU citizens', sometimes even widening the gap between authorities than bridging it. It shows the significance of the different positions, resulting in different discourses, causing a wide range of varied institutional actions.

As argued above, our analysis shows little evidence of effective multi-level governance, in spite of intra-European movement clearly being a policy area that is characterized by a multi-level setting. The absence of common basic understanding of intra-European movement obstructs the development of a common or even coordinated approach across various levels. The different logics (political, social and sometimes economic) per governance level appear so strong that the logic of governance in this area is primarily 'horizontal' (per level) rather than 'vertical' (across levels). This shows that the concept of multi-level governance should not be used too light; it remains an empirical question whether multi-level governance is actually achieved *across* levels. We have seen efforts, especially by local governments acting as policy entrepreneurs, to establish such multi-level governance relations, but this has not resulted (at least not yet) in strong horizontal governance logics per level.

As a consequence, this book finds many illustrations of 'disjointed' or 'decoupled' governance and points out the need for much more work to understand why governance decoupling occurs and what the effects may be. However, this book clearly shows that the dominance of level-specific factors (including legal and political principles such as free movement) seem to be much stronger than the will to cooperate across levels. It also shows that the overall effectiveness of the governance of intra-European movement decreases because of this decoupling. For instance, issues of social integration at the local level can be much less addressed for intra-European movers than for instance for TCN migrants, which may in itself also pose an impediment to achieve free movement in the EU itself.

Besides consequences in terms of disjointed governance, the failure of multi-level governance also has consequences for intra-European movers themselves. It stimulates the dominance of a *hospitality paradigm* on the national level by the discourse of welfare chauvinism. This crucial point, made by Balch in Chap. 8, reminds us that "*the result of conflicts and compromise over intra-European mobility has been to construct a kind of social denizenship for mobile European citizens by those Member States that have been the main recipients of this kind of migration*". The continued dominance of such national paradigms rearticulate the dividing lines between the excluded and included ones based on nationality. Consequentially, this causes that despite legal and regulatory European frameworks to equalize the rights of European citizens, the position of a substantive group of European 'mobile workers' stays precarious and vulnerable (Sennet 1998; Beck 1992). It means that the labour market position of European mobile workers, especially in low skilled positions, does not extremely differ from that of undocumented or irregular migrants such as Third Country Nationals (Ruhs and Anderson 2010; Bommes and Sciortino 2011; Favell 2008; Standing 2011; van Ostaijen et al. 2017). This demonstrates the relevance of a more differentiated perspective on the downsides and benefits of European free movement.

13.7 Intra-European Movement as a Critical Case in Migration Studies, Governance Studies and European Studies

Finally, we conclude this volume by a concise discussion about how the case of intra-European movement speaks more broadly to theoretical developments in migration studies, governance studies and European studies. For migration studies, intra-European movement invokes not only an important topic in terms of its size and degree of public contestation (as seen for instance in Brexit debates), but also touches upon one of the most fundamental questions in this research field; how to conceptualize migration. Thus far, migration scholars have been able to ground their analyses on a clear distinction between domestic and international movement. Intra-European movement defies this simple distinction, and shows that different political contestations (such as within the EU) matter to the conceptualization of what can be seen as migration. It also shows the importance of the political setting to understand how migration is framed for the 'migrants' involved and its governance. This means that migration studies will increasingly need to problematize the political constitution of anything as 'migration' to understand such a phenomenon.

This also raises a further need for cross-disciplinary work between migration studies and governance studies, and touches upon various questions of broader relevance to governance studies. This book shows that the issue of intra-European movement raises issues that apply at the EU as well as the national and the local (urban) level. This makes intra-European movement into a critical case for the study of multi-level governance in Europe. Reaching beyond traditional state-centric views on policymaking or top-down perspectives on Europeanization, multi-level governance is positioned in the literature (and in policy discourse) as a response to those complex policy issues that call for a broader approach across policy levels. However, this book shows that multi-level governance appears more as an ideal type than as a reality when it comes to intra-European movement. This can be attributed towards the dominant policy logics per level ('horizontally') but also because of the lack of a shared understanding of intra-European movement that would allow cross-level ('vertical') interactions. For governance studies, this raises questions how multi-level governance could be designed in more effective ways especially in the context of such a complex multi-layered policy systems as the European Union.

To conclude, this brings us to a final contribution, which applies in particular to European Studies. Intra-European movement perhaps touches upon the most fundamental 'pillars' of the European project, which is free movement. While this book and this research has not been an attempt to undermine the 'fundamental' belief in this 'pillar' of free movement, it delivers empirical insights that inform such beliefs in free movement and the European project. This book shows that free movement invokes fundamental questions at the local level regarding 'integration' issues of intra-European movers. Regardless of how such questions will be addressed, which is in itself a political decision, our research shows that the local implications of intra-European movement are in many ways in conflict with the ideal of free movement. In fact, this book has shown that intra-European movement can also work out rather negatively for intra-European movers involved. This ranges from a lack of access to information and services to more extreme cases of exploitation of intra-European workers. Despite new European legal and regulatory frameworks to equalize the rights of European citizens, this book shows that the position of a substantive group of European 'mobile workers' stays precarious and vulnerable (Sennet 1998; Beck 1992). Their precariousness and vulnerability carries some resemblances pointing at a 'new Victorian servant class' or a 'new precariat', characterized by a lack of agency, stability and security (Favell 2008; Standing 2011). It means that the labour market position of European mobile workers, especially in low skilled positions, does not extremely differ from that of undocumented or irregular migrants such as Third Country Nationals leading to *exploitative* and *greedy* relationships in many countries (Favell 2008; Standing 2011; Ruhs and Anderson 2010; Bommes and Sciortino 2011; van Ostaijen et al. 2017). As such, this volume contributes to a more balanced understanding of the 'shadow sides' of European free movement, as it shows that not all free movement of persons is totally free (Ciupijus 2011). Moreover, instead of bold political statements, this book demonstrates the relevance of a more differentiated perspective on the downsides and benefits of European free movement. We hope this volume gives constructive empirical insights and critical theoretical substance for various publics and speaks to the daily reality of those readers involved in this topic personally and professionally.

References

Asscher, L. and Goodhart, D. (2013). Code oranje voor vrij werkverkeer binnen de EU. *De Volkskrant* 17-08-2013.

Bache, I., & Flinders, M. (2004). *Multi-Level governance*. Oxford: Oxford University Press.

Beck, U. (1992). *Risk society: Towards a new modernity*. London: Sage.

Bommes, M., & Sciortino, G. (2011). *Foggy social structures*. Amsterdam: University Press.

Ciupijus, Z. (2011). Mobile central eastern Europeans in Britain: Successful European Union citizens and disadvantages labour migrants? *Work Employment and Society, 25*(3), 540–550.

Engbersen, G. (2012). Migration transitions in an era of liquid migration. In M. Okolski (Ed.), *European immigrations: Trends, structures and policy implications IMISCOE research* (pp. 91–105). Amsterdam: Amsterdam University Press.

EY. (2014). *Evaluation of the impact of free movement of EU citizens at local level – Final report*. Ernst and Young: Brussels.

Favell, A. (2008). The new face of East–West migration in Europe. *Journal of Ethnic and Migration Studies, 34*(5), 701–716.

Hansen, P. (2015). Undermining free movement: Migration in an age of austerity, *Eurozine*. http://www.eurozine.com/articles/2015-02-06-hansenp-en.html

Hooghe, L., & Marks, G. (2003). Unraveling the central state, but how? Types of multi-level governance. *American Political Science Review, 97*, 233–243.

Hundstorfer, R., Peeters, K., Rebsamen, F., Nahles, A., Schmit, N., Asscher, L., Johansson, Y. (2015). Letter to Ms. Thyssen. Posting of workers Directive. 18-06-2015.

McKenzie, R., & Forde, C. (2009). The rhetoric of the 'good worker' versus the realities of employers' use and the experiences of migrant workers. *Work, Employment and Society, 23*(1), 142–159.

Mikl-Leitner, J., H.P. Friedrich, F. Teeven, and H.T. May. (2013). Letter to Alan Shatter, Presidency of European Council.

Ostaijen, M.v., Reeger, U., & Zelano, K. (2017). The commodification of mobile workers in Europe. A comparative perspective on capital and labour in Austria, the Netherlands and Sweden. *Comparative Migration Studies, 5*(6).

Piattoni, S. (2010). *The theory of multi-level governance: Conceptual, empirical and normative challenges*. Oxford: Oxford University Press.

Reding, V. (2013). *Main Message: Trieste Citizens' Dialogue*. Speech/13/706. European Commission, 16-09-2013. www.europa.eu/rapid/press-release_SPEECH-13-706_en.htm

Reding, V. (2014). *Free movement of EU citizens: Turning challenges into opportunities at local level.* Speech Conference for Mayors on EU Mobility at local level. Brussels, 11 February 2014.

Ruhs, M., & Anderson, B. (2010). Semi-compliance and illegality in migrant labour markets: An analysis of migrants, employers and the state in the UK. *Population Space Place, 16*, 195–211.

Sennet, R. (1998). *The corrosion of character*. New York: Norton.

Standing, G. (2011). *The precariat; the new dangerous class*. London: Bloomsbury Academic.

van Ostaijen, M. (2016). Between migration and mobility discourses: The performative potential within 'intra-European movement'. *Critical Policy Studies*.

Zuidervaart, B. (2010). Zelfs mislukte Polen blijven gewoon in Nederland. *Trouw*, 01-11-10.

Chapter 14
The New European Migration Laboratory: East Europeans in West European Cities

Adrian Favell

The IMAGINATION project and its varied outputs represent the fruition of a research agenda that ought to be substantially shifting the mainstream paradigm of research on international migration (for the developing agenda see: Wallace and Stola 2001; Favell and Hansen 2002; Favell 2008a; Black et al. 2010; Crul 2016; Lafleur and Stanek 2016). The new European migrations heralded by European economic integration, in particular the Eastern enlargements of 2004 and 2007, represent a challenge to assumptions about immigration and citizenship, framed as they are by a legal-institutional transformation of the notion of international migration within and across the European regional territory. East European (CEE) populations, hitherto a peripheral part of the continent, had historically been a source of immigrant labour to their richer West European neighbours (Olsson 1996). For many years, then, movement Westwards was restricted by the barriers of the Cold War. In the post 1989 period, they still faced substantial restrictions on mobility. With the accession of eight new members in 2004, followed by Romania and Bulgaria in 2007 and Croatia in 2013, these populations all became putative EU citizens and post-national members (Soysal 1994, 2012). On paper they would be equal with all West Europeans before international law, and free to choose to move as individuals, to travel, study, live and work in all other member states of the European Union. In other words, they would be free of the restrictions of immigration legislation and categories—as have been West Europeans for many years. As international migrants they would thus become co-citizens and "free movers", in theory at least. Once transitional barriers were also down, older assumptions about one-way migration systems from poorer to richer countries – via lower-end incorporation in (typically) exploitative or exclusionary labour markets, followed by settlement, integration, and eventually change of nationality (citizenship) – would be called into question (for classic discussions see Massey et al. 1998; Castles and Miller 2003;

A. Favell (✉)
University of Leeds, Leeds, UK
e-mail: a.favell@leeds.ac.uk

P. Scholten, M. van Ostaijen (eds.), *Between Mobility and Migration*, IMISCOE Research Series, https://doi.org/10.1007/978-3-319-77991-1_14

see Penninx in this volume for a comparison of the old and new migration systems in Europe). For the regional integration of the continent and its open borders, would create also, in theory, a new space of mobility. In this space, temporary and pendular movements, and long term life and work as a foreigner based on European membership rights, without the need for settlement or change of citizenship, would all become more likely, along with a healthy transnational flow of capital and populations back and forth between receiving and sending countries (Garapich 2008). The emergence of new South-North flows alongside the East-West system after the financial crisis of 2008 has further complexified this new European map of migration (King 2002; King et al. 2016)

My own work on free movement was initially about West European movers in West European cities: the young, highly mobile, mostly professional pioneers taking their opportunities as EU citizens in the post Maastricht era in the classic European hubs of Amsterdam, Brussels and London (Favell 2008b). With the PIONEUR project, this ethnographic work was complemented with an extensive quantitative survey which revealed a broader typology of free movers, including ongoing lower-end labour migrants and retirees (Recchi and Favell 2009). It also included a qualitative study which suggested the experiences of Polish and Romanian movers were different, and a lot more negative than the ideal theory might suggest (Favell and Nebe 2009). In subsequent work, which engaged with a large project (KNOWMIG) Christina Boswell was conducting at the Hamburg Institute for International Economics, I extended the framework of my work on Eurostars to the "new face" of CEE movers now able to move, live and work as EU citizens across the EU (Favell 2008a; Favell 2009). The 2008 and 2009 articles – which are taken as a starting point for the IMAGINATION project – posed the issue as a hypothesis driven by the normative-legal logic of European free movement accords. "Textbook narratives, in terms of standard accounts of immigration, integration and citizenship based on models of postcolonial, guestworker and asylum migration, will need to be rethought," I wrote (Favell, 2008a: 701). Free movement for East Europeans offered the potential of a transformation of lowly classified "immigrants" into newly equalized "free moving" European co-citizens, and the realisation of a kind of "post-national" space of mobility at a European regional scale. The transformation here would be more than just the end of the East/West division of the continent; it was also potentially a fundamental challenge to the very order of a nation-state centred Western world, divided into self-contained bordered territories built on a distinction between citizens and foreigners, and ordered by a hierarchy of privilege between rich and dominant receiving states, and poor, subordinate sending states—with an always ready abundance of willing migrant workers on hand to serve their colonial masters. The integration of the European Union – at least in the principle of "non-discrimination" by nationality it instituted between citizens of all member states – offered not only the image of a unified Europe beyond the Cold War, but the glimpse of a viable, de-colonialised world of borderless free movement—albeit on a European scale, and heavily reliant on other borderings and hierarchies at, and beyond, its outer edge.

That at least was the theory. Sociologically speaking, the work on the "new face" of EU migration took seriously that it was an empirical question *how much* this legal-normative ideal for the new European citizens would be realised. In a more extended version of the article published recently, I laid out four hypothetical scenarios, stated in political economy terms, in which the exploitation and/or exclusion of, i.e., Polish and Romanian movers in distinct West European locations, could be measured to determine the precise degree of citizenship status achieved within the European regional integration proposed by the Eastern enlargements (Favell 2015: 176–178). In the first, "neo-liberal" Europe, the migration is demand driven, leading to a successful top end selection of highly employable movers and their settlement and inclusion as immigrants in their new countries, but with a substantial brain drain and growing inequalities across Europe. In the second, "exclusionary" Europe, the East European migrants encounter substantial racialisation, and fall into negative competition with existing migrant-origin ethnic and racial groups in receiving countries as unwanted newcomers. In the third, "EU" Europe, there is a Panglossian outcome of migrants moving successfully West according to temporary and pendular patterns, leading to rising investment in the East, economic equilibrium and decreasing economic imbalances between West and East. In the fourth, "exploitative" Europe, East Europeans move and find work, but encounter significant downward evaluation by the market, as they are exploited and marginalised as a new flexible labour force.

As clearly underlined in this volume, the answer to what in fact happened has in large part been negative, and mostly in line with the fourth scenario; although there are elements of all four when the experiences of different nationalities with different education levels, gender, and cultural backgrounds in different national locations are compared. Yet the overall picture is rather clear. CEE movers were indeed "cadet" Eurostars, but cultural distinctions and (even) racialised subordinations have been commonplace among the experiences of CEE movers, even among the more highly educated (Csedö 2008; Morosanu and Fox 2013). Moreover, as this volume also stresses, the idea of all migrations from the East to the West embodying a new logic of temporary, pendular and "free" free movement, has certainly been confounded by the many types and distinctions found among intra-EU migrants in this study. The idealised economists' labour market, driven entirely by supply and demand moving West, and matched by a balancing flow of capital investment East, gives way to a complex, differentiated patchwork of migrants and movers on a continuum from knowledge workers and students, through informal employees, to sex workers, beggars and the homeless. And across the six West European regions studied (I leave aside the Turkey case, driven by rather different sources and patterns), we find national and local governments reacting quite differently to the rather varied mixes of migrants attracted to these cities.

The present volume offers an invaluable documentation of these new migrants and the strategies of governance engaged by receiving regional governments. In this, and the accompanying published policy formulations (Fermin et al. 2016), it seeks to aid the recovery of a missing degree of multi-levelled governance, which ought to be hooking up EU and local level responses, over and beyond the pervasive national level government of "classic" immigration politics. Thus, the volume contributes not only to a more nuanced sociology of intra-EU migration – a "next generation" on from the initial work of the 2000s – but also offers rich material for political scientists looking to grapple with the multi-levelled political economy and policy terrain of immigration and diversity politics (Hepburn and Zapata-Barrero 2014; Barker 2015). A welcome dimension of this is that it is focused on less heavily studied mid-sized nations – and their component metropolitan regions – which often have mixed, patchwork approaches to migrant diversity, rather than coherent national "philosophies" (Favell 1998). It is a complement, for example, to Barbulescu's (2018) study of migration governance in Italy and Spain, which itself added new perspectives at national and local level to the classic cases of the UK, France, Germany or Switzerland (Ireland 1994; Garbaye 2005).

Godfried Engbersen's notion of "liquid migration" captures the fluid sense of new migration types, patterns and social/political formations signalled by the new East European migrations in West European urban contexts. Its association with Zygmunt Bauman's metaphor of "liquid modernity" may be misleading, however, in that the veteran social theorist's terminology in fact signalled his rather despairing take on the old Marxist adage that "all that is solid melts into air" (Berman 1992). It was an anti-empiricist stance; that the old apparatus and tools of classic sociological theory and measurements of social structures, social class, social institutions and social groups (etc.) – were now blunt and unable to adapt to the new, fluid, postmodern environment. All that remained to grasp this change faster and more complex than any science could capture, were the literary metaphors that could still be invented by a suitably soundbite-driven "mobile" social theory (Urry 2000). This exaggerated epistemological position is not Engbersen's, who is clearly engaged still in the empirical business of typologising, classifying and hypothesising the new migrations against the evidence found, albeit against a quite different potential range of migration systems. As Engbersen confirms in his chapter here, though, 5 million new CEE migrants in Western Europe between 2004 and 2010 does constitute a seismic population shift in the continent—and we are right to focus on how that ought to shift our standard migration theories and paradigms. In 2008, I argued that the new intra-EU migrations could be conceptualised with the help of models and theories from North America that had evolved around Latin and Central American migration to the US—itself a particular kind of fluid, transnational system born of a regional integration, open bordered in more informal and ambiguous ways that the European legal regime (Massey et al. 2002). My optimism at a shift in international migration scholarship was, perhaps, unwarranted. Although it would provide perfect material for rethinking the methodological nationalism of standard immigration studies, East-West migration and EU free movement does not feature in some of the most sophisticated reflections rethinking immigration research in the context of US sociology (Wimmer 2013; Waldinger 2015). And, among those North American scholars interested in applying comparatively US models and theory on immigration in Europe, there is a lack of awareness of the distinctiveness of intra-EU migration to "classic" non-European immigration and settlement patterns—even if in many situations, EU migration is more numerous and more dramatic in its consequences (for example, Alba and Foner 2015; see Favell 2016). As yet, there is little or no sign of such classic models of nation-centred immigration and citizenship, and the methodological nationalism on which it is built, being shifted in transatlantic comparative work.

This is an area indeed where the present volume's focus could be profitably extended. While intra-EU movements "between mobility and migration" is noted as a challenge to standard conceptions of immigration and settlement across national borders, there is not much attempt to compare the intra-EU migrants to other non-European migrants or other ethnic and racial minorities, who may well take up similarly marginalised social, economic and cultural positions in the receiving cities. Many of the "integration" and "incorporation" reflexes of local governance indeed are caused by the fact that local policy makers and stakeholders have simply applied the same tried and testing policy thinking and methods to these new migrants as to older immigrants—however ill-suited or inappropriate. This may apply to anti-discrimination efforts, coercive functional or normative integration expectations and obligations, or (even) minority cultural provisions. It should come as no surprise that there is no one size fits all "integration" policy likely to work for, at once, a single, skilled, pendular Polish entrepreneur in his 30s, and the stay-at-home young teenage spouse of a South Asian Muslim shop worker. Issues to do with race discrimination meanwhile are heavily complicated by the distinctly "white" status – and sometimes attitudes – of CEE movers finding themselves in the multi-racial super-diversity of many West European cities (Crul et al. 2013). The ambivalence of CEE migrants often lies in their tangential postion in the usual post-colonial hierarchies. They are new migrants and so may face disadvantages as newcomers in comparison to established racial and ethnic minorities with a longer standing place in the diversity of the host nation (Fox et al. 2012); but at the same time they are white Europeans, who can find themselves more easily in an advantaged "invisible" position in the host country, contributing in some cases to the ongoing racialising discriminations of others (Datta 2009; Fox 2012).

The recent experiences of a case not much mentioned in the book – yet crucial to its message given the sheer size of the CEE population – i.e., the UK – could here be of great significance. These have been sharpened by the "Brexit" vote in June 2016 to leave the European Union, a vote driven in substantial part by reactions amongst British citizens against the new European resident population in the UK (Clarke et al. 2016). The UK and the EU is now faced with retrenchment in European citizenship rights, in which European citizenship will be stripped from the over 3 million foreign EU residents in the UK, as well as the British population as a whole. This again constitutes an extraordinary natural laboratory of potential social science research into the social effects as well legal-political accommodations of this situation. What has been clear for some time in the parts of the UK (mainly England), which have voted heavily UKIP and then for Brexit, is that this is fuelled considerably by anti-EU migrant sentiment, including sometimes among British Black, Asian and Minority Ethnic populations (BAME), and notably also among many working class Labour supporters. This explosive mix can be seen in some particular provincial areas of the UK where there is a substantial presence of ethnic minority

British alongside CEE workers, such as some of the post-industrial towns of the North and the West Midlands, many of which voted heavily for Brexit. To these can be joined agricultural towns in the East of England—where there are substantial numbers of casual CEE workers; and many poor, mainly white coastal towns in the South East—again, where CEE families have often settled. London, and other major cities, on the other hand, as well as smaller university towns, voted to stay in the EU. This observation suggests that the real place to be studying the dynamics of migrant and immigrant relations and "exclusion"/"integration" may be provincial locations, rather than the big cities featured in this study. It is a question about the urban versus non-urban conditions of cosmopolitanism.

As a collected project, IMAGINATION, offers a comprehensive synthesis of the best research on intra-EU migration of the last decade, as well as a handbook of policy responses. It is clearly also "impact" related current affairs research of the most intense interest, having established extensive relations and cooperation with many of the cities and migrant groups involved. The signs are, pessimistically, that policy responses to the innovation and progressive promise are being swallowed back into standard, national, security- and restriction- driven responses, that will rip from the idea of European citizenship the non-discrimination of all European citizens that lay at its (post-national) heart (Hansen 2015). East European EU citizens are facing differentiation and relegation to a subordinate status within a more "controlled" Europe; and, increasingly, the hitherto "invisible" new movers from the South of Europe to the North West are also being cast as unwanted "immigrants". If this signals the end of non-discrimination by nationality within the EU, then the legal-political experiment that was tried in the laboratory of European migrations with the East European accessions, will leave a bitter taste of failure for those who believed in a unified European future. Yet it may still point the way forward to progressive alternatives to the question of international and regional inequality between populations which surely will be demanded again someday.

References

Alba, R., & Foner, N. (2015). *Strangers no more: Immigration and the challenges of integration in North America and Western Europe*. Princeton: Princeton University Press.

Barbulescu, R. (2018). *Migrant integration in a changing Europe: immigrants, European citizens and co-ethnics in Italy and Spain*. Notre Dame, IN: Notre Dame University Press.

Barker, F. (2015). *Nationalism, identity and the governance of diversity: Old politics, new arrivals*. London: Palgrave Macmillan.

Berman, M. (1992). *All that is solid melts into air*. New York: Verso.

Black, R., Engbersen, G., Marek, O., & Pantiru, C. (Eds.). (2010). *A continent moving west? EU enlargement and labour migration from central and Eastern Europe*. Amsterdam: University of Amsterdam Press.

Castles, S., & Miller, M. (2003). *The age of migration: International population movements in the modern world* (3rd ed.). London: Palgrave Macmillan.

Clarke, H, Goodwin, M & Whiteley, P. (2016). Why Britain voted for Brexit: An individual level analysis of the 2016 referendum. Paper presented at the EPOP conference, Sept 10. https://blogs.kent.ac.uk/epop/files/2016/07/Clarke-Goodwin-and-Whiteley.pdf.

Crul, M., Schneider, J., & Lelie, F. (2013). *Super-diversity: A new perspective on integration*. Amsterdam: VU Press.

Crul, M. (2016). Super-diversity vs. assimilation: How complex diversity in majority–minority cities challenges the assumptions of assimilation. *Journal of Ethnic and Migration Studies, 42*(1), 54–68.

Csedö, K. (2008). Negotiating skills in the global city: Hungarian and Romanian professionals and graduates in London. *Journal of Ethnic and Migration Studies, 34*(5), 803–823.

Datta, A. (2009). Places of everyday cosmopolitanisms: East European construction workers in London. *Environment and Planning A, 41*(2), 353–370.

Favell, A. (1998). *Philosophies of integration: immigration and the idea of citizenship in France and Britain*. London/New York: Macmillan-Palgrave and St Martin's Press.

Favell, A., & Hansen, R. (2002). Markets against politics: Migration, EU enlargement and the idea of Europe. *Journal of Ethnic and Migration Studies, 28*(4), 581–601.

Favell, A. (2008). The new face of East-West migration in Europe. *Journal of Ethnic and Migration Studies, 34*(5), 701–716.

Favell, A. (2008b). *Eurostars and Eurocities: Free movement and mobility in an integrating Europe*. Oxford: Blackwell.

Favell, A. (2009). Immigration, migration and free movement in the making of Europe. In J. Checkel & P. Katzenstein (Eds.), *European identity* (pp. 167–189). Cambridge: Cambridge University Press.

Favell, A. (2015). The new face of East-West migration in Europe [revised]. In A. Favell (Ed.), *Immigration, integration and mobility: New agendas in migration studies. Essays 1998–2015* (pp. 169–184). Colchester: ECPR Press.

Favell, A. (2016). Just like the USA? Commentary on Richard Alba and Nancy Foner, Strangers no more: Immigration and the challenges of integration in North America and Western Europe (2015). *Ethnic and Racial Studies, 39*(6), 2352–2360.

Favell, A., & Nebe, T. (2009). Internal and external movers: East-West migration and the impact of EU enlargement. In E. Recchi & A. Favell (Eds.), *Pioneers of European integration* (pp. 205–223).

Fermin, A., et al. (2016). Handbook of urban governance of free movement in the EU. Facts. In *Implications and policies*. The Hague: EUKN.

Fox, J. (2012). The uses of racism: Whitewashing new Europeans in the UK. *Ethnic and Racial Studies, 36*(11), 1871–1889.

Fox, J., Morosanu, L., & Szilassy, E. (2012). The racialization of the new European migration to the UK. *Sociology, 46*(4), 680–695.

Garapich, M. (2008). The migration industry and civil society: Polish immigrants in the United Kingdom before and after EU enlargement. *Journal of Ethnic and Migration Studies, 34*(5), 735–752.

Garbaye, R. (2005). *Getting into local power: The politics of ethnic minorities in British and French cities*. Oxford: Blackwell.

Hansen, Peo. (2015). Undermining free movement: Migration in an age of austerity, *Eurozine*. http://www.eurozine.com/articles/2015-02-06-hansenp-en.html

Hepburn, E., & Zapata-Barrero, R. (Eds.). (2014). *The politics of immigration in multi-level states: Governance and political parties*. London: Palgrave.

Ireland, P. (1994). *The policy challenge of ethnic diversity*. Cambridge, MA: Harvard University Press.

King, R. (2002). Towards a new map of European migration. *International Journal of Population Geography, 8*, 89–106.

King, R., Lulle, A., Conti, F., & Mueller, D. (2016). Eurocity London: A qualitative comparison of graduate migration from Germany, Italy and Latvia. *Comparative Migration Studies, 4*(3).

Lafleur, J.-M., & Stanek, M. (Eds.). (2016). *South-North migration of EU citizens in times of crisis*. Amsterdam: Springer.
Massey, D., Arango, J., Hugo, G., Kouaouci, A., Pellegrino, A., & Taylor, J. E. (1998). *Worlds in motion: Understanding international migration at the end of the Millenium*. Oxford: Clarendon Press.
Massey, D., Durand, J., & Malone, N. (2002). *Beyond smoke and mirrors: Mexican migration in an era of economic integration*. New York: Russell Sage.
Morosanu, L., & Fox, J. (2013). No smoke without fire': Strategies of coping with stigmatised migrant identities. *Ethnicities, 13*(4), 438–456.
Olsson, L. (1996). Labor migration as a prelude to World War I. *International Migration Review, 30*(4), 875–900.
Recchi, E., & Favell, A. (Eds.). (2009). *Pioneers of European integration: Citizenship and mobility in the European Union*. Cheltenham: Edward Elgar.
Soysal, Y. N. (1994). *Limits of citizenship: Migrants and post-national membership in Europe*. Chicago: Chicago University Press.
Soysal, Y. N. (2012). Citizenship, immigration and the European social project: Rights and obligations of individuality. *British Journal of Sociology, 63*(1), 1–21.
Urry, J. (2000). *Sociology beyond societies*. London: Routledge.
Waldinger, R. (2015). *The cross-border connection: Immigrants, emigrants and their homelands*. Cambridge, MA: Harvard University Press.
Wallace, C., & Stola, D. (Eds.). (2001). *Patterns of migration in Central Europe*. London: Palgrave.
Wimmer, A. (2013). *Ethnic boundary making: Institutions, power, networks*. New York: Oxford University Press.